HIGH COURT CASE SUMMARIES

HEALTH LAW

Keyed to Furrow's Casebook on Health Law, 6th Edition

WEST®

A Thomson Reuters business

Mat #40870056

© West, a Thomson business, 2002, 2006
© 2009 Thomson Reuters

    610 Opperman Drive

    St. Paul, MN 55123

    1–800–313–9378

Printed in the United States of America

ISBN: 978–0–314–90531–4

Table of Contents

TABLE OF CONTENTS

*

Alphabetical Table of Cases

CHAPTER ONE

Introduction to Health Law and Policy

Katskee v. Blue Cross/Blue Shield of Nebraska

Instant Facts: Insurance company denied coverage for preventative surgery in woman diagnosed with breast-ovarian carcinoma syndrome (putting her at great risk of getting cancer) on the ground that the syndrome is not an illness and therefore is not covered by the policy.

Black Letter Rule: An abnormal physical condition is an illness when it is such that in its probable and natural progression it may be expected to be a source of mischief.

Berry v. Cardiology Consultants, P.A.

Instant Facts: Following heart surgery, Berry's (P) cardiologist administered Amiodarone after he suffered atrial fibrillation, which led to Berry's (P) death by Amiodarone toxicity.

Black Letter Rule: Scientific evidence is relevant if it is probative of an issue in the case, such as the standard of care.

Newman v. Sathyavaglswaran

Instant Facts: The corneas were removed from the body of Newman's (P) son after his death, but Newman (D) was not informed of their removal beforehand.

Black Letter Rule: The property interests of the next of kin in the bodies of their family members are firmly entrenched, and the state may not alter those interests via exceptions to the general rule that lack a firm basis in traditional property principles.

Jacobson v. Massachusetts

Instant Facts: The city of Cambridge adopted a regulation requiring immunization against smallpox, pursuant to a state law that allowed such regulations.

Black Letter Rule: Public health laws are within the police powers of the states, and the state is given broad discretion in making those laws.

Katskee v. Blue Cross/Blue Shield of Nebraska

(Insured) v. *(Medical Insurer)*

245 Neb. 808, 515 N.W.2d 645 (1994)

AN ILLNESS IS A PHYSICAL STATE THAT IS SIGNIFICANTLY DIFFERENT FROM THE PHYSICAL STATE OF A HEALTHY, NORMAL PERSON

■ **INSTANT FACTS** Insurance company denied coverage for pre-ventative surgery in woman diagnosed with breast-ovarian carcinoma syndrome (putting her at great risk of getting cancer) on the ground that the syndrome is not an illness and therefore is not covered by the policy.

■ **BLACK LETTER RULE** An abnormal physical condition is an illness when it is such that in its probable and natural progression it may be expected to be a source of mischief.

■ **PROCEDURAL BASIS**

Appeal from district court's grant of summary judgment on matter of contract interpretation.

■ **FACTS**

Sindee Katskee (P) is suing Blue Cross/Blue Shield of Nebraska (BCBS) (D) for breach of contract for refusal to cover major surgery under a medical insurance policy. Upon the advice of her gynecologist (Dr. Roffman), Katskee (P) consulted with Dr. Henry Lynch regarding her family's history of breast and ovarian cancer. After examining Katskee (P), Dr. Lynch diagnosed her as suffering from a genetic condition known as breast-ovarian carcinoma syndrome. Women with the syndrome are at greatly increased risk for breast or ovarian cancer. Based on this diagnosis, Dr. Lynch recommended that Katskee (P) have surgery to remove her uterus, ovaries, and fallopian tubes. Dr. Roffman agreed that this was the most medically appropriate treatment available. Prior to surgery, Katskee (P) filed a claim with BCBS (D). Both doctors wrote to BCBS (D) explaining the diagnosis and their basis for recommending the surgery. Katskee's (P) insurance policy with BCBS (D) covers services that are medically necessary. In relevant part, the policy defines "medically necessary" to mean the "services, procedures, drugs, supplies or durable medical equipment provided by the physician, hospital or other health care provider, in the diagnosis or treatment of the covered person's *illness,* injury or pregnancy." The policy broadly defines "illness" as a bodily disorder or disease, but does not provide definitions for either "bodily disorder" or "disease." The policy gives BCBS (D) the right to determine whether a service is medically necessary. Two weeks before the surgery, Dr. Charles Mason, chief medical officer for BCBS (D), wrote to Katskee (P) and stated that the BCBS (D) policy would not cover the cost of the surgery. He stated that Katskee's (P) condition did not constitute an "illness" and thus the surgery was not medically necessary. Katskee (P) had the surgery anyway. Katskee (P) then filed this action for breach of contract, seeking to recover $6,022.57 in costs associated with the surgery. The district court granted BCBS's (D) motion for summary judgment.

■ **ISSUE**

Does a physical predisposition toward certain diseases (such as cancer) constitute an illness?

■ **DECISION AND RATIONALE**

(White, J.) Yes. An insurance policy is subject to the same rules of construction as all other contracts. It must be construed to give effect to the intentions of the parties at the time the contract was made.

Where the language of the policy is unambiguous, we give the terms contained in the policy their plain and ordinary meaning. The language of the policy in this case is not ambiguous. The plain and ordinary meaning of the terms "bodily disorder" and "disease" as they are used in the policy to define illness encompasses any abnormal condition of the body or its components of such a degree that in its natural progression would be expected to be problematic. BCBS (D) characterizes Katskee's (P) condition, breast-ovarian carcinoma syndrome, as a predisposition to an illness (cancer), but does not address the question at hand: whether the syndrome itself is an illness. Dr. Mason, the person at BCBS (D) who was responsible for the denial, lacks experience in this specialized field of cancer research and yet failed to consult any medical literature to determine the exact nature of Katskee's (P) condition. We believe that in order to determine whether the syndrome is an illness, we must first understand the nature of the syndrome. Breast and ovarian cancer are hereditary and are related to a woman's genetic make-up. While no conclusive physical test exists to determine the presence of the syndrome in any particular woman, it can be diagnosed by tracing the occurrences of hereditary cancer throughout the patient's family. Women diagnosed with the syndrome have at least a 50% chance of developing breast or ovarian cancer, whereas unaffected women have only a 1.4% chance. There is no way to detect ovarian cancer until it reaches an advanced stage, and therefore treatment of ovarian cancer is relatively unsuccessful. Dr. Lynch testified that the presence of the syndrome is the result of a genetic deviation from the normal, healthy state and that the recommended surgery treats that condition by eliminating or significantly reducing the presence of the syndrome and its likely development. Thus, we find the syndrome to be an illness as defined by the policy. Katskee's (P) condition is a deviation from what is considered a normal, healthy physical state or structure, which arises from her genetic make-up. Not every condition that constitutes a predisposition to another illness is necessarily an illness within the meaning of an insurance policy. However, when a condition is such that in its probable and natural progression it may be expected to be a source of mischief, it may reasonably be described as a disease or an illness. In this case, the syndrome is an illness distinct from the cancer that it causes. The record establishes that the syndrome was manifest, at least in part, from the genetic deviation and evident from the family medical history. The condition was such that one learned in medicine could with a reasonable degree of accuracy diagnose it. The medical evidence in this case persuades us that breast-ovarian carcinoma syndrome is a bodily disorder or disease and thus an illness as defined by the policy. Reversed.

Analysis:

In modern society, we have come to focus more and more on concepts of "wellness"—on how we are doing mentally, physically, and spiritually. Under this expansive, modem approach, problems like alcoholism and obesity, which were traditionally considered as behavioral disorders, seem to fall under the category of illness. There are economic consequences to adding to the list of what is an illness—it makes the cost of health insurance go up. which puts it out of reach for some people. This is surely not the desired result—to increase coverage for some at the cost of denying coverage to others. There is also a question about the court's definition of illness because it leaves out the concept of culpability. It seems well accepted that any definition of illness should include a lack of culpability. However, the concepts of culpability and personal responsibility carry their own problems—there is debate about, for example, whether drug addiction or anorexia are diseases or choices. Therefore, the definition of illness may be as elusive as the definition of obscenity—you know it when you see it, but this is not particularly satisfying as a legal standard.

■ CASE VOCABULARY

ILLNESS: The definition will vary between jurisdictions—some defining more broadly than others—but is generally some variation from the normal, healthy state that can be diagnosed with relative certainty.

Berry v. Cardiology Consultants, P.A.

(Patient's Estate) v. *(Physicians)*

909 A.2d 611 (Del. Super. Ct. 2006)

MEDICAL EVIDENCE ESTABLISHING THE STANDARD OF CARE IS ADMISSIBLE

This is a really tough case.
Raise your hand if you know what an "algorithm" is.

■ **INSTANT FACTS** Following heart surgery, Berry's (P) cardiologist administered Amiodarone after he suffered atrial fibrillation, which led to Berry's (P) death by Amiodarone toxicity.

■ **BLACK LETTER RULE** Scientific evidence is relevant if it is probative of an issue in the case, such as the standard of care.

■ **Procedural Basis**

Trial court consideration of a motion for a new trial.

■ **FACTS**

For twelve years prior to his death, Berry (P) had seen Dr. Doorey (D) at Cardiology Consultants, P.A. (D) for a variety of heart problems, including several heart attacks. In November 2002, Berry (P) experienced an episode of atrial fibrillation, for which the surgical staff administered Amiodarone. After several recurrences of atrial fibrillation over the next few days, Doorey (D) prescribed continued administration of Amiodarone beyond Berry's (P) discharge. At a December 2002 postoperative evaluation, Doorey (D) again prescribed Amiodarone, allegedly explaining to Berry (P) what dosage he should take and that his dosage should be reduced after one month. In February 2003, Berry (P) returned to the hospital with pulmonary complaints and was seen by a different cardiologist, who noted no signs of Amiodarone toxicity, but detected some signs of early Amiodarone effects. Berry (P) was directed to discontinue Amiodarone and was discharged. Five days later, Berry (P) again experienced pulmonary complaints. A pulmonary biopsy was performed and the results were referred to a Harvard physician for examination. The physician admitted that it was a difficult case, but he diagnosed Berry (P) with Amiodarone pneumonitis. Berry (P) died on March 23, 2003. The certificate of death indicated the cause of death as acute pneumonitis and Amiodarone toxicity.

Berry's estate (P) sued both Doorey (D) and the hospital (D), claiming Doorey (D) negligently prescribed Amiodarone to treat atrial fibrillation, Doorey (D) negligently prescribed an excessive dosage of Amiodarone, and Doorey (D) failed to adequately inform Berry (P) of the dangers of Amiodarone. The defendants countered that Amiodarone is an accepted treatment for atrial fibrillation, that the prescribed dosage was within established amounts, and that Doorey (D) adequately informed Berry (P) of the risks before administering Amiodarone.

At trial, the plaintiffs produced expert testimony that Berry's (P) Amiodarone dosage was double that called for by the standard of care established by an algorithm contained in a Cardiac Surgery Service Manual ("CSSM") followed by the hospital (D). In response, Doorey (D) explained that while the algorithm calls for a lower dosage than that prescribed, the CSSM algorithm merely contains guidelines designed to enable the support team to get something started at a time when a specialist is not available. They are not provided to nor followed by cardiologists like Doorey (D) and do not establish the standard of care. The defense offered expert testimony that no specific Amiodarone dosage had been established at the time of Berry's (P) treatment. The defense expert testified that when Amiodarone treatment for atrial fibrillation gained acceptance, the American College of Cardiology ("ACC")

---

published and distributed guidelines for atrial fibrillation treatment. This algorithm and other supporting materials indicated that no recommended dosage for Amiodarone had been established, and the expert opined that Berry's (P) dosage level fell within the standard of care. The ACC algorithm was admitted into evidence and presented to the jury for consideration. After trial, the jury issued its verdict in favor of the defense. The plaintiffs moved for a new trial, claiming error in the admission of the ACC algorithm and challenging the verdict as unsupported by the evidence.

■ ISSUE

Did the court err in admitting the ACC algorithm into evidence?

■ DECISION AND RATIONALE

(Del Pesco, J.) No. Scientific evidence is relevant if it is probative of an issue in the case, such as the standard of care. Here, the ACC algorithm serves as an analytical path that demonstrated that Amiodarone was both appropriate for treatment of atrial fibrillation and given to Berry (P) in an appropriate dosage. Whether or not Berry's (P) specific condition was within the scope of the algorithm is a question of fact to be determined by the jury. The jury properly evaluated the evidence from both parties and fulfilled its function in returning its verdict. Motion denied.

Analysis:

Although the plaintiff lost the post-trial battle, it eventually won the war. On appeal, the Supreme Court of Delaware reversed and remanded the case, ruling that while the trial court judge appropriately allowed the ACC algorithm into evidence as a learned treatise, it erred in permitting the algorithm to be presented to the jury for review during deliberation. *See Berry v. Cardiology Consultants, P.A.*, 935 A.2d 255 (Del. 2007). Learned treatises may be read into the record by an expert, but may not be physically presented to the jury, because to do so invites too much jury speculation contrary to the expert testimony presented.

■ CASE VOCABULARY

LEARNED–TREATISE RULE: An exception to the hearsay rule, by which a published text may be established as authoritative, either by expert testimony or by judicial notice. Under the Federal Rules of Evidence, a statement contained in a published treatise, periodical, or pamphlet on sciences or art (such as history and medicine) can be established as authoritative—and thereby admitted into evidence for the purpose of examining or cross-examining an expert witness—by expert testimony or by the court's taking judicial notice of the authoritative nature or reliability of the text. If the statement is admitted into evidence, it may be read into the trial record, but it may not be received as an exhibit. Fed. R. Evid. 803(18).

RELEVANT EVIDENCE: Evidence tending to prove or disprove a matter in issue. Relevant evidence is both probative and material and is admissible unless excluded by a specific statute or rule. Fed. R. Evid. 401–403.

STANDARD OF CARE: In the law of negligence, the degree of prudence that a reasonable person should exercise.

Newman v. Sathyavaglswaran

(Parent) v. *(Coroner)*

287 F.3d 786 (9th Cir. 2002)

THE DECEDENT'S NEXT OF KIN HAVE A PROPERTY INTEREST IN THE DEAD BODY

Today I bury my son...

...or at least the parts of him that weren't stolen by the State.

stus.com

■ **INSTANT FACTS** The corneas were removed from the body of Newman's (P) son after his death, but Newman (D) was not informed of their removal beforehand.

■ **BLACK LETTER RULE** The property interests of the next of kin in the bodies of their family members are firmly entrenched, and the state may not alter those interests via exceptions to the general rule that lack a firm basis in traditional property principles.

■ **PROCEDURAL BASIS**

Appeal from an order dismissing a complaint for failure to state a claim.

■ **FACTS**

Newman's (P) son and Obarski's (P) son both died in October 1997. In accordance with state law, Sathyavaglswaran (D), the Los Angeles County Coroner, obtained possession of the bodies and removed the corneas for use by a non-profit eye bank. The statute authorized the coroner to remove the corneas without notification or consent of the next of kin, as long as the coroner had no knowledge of any objection to the removal. No attempt was made to notify Newman (P) or Obarski (P), and neither of them knew of the removal beforehand.

Newman (P) and Obarski (P) learned of the removal of the corneas in 1999 and brought an action under 42 U.S.C. § 1983. The complaint alleged a deprivation of property without due process of law. The trial court dismissed the complaint for failure to state a claim.

■ **ISSUE**

Do a decedent's next of kin have a property right in the decedent's body that is protected by the Fourteenth Amendment?

■ **DECISION AND RATIONALE**

(Fisher, J.) Yes. The property interests of the next of kin in the bodies of their family members are firmly entrenched, and the state may not alter those interests with exceptions to the general rule that lack a firm basis in traditional property principles. Those property interests are based on long-standing legal principles. Historically, the common law did not refer to the rights of the next of kin as a property right. The right of the next of kin was the right to receive the body in order to provide it with a funeral. Gradually, cases began to refer to a property right of the next of kin. The recognition of a property right, or a quasi-property right, increased as cases involving the unauthorized mutilation or disposition of bodies increased, along with the demand for cadavers for medical research and the use of cremation as an alternative to burial.

Organ transplantation led to an expansion of the rights of next of kin. The Uniform Anatomical Gift Act (UAGA) granted to the next of kin the right to transfer the parts of bodies in their possession to others for medical or research purposes. The right to transfer is limited, and both federal and state laws

---

prohibit the sale of body parts. As the demand for organs for transplantation increased, the requirement of consent from the next of kin (or the decedent, prior to death) before organs could be removed was regarded as a hindrance. Many states, including California, enacted so-called "presumed consent" laws that allowed the taking and transfer of body parts without the consent of the next of kin as long as no objection to the removal is known.

Modern case law is split on the question of whether a presumed consent law infringes on a constitutionally protected right. The Florida and Georgia courts have held that the rights of the next of kin are "quasi property" rights. The public health interest in corneal transplants was balanced against the minimal intrusion of their removal. The Sixth Circuit has held, however, that the interests of the next of kin are sufficient to allow them to bring a § 1983 action for the unauthorized removal of corneas. Under traditional common law principles, Newman (P) and Obarski (P) had exclusive and legitimate claims of entitlement to prevent the violation of the corneas and the rest of the bodies of their deceased children. By adopting the UAGA, California has recognized the parents' right to make the decision whether to allow the transfer of parts of the bodies of their deceased children. In addition, the presumed consent law implicitly recognizes the ongoing property interests of the next of kin, by prohibiting the removal of corneas if the coroner knows of an objection to the removal. It does not matter that body parts may not be traded for profit. The courts have never held that a physical item is not property simply because it has no economic or market value.

Nonetheless, the state has significant interests in promoting the public health. When the rights of citizens are invaded, it is up to the state to assert those rights, and subject them to scrutiny. The case will be remanded to the district court to allow consideration of the state's asserted justification. Reversed and remanded.

Analysis:

The "presumed consent" laws give little meaningful opportunity to register an objection. A coroner is not required to notify the next of kin, so it seems that, unless there is someone physically present, or the decedent has something on his or her person clearly indicating non-consent to the removal of body parts, there is no reason for the coroner not to proceed with a removal. Intuitively, this would seem wrong to many people.

■ CASE VOCABULARY

DUE PROCESS: The conduct of legal proceedings according to established rules and principles for the protection and enforcement of private rights, including notice and the right to a fair hearing before a tribunal with the power to decide the case.

NEXT OF KIN: The person or persons most closely related to a decedent by blood or affinity; an intestate's heirs—that is, the person or persons entitled to inherit personal property from a decedent who has not left a will.

Jacobson v. Massachusetts

(Vaccination Objector) v. *(Prosecuting Government)*

197 U.S. 11, 25 S.Ct. 358, 49 L.Ed. 643 (1905)

STATES HAVE BROAD AUTHORITY TO MAKE LAWS RELATING TO PUBLIC HEALTH

I don't want a vaccination!

And we don't want to catch smallpox from you.

CITY COUNCIL

stus.com

■ **INSTANT FACTS** The city of Cambridge adopted a regulation requiring immunization against smallpox, pursuant to a state law that allowed such regulations.

■ **BLACK LETTER RULE** Public health laws are within the police powers of the states, and the state is given broad discretion in making those laws.

■ **PROCEDURAL BASIS**

Appeal from an order sustaining a conviction for failure to be vaccinated.

■ **FACTS**

A statute enacted in Massachusetts (P) allowed cities to require vaccination of adult inhabitants, if deemed necessary for the public health or safety. The statute required that vaccinations be provided free of charge. The Board of Health of Cambridge adopted a regulation that required all inhabitants of the city to be vaccinated or revaccinated against smallpox. Jacobson (D) refused to be vaccinated and was convicted and fined five dollars. Jacobson (D) claimed that the state statute was unconstitutional.

■ **ISSUE**

Was the state statute allowing cities to implement mandatory vaccination regulations unconstitutional?

■ **DECISION AND RATIONALE**

(Harlan, J.) No. Public health laws are within the police powers of the states, and the state is given broad discretion in making those laws. As a part of this power, the state may give local bodies the authority to take steps to safeguard the public health and safety. The state's authority is subject only to the condition that no rule or regulation contravenes the U.S. Constitution or infringe on any right granted or secured by the Constitution. The state statute at issue here does not infringe on any constitutional right. The Constitution does not guarantee an absolute right to be free from all restraint. Individuals are subject to many restraints for the common good, and the state legislature is the primary judge of the common good.

In this case, the vaccinations are required only when a local authority determines that they are necessary. It was appropriate to give the Board of Health the authority to determine the necessity of vaccinations. The courts would usurp the functions of another branch of government if they were to determine that the method used to protect the people of Cambridge from smallpox was arbitrary and not justified by the necessities of the case. Reference is made to the "necessities of the case," because it is possible that the power of a community to protect itself against an epidemic might be exercised in such an arbitrary and unreasonable manner in reference to particular persons, or might go so far beyond what was reasonably required for the protection of the public, that the courts would be justified in intervening for the protection of those persons. Although there is a sphere within which an individual may assert the supremacy of his or her will and dispute the authority of any government to interfere with the exercise of that will, it is also true that the rights of the individual may, in times of danger, be subject to such restraint as the safety of the public may demand.

At trial, Jacobson (D) offered to introduce evidence that some members of the medical profession doubt the usefulness of vaccination, or that vaccination causes other diseases. It must be assumed that the Massachusetts Legislature was aware of these competing theories when it enacted the statute in question and was compelled to choose between them. It was not required to submit the matter to the determination of the court or a jury. The courts have the power to review this decision only when the statute enacted has no real or substantial relation to the object of the law or constitutes a violation of constitutional rights. The statute in question here does not violate the Constitution, and it cannot be said that it has no real or substantial relation to the goal of eradicating smallpox. The minority of citizens in a community does not have the power to defy the will of the authorities, acting in good faith for the protection of all.

It is, of course, easy to imagine extreme cases where the courts would be justified in intervening in order to prevent wrong and oppression. For example, one could imagine an individual whose health was in such a state that it would be cruel and inhuman to subject him or her to vaccination. The statute was not intended to be applied in such a situation; if it were, it cannot be said that the courts would be incompetent to intervene and protect the life and health of the individual concerned.

Analysis:

Justice Harlan's opinion seems to give government a free hand in making laws, as long as they can be justified under the rubric of "public health." Nevertheless, the opinion goes to some lengths to note that the possibility of judicial scrutiny is never to be ruled out. The public health laws must have some real or substantial relation to the goal of the statute, and there may be individual cases in which the courts would prevent the application of the statute. In this case, Jacobson's (D) only objection seems to be that he does not think that the vaccination will work, or that it will have some side effects. The Court refuses to allow such second-guessing.

CHAPTER TWO

Quality Control Regulation: Licensing of Health Care Professionals

In Re Williams

Instant Facts: Doctor was suspended from practice due to prescription of drugs to weight loss patients.

Black Letter Rule: An agency's determination must be supported by reliable, probative, and substantial evidence.

Hoover v. The Agency for Health Care Administration

Instant Facts: A doctor was disciplined by the Board of Medicine for over-prescribing controlled substances for patients with intractable pain, despite a hearing officer's original determination that that doctor had not fallen below the applicable standard of care.

Black Letter Rule: Where the evidence is inadequate to do so, the Board of Medicine may not overrule a hearing officer's finding of fact.

State Board of Registration for the Healing Arts v. McDonagh

Instant Facts: McDonagh (D) used chelation therapy to treat vascular disease, and the Board of Registration (P) claimed that treatment constituted repeated negligence.

Black Letter Rule: The appropriate standard of care is the degree of skill and learning used by members of the profession in similar circumstances.

State Board of Nursing and State Board of Healing Arts v. Ruebke

Instant Facts: The Kansas medical and nursing boards sought a temporary injunction to stop a midwife from practicing her trade without a medical or nursing license.

Black Letter Rule: Midwifery does not fit the definition of either a healing art or nursing, and thus a lay midwife is not required to be licensed as long as she limits her practice to activities that do not constitute a healing art (unless supervised by a licensed physician.)

Sermchief v. Gonzales

Instant Facts: Nurses who engaged in the assessment and diagnosis of patients were threatened with being charged with the unauthorized practice of medicine.

Black Letter Rule: The statutory concept of professional nursing is broad and expansive, and nursing activity is not unauthorized practice of medicine as long as the nurse acts within his or her training and skill level.

In re Williams

(Medical Board) v. *(Doctor)*

60 Ohio St.3d 85, 573 N.E.2d 638 (1991)

THE MEDICAL BOARD HAS SUBSTANTIAL DISCRETION IN DETERMINING THE STANDARD OF PRACTICE FOR DOCTORS

■ **INSTANT FACTS** Doctor was suspended from practice due to prescription of drugs to weight loss patients.

■ **BLACK LETTER RULE** An agency's determination must be supported by reliable, probative, and substantial evidence.

■ **PROCEDURAL BASIS**

Appeal from lower courts' reversal of an administrative agency's determination.

■ **FACTS**

From 1983–1986, Dr. Williams (D) prescribed certain controlled substances for 50 patients as part of a weight control program. In November 1986, the Ohio State Medical Board (Board) (P) promulgated a regulation that prohibited the prescription of these drugs for weight control purposes. Dr. Williams (D), in conformity with the regulation, stopped prescribing the drugs. In 1987, the Board (P) charged Dr. Williams (D) with failing to conform to minimal standards of medical practice because he had prescribed these drugs for long-term weight loss treatment. A hearing on the matter was held before a Board examiner. The Board (P) introduced evidence from the Physician's Desk Reference recommending that the drugs that Dr. Williams (D) was prescribing should only be used for a few weeks in the treatment of obesity. This was the only evidence that the Board (D) introduced. Dr. Williams (D) presented expert testimony from two prominent doctors that there were two schools of thought regarding the use of these drugs for weight control. The majority view is that they should only be used for short periods. The minority view is that long-term use is acceptable if properly supervised. Both experts testified that Dr. Williams's (D) application of the minority protocol was not substandard medical practice. Based on this evidence, the hearing examiner found that Dr. Williams (D) had been practicing substandard medicine and recommended a three-year probationary period. The Board (P) modified the penalty suspending Dr. Williams's (D) license for one year followed by a five-year probationary period. Dr. Williams (D) appealed to the courts, and the Court of Common Pleas and Court of Appeals found that the Board's (P) order was not supported by reliable, probative and substantial evidence.

■ **ISSUE**

Should the physician's regulatory board have the final say in what constitutes substandard medical practice?

■ **DECISION AND RATIONALE**

(Brown, J.) No. In an appeal from an administrative agency, a reviewing court is bound to uphold the agency's order if it is supported by reliable, probative, and substantial evidence and is in accordance with the law. The Board (P) contends that the case of *Arlen v. Ohio State Medical Bd,* is dispositive precedent. In *Arlen*, a physician was disciplined because he had written prescriptions for controlled substances to a person who the physician knew was redistributing the drugs to others. In that case we

---

held that the Board (P) is not required to present expert testimony on the acceptable standard of medical practice in every case before it can find that a physician's conduct falls below this standard. Since the majority of Board (P) members are themselves experts in the medical field, they often already possess the specialized knowledge needed to determine the acceptable standard of general medical practice. However, even though the Board (P) does not need to present expert testimony in every case, a charge against a doctor must still be supported by some reliable, probative and substantial evidence. Here, Dr. Williams (D) dispensed controlled substances in what was, at the time, a legally permitted manner. The only evidence in the record on the issue was the testimony of Dr. Williams's (D) expert witnesses that his use of the drugs in a weight control program did not fall below the acceptable standard of medical practice. We note that where a particular medical practice is proscribed by a statute or an administrative rule, even the existence of a body of expert opinion supporting that practice would not excuse a violation. Here, however, there is insufficient evidence to support the charges against Dr. Williams (D). The Board (P), though it does possess special knowledge, does not have unbridled discretion. Affirmed.

■ DISSENT

(Wright, J.) We send today to the medical community's regulators a message that would never be tolerated if it were sent to the legal community. We are telling those in charge of policing the medical community that their expertise as to what constitutes the acceptable standard of medical practice is not enough to overcome a doctor's assertion otherwise.

Analysis:

The tension in this case centers on how much discretion the state regulatory agency (the state medical board) has when it comes to deciding standards of practice. The majority says that there is some limit as to the board's discretion, but the minority seems to want to allow the medical community to be completely self-disciplined. There is debate about allowing doctors to self-regulate the health care profession. The purported goal of licensing and physician discipline by peer review is quality control and public protection. The idea is that since medical care is too complex for consumers to effectively evaluate, medical boards should oversee physicians to insure that they live up to certain minimum standards of competence. However, this system has been criticized as paternalistic, allowing physicians to protect their monopoly on health care, discriminating against allowing minorities into the system, raising the price of service, slowing innovation in health care by mandating uniformity in education and care, and it operating as an "old boys' club"; as such, it is ineffective in assuring quality control.

■ CASE VOCABULARY

ADMINISTRATIVE RULEMAKING: Administrative agencies (such as the medical board), if they have the proper authority and follow the proper procedures, can make rules that are binding on the public just as if the rules were statutes that had been enacted by the legislature.

PHYSICIAN'S DESK REFERENCE: A text that is commonly used by physicians all over the United States which is a treatise on prescription drugs, their proper use and their effects.

Hoover v. The Agency For Health Care Administration

(Doctor) v. *(Oversight Agency)*
676 So.2d 1380 (Fla. Ct. App. 1996)

A HEARING OFFICER'S FACTUAL FINDINGS ARE ENTITLED TO GREAT DEFERENCE

■ **INSTANT FACTS** A doctor was disciplined by the Board of Medicine for over-prescribing controlled substances for patients with intractable pain, despite a hearing officer's original determination that that doctor had not fallen below the applicable standard of care.

■ **BLACK LETTER RULE** Where the evidence is inadequate to do so, the Board of Medicine may not overrule a hearing officer's finding of fact.

■ **PROCEDURAL BASIS**

Appeal from administrative discipline of a doctor.

■ **FACTS**

Dr. Hoover (D) was accused of inappropriately and excessively prescribing controlled substances to seven patients in her care. This led to the charge that Dr. Hoover (D) had violated a state statute in that the care that she had given fell below that level of care, skill, and treatment that would be exercised by a reasonably prudent physician under similar circumstances. All seven patients had been treated by Dr. Hoover (D) for intractable pain arising from various noncancerous illnesses. At the administrative hearing, the Agency for Health Care Administration (the agency) (P) presented the testimony of two expert witnesses. Neither had examined any of the patients or their medical records. Neither of the agency's (P) experts specialized in the care of chronic pain. In fact, both experts referred any patient who had chronic pain to other doctors [perhaps in an effort to avoid prosecutions like this one]. Both of the experts testified that without looking at the patients' medical records they could not tell whether alternative medications had been tried or were appropriate or whether testing had been done to support Dr. Hoover's (D) medical treatment. Despite this paucity of evidence, lack of familiarity, and seeming lack of expertise, both of the agency's (P) physicians testified that Dr. Hoover (D) had prescribed excessive, perhaps lethal, amounts of narcotics and had practiced below the standard of care. Dr. Hoover (D) also testified in great detail concerning each of the patients, her diagnoses and treatment, alternatives attempted, the patients' need for medication, the uniform improvement in patient function on the medication prescribed, and her ability to closely monitor each patient. She presented corroborating physician testimony supporting the appropriateness of Dr. Hoover's (P) treatment. The hearing officer concluded that the agency (P) had failed to meet its burden of proof and could not show that Dr. Hoover (D) had failed to meet the requisite standard of care. The hearing officer found Dr. Hoover's (D) treatment to be appropriate based on Dr. Hoover's (D) testimony, the corroborating testimony of another physician, and federal guidelines for treatment of intractable pain in cancer patients (even though none of her patients were suffering from cancer). The agency (P) appealed to the Board of Medicine, which adopted wholesale the agency's (P) position. In particular, the Board of Medicine adopted the agency's (P) argument that the hearing officer's findings were erroneously based on irrelevant federal guidelines and that the agency's (P) physicians' testimony was that Dr. Hoover (P) had fallen below the proper standard of care. The Board of Medicine levied the agency's (P) recommended penalties: a reprimand, a $4,000 fine, continuing medical education on abusable drugs, and two years probation. This appeal follows.

■ ISSUE

Must a reviewing administrative agency defer to the hearing officer's findings of fact if they are supported by evidence in the record?

■ DECISION AND RATIONALE

(Jorgenson, J.) Yes. The Board of Medicine made two mistakes in rejecting the findings of the hearing officer. First, it mischaracterized the hearing officer's reference to the federal guidelines. It is true, as the hearing officer noted, that the federal guidelines address the use of controlled substances in treating pain in cancer patients. However, the hearing officer did not, as the board suggests, rely solely upon the federal guidelines in determining that Dr. Hoover's (D) prescription practices were not excessive. Rather, he used the federal guidelines to buttress his independent determination of the persuasiveness and credibility of the expert witnesses on both sides. For example, one of the agency's (P) physicians opined that the number of pills that Dr. Hoover (D) had prescribed to one patient would be lethal, even though the amount that Dr. Hoover (D) had prescribed fell well within the federal guidelines. Such use of the federal guidelines was relevant and reasonable. Second, the hearing officer was entitled to believe Dr. Hoover's (D) testimony and doubt the testimony of the agency's (P) experts. Dr. Hoover (D) testified in great detail about the treatment of each patient. The hearing officer was entitled to give this testimony greater weight than that of the agency's (P) witnesses, who did not examine these patients or regularly engage in the treatment of intractable pain. Reversed.

Analysis:

In this case, the medical board acts as the investigator, prosecutor, and judge at the hearing. Thus, it is kind of like having the judge on the same team as one of the parties. Therefore, judicial review (review of the board's decision by a neutral adjudicator) seems particularly appropriate, and is the doctor's right upon an adverse determination. However, judges usually give broad deference to the decisions of the board, requiring only that the charges be supported by some sort of evidence. Courts generally do not do a de novo review. Rather, they review the board for abuse of discretion. There are many different grounds for physician discipline. In this case, the charge against the doctor amounted to one of incompetence, but incompetence is not the only ground for discipline, nor is it the most common. There are more disciplinary actions against doctors due to the use of drugs or alcohol. Other grounds include conviction of some crime rendering the doctor unfit for the practice of medicine and sexual relations with patients.

■ CASE VOCABULARY

INTRACTABLE: Difficult to manage, relieve or cure.

State Board of Registration for the Healing Arts v. McDonagh

(Disciplinary Board) v. *(Physician)*

123 S.W.3d 146 (Mo. 2003)

DOCTORS MUST EXERCISE THE STANDARD OF CARE APPLIED BY PHYSICIANS IN SIMILAR CIRCUMSTANCES

■ **INSTANT FACTS** McDonagh (D) used chelation therapy to treat vascular disease, and the Board of Registration (P) claimed that treatment constituted repeated negligence.

■ **BLACK LETTER RULE** The appropriate standard of care is the degree of skill and learning used by members of the profession in similar circumstances.

■ **PROCEDURAL BASIS**

Appeal from an order of the circuit court, affirming a finding of no violation.

■ **FACTS**

McDonagh (D), a licensed osteopathic physician, used chelation therapy to treat various vascular conditions. He followed a protocol developed by the American College for the Advancement of Medicine. The FDA had not approved chelation therapy for such treatments, and the American Medical Association had issued a study saying that there was no evidence that chelation therapy was effective. No rule was adopted forbidding the use of the therapy, however. McDonagh (D) continued to use chelation therapy, and recommended that his patients follow a diet and exercise regimen. He did not discourage his patients from seeing other physicians, and he had his patients sign an informed consent form. The form explained, among other things, that chelation therapy was not approved for the treatment of vascular disease.

After inquiries about his use of chelation therapy, the Board of Registration (P) filed a complaint against McDonagh (D) in 1994, but that complaint was dismissed. A second complaint was filed in 1996. That complaint alleged, among other things, repeated negligence because of the use of chelation therapy. At the hearing, the Board (P) introduced expert testimony that the use of chelation therapy was not generally accepted in the field of treatment of vascular disease and did not meet the standard of care for the treatment of vascular disease. McDonagh (D) introduced expert testimony of his own that supported the use of chelation therapy to treat vascular disease. The Administrative Hearing Commission (AHC) found no evidence of harm from McDonagh's (D) use of chelation therapy, dismissed all thirteen counts of the complaint, and found no cause to discipline McDonagh (D). The circuit court affirmed the AHC finding.

On appeal, the Board (P) argued that, in order to counter the Board's (P) experts, McDonagh (D) was required to introduce evidence that he met the standard of care generally accepted in the medical profession. According to the Board (P), this meant that McDonagh (D) was negligent if he used treatments other than those generally offered by doctors in the field. McDonagh (D) argued that the proper standard of care was the standard set by physicians who use chelation therapy. Since he followed the protocols set by those physicians, McDonagh (D) argued, he was not negligent.

In 2001, the Board of Registration (P) issued a statement that said chelation therapy was ineffective, but that it would not seek to discipline physicians who used it to treat vascular conditions, provided the physician's patients signed an approved informed consent form. The consent form was similar to the one used by McDonagh (D).

■ ISSUE

Is the proper standard of care to be used in determining if a physician is negligent in his choice of treatments the standard generally accepted in the medical profession?

■ DECISION AND RATIONALE

(Denvir Stith, J.) No. The appropriate standard of care is the degree of skill and learning used by members of the profession in similar circumstances. The standard by which to judge McDonagh's (D) actions is the standard of care used by doctors treating vascular disease.

Physicians may make different determinations on the appropriate treatment for a condition. That does not necessarily mean that one physician is negligent. Instead, it could simply mean that different physicians have used their skill and training to come to different conclusions. It does not matter that a treatment selected is not the most popular. This approach would penalize physicians who pursue unconventional courses of treatment, or who use a medicine for off-label purposes.

In this case, if McDonagh's (D) treatment, including the diet and exercise regimen, and the lack of evidence of harm from his approach, demonstrates the degree of skill and learning ordinarily used by members of the profession, there are no grounds for discipline. The AHC, however, relied on McDonagh's (D) expert testimony regarding the standard used by physicians who use chelation therapy. This evidence did not show whether the experts applied the proper standard of care, so the case must be remanded to the AHC for further consideration.

■ CONCURRENCE IN PART, DISSENT IN PART:

(Wolff, J.) The Board (P) is attempting to use the disciplinary process to impose its own sense of orthodoxy. After several days of testimony and a great deal of evidence, the AHC issued seventy pages of findings of fact and conclusions of law that found no cause for discipline. Specifically, the AHC concluded that McDonagh's (D) use of chelation therapy caused no one to suffer any harm, gave some benefit to many, and was provided with the informed consent of the patients who received the treatment.

At the time McDonagh (D) administered his treatments, the Board (P) had no rule against providing chelation therapy for vascular ailments. The Board (D) did not adopt its rule until several years after McDonagh's (D) treatments. The Board (D) specifically declared that it would not seek discipline against physicians who use chelation therapy. The question then becomes, is the unapproved use of chelation therapy negligence, or can so-called acts of negligence be the grounds for discipline when there is no evidence that anyone was harmed by them?

Physicians are given broad leeway in determining an appropriate treatment. Negligence does not seem to fit the case where a physician has studied a condition and made a treatment recommendation. Failure of the FDA to approve a treatment does not necessarily mean it is inappropriate or dangerous. If chelation therapy were in fact dangerous, the Board's (P) rule refusing to discipline physicians for using it would be unconscionable.

Analysis:

Some of the common policy arguments advanced against allowing patients to receive unconventional treatments that are at best harmless is that the patients do not know what they are getting, and they are dissuaded from seeking more conventional, and possibly more effective, treatments. McDonagh (D) seems to have gone to some lengths to counter those objections. The court notes that he did not discourage patients from seeing other physicians, and his implied consent form told patients that chelation therapy may not work for them. In addition, the evidence introduced by McDonagh (D) was limited to scientific studies. He did not dispute the medical efficacy of other treatments or claim a "conspiracy" to "silence" him—claims that are sometimes made by practitioners who use unconventional treatments.

State Board of Nursing and State Board of Healing Arts v. Ruebke

(*Licensing Boards*) v. (*Midwife*)

259 Kan. 599, 913 P.2d 142 (1996)

PRACTICES THAT COMPETE WITH THOSE OF A LICENSED PHYSICIAN DO NOT NECESSARILY BECOME THE PRACTICE OF MEDICINE.

■ **INSTANT FACTS** The Kansas medical and nursing boards sought a temporary injunction to stop a midwife from practicing her trade without a medical or nursing license.

■ **BLACK LETTER RULE** Midwifery does not fit the definition of either a healing art or nursing, and thus a lay midwife is not required to be licensed as long as she limits her practice to activities that do not constitute a healing art (unless supervised by a licensed physician.)

■ **PROCEDURAL BASIS**

Appeal from denial of a temporary injunction.

■ **FACTS**

The Board of Healing Arts (Healing Arts) (P) and the Board of Nursing (Nursing) (P) sought a temporary injunction to stop E. Michelle Ruebke (D) from continuing her alleged practice of nursing and medicine. Ruebke (D) is a lay midwife, comprehensively assisting pregnant women with prenatal care, delivery, and postpartum care. She follows the standards of care promulgated by the Kansas Midwives Association, which include assessing family medical history, establishing prenatal care plans, assisting in births, and post-partum care. She works with supervising physicians who are aware of her mode of practice and are available for consultation and perform many of the medical tests incident to pregnancy. At the hearing, Dr. Debra Messamore, an obstetrician/gynecologist, testified that the standards of the Kansas Midwives Association were similar to the standards that she used in the practice of obstetrics and that the prenatal and post-partum assessments made by Ruebke (D) were medical judgments. Dr. Messamore also testified that many of the procedures that Ruebke (D) performed could be performed by a nurse. Ginger Breedlove, a nurse practitioner and nurse-midwife, reviewed the records of two births and testified that nursing functions were involved. The court below found that the provisions of the healing arts act and nursing act were unconstitutionally vague, that Ruebke's (D) practice did not fall under the provisions of either act, and that, in the alternative, Ruebke's (D) practice fell within exceptions to the acts. The district court denied the temporary injunction.

■ **ISSUE**

Do midwives perform the type of activities that are the "practice of medicine?"

■ **DECISION AND RATIONALE**

(Larson, J.) No. We start with a brief look at the history of midwifery. Women have been practicing as midwives since Biblical times. In early American society, Midwives often occupied positions of great prestige. In the 19th and 20th centuries, doctors lobbied for more restrictive licensing laws. The Kansas Legislature adopted its first restrictions on the practice of medicine in 1870, though there is a notable absence of any attempt to specifically target midwives. At that time, there were not enough licensed physicians to deliver all of the children born in the state. In fact, until 1910 approximately half of all births in this country were midwife assisted. Although obstetricians held themselves out as a specialized branch of medicine as early as 1868, midwives were not seen engaged in the practice of obstetrics. Currently 25 states have laws regulating the practice of midwifery and 12 states, including Kansas, place no prohibition, either direct or indirect, on the practice. In 1978 the Kansas Legislature created a new classification of nurses known as Advanced Registered Nurse Practitioner, of which one subclass is a certified nurse midwife. Although this arguably demonstrates the legislature's intent to prohibit the practice of lay midwives, this contention has been rejected elsewhere. Both the Kansas Attorney General and Healing Arts (P) have written opinions that midwifery is the practice of medicine and therefore requires licensure. Neither opinion is binding on the courts. With this history in mind, we consider the initial question of whether the healing arts act is unconstitutionally vague. A statute is unconstitutionally vague if a person of ordinary intelligence cannot understand what conduct is prohibited and it fails to guard against arbitrary and discriminatory enforcement. In relevant part, the healing arts act requires licensure of any person who practices a "healing art," which is defined as "any system, treatment, operation, diagnosis, prescription, or practice for the ascertainment, cure, relief, palliation, adjustment, or correction of any human disease, ailment, deformity, or injury." *K.S.A. 65-2802(a).* We hold that this definition uses words that have ordinary, definite, and ascertainable meanings, and therefore the act is not unconstitutionally vague. However, though the act is not vague, we find that the definitional provisions of the healing arts act do not cover midwifery. The act focuses exclusively on pathologies (i.e., disease) and abnormalities (i.e., ailments, deformities, or injuries). Pregnancy and childbirth are neither pathologies nor abnormalities. Healing Arts (P) has argued that since obstetrics is a branch of medicine and obstetricians perform functions commonly performed by midwives, that midwifery is also the practice of medicine. However, history clearly shows that obstetrics and midwifery coexisted separately for many years. It is true that many pregnant women prefer that physicians assist during the birth of their children. But the fact that a person with medical training provides services in competition with someone with no medical degree does not transform the latter's practices into the practice of medicine. Although we conclude that midwifery itself is not the practice of medicine, this does not mean that lay midwives may perform any activity whatsoever on pregnant women. Lay midwives must take care to avoid activities that are regulated under the healing arts act. However, we need not decide the exact definition of healing arts at this juncture. It is uncontested that Ruebke (D) was working under the supervision of licensed physicians, which puts her squarely within an exception to the licensure requirement. Nursing (P) also claims that Ruebke's (D) practice of midwifery violates the nursing act, which requires licensure of persons who hold themselves out as having specialized knowledge in areas of the biological, physical, and behavioral sciences and educational preparation within the field of the healing arts. Ruebke (D) claims no such specialized knowledge. Rather, her assistance is sought because she, like generations of midwives before her, has practical experience assisting in childbirth. Even though the Legislature has the authority to place lay midwifery within the practice of nursing, it has not done so. Affirmed.

Analysis:

This case addresses the question of exactly what constitutes the "practice of medicine." Since the licensing of physicians falls within the state's police power, the practice of medicine is defined by state legislatures. Statutes defining the practice of medicine have historically been very broad in scope. The traditional acts of medical diagnosis (as opposed to nursing diagnosis), medical treatment, and writing prescriptions are generally thought of as the practice of medicine. However, not every activity aimed at producing good (or at least better) health is the practice of medicine. Thus, advising a person on which brand of cough syrup works best is not the practice of medicine (or else every pharmaceutical company that advertises its cough remedies on television would be guilty of unlicensed practice). Some have suggested, as this opinion hints at, that the distinction is whether one holds oneself out to the public as having the requisite education to diagnose and treat diseases.

■ CASE VOCABULARY

MIDWIFE: A person (usually a woman) who is not a doctor and who assists women in childbirth.

NURSE PRACTITIONER: A person trained in the nursing arts who has more education than a nurse and is generally given more responsibility and autonomy in diagnosing and treating patients.

Sermchief v. Gonzales

(Licensing Board) v. *(Nurses)*

660 S.W.2d 683 (Mo. 1983)

THERE IS A THIN LINE BETWEEN THE PRACTICE OF NURSING AND THE PRACTICE OF MEDICINE

■ **INSTANT FACTS** Nurses who engaged in the assessment and diagnosis of patients were threatened with being charged with the unauthorized practice of medicine.

■ **BLACK LETTER RULE** The statutory concept of professional nursing is broad and expansive, and nursing activity is not unauthorized practice of medicine as long as the nurse acts within his or her training and skill level.

■ PROCEDURAL BASIS

Appeal from refusal to grant declaratory judgment and injunction.

■ FACTS

Two nurses (P) and five physicians (P) are employed at the East Missouri Action Agency (the Agency), which provides medical services in the fields of family planning, obstetrics and gynecology to low income individuals. The nurses (P) are duly licensed as nurses, and the physicians (P) are licensed by the Missouri State Board of Registration for the Healing Arts (the Board) (D). The nurses (P) routinely provide such services as taking medical histories, breast and pelvic examinations, PAP smears, gonorrhea cultures and blood serology, providing information about contraception, dispensing certain medication, counseling services, and community education. There is no evidence that any action of the nurses (P) has caused harm to any patient. All acts of the nurses (P) are taken pursuant to written standing orders and protocols signed by the physicians (P). The Board (D) threatened to order the nurses (P) to show cause why they should not be found guilty of the unauthorized practice of medicine, and the physicians (P) guilty of aiding and abetting the unauthorized practice of medicine. The nurses (P) and physicians (P) brought this action for a temporary injunction and declaratory judgment, asking this court to declare that the nurses (P) are not engaging in the unauthorized practice of medicine.

■ ISSUE

Do nurses who assess and diagnose patients' symptoms engage in the practice of medicine?

■ DECISION AND RATIONALE

(Welliver, J.) No. We have been asked to define that thin line that separates the practice of medicine from the practice of nursing. We decline to do so because we believe that this would serve no purpose but to invite an avalanche of medical and nursing malpractice suits that would hinder the delivery of health services. Therefore, we consider only whether the acts of these particular nurses (P) constitute the practice of medicine. In 1975, the legislature substantially expanded the definition of "professional nursing" in our statutes, thereby expanding the scope of a nurse's duties. For example, the current legislation has eliminated the requirement that a physician directly supervise all nursing staff. Another significant change is that the legislature formulated an open-ended definition of professional nursing. The old statute limited nursing to services in care of the sick, in the prevention of disease or in the conservation of health. The new act defines a much broader spectrum of nursing functions (teaching patients about health care, administration of medications, assessment and nursing diagnosis of patients, coordination of a health care plan, and teaching and supervising other nurses) and in addition it qualifies the definition as "including, but not limited to" these functions. We believe that this was meant to avoid constraints on the evolution of new responsibilities for nurses, so long as those responsibilities are consistent with the nurse's specialized education, judgment and skill based on knowledge and application of principles derived from the biological, physical, social and nursing sciences—as is required by the statute. The acts of the nurses (P) clearly fall within this standard. All acts were performed pursuant to the physicians' (P) standing orders and protocols, which was a standard practice at the time the current statute was enacted. There is nothing in the statute that would restrict or limit their continued use. We believe that the type of acts that the nurses (P) are performing are precisely the type of acts that the legislature contemplated when it granted nurses the right to make assessments and nursing diagnoses. Reversed.

Analysis:

This case looks at where the practice of nursing ends and the practice of medicine begins. Vagueness in practice of medicine statutes makes them open to constitutional attack (though the attacks are usually unsuccessful). Under modern statutes, nurses are allowed to do many of the same things that doctors do, such as diagnosis and counseling of patients, but the limits of that overlap are unclear. Here, the court seems to be unwilling to limit what a nurse can do, so long as the nurses are clearly subordinate to the doctors.

CHAPTER THREE

Quality Control Regulation of Health Care Institutions

Mauceri v. Chassin

Instant Facts: The Department of Health (D) is requiring an agency which provides the names of health care aides for patients to comply with statutory licensing requirements.

Black Letter Rule: The construction given to a statute by the agency charged with implementing it should be upheld if not irrational.

In Re the Estate of Michael Patrick Smith v. Heckler

Instant Facts: The plaintiffs brought a class action on behalf of Medicaid recipients residing in nursing homes in an effort to improve the deplorable conditions at many nursing homes.

Black Letter Rule: The Secretary of Health and Human Services has a duty to establish a system to adequately inform herself as to whether the facilities receiving federal money are satisfying the requirements of the Medicaid Act, including providing high quality patient care.

Fairfax Nursing Home, Inc. v. U.S. Dep't of Health & Human Services

Instant Facts: Civil fines were imposed on Fairfax (D) for failure to comply with patient care regulations, and Fairfax (D) claimed that the fines were excessive.

Black Letter Rule: When imposing sanctions for deficient care, the situation of all similar patients at a facility must be considered, not just the status of an individual patient or patients.

Mauceri v. Chassin

(Home Health Aide Agent) v. *(Dept. of Health)*
156 Misc.2d 802, 594 N.Y.S.2d 605 (Sup. Ct. 1993)

PROVIDING THE NAMES OF PEOPLE WILLING TO PROVIDE NURSING SERVICES MAY BE REGULAT-
ED

■ **INSTANT FACTS** The Department of Health (D) is requiring an agency which provides the names of health care aides for patients to comply with statutory licensing requirements.

■ **BLACK LETTER RULE** The construction given to a statute by the agency charged with implementing it should be upheld if not irrational.

■ **PROCEDURAL BASIS**

Action brought by the plaintiff in objection to a statutory licensing requirement.

■ **FACTS**

Mauceri (P) has operated a business out of her home for over ten years, providing patients and their families with the names of home health aides. It is up to the patient or the family to contact the aide and work out the specific pay scale, hours, and duties. Mauceri (P) receives compensation directly from the patient or the family at a flat rate of 80 cents per hour for each hour the aide works for the client. Mauceri (P) does not conduct an investigation as to the qualifications of the aides, nor does she create a care plan for the patient, or maintain medical records. The Department of Health (D) received a complaint that Mauceri (P) was referring home health aides without being licensed as a home health care services agency.

■ **ISSUE**

Do the services rendered by the plaintiff require that she be licensed as a home care services agency?

■ **DECISION AND RATIONALE**

(Not Stated) Yes. The construction given to a statute by the agency charged with implementing it should be upheld if not irrational. Public Health Law Section 3602(2) provides that "home care services agency" means "an organization primarily engaged in arranging and/or providing directly or through contract arrangement" with "home health aide services." Mauceri (P) claims that her services are not encompassed by this statutory definition, however the Department of Health (D) disagrees. Clearly, Mauceri's (P) business is an organization engaged in arranging for home health services. She receives compensation for providing the names of health care providers to patients seeking such. Since the Department of Health's (D) interpretation of the statute is not irrational, it will be upheld. That being the case, Mauceri will be enjoined from operating her home health care referral service until such time as she has been licensed under article 36.

Analysis:

A state agency may regulate only under its statutory authority; if there is no legislative authorization for the regulation of a specific institution, the state may not reach that entity. However, if an agency does have statutory authority, its construction of a statute should be upheld if it is not irrational. In this case, Mauceri's (P) business clearly fits within the statute. The fact that she does not provide or supervise the health services does not mean that she is not arranging for them when she provides her clients with a list of home health aides. As such, it is not irrational to interpret Public Health Law § 3602(2) as encompassing Mauceri's (P) business. Thus, the court correctly held that she must comply with the licensing requirements of the statute.

■ **CASE VOCABULARY**

ENJOINED: Prevented; stopped.

In re the Estate of Michael Patrick Smith v. Heckler

(*Medicaid Recipients*) v. (*Secretary of Health and Human Services*)

747 F.2d 583 (10th Cir. 1984)

THE SECRETARY MUST INSURE THAT STATES COMPLY WITH THE CONGRESSIONAL MANDATE TO PROVIDE HIGH QUALITY MEDICAL CARE AND REHABILITATIVE SERVICES

■ **INSTANT FACTS** The plaintiffs brought a class action on behalf of Medicaid recipients residing in nursing homes in an effort to improve the deplorable conditions at many nursing homes.

■ **BLACK LETTER RULE** The Secretary of Health and Human Services has a duty to establish a system to adequately inform herself as to whether the facilities receiving federal money are satisfying the requirements of the Medicaid Act, including providing high quality patient care.

■ PROCEDURAL BASIS

Appeal from the District Court's judgment in favor of the defendant.

■ FACTS

The plaintiffs brought this class action under the Medicaid Act on behalf of Medicaid recipients residing in nursing homes in an effort to improve the deplorable conditions at many nursing homes. They provided evidence of the lack of adequate medical care and of the widespread knowledge that care is inadequate. They alleged that the Secretary of Health and Human Services (D) has a statutory duty under the Medicaid Act to develop and implement a system of nursing home review and enforcement designed to ensure that Medicaid recipients residing in Medicaid-certified nursing homes actually receive the optimal medical and psychosocial care that they are entitled to under the Act. The plaintiffs contended that the enforcement system developed by the Secretary (D) is "facility-oriented," not "patient-oriented" and thereby fails to meet the statutory mandate. The district court found that although a patient care or "patient-oriented" management system is feasible, the Secretary (D) does not have a duty to introduce and require the use of such a system.

■ ISSUE

Does the Secretary of Health and Human Services have a statutory duty to develop and implement a system of nursing home review and enforcement, which focuses on and ensures high quality patient care?

■ DECISION AND RATIONALE

(McKay, C.J.) Yes. The purpose of the Medicaid Act is to enable the federal government to assist states in providing medical assistance to aged, blind or disabled individuals, whose income and resources are insufficient to meet the costs of necessary medical services, and rehabilitation and other services to help such individuals to attain or retain capabilities for independence or self care. To receive funding, a state must submit to the Secretary (D) and have approved by the Secretary (D), a plan for medical assistance, which meets the requirements of the Act. Congress gave the Secretary (D) a general mandate to promulgate rules and regulations necessary to the efficient administration of the functions with which the Secretary (D) is charged by the Act. Pursuant to this mandate, the Secretary (D) has promulgated standards for the care to be provided by skilled nursing facilities and intermediate care facilities. The Secretary (D) has established a procedure for determining whether state plans comply with the standards set out in the regulations. This enforcement mechanism is known as the "survey/certification" inspection system. Under this system, the states conduct reviews of nursing homes, and the Secretary (D) then determines, on the basis of the survey results, whether the nursing home surveyed is eligible for certification and, thus, eligible for Medicaid funds. The states must use federal standards, forms, methods, and procedures in conducting the survey. At issue in this case is the form SSA-1569, which the Secretary (D) requires the states to use to show that the nursing homes participating in Medicaid under an approved state plan meet the conditions of participation contained in the Act and the regulations. Plaintiffs contend that the form is "facility-oriented," in that it focuses on the theoretical capability of the facility to provide high quality care, rather than "patient-oriented," which would focus on the care actually provided. After carefully reviewing the statutory scheme of the Medicaid Act, the legislative history, and the district court's opinion, we conclude that the district court improperly defined the Secretary's (D) duty under the statute. The federal government has more than a passive role in handing out money to the states. The district court erred in finding that the burden of enforcing the substantive provisions of the Medicaid Act is on the states. The Secretary (D) has a duty to establish a system to adequately inform herself as to whether the facilities receiving federal money are satisfying the requirements of the Act, including providing high quality patient care. This duty to be adequately informed is not only a duty to be informed at the time a facility is originally certified, but is a duty of continued supervision. Being charged with this function, we must conclude that a failure to promulgate regulations that allow the Secretary (D) to remain informed, on a continuing basis, as to whether facilities receiving federal money are meeting the requirements of the Act, is an abdication of the Secretary's (D) duty. While the Medicaid Act is admittedly very complex and the Secretary (D) has exceptionally broad authority to prescribe standards for applying certain sections of the Act, the Secretary's authority cannot be interpreted so as to hold that that authority is merely permissive authority. The Secretary (D) must insure that states comply with the congressional mandate to provide high quality medical care and rehabilitative services. Reversed and remanded.

Analysis:

Nothing in the Medicaid Act indicates that Congress intended the physical facilities to be the end product. Rather, the purpose of the Act is to provide medical assistance and rehabilitative services. The Act repeatedly focuses on the care to be provided, with facilities being only part of that care. While the district court correctly noted that it is the state that develops specific standards and actually conducts the inspection, there is nothing in the Act to indicate that the state function relieves the Secretary (D) of all responsibility to ensure that the purposes of the Act are being accomplished. The Secretary (D), not the state, determines which facilities are eligible for federal funds. While participation in the program is voluntary, states that choose to participate must comply with federal statutory requirements.

■ CASE VOCABULARY

CLASS ACTION: A means by which, where a large group of persons are interested in a matter, one or more may sue or be sued as representatives of the class without needing to join every member of the class.

Fairfax Nursing Home, Inc. v. U.S. Dep't of Health & Human Services

(Skilled Nursing Facility) v. *(Regulator)*

300 F.3d 835 (7th Cir. 2002), *cert. denied*, 537 U.S. 1111, 123 S.Ct. 901, 154 L.Ed.2d 784 (2003)

SANCTIONS FOR DEFICIENT CARE MUST CONSIDER THE LEVEL OF CARE FOR ALL PATIENTS AT A FACILITY

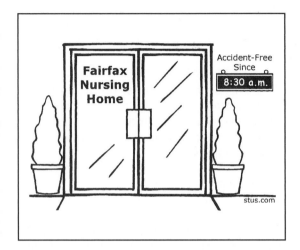

■ **INSTANT FACTS** Civil fines were imposed on Fairfax (D) for failure to comply with patient care regulations, and Fairfax (D) claimed that the fines were excessive.

■ **BLACK LETTER RULE** When imposing sanctions for deficient care, the situation of all similar patients at a facility must be considered, not just the status of an individual patient or patients.

■ PROCEDURAL BASIS

Appeal from an order of the appellate division affirming a civil monetary penalty.

■ FACTS

As a skilled nursing facility, Fairfax (D) was subject to unannounced surveys by state regulators. After one such survey, it was determined that Fairfax (D) engaged in acts and omissions that posed "immediate jeopardy" to the health and safety of its residents. Five specific incidents were noted. The first, which happened on December 20, 1996, involved a ventilator-dependent patient whose ventilator was turned off during an emergency. The ventilator was not turned back on after emergency care was given, and the patient died. Fairfax (D) developed a policy for the care of ventilator-dependent residents after that incident. The second incident was on March 2, 1997. Contrary to Fairfax's (D) policy, the patient's chart did not show whether a doctor's instructions regarding a patient's care were followed. The patient died shortly afterwards. The third incident, on March 5, 1997, involved a failure to make a complete assessment of a patient's condition or to take the patient's vital signs, failure to make follow-up assessments, and failure to contact a physician. There was no record that the patient was properly treated. The patient had a severe infection and died on March 27. The fourth incident, on March 23, 1997, involved a failure to monitor a patient's condition. The fifth incident, on April 2, 1997, involved the failure to use sterile procedures while performing tracheostomy care on two patients.

Fairfax (D) was found to have violated the rules relating to the special care of ventilator-dependent patients. A civil monetary penalty of $3,050 per day, from December 20, 1996, through April 3, 1997, was imposed based on the conclusion that the deficiencies constituted immediate jeopardy. Fairfax (D) claimed that the penalty was excessive. Fairfax (D) argued that the Administrative Law Judge who imposed the penalties used the term "potential" in several findings to describe the probability of harm, and that the term "potential" justified a lower range of penalties.

■ ISSUE

Was the penalty imposed against Fairfax (D) excessive?

■ DECISION AND RATIONALE

(Ripple, J.) No. When imposing sanctions for deficient care, the situation of all similar patients at a facility must be considered, not just the status of an individual patient or patients. It is clear that the ALJ applied the proper standard in fixing the penalty. Although the ALJ used the term "potential," the findings all concluded that Fairfax's (D) actions or inactions caused or were likely to cause serious injury or death. The ALJ's opinion focused on the entire state of readiness at Fairfax (D), and not just on the situation of each individual patient. A respiratory patient at Fairfax's (D) facility was in continuous jeopardy of serious injury or death because of the incapacity of the facility.

There is adequate evidence to support the findings. There are numerous documented instances of Fairfax's (D) failure to properly care for ventilator-dependent patients. The common thread is a lack of follow-up and monitoring of patients in respiratory distress. The record supports the determination that a state of immediate jeopardy to patient health or safety existed. Affirmed.

Analysis:

The purpose of unannounced surveys is not so much to catch specific incidents, but to assess the overall quality and compliance of a facility. It is always possible to argue that there is no connection between incidents with different patients, but in this case, there was a common thread. The punishment was levied for the entire situation at Fairfax (D), not just what happened to the individual patients. The occurrences with each patient are, in a sense, evidence of that overall situation.

■ CASE VOCABULARY

ADMINISTRATIVE LAW JUDGE: An official who presides at an administrative hearing and who has the power to administer oaths, take testimony, rule on questions of evidence, and make factual and legal determinations.

CIVIL PENALTY: A fine assessed for a violation of a statute or regulation.

CHAPTER FOUR

The Professional–Patient Relationship

Esquivel v. Watters

Instant Facts: Esquivel's (P) baby died after Watters (P) failed to inform Esquivel of a serious irregularity noted in a gender-determination sonogram.

Black Letter Rule: No legal duty to provide medical treatment, diagnosis, or advice exists outside the physician-patient relationship.

Millard v. Corrado

Instant Facts: Summary judgment was entered in favor of Dr. Corrado (D) in Millard's (P) malpractice and general negligence suit against him because there was no physician-patient relationship between them.

Black Letter Rule: In a negligence case, a physician may have a duty of due care to a non-patient if the physician's allegedly negligent acts or omissions do not involve matters of medical science, and where public policy favors the existence of a duty or the harm is particularly foreseeable.

Mills v. Pate

Instant Facts: Dr. Pate (D) guaranteed that Mills (P) would be beautiful and have smooth skin if she underwent liposuction surgery.

Black Letter Rule: A negligence action may not be recast as a contractual claim so as to avoid statutory requirements governing healthcare liability claims.

Tunkl v. Regents of Univ. of California

Instant Facts: A lawsuit arose over a charitable research hospital's requirement that as a condition of admission all patients release the hospital from liability for negligence.

Black Letter Rule: Even charitable research hospitals may not, consistent with California law, impose as a condition of admission a requirement that patients release the hospital from future liability for negligence.

Shorter v. Drury

Instant Facts: A woman died from loss of blood when, in accord with her religious convictions, she refused to accept a blood transfusion during a surgery gone wrong.

Black Letter Rule: Given the problems that arise when a patient on religious grounds refuses to permit necessary blood transfusions during a surgery, it is not inappropriate for a physician dealing with such a patient to require him or her to sign a release relieving the physician from responsibility for unfavorable consequences resulting from the refusal of blood.

Canterbury v. Spence

Instant Facts: A back-surgery patient sued his doctor and the hospital in which the surgery was performed when he became paralyzed just following the surgery.

Black Letter Rule: A physician's obligation to his or her patient imposes upon the physician a duty to disclose all treatment options available and the dangers inherently and potentially involved with each.

Johnson v. Kokemoor

Instant Facts: A patient filed suit against her physician claiming that his failure to honestly disclose the extent of his experience performing a certain surgery violated the doctrine of informed consent.

Black Letter Rule: A patient cannot make an informed, intelligent decision regarding suggested treatment unless the physician discloses all of the viable alternatives and risks of the treatment proposed, including the physician's experience in performing a particular procedure, his or her risk statistics as compared with those of other physicians who perform the procedure, and the availability of other physicians better able to perform the procedure.

Arato v. Avedon

Instant Facts: A widow and her two children sued their husband/father's former doctor for malpractice, claiming that his failure to inform the patient of his life expectancy was a breach of the physician's duty to fully disclose all material information regarding proposed treatment.

Black Letter Rule: While physicians have a duty to disclose all available choices with respect to proposed therapy and the dangers inherently and potentially involved in each, it is unwise to require, as a matter of law, that a particular species of information such as mortality rates associated with a particular condition always be disclosed.

Moore v. Regents of the University of California

Instant Facts: A patient filed suit against his doctor and the doctor's employer when it became known that, despite prior protestations to the contrary, they were using the patient's cells for their own personal economic gain.

Black Letter Rule: A physician who is seeking a patient's consent for a medical procedure must, in order to satisfy his fiduciary duty and to obtain the patient's informed consent, disclose personal interests unrelated to the patient's health, whether research or economic, that may affect his medical judgment.

Canterbury v. Spence

Instant Facts: A back-surgery patient sued his doctor and the hospital in which the surgery was performed when he became paralyzed just following the surgery.

Black Letter Rule: A causal connection between nondisclosure and harm to the patient exists only when disclosure of significant risks incidental to treatment would have resulted in a decision against accepting that treatment, as demonstrated by a showing of what a reasonable person would do under similar circumstances.

Tisdale v. Pruitt, Jr., M.D.

Instant Facts: A lawsuit was filed when a physician performed a dilation and curettage (D & C) in his office; had the physician looked closely at the patient's chart, he would have discovered that she was not there to have the procedure performed, but only to get a second opinion about its necessity.

Black Letter Rule: In a medical malpractice action, punitive damages are only available when there is evidence of wilful, wanton, or reckless conduct on the part of the physician.

Canterbury v. Spence

Instant Facts: A back-surgery patient sued his doctor and the hospital in which the surgery was performed when he became paralyzed just following the surgery.

Black Letter Rule: A physician can treat a patient without making all material disclosures when: (1) the patient is unconscious or otherwise incapable of consenting, and the harm from a failure to treat is imminent and outweighs any harm threatened by the proposed treatment, or (2) the disclosure of the risks poses such a threat of detriment to the patient that it becomes improper from a medical point of view.

Humphers v. First Interstate Bank of Oregon

Instant Facts: A woman sued her former doctor when he revealed her identity to a daughter whom she had given up for adoption over twenty years earlier.

Black Letter Rule: An unauthorized and unprivileged disclosure of confidential information obtained in a confidential relationship can give rise to tort damages.

Doe v. Medlantic Health Care Group, Inc.

Instant Facts: A hospital employee (D) told Doe's (P) co-workers that Doe (P) was HIV positive.

Black Letter Rule: The tort of breach of a confidential relationship consists of the unconsented, unprivileged disclosure to a third party of nonpublic information learned within a confidential relationship.

Herman v. Kratche

Instant Facts: A clinic disclosed a patient's non-work-related medical records to the patient's employer without her consent.

Black Letter Rule: A healthcare provider can be held liable for the unauthorized disclosure of patient medical records if a fiduciary relationship is breached, causing the patient's damages.

Acosta v. Byrum et al.

Instant Facts: The plaintiff's confidential medical and psychiatric records were impermissibly accessed and disseminated to third parties.

Black Letter Rule: Although HIPAA confers no private right of action, HIPAA requirements may be relied upon to establish the standard of care for a negligence claim.

Esquivel v. Watters

(Patient) v. *(Sonogram Technician)*

154 P.3d 1184 (Kan. Ct. App. 2007)

A SONOGRAM TECHNICIAN OWES NO DUTY TO PROVIDE MEDICAL TREATMENT

The good news is you're having a boy!

The bad news, I'll let your doctor tell you...

stus.com

■ **INSTANT FACTS** Esquivel's (P) baby died after Watters (P) failed to inform Esquivel of a serious irregularity noted in a gender-determination sonogram.

■ **BLACK LETTER RULE** No legal duty to provide medical treatment, diagnosis, or advice exists outside the physician-patient relationship.

■ **Procedural Basis**

On appeal to review a trial court decision granting the defendants' motion for summary judgment.

■ **FACTS**

Esquivel (P) obtained obstetric counseling from Ark City Clinic, which supplied her with a certificate for a free gender-determination sonogram from the South Central Kansas Regional Medical Center ("SCKRMC") (D). With her certificate, Esquivel (P) went to SCKRMC (D) for her free sonogram. Before the procedure, Esquivel (P) signed a consent form acknowledging that the purpose of the procedure was "to attempt to determine the sex of [her] unborn baby" and "not to determine any fetal abnormality or any other complication of pregnancy." SCKRMC (D) technician David Hazlett performed the sonogram and noted that Esquivel's (P) baby suffered from gastroschisis, a condition in which the baby's bowel is outside of its body. Hazlett, who was not a doctor, did not inform Esquivel (P) of his findings, but did orally report the irregularity to Watters (D), Esquivel's obstetrician. Because nothing was written in Esquivel's (P) medical records, Watters (D) forgot about Hazlett's oral report and never informed Esquivel (P) of the irregularity, despite some earlier efforts to communicate with her. Esquivel (P) learned of the gastroschisis when she gave birth to her son by emergency caesarean section. The baby died of the condition ten days later. Esquivel (P) sued Watters (D) and SCKRMC (D), among others, for wrongful death. The trial court granted the defendants' (D) motion for summary judgment because SCKRMC owed no duty to Esquivel (P) or her son that would support her claims.

■ **ISSUE**

Does a medical provider who undertakes a duty to perform a gender-determination sonogram owe the patient a legal duty to disclose known irregularities incidentally determined during the procedure?

■ **DECISION AND RATIONALE**

(Judge Undisclosed.) No. No legal duty to provide medical treatment, diagnosis, or advice exists outside the physician-patient relationship. In a medical malpractice claim like this, the existence of a legal duty is fundamental. Without a duty to act, a defendant cannot be held liable for negligence. As a long line of cases illustrates, the contours of the duty owed to a patient are shaped by the relationship developed between them. While a doctor-patient relationship is fiduciary in nature, a hospital-patient relationship is not. Here, SCKRMC (D) and Esquivel (P) were not in a healthcare provider-patient relationship. As the consent form makes clear, SCKRMC's (D) only duty was to refrain from negligence in determining the gender of Esquivel's (P) baby. Because there is no evidence suggesting Watters (D) committed negligence in performing the sonogram, summary judgment for lack of duty was appropriate. Affirmed.

Analysis:

As the case illustrates, a medical malpractice claim is, at its core, merely a negligence claim. Just as with other claims, a plaintiff asserting a cognizable malpractice claim must establish a duty owed by the defendant, a breach of that duty, probable cause, and damages. Without a breach of a duty, no malpractice claim exists. Here, consider whether the case would have come out the same way if the treating obstetrician were the defendant.

■ CASE VOCABULARY

DUTY: A legal obligation that is owed or due to another and that needs to be satisfied; an obligation for which somebody else has a corresponding right.

Millard v. Corrado

(Patient) v. *(Surgeon)*

14 S.W.3d 42 (Mo. Ct. App. 1999)

LACK OF A PHYSICIAN–PATIENT RELATIONSHIP IS NO BAR TO A NEGLIGENCE ACTION AGAINST A PHYSICIAN

But I thought playing hooky from work would actually PROTECT me from committing malpractice that day...

stus.com

■ **INSTANT FACTS** Summary judgment was entered in favor of Dr. Corrado (D) in Millard's (P) malpractice and general negligence suit against him because there was no physician-patient relationship between them.

■ **BLACK LETTER RULE** In a negligence case, a physician may have a duty of due care to a non-patient if the physician's allegedly negligent acts or omissions do not involve matters of medical science, and where public policy favors the existence of a duty or the harm is particularly foreseeable.

■ **Procedural Basis**

Appeal from an order granting summary judgment to the defendant.

■ **FACTS**

Dr. Corrado (D) was a general surgeon with staff privileges at Audrain Medical Center. Audrain held itself out as having a twenty-four hour emergency room with an in-house emergency room physician and a general surgeon on call. On November 5, Corrado (D) was scheduled to be the only general surgeon on call at the hospital. He also planned to attend a professional meeting in another city. Prior to leaving for the meeting, Corrado (D) asked Dr. Jolly, an orthopedic surgeon, to cover his calls during the four hours Corrado (D) would be at the meeting. Jolly agreed, even though he did not have general surgery privileges at the hospital. Corrado (D) left for the meeting without telling anyone at the hospital other than Jolly that he would be unavailable to provide general surgery to emergency room patients.

Later that morning, Millard (P) was involved in a car accident in which she suffered severe injuries. The accident occurred approximately fourteen miles from Audrain Medical Center and twenty-five miles from the University of Missouri Medical Center. An ambulance arrived on the scene, and the crew decided to transport Millard (P) to Audrain based on the proximity and on the belief that Audrain had a twenty-four hour emergency room with a surgeon on call. The ambulance crew radioed Audrain that they were transporting a critically injured patient to the emergency room, but Audrain did not reply.

Millard (P) was examined after she arrived at Audrain. A technician paged Corrado (D), because he was listed as the surgeon on call. A few minutes later, the emergency room physician examined Millard (P) and tried to page Corrado (D), but Corrado (D) still did not respond. Audrain staff tried to arrange to have Millard (P) transported by helicopter to the University of Missouri, but the weather was too bad for the flight. Jolly examined Millard (P) approximately one hour after she arrived at Audrain and concluded that she needed surgery, but he was not qualified to perform the surgery. In addition, Jolly did not have general surgery privileges at Audrain. Corrado (D) finally responded to his pages after Millard (P) had been at Audrain for nearly one and a half hours. It was agreed that Millard (P) should be transferred to the University of Missouri Medical Center. Corrado (D) testified that the decision to transfer her had

---

already been made when he called Audrain. Miller was transferred to the University, where she underwent surgery approximately four hours after the accident.

Millard (P) brought suit against Corrado (D), alleging that the delay in her treatment caused her to sustain injuries and also aggravated her existing injuries. Corrado (D) moved for, and was granted, summary judgment on the grounds that no physician-patient relationship existed between him and Millard (P).

■ ISSUE

Must a plaintiff prove the existence of a physician-patient relationship in a negligence action against a physician?

■ DECISION AND RATIONALE

(Dowd, J.) No. In a negligence case, a physician may be found to have a duty of due care to a non-patient if the physician's allegedly negligent acts or omissions do not involve matters of medical science, and where public policy favors the existence of a duty or the harm is particularly foreseeable. This duty exists independent of any physician-patient relationship.

When deciding the existence of a duty based on public policy, the courts should consider the social consensus that an interest is worth protecting, the foreseeability of harm and the degree of certainty that the protected person suffered the injury, the moral blame society assigns to the conduct, the prevention of future harm, the cost and the ability to spread the risk of loss, and the economic burden on the actor and the community. The application of these factors leads to a conclusion that Corrado (D) owed a duty to Millard (P). A regulation adopted by the General Assembly required on-call emergency room physicians to arrive at the hospital within thirty minutes, which shows the social consensus. It does not matter that the regulation was adopted after Millard's (P) accident; indeed, the Legislature acts largely in response to existing social consensus. Imposing a duty on emergency room physicians to respond to calls is not unduly burdensome. The inconvenience of responding is outweighed by the substantial risk to emergency room patients when a physician does not respond.

A duty will be recognized if harm is particularly foreseeable. A court will recognize a duty if, under the circumstances, a reasonable person would have anticipated danger and guarded against it. The harm to which Millard (P) was exposed by Corrado's (D) actions was reasonably foreseeable. Corrado's (D) attempt to delegate his responsibilities was conclusively ineffective, because Jolly was not qualified to perform general surgery, and he had no general surgical privileges at Aurain. Corrado's (D) failure to notify the hospital of his absence delayed Millard's (P) care. Under the circumstances, a reasonably prudent person would have foreseen that such conduct would create a substantial risk of harm to emergency room patients.

The fear that imposition of a duty to respond in a timely manner will cause fewer physicians to agree to be on call is unfounded. Physicians are not obligated to take on-call assignments. It is not a patient's expectation that a physician will be available that creates the duty; it is the physician's agreement to be available without reservation that creates the duty. There is no public interest that is furthered by allowing a physician who is on call to leave town without notifying the hospital that he or she will be unavailable.

The concurring opinion cites Restatement (Second) of Torts § 324A in support of Millard's (P) claim. Although no Missouri case applies § 324A in a medical negligence context, the Restatement is consistent with the conclusion in this case. Other jurisdictions have applied § 324A in medical negligence cases and create the same duty through application of the foundational principles of public policy and foreseeability that apply to all duties rooted in negligence.

However, if there is no physician-patient relationship, a medical malpractice claim must fail. The law defines a physician-patient relationship as a consensual relationship where the patient or someone acting on the patient's behalf knowingly employs a physician who consents to treat the patient. A physician-patient relationship is created only where the physician personally examines the patient, although courts have recognized a physician-patient relationship in the absence of any personal contact between the physician and patient. In *Corbet v. McKinney*, 980 S.W.2d 166 (Mo. Ct. App. 1998), for instance, the court stated that a physician-patient relationship exists between a patient and a consultant physician "where the physician is contractually obligated to provide assistance in the patient's diagnosis or treatment and does so." Millard (P) presented evidence to support finding a contractual obligation on the part of Corrado (D) to respond to calls within thirty minutes. Specifically, the response details Aurain staff bylaws relating to on-call physician responsibilities, and deposition testimony from Aurain's CEO Richard Jansen and other hospital personnel indicating such a duty. After examining the section of the bylaws before the trial court and the testimony of Jansen, we conclude that, absent contrary evidence, Millard (P) is entitled to the reasonable inference that Corrado (D) contracted to treat all general surgery patients who presented to the emergency room. Millard (P) therefore adequately pleaded both a general negligence claim and a medical negligence claim.

■ CONCURRENCE

(Crahan, J.) A claim for negligence against Corrado (D) is stated regardless of the existence of a physician-patient relationship. Missouri courts have applied the rule of Restatement (Second) of Torts § 324A, which provides that a person who undertakes to render services to another that he should recognize as necessary for the protection of a third person or his property is liable for physical harm if his failure to exercise due care increased the risk of harm. The Millards (P) have provided sufficient evidence to allow a jury to find all of the elements required for recovery.

Analysis:

It is unclear why the majority did not take the seemingly simpler route of adopting the analysis of Restatement § 324A. The majority does not reject the reasoning of the Restatement or the result that would be reached; in fact, the majority seems to say that § 324A is based on the same reasoning used by the majority. The majority draws a distinction between "general negligence" and "medical malpractice" that is not explained. Specifically, there is no explanation offered as to why § 324A, which has been applied by Missouri courts in negligence cases, should not be explicitly adopted solely because the negligence at issue was in a medical situation.

Mills v. Pate

(Patient) v. *(Physician)*

225 S.W.3d 277 (Tex. Ct. App.—El Paso 2006)

PHYSICIANS' GUARANTEES CAN CREATE COMMON LAW LIABILITY FOR BREACH OF WARRANTY

Beauty is only skin deep. Litigiousness, however, is ugly from the inside.

stus.com

■ **INSTANT FACTS** Dr. Pate (D) guaranteed that Mills (P) would be beautiful and have smooth skin if she underwent liposuction surgery.

■ **BLACK LETTER RULE** A negligence action may not be recast as a contractual claim so as to avoid statutory requirements governing health-care liability claims.

■ **Procedural Basis**

On appeal to review a trial court decision granting the defendant's motion for summary judgment.

■ **FACTS**

In 1999, Mills (P) contacted Dr. Pate (D) about a liposuction procedure to removed fat bulges in her abdomen, hips, and thighs. During their initial consultation, Pate (D) told Mills (P) that after the procedure, she would be beautiful with smooth skin and wonderful skin tone. Pate (D) never told Mills (P) of any possible irregularities or complications that could result from the procedure, such as sagging skin or rippling. On November 17, 1999, Mills (P) signed an informed consent form that acknowledged that a small percentage of patients require additional cosmetic follow-up procedures and listed possible side effects that may result. However, the form did not disclose that Mills's (P) skin quality could change or that she may experience rippling, indentations, or other abdominal abnormalities. Mills (P) underwent the procedure in December 1999, experiencing considerable swelling in the weeks that followed. As the swelling subsided three to four months later, Mills (P) noticed two rolls on her abdomen and sagging of the skin on her thighs. Although Pate (D) claimed these irregularities were due to swelling and would resolve with time, Mills (P) expressed her dissatisfaction to Pate (D), who demanded to be paid to perform a second surgery for the medial thigh lift and touch-ups. In January 2001, Mills (P) underwent the second surgery, which she understood to involve only minor touch-up work to lift the sagging skin on her thighs. For several months, Mills (P) did not look the way she expected to look based on Pate's (D) representations.

After meeting with Pate (D) several times following her second procedure, Mills (P) consulted Dr. Miller, a plastic surgeon. Miller informed Mills (P) that he could resolve the rippling of her abdomen and unevenness in her thighs with a minimum of three surgeries. After consulting with a third doctor, Mills (P) eventually underwent a body lift, a procedure much more extensive than liposuction. After recovering, Mills (P) was happy with the shape of her body. In January 2002, Mills (P) notified Pate (D) of her intent to sue as required by the state's Medical Liability and Insurance Improvement Act ("the Act") and she filed suit one year later. While the suit was pending, Mills (P) amended her complaint to add a claim for breach of express warranty. On Pate's (D) motion, the trial court dismissed the breach of express warranty claim, ruling that it was an attempt to recast her negligence claim as a breach of contract claim.

■ **ISSUE**

Did the plaintiff merely recast her negligence claim as a breach of contract claim?

■ DECISION AND RATIONALE

(Judge Undisclosed.) No. A negligence action may not be recast as a contractual claim so as to avoid statutory requirements governing healthcare liability claims. Under the Act, a healthcare liability claim exists if it is based on a claimed departure from an accepted standard of medical care, healthcare, or safety of the patient, whether it sounds in contract or tort. The requirements of the Act cannot be avoided by recasting a healthcare liability claim as a claim that otherwise is not included within the Act. Accordingly, the plaintiff's breach of express warranty claim is inseparable from her negligence claim if it requires proof of the defendant's breach of an accepted standard of medical care.

Here, Mills (P) alleged that Pate (D) represented that (1) she was a suitable candidate for cosmetic surgery and (2) that she would look beautiful and would have smooth skin following liposuction surgery. These representations, Mills (P) alleges, did not conform to the character and quality of the services, constituting a breach of warranty. This claim, if supported by the evidence, does not require proof of a deviation from an acceptable standard of medical care, and therefore is not merely a negligence claim recast as a contract claim. Mills's (P) evidence establishes a genuine issue of material fact as to each element of the claim. The court incorrectly dismissed the breach of express warranty claim. Affirmed in part, reversed in part, and remanded.

Analysis:

Ordinarily, the physician-patient relationship implies only that the physician warrants the necessary skill and expertise to properly render medical treatment. Recovery for physician guarantees, therefore, requires proof that the physician made a specific, direct statement of the outcome of the procedure. Mere assurances to a patient that improvement is likely or expected, however, are generally expected as part of ordinary medical care and are an insufficient basis for physician liability.

■ CASE VOCABULARY

EXPRESS WARRANTY: A warranty created by the overt words or actions of the seller.

MALPRACTICE: An instance of negligence or incompetence on the part of a professional.

NEGLIGENCE: The failure to exercise the standard of care that a reasonably prudent person would have exercised in a similar situation; any conduct that falls below the legal standard established to protect others against unreasonable risk of harm, except for conduct that is intentionally, wantonly, or willfully disregardful of others' rights.

WARRANTY: An express or implied promise that something in furtherance of the contract is guaranteed by one of the contracting parties; especially, a seller's promise that the thing being sold is as represented or promised.

Tunkl v. Regents of Univ. of California

(Patient) v. *(Hospital)*

60 Cal.2d 92, 32 Cal.Rptr. 33, 383 P.2d 441 (1963)

CONTRACTS PURPORTING TO RELEASE A HOSPITAL FROM LIABILITY FOR FUTURE NEGLIGENCE ARE AGAINST THE PUBLIC INTEREST AND ARE THEREFORE INVALID

■ **INSTANT FACTS** A lawsuit arose over a charitable research hospital's requirement that as a condition of admission all patients release the hospital from liability for negligence.

■ **BLACK LETTER RULE** Even charitable research hospitals may not, consistent with California law, impose as a condition of admission a requirement that patients release the hospital from future liability for negligence.

■ **PROCEDURAL BASIS**

Appeal to the Supreme Court of California of a trial court order sustaining the validity of a contract releasing a research hospital from liability for future negligence.

■ **FACTS**

On July 11, 1956, the University of California at Los Angeles (UCLA) Medical Center, a research and education hospital, admitted Hugo Tunkl (P) as a patient. The hospital, which was operated by the Regents of the University of California (D), was not open to all patients, but only to those whose conditions were consistent with the research and education purposes of the hospital. At the time of his admission, Tunkl (P) signed a document purporting to release the hospital from "any and all liability for the negligent or wrongful acts or omissions of its employees, if the hospital has used due care in selecting its employees." Tunkl (P) was injured as a result of physician negligence and filed suit against the hospital and its operators. Tunkl (P) died before the suit could be completed, and his wife was substituted as plaintiff. At trial, the trial judge submitted to the jury the question of the validity of the exculpatory agreement. The jury returned a verdict upholding the agreement, and the court entered judgment in that manner. Tunkl (P) appealed.

■ **ISSUE**

May a hospital, as a condition of admission, require that entering patients release the hospital from liability for future negligence?

■ **DECISION AND RATIONALE**

(Tobriner, J.) No. Cal. Civ. Code § 1668 states: "All contracts which have for their object . . . to exempt anyone from responsibility for his own fraud, or willful injury to the person or property of another, or violation of law, whether willful or negligent, are against the policy of the law." The cases interpreting this provision have consistently held that the exculpatory provision may stand only if it does not involve "the public interest." The question, then, is what constitutes the public interest? The following factors help answer that question. The public interest concerns a business of a type generally thought suitable for public regulation. The party seeking exculpation is engaged in performing a service of great importance and necessity to the public. The party holds itself out as willing to perform the service for any member of the public coming within certain established standards. As a result of the essential nature of the service, in the economic setting of the transaction, the party invoking exculpation possesses a decisive advantage of bargaining strength against any member of the public who seeks his services. In exercising that power, the party confronts the public with a standardized adhesion contract of exculpation, and makes no provision whereby a purchaser may obtain protection against negligence. Finally, as a result of the transaction, the person or property of the purchaser is placed under the control of the seller, subject to the risk of the seller's carelessness. The hospital-patient contract at issue here clearly falls within the category of agreements affecting the public interest. To meet that test, the agreement need only fulfill some of the characteristics outlined above; here, the relationship fulfills all of them. Thus the contract of exculpation involves an institution suitable for public regulation. To wit, the hospital provides the public with necessary services. It likewise holds itself out as willing to perform services for those persons who qualify for its research and training facilities. In insisting that the patient accept the provision of waiver in the contract, the hospital certainly exercises a decisive advantage in bargaining, as the would-be patient is in no position to reject the proffered agreement or to bargain with the hospital. In sum, we cannot but conclude that the instant agreement manifests the characteristics of an adhesion contract. When Tunkl (D) signed the contract he completely placed himself in the control of the hospital, subjecting himself to the risk of its carelessness. To protect the hospital from liability for negligence in such a situation would violate public policy. The Regents (D) contend that while the public interest may possibly invalidate the exculpatory provision as to a paying patient, it certainly cannot do so as to a charitable one. This argument has no merit. In *Malloy* we did away with the doctrine of charitable immunity. We must follow that precedent here. Reversed.

Analysis:

The seminal case in the area, *Tunkl* stands for the proposition that exculpatory clauses and other attempts to get patients to waive physician or hospital liability in the event of future negligence are disfavored by the courts. And as this case shows, this is true even when treatment is given at a very low cost or even for free. Some exceptions may apply. For example, at least one court has held that exculpatory agreements should be upheld when the treatment is experimental and the patient's last hope of survival. Other cases have allowed waivers of the right to seek punitive damages and liquidated damages clauses. Furthermore, while they are scrutinized carefully, courts will generally uphold arbitration agreements so long as the six *Tunkl* factors are not compromised. And finally, some legislatures have provided at least partial tort immunity for doctors or others who provide no cost health care services by allowing suit only upon a finding of gross negligence.

■ CASE VOCABULARY

ADHESION CONTRACT: A standardized contract favorable to the party with greater bargaining power that is presented to the weaker party for signature; the weaker party generally has no power to negotiate for different, less-oppressive terms.

Shorter v. Drury

(Husband of Deceased Patient) v. (Doctor)

103 Wash.2d 645, 695 P.2d 116 (1985)

A RELEASE OF PHYSICIAN LIABILITY FOR CONSEQUENCES STEMMING FROM A PATIENT'S REFUSAL TO ACCEPT NECESSARY BLOOD TRANSFUSIONS DURING SURGERY IS VALID AND CREATES A PARTIAL LIMITATION ON A PATIENT'S RIGHT TO SUE THE PHYSICIAN

■ **INSTANT FACTS** A woman died from loss of blood when, in accord with her religious convictions, she refused to accept a blood transfusion during a surgery gone wrong.

■ **BLACK LETTER RULE** Given the problems that arise when a patient on religious grounds refuses to permit necessary blood transfusions during a surgery, it is not inappropriate for a physician dealing with such a patient to require him or her to sign a release relieving the physician from responsibility for unfavorable consequences resulting from the refusal of blood.

■ **PROCEDURAL BASIS**

Appeal by a wrongful death plaintiff to the Supreme Court of Washington of a trial court's judgment on a jury verdict reducing the wrongful death plaintiff's damages by 75% under the doctrine of assumption of the risk; appeal by the defendant doctor on the ground that the deceased had signed a release form purportedly barring any recovery for wrongful death.

■ **FACTS**

Doreen Shorter, a Jehovah's Witness, became pregnant in the summer of 1979. In October her physician, Dr. Robert Drury (D), diagnosed her as having had a "missed abortion," which occurs when a fetus dies but is not discharged from the uterus. When a missed abortion occurs, it is prudent to have the fetus removed and the uterus cleansed. Dr. Drury (D) recommended a procedure known as a "dilation and curettage" (D and C), and recommended that it be performed by means of a curette, a metal instrument with a sharp-edged hoop on the end. When he recommended this procedure to Mrs. Shorter and her husband (P), who was also a Jehovah's Witness, Dr. Drury (D) did not inform them that a D and C could also be performed by means of a suction device or a vaginal suppository containing a chemical known as prostaglandin. Each method involved the possible loss of blood, the use of the curette posing the greatest risk of blood loss. As a Jehovah's Witness, Mrs. Shorter was precluded from accepting a blood transfusion. Aware that blood loss might occur during the course of the surgery, Mrs. Shorter, upon entering the hospital, signed a form stating her intent to refuse a blood transfusion should it be necessary. The form, co-signed by her husband, also purported to release the hospital and the attending physician from any responsibility for unfavorable consequences resulting from the refusal to accept a blood transfusion. The operation did not go well, and as a result of several lacerations caused by Dr. Drury's (D) use of the curette, Mrs. Shorter began to bleed. She refused a blood transfusion, and her husband refused to allow one to take place. Mrs. Shorter died shortly thereafter from loss of blood. After his wife's death, Mr. Shorter (P) filed a wrongful death action against Dr. Drury (D) and the hospital. At trial, a jury found Dr. Drury's (D) negligence to be the cause of Mrs. Shorter's death, and found damages in the amount of $412,000. The jury reduced that amount by 75%, however, because it felt that the Shorters had assumed the risk of Mrs. Shorter bleeding to death. As such, the award was reduced to $103,000. Both Mr. Shorter (P) and Dr. Drury (D) appealed.

■ ISSUE

When a patient refuses to accept necessary blood transfusions during surgery, will a release of physician liability for consequences stemming from that refusal be upheld and enforced?

■ DECISION AND RATIONALE

(Dolliver, J.) Yes. Shorter (P) argues that the purpose of the refusal was only to release Dr. Drury (D) from liability for not transfusing blood into the deceased had it been required during the course of a non-negligently performed operation. He further argues that to allow it to act as a release of Dr. Drury's (D) negligence would violate public policy. Dr. Drury (D) concedes that the refusal does not release him from his negligence. However, he does argue that it does release him from the consequences arising out of Mrs. Shorter's voluntary refusal to accept blood, which in this case was death. The refusal does not address Dr. Drury's (D) negligence, and so cannot be considered a release from liability for negligence. Contrary to Shorter's (P) argument, however, the document is more than a simple declaration that the signer would refuse blood only if there was no negligence. It is a valid refusal that by itself does not violate public policy. The refusal was an agreement that Mrs. Shorter receive no blood or blood derivatives. In signing the refusal, the Shorters specifically accepted the risk which might flow from a refusal to accept blood. Given the particular problems faced when a patient on religious grounds refuses to permit necessary blood transfusions, the use of a release such as that signed here is appropriate. The alternatives would be to require the doctor to get a court order, which would be cumbersome, or refusal of service to Jehovah's Witnesses, which would be repugnant to society. The procedure used here-the voluntary execution of a document protecting the physician and hospital-is an appropriate alternative and not contrary to the public interest. Contrary to Shorter's (P) contention, the refusal is not a complete bar to his wrongful death claim. It does not release Dr. Drury (D) from his negligence, but simply raises the issue of assumption of the risk. The jury properly addressed that issue, and properly allocated some responsibility for Mrs. Shorter's death to the decision not to accept blood. As such, their decision should be upheld. And because no state action was present, the submission of the issue of assumption of the risk to the jury did not violate the free exercise clause of the First Amendment. Affirmed.

Analysis:

Tunkl v. Regents of the University of California provides the majority rule for contracts limiting the liability of a physician for potential negligence during the course of treatment, holding that such contracts are unenforceable as they violate public policy. *Shorter v. Drury* provides an exception to that majority rule, upholding a partial limitation on a plaintiff's right to recover for physician negligence. The release at issue in *Shorter* created only a partial limitation on the right to recover because it did not completely bar Mr. Shorter's (P) right to sue Dr. Drury (D). Contrary to Mr. Shorter's (P) protestations, the release did not wholly relieve Dr. Drury (D) from responsibility for his negligence, a result that would have violated the rule in *Tunkl*. In fact, Dr. Drury (D) did have to pay $103,000 for his mistakes. The effect of the release was to simply raise the issue of assumption of the risk and limit Mr. Shorter's (P) recovery for Dr. Drury's (D) undisputed negligence. Also significant is the fact that, as the court points out, this decision protects Jehovah's Witnesses from being refused treatment. Certainly any doctor concerned about malpractice liability would avoid treating people who will not accept blood transfusions if the *Shorter* court had come out the other way, meaning many Jehovah's Witnesses might have been refused treatment.

■ CASE VOCABULARY

CURETTE: A metal instrument with a sharp-edged hoop on the end that is used to clean out a woman's uterus during a D and C.

DILATION AND CURETTAGE (D AND C): A medical procedure that involves the cleansing of a woman's uterus.

MISSED ABORTION: A condition in which a fetus dies but is not discharged from the uterus.

PROSTAGLANDIN: A chemical that causes a woman to have artificial labor contractions.

SUPPOSITORY: A meltable piece of medicated material that, for various purposes, is placed into a body cavity.

Canterbury v. Spence

(Patient) v. *(Doctor)*
464 F.2d 772 (D.C. Cir. 1972)

DOCTORS MUST PROVIDE PATIENTS WITH ENOUGH INFORMATION TO ALLOW THEM TO MAKE INTELLIGENT AND INFORMED DECISIONS REGARDING TREATMENT

■ **INSTANT FACTS** A back-surgery patient sued his doctor and the hospital in which the surgery was performed when he became paralyzed just following the surgery.

■ **BLACK LETTER RULE** A physician's obligation to his or her patient imposes upon the physician a duty to disclose all treatment options available and the dangers inherently and potentially involved with each.

■ **PROCEDURAL BASIS**

Appeal to the D.C. Circuit Court of Appeals of a district court's decision to grant a directed verdict in favor of a physician and a hospital accused of negligence.

■ **FACTS**

In December of 1958, Canterbury (P) began to experience severe back pain. After other treatments failed, Canterbury (P) approached Dr. Spence (D), a neurosurgeon. Dr. Spence (D) was unable to find anything wrong with Canterbury (P) after an office examination and x-rays, so he ordered a myelogram. The myelogram revealed a "filling defect" in the area of the fourth thoracic vertebrae. Upon making this finding, Dr. Spence (D) told Canterbury (P) that he would have to undergo a laminectomy to correct what he suspected was a ruptured disk. Canterbury (P) did not ask and was not told about the nature of the laminectomy. Nor was he told of its potential risks. Prior to the surgery Dr. Spence (D) also spoke with Canterbury's (P) mother. When she asked about the seriousness of the surgery she was simply told that it was "not any more [serious] than any other operation." She too was not told of the risks inherent in a laminectomy. The surgery revealed some unique problems with Canterbury's (P) back which Dr. Spence (D) attempted to fix. For the first twenty-four hours following the surgery, Canterbury (P) recovered normally. He then suffered a fall, however, and an immediate setback. It is unclear why exactly Canterbury (P) fell, but it was determined that he had been left unattended in a bed without rails. Within a matter of hours after the fall, Canterbury (P) began to have trouble breathing. He also became paralyzed from the waist down. Dr. Spence (D) was rushed to the hospital and performed another surgery to allow the spinal cord more room to pulsate. After the second surgery Canterbury (P) was able to exercise almost-normal control over his lower body muscles, but he was unable to void properly. From that point forward Canterbury (P) had to make frequent visits to a urologist and other specialists, and suffered from continued urinal incontinence and paralysis of the bowels. Canterbury (P) also had difficulty finding work because he needed to remain seated at almost all times and had to be very close to a bathroom. In 1968, approximately nine years after the initial surgery, Canterbury (P) filed suit against Dr. Spence (D) and the Washington Hospital Center in the Federal District Court for the District of Columbia, seeking recovery for pain and suffering, medical expenses, and lost earnings. At the close of Canterbury's (P) case-in-chief both Dr. Spence (D) and the hospital moved for directed verdicts. Both were granted on the ground that Canterbury (P) had not shown that the actions of each defendant were in any way medically responsible for his condition. Canterbury (P) appealed.

■ ISSUE

Does a physician have any obligation to his or her patient with respect to the disclosure of information regarding the patient's condition, treatment options, dangers involved in treatment, or the like?

■ DECISION AND RATIONALE

(Robinson, J.) Yes. To give true consent to a medical procedure, a patient must have an opportunity to evaluate knowledgeably the options available and the risks attendant to that procedure. Because the average patient has no significant understanding of the practice of medicine, the physician is under an obligation to communicate specific information to the patient so that an intelligent decision can be made. If circumstances require it, this obligation may require a physician to tell the patient of the exact nature of his or her condition, to inform the patient that treatment is not working, and to present alternative treatment options. Due care will also require that the physician warn the patient of any risks to his well-being which contemplated therapy may involve. This duty of risk-disclosure arises when it must be decided whether a particular treatment is to be undertaken. It is the prerogative of the patient, not the physician, to determine the direction of treatment. As such, physician disclosure of alternative treatments and their hazards is essential. Many of the courts that have held that a duty to disclose exists have made the duty depend on whether it was the custom of physicians practicing in the community to make a particular disclosure. We agree that physician noncompliance with a professional custom to reveal may give rise to liability. We do not agree, however, that the patient's cause of action is dependent upon the existence and nonperformance of a relevant professional tradition. Respect for the patient's right of self-determination on particular therapy demands a standard set by law for physicians rather than one which physicians may or may not impose upon themselves. Furthermore, the decision to unveil the patient's condition and the chances as to remediation is oftentimes a non-medical judgment and therefore is a decision outside the ambit of any special industry standard. Prevailing medical practice has evidentiary value in making determinations as to what the specific criteria measuring challenged professional conduct are and whether they have been met, but does not itself define the standard. Thus we distinguish, for the purposes of duty to disclose, the special and general standard aspects of the physician-patient relationship. When medical judgment enters the picture and for that reason the special standard controls, prevailing medical practice must be given its just due. In all other instances, however, the general standard exacting ordinary care applies, and that standard is set by law. In sum, the physician's duty to disclose is governed by the same legal principles applicable to others in comparable situations, with modifications only to the extent that medical judgment enters the picture. We hold that the standard measuring performance of that duty by physicians, as by others, is conduct which is reasonable under the circumstances. Once circumstance gives rise to a duty on the part of the physician to inform his patient, the next inquiry is the scope of the disclosure the physician is legally obliged to make. The courts that have addressed the issue have reached different conclusions, and have thus applied many different standards. In our view, the patient's right of self-decision shapes the boundaries of the duty to reveal. That right can be effectively exercised only if the patient possesses enough information to enable an intelligent choice. The scope of the physician's communications to the patient, then, must be measured by the patient's need, and that need is the information material to the decision. Thus the test for determining whether a particular peril must be divulged is its materiality to the patient's decision; all risks potentially affecting the decision must be unmasked. And to safeguard the patient's interest in achieving his own determination on treatment, the law, and not professional custom, must set the standard for adequate disclosure. This being said, the physician's liability for nondisclosure is to be determined on the basis of foresight, not hindsight; the issue of nondisclosure must be approached from the viewpoint of the reasonableness of the physician's divulgence in terms of what he knows or should know to be the patient's informational needs. If, but only if, the fact-finder can say that the physician's communication was unreasonably inadequate is an imposition of liability legally justified. Of necessity, the content of the disclosure rests in the first instance with the physician, who is in a position to identify particular dangers. He cannot know exactly what the patient would consider important to his decision, but on the basis of his medical training and experience he can sense how the average, reasonable patient generally would react. From these considerations we derive the breadth of the disclosure of risks legally to be required. The scope of the standard remains objective with due regard for the patient's informational needs and with suitable leeway for the physician's situation. In broad outline, a risk is material when a reasonable person knowing what the physician knows or should know to be the patient's position would likely attach significance to the risk or cluster of risks in deciding whether or not to forego the proposed therapy. The topics demanding a communication of information include the inherent and potential hazards of a proposed treatment, any alternatives to that treatment, and the results likely if the patient remains untreated. Further, a physician must disclose the incidence of injury and the degree of harm threatened, any chance of death or serious disablement, any potential disability which dramatically outweighs the potential benefit of therapy, and the detriments of the existing malady. There is no bright line separating the significant from the insignificant; the answer in any case must abide a rule of reason. The disclosure doctrine is a requirement of conduct prudent under the circumstances. Whenever nondisclosure of particular risk information is open to debate by reasonable-minded men, the issue is for the finder of fact. Reversed.

Analysis:

In the United States there are two general standards for informed consent. As articulated by the *Canterbury* court, the reasonable patient standard requires a doctor to provide that degree of information that a reasonable patient would expect to have in order to make an informed decision about treatment. The second standard accepted in the United States (and rejected by *Canterbury*) is the professional disclosure standard. Under that standard, a physician is liable to the patient under the doctrine of informed consent only when he or she discloses less than the degree of information that the reasonable physician in the same practice area and community would disclose. The difference between the two standards is important. Under the second standard, a physician can prevail by providing expert testimony regarding the professional standards for the community in which he or she practices. Under the patient-centered standard, however, a doctor can potentially lose even if expert testimony shows that he or she went well beyond what the average physician would do. To patients, then, the reasonable patient standard is clearly preferable because the burden of proof is easier to satisfy.

■ CASE VOCABULARY

INCONTINENCE: An inability to control the excretion of waste from the body.

LAMINECTOMY: The excision of the posterior arch of the vertebra.

MYELOGRAM: A procedure used to detect disease or other disorders in the spinal column in which dye is injected into the spinal column and then traced.

VOID: The excretion of solid or liquid waste from the body.

Johnson v. Kokemoor

(Patient) v. *(Doctor)*

199 Wis.2d 615, 545 N.W.2d 495 (1996)

WHEN A PHYSICIAN'S LACK OF EXPERIENCE IS LIKELY TO HAVE A SIGNIFICANT EFFECT ON THE OUTCOME OF A SURGERY, THE PHYSICIAN HAS A DUTY TO DISCLOSE THAT LACK OF EXPERIENCE TO THE PATIENT

■ **INSTANT FACTS** A patient filed suit against her physician claiming that his failure to honestly disclose the extent of his experience performing a certain surgery violated the doctrine of informed consent.

■ **BLACK LETTER RULE** A patient cannot make an informed, intelligent decision regarding suggested treatment unless the physician discloses all of the viable alternatives and risks of the treatment proposed, including the physician's experience in performing a particular procedure, his or her risk statistics as compared with those of other physicians who perform the procedure, and the availability of other physicians better able to perform the procedure.

■ **PROCEDURAL BASIS**

Appeal to the Wisconsin Supreme Court of an appellate court decision to disallow the admission at trail of evidence regarding a physician's inexperience and the mortality.

■ **FACTS**

When Donna Johnson (P) began experiencing headaches, her family physician referred her to neurosurgeon Richard Kokemoor (D). Dr. Kokemoor (D) diagnosed Johnson (P) as having an enlarging aneurysm at the rear of her brain. He recommended basilar bifurcation aneurysm surgery to clip the aneurysm, which he later performed in a community hospital in October of 1990. Though technically a success, the surgery rendered Johnson (P) an incomplete quadriplegic unable to control her bowel or bladder movements. Johnson's (P) speech, vision, walking ability, and upper body coordination were also impaired. Johnson (P) sued Kokemoor (D). At trial, Johnson (P) introduced evidence that Kokemoor (D) had overstated the urgency of her need for the surgery. Johnson (P) also introduced evidence that Kokemoor (D) had overstated his qualifications and experience performing the type of aneurism surgery that she needed. Johnson (P) further presented evidence that Kokemoor (D) had understated the mortality rate associated with the surgery that she needed. According to the evidence, Kokemoor (D) had represented that the surgery carried a 2% risk of death. At trial, evidence was presented that the actual risk of death was closer to 15%, and that for a physician of Kokemoor's (D) limited experience it was closer to 30%. Finally, Johnson (P) introduced evidence showing that a reasonable physician in Kokemoor's (D) position would have referred her to more experienced surgeons who had access to a tertiary care center, which would contain the proper equipment needed to successfully perform the surgery. Kokemoor (D) presented evidence disputing Johnson's (P) allegations and expert testimony, though one of his experts did testify that he personally would have provided more information to a patient regarding the extent of his experience in relation to the experience of other physicians performing similar operations.

ISSUE

Does a physician contemplating performing a certain surgery ever have a duty to disclose to the patient his or her degree of experience (or inexperience) in performing the surgery, as well as the mortality rates associated with surgery performed by doctors of that level of experience as compared with others of greater experience?

DECISION AND RATIONALE

(Abrahamson, J.) Yes. Information regarding a physician's experience may be important to a patient's decision whether to give consent to a certain medical procedure. In this case, Johnson (P) introduced evidence that had a reasonable person in her position been aware of Kokemoor's (D) lack of experience in performing basilar bifurcation aneurysm surgery, that person would not have undergone surgery with him. According to the record, Johnson (P) made inquiry regarding Kokemoor's (D) experience with surgery like hers. In response to her questions, he untruthfully responded that he had operated on aneurysm comparable to hers "dozens" of times. Evidence was also introduced that Johnson's (P) surgery is among the most difficult aneurysm surgery in all of neurosurgery. As a reasonable person in Johnson's (P) position would have considered such information material in making an intelligent decision about the surgery, it was not error to allow it to be presented at trial. Kokemoor (D) next argues that the trial court erred in allowing Johnson (P) to introduce evidence of mortality rates associated with the surgery at issue, including the rates of physicians with various degrees of experience. Expert testimony indicated that the mortality rate for the type of surgery at issue here is significantly higher when a surgeon of Kokemoor's (D) experience performs the surgery as compared to a more experienced surgeon. Kokemoor (D) asserts that the admission of these mortality rates would lead the jury to find him liable for failing to perform at the level of the masters rather than for failing to adequately inform Johnson (P) regarding the risks associated with her surgery. Further, he contends that the statistics are inaccurate and misleading. Despite Kokemoor's (D) protestations, we reject a bright line rule excluding evidence of comparative risk relating to the medical provider. The evidence indicates that Kokemoor (D) downplayed the risks associated with Johnson's (P) surgery, providing her with a mortality rate much lower than the actual rate. Had a reasonable person in Johnson's (P) position been made aware that being operated upon by Kokemoor (D) significantly increased the risk one would have faced in the hands of another surgeon performing the same operation, that person might well have elected to forego surgery with Kokemoor (D). In sum, when different physicians have substantially different success rates, whether surgery is performed by one rather than another represents a choice between alternate, viable medical modes of treatment. As this information is material to the patient's exercise of an informed consent regarding treatment options, a court may conclude that the information is admissible. Our decision will not always require physicians to give patents comparative risk evidence in statistical terms to obtain informed consent. Rather, we hold that evidence of the mortality outcomes of different physicians was admissible under the circumstances of this case. With respect to other cases, questions regarding whether statistics are sufficiently material to a patient's decision to be admissible and sufficiently reliable to be non-prejudicial are best resolved on a case-by-case basis. Dr. Kokemoor (D) asserts that the trial court also erred in allowing Johnson (P) to introduce expert testimony that because of the difficulties associated with operating on Johnson's (P) aneurysm, he should have referred her to a tertiary care center containing better facilities, tools, and surgeons. In a breach of the duty of informed consent action, the pertinent inquiry concerns what information a reasonable person in the patient's position would have considered material to an exercise of intelligent consent. Under the facts in this case, the trial court could declare, in the proper exercise of its discretion, that evidence of referral would have been material to the ability of a reasonable person in Johnson's (P) position to render informed consent. Johnson's (P) medical experts testified that given the nature and difficulty of the surgery at issue, Johnson (P) could not make an intelligent decision or give an informed consent without being made aware that surgery in a tertiary facility would have decreased the risk she faced. Medical literature supports this view. Hence, under the materiality standard that governs this case, the trial court properly exercised its discretion in admitting evidence that Kokemoor (D) should have advised Johnson (P) of the possibility of undergoing the surgery elsewhere. Finally, Kokemoor (D) argues that if his duty to procure Johnson's (P) informed consent includes an obligation to disclose that she consider seeking treatment elsewhere, then there will be no logical stopping point to what the doctrine of informed consent might encompass. We disagree. As Johnson (P) noted, it is a rare exception when the vast body of medical literature and expert opinion agree that the difference in experience of a surgeon in performing an operation will impact the risk of mortality, as was the case here, thereby requiring a referral. Under most circumstances, whether or not a physician referred a patient elsewhere would be utterly irrelevant in an informed consent case. Moreover, we have already concluded that comparative risk data distinguishing Kokemoor's (D) mortality rate from the rate of more experienced physicians was properly before the jury. A close link exists between such data and the propriety of referring a patient elsewhere. When the duty to share comparative risk data is material to a patient's exercise of informed consent, an ensuing referral will often represent no more than a modest and logical next step. The trial court did not erroneously exercise its discretion in admitting the evidence at issue. Reversed.

Analysis:

As stated in prior cases in this chapter, the doctrine of informed consent requires a physician to disclose all material information regarding a potential treatment to a patient contemplating undergoing that treatment. *Johnson* expands on this rule by setting forth the principle that, in some cases, a doctor's level of experience and the likely effects of that experience or inexperience on the surgery can, in certain cases, be a material fact that must be disclosed. Specifically, the doctor's degree of experience must be disclosed when the difference in the expected result of the surgery when performed by an experienced rather than an inexperienced physician is significant. When there is no significant difference, meaning the results will basically be the same regardless of the physician's experience, the doctrine of informed consent will not require disclosure of the physician's level of experience.

Arato v. Avedon

(Patient) v. *(Doctor)*

5 Cal.4th 1172, 23 Cal.Rptr.2d 131, 858 P.2d 598 (1993)

IN DETERMINING WHAT INFORMATION TO DISCLOSE TO A PATIENT, A PHYSICIAN NEED NOT TAKE INTO ACCOUNT THE PATIENT'S FINANCIAL AFFAIRS AND OTHER NONMEDICAL RIGHTS AND INTERESTS

■ **INSTANT FACTS** A widow and her two children sued their husband/father's former doctor for malpractice, claiming that his failure to inform the patient of his life expectancy was a breach of the physician's duty to fully disclose all material information regarding proposed treatment.

■ **BLACK LETTER RULE** While physicians have a duty to disclose all available choices with respect to proposed therapy and the dangers inherently and potentially involved in each, it is unwise to require, as a matter of law, that a particular species of information such as mortality rates associated with a particular condition always be disclosed.

■ PROCEDURAL BASIS

Appeal to the California Supreme Court of an appellate court reversal of a trial court's decision not to give a medical malpractice jury two pro-plaintiff jury instructions.

■ FACTS

In 1980, Miklos Arato's internist diagnosed him as having a failing kidney. In July of that year, Arato had surgery to remove the kidney. During that surgery doctors discovered a tumor on the distal portion of Arato's pancreas. The tumor was removed and found to be malignant, and Arato was referred to an oncologist. During the initial visit to the oncologist, Arato filled out a questionnaire, one answer on which indicated his desire to be told the truth about his condition. In discussing Arato's condition with him on a number of different occasions, the oncologists provided Arato with a great detail of information about the disease and potential treatments. At no time, however, did they provide him with statistical information regarding the high mortality rate associated with pancreatic cancer. This they refrained from doing on two grounds. First, his surgeon testified that Arato had exhibited such great anxiety over his condition that it was determined that it would be inappropriate to disclose the high mortality rates to him. The oncologists testified that they did not want to overwhelm Arato, and so they intentionally danced around the issue, making statements that, in their opinion, would have caused one who wanted to know to ask "how long do I have to live?" Arato never asked that question during any of his 70 plus visits to the oncologists, so they did not provide that information. The oncologists treated Arato with a combination of drugs and chemotherapy. The treatment initially worked, but the cancer returned. In July of 1981, Arato died. Following his death, Arato's widow and children (P) filed suit against his doctors, claiming that by not providing Arato with statistical information regarding the high mortality rates for pancreatic cancer patients, they had breached their duty of full disclosure. The widow and children (P) further contended that had Arato known of his likelihood of death, he would have spent his last days arranging his business and other affairs such that his survivors would have been better provided for. In short, they claimed that by not providing Arato with the mortality rates, the doctors (D) gave him false hope of survival. Near the end of trial, Arato's survivors (P) asked the judge to give the jury two special instructions: (1) "A physician has a fiduciary duty to a patient to make a full and fair disclosure to the patient of all facts which materially affect the patient's rights and interests;" and (2) "The scope of the physician's duty to disclose is measured by the amount of knowledge a patient needs in order to make an informed choice. All information material to the patient's decision should be given." The trial judge declined to give either of these instructions, choosing instead to read to the jury a modified version of BAJI No. 611, which is drawn from the case of *Cobbs v. Grant.* The jury found for the physicians (D), and an appeal ensued.

■ ISSUE

When a patient's life expectancy is shortened by a disease or other condition, does the patient's physician have a duty to always inform the patient of that life expectancy?

■ DECISION AND RATIONALE

(Arabian, J.) No. The question that we must address is whether our holding in *Cobbs v. Grant*—that physicians have a duty of reasonable disclosure of the available choices with respect to proposed therapy and of the dangers inherently and potentially involved in each—accurately conveys to juries the legal standard under which they assess the evidence in determining the adequacy of a physician's disclosures in a particular case, or whether, as the court of appeals concluded, specific disclosures such as patient life expectancy as revealed by mortality statistics must always be made. One of the merits of BAJI No. 6, which embodies our holding in *Cobbs*, is its recognition of the importance of the overall medical context that juries ought to take into account in deciding whether a challenged disclosure was reasonably sufficient to convey to the patient information material to an informed treatment decision. The contexts in which the physician and patient interact and exchange information material to the therapeutic decisions to be made are so multifarious, and the informational needs and degree of dependency of individual patients so various, that it is unwise to require, as a matter of law, that a particular species of information always be disclosed. This sensitivity to context seems all the more appropriate in the case of life expectancy projections based on statistical samples. The testimony of every physician-witness at trial confirmed that statistical morbidity values are inherently unreliable and offer little assurance regarding the fate of the individual patient. Further, the jury here certainly heard evidence of articulable grounds for the conclusion that the particular features of Arato's case distinguished it from the typical population of pancreatic cancer sufferers and their dismal statistical probabilities—a fact that Arato's survivors (P) admitted at trial. Rather than mandate the disclosure of specific information as a matter of law, the better rule is to instruct the jury that a physician is under a legal duty to disclose all material information needed to make an informed decision regarding a proposed treatment. That, of course, is the formulation embodied in BAJI No. 6.11, which was given in this case. Having been properly instructed, the jury returned a defense verdict. Because we leave the ultimate judgment as to the factual adequacy of a challenged disclosure to the jury, and the evidence here has been more than sufficient to support the jury's pro-defense finding, we decline to intrude into this matter further. The instructions given to the jury were an accurate statement of the law, and resulted in a fairly litigated verdict. We will not alter that verdict. The deceased's family (P) contends that the treating physicians (D) should have disclosed statistical life expectancy data to Arato because it was material to his nonmedical interests-his business and investment affairs. The family (P) relies on the following statement in *Bowen v. McPheeters*: "As fiduciaries it was the duty of defendants [physicians] to make a full and fair disclosure to plaintiff of all facts which materially affected his rights and interests." The family (P) contends that since Mr. Arato's contracting and real estate affairs are among his "rights and interests," the physicians (D) were under a legal duty to disclose all material facts that might affect them. We reject this claim. A physician is not a patient's financial adviser. The conditions for the exercise of the patient's right of self-decision presupposes a therapeutic focus. The fact that a physician has "fiducial" obligations which prohibit misrepresenting the nature of the patent's medical condition does not mean that he or she is under a duty to disclose every contingency that might affect the patient's nonmedical "rights and interests." Finally, the family (P) makes much of the fact that in his initial visit to Dr. Avedon's (D) office, Arato indicated that he "wish[ed] to be told the truth about [his] condition." We do not see how a request to be told the "truth" in itself heightens the duty of disclosure imposed on physicians as a matter of law. The final issue concerns the use of expert testimony at trial. The court of appeals concluded that expert testimony offered in behalf of the doctors (D) went beyond what was appropriate in support of the therapeutic exception to the physician's duty of disclosure. Over the family's (P) objection, the trial court admitted the testimony of two medical experts who testified that the standard of medical practice cautioned against disclosing to pancreatic cancer patients specific life expectancy data unless the patient directly requested such information and that this standard was complied with in this case. A physician must reveal the potential for death or serious harm known to be inherent in a given procedure and an explanation of the complications that might occur. In addition, a physician must also reveal any additional information as a skilled practitioner of good standing would provide under similar circumstances. In reckoning the scope of disclosure, the physician will generally be guided by the patient's decisional needs. A physician, however, evaluates the patient's decisions needs against a background of professional understanding that includes a knowledge of what information beyond the significant risks associated with a given treatment would be regarded by the medical community as appropriate for disclosure under the circumstances. Situations will sometimes arise in which the trier of fact is unable to decide the ultimate issue of adequacy of disclosure without an understanding of the standard of practice within the relevant medical community. As such, the testimony of medical experts qualified to offer an opinion regarding what disclosures would be made to a the patient by a skilled practitioner in the relevant medical community under the circumstances is relevant and admissible. Expert testimony has a limited and essentially subsidiary role in informed consent litigation. Nevertheless, there may be a limited number of occasions where the adequacy of disclosure may turn on the standard of practice in the relevant medical community. In such instances, expert testimony is generally appropriate. Because statistical life expectancy data is information that lies outside the significant risks associated with a given treatment, it falls within the scope of the additional information a skilled practitioner would provide. And since the question of whether a physician should disclose such information turns on the standard of practice within the medical community, the trial court did not err in permitting expert testimony directed at that issue. Reversed.

Analysis:

Arato teaches three important principles. First, *Arato* subscribes to the view that it would be improper for the law to require that the mortality rates associated with a particular condition always, without question, be disclosed to the patient. This view is consistent with one of the generally recognized exceptions to the disclosure requirements—that of the physician's right to refrain from disclosing information that he or she feels will be of more harm to the patient than good. For example, if knowing that death is close at hand will cause a patient to lose all ability to think rationally, the law does not require that disclosure. Second, *Arato* teaches that physicians base their disclosure decisions on medical need. While physicians have a fiduciary duty to patients, they need not take into account the patient's financial affairs when deciding what information to disclose and what not to disclose. This is certainly the better view, as any doctor with a good practice does not have the time to investigate all of his or her patients' finances. And finally, *Arato* teaches the value of expert testimony in medical malpractice cases. *Canterbury v. Spence* introduced the reasonable patient standard for physician disclosures. Under that standard, a physician must disclose the amount and type of information that a reasonable patient would need to make an informed decision regarding medical treatment. *Arato* arguably applies a different standard—the professional disclosure standard. Under that standard, a physician is liable for nondisclosure only when he or she fails to disclose information that the average physician in the same practice area in the same community would disclose.

■ CASE VOCABULARY

INTERNIST: A physician who specializes in internal medicine.

ONCOLOGY: The study of tumors.

Moore v. Regents of the University of California

(Patient) v. *(Hospital Directors)*

51 Cal.3d 120, 271 Cal.Rptr. 146, 793 P.2d 479 (1990)

DOCTORS HAVE A DUTY TO DISCLOSE TO THEIR PATIENTS ANY CONFLICTS OF INTEREST THAT MIGHT AFFECT THEIR DECISIONS OR RECOMMENDATIONS REGARDING MEDICAL TREATMENT

■ **INSTANT FACTS** A patient filed suit against his doctor and the doctor's employer when it became known that, despite prior protestations to the contrary, they were using the patient's cells for their own personal economic gain.

■ **BLACK LETTER RULE** A physician who is seeking a patient's consent for a medical procedure must, in order to satisfy his fiduciary duty and to obtain the patient's informed consent, disclose personal interests unrelated to the patient's health, whether research or economic, that may affect his medical judgment.

■ **PROCEDURAL BASIS**

Appeal to the California Supreme Court of a superior court finding that no cause of action had been stated in an informed consent lawsuit involving the nondisclosure of a physician and his hospital's economic interests in a particular patient.

■ **FACTS**

In 1976, John Moore (P) was diagnosed with hairy-cell leukemia. He sought treatment for the disease at the UCLA Medical Center. While there, Moore (P) was treated by Dr. David Golde (D). Also involved in his treatment was Shirley Quan (D), a researcher at the university. At the time that he began treating Moore (P), Golde (D) was aware that certain of Moore's (P) "blood products and blood components were of great value in a number of commercial and scientific efforts." Golde (D) was also aware that access to Moore's (P) blood provided certain "competitive, commercial, and scientific advantages." Part of Dr. Golde's (D) proposed treatment was the performance of a splenectomy. Moore (P) consented to the splenectomy, however he did not consent to Golde's (D) undisclosed plan to use the removed spleen for research. Moore (P) did not consent to the research because he did not know about it. Following the surgery, Moore (P) made several return visits to the UCLA Medical Center from his home in Seattle. He did so because Golde (D) told him that it was necessary for his health and well-being. During each visit, Golde (D) withdrew blood, blood serum, skin, bone marrow aspirate, and sperm from Moore (P). At no time, however, did he tell Moore (P) that he was using these substances for research unrelated to the treatment of Moore's (P) leukemia. Golde (D) benefitted financially from the removal of Moore's (P) cells. He produced a cell line on which he, Quan (D), and the Medical Center were granted a patent. He also negotiated for commercial development of the cell line and products derived from it, for which he and the Medical Center were given over $300,000 during a three year period. Moore (P) was never told about any of this, and filed suit when he found out.

■ **ISSUE**

Does a physician seeking a patient's consent for a medical procedure have a duty to disclose any personal interests unrelated to the patient's health that might affect his medical judgment?

■ DECISION AND RATIONALE

(Authoring Judge Not Stated) Yes. Moore (P) alleges that Dr. Golde (D) failed to disclose the extent of his research and economic interests in Moore's (P) cells before obtaining consent to the medical procedures by which the cells were extracted. These allegations state a cause of action against Golde (D) for invading a legally protected interest of his patient. Our analysis begins with three well-established principles. First, a person of adult years has the right to determine whether or not to submit to lawful medical treatment. Second, the patient's consent to treatment must be an informed consent. Third, in soliciting the patient's consent, a physician has a fiduciary duty to disclose all information material to the patient's decision. These principles lead to the following conclusions: (1) a physician must disclose personal interests unrelated to the patient's health, whether research or economic, that may affect the physician's professional judgment; and (2) a physician's failure to disclose such interests may give rise to a cause of action for performing medical procedures without informed consent or breach of fiduciary duty. The concept of informed consent is broad enough to encompass allegations that the physician had a personal interest. "The scope of the physician's communication to the patient . . . must be measured by the patient's need, and that need is whatever information is material to the decision." *Cobbs v. Grant.* Indeed, the law recognizes that a reasonable patient would want to know whether a physician has an economic interest that might affect the physician's professional judgment. It is important to note that no law prohibits a physician from conducting research in the same area in which he practices. Yet a physician who treats a patient in whom he also has a research interest has potentially conflicting loyalties. For example, he may be tempted to order a scientifically useful procedure that offers marginal or no benefits to the patient. The possibility that an interest extraneous to the patient's health has affected the physician's judgment is something that a reasonable patient would want to know in deciding whether to consent to a proposed course of treatment. It is thus a prerequisite to informed consent. Golde (D) argues that the scientific use of cells that have already been removed cannot possibly affect the patient's medical interests. The argument is correct in one instance but not in another. If a physician has no plans to conduct research on a patient's cells at the time he recommends the procedure by which they are taken, the patient's medical interests have not been impaired. In that instance, the argument is correct. On the other hand, a physician who does have a preexisting research interest might take that into consideration in recommending the procedure. In that instance the argument is incorrect: the physician's extraneous motivation may affect his judgment and is thus material to the patient's consent. Accordingly, we hold that a physician who is seeking a patient's consent for a medical procedure must, in order to satisfy his fiduciary duty and to obtain the patient's informed consent, disclose personal interests unrelated to the patient's health, whether research or economic, that may affect his medical judgment. We now turn to a determination of whether Moore (P) has stated a cause of action. Moore (P) alleges that, prior to the surgical removal of his spleen, Golde (D) formed the intent to obtain portions of Moore's (P) spleen in connection with his desire to have regular and continuous access to Moore's (P) unique and rare blood cells. Moore (P) was never informed, prior to the splenectomy, of Golde's (D) prior formed intent. In our view, these allegations adequately show that Golde (D) had an undisclosed research interest in Moore's (P) cells at the time he sought Moore's (P) consent to the surgery. Accordingly, Moore (P) has stated a cause of action for breach of fiduciary duty, or lack of informed consent. We next discuss the adequacy of Golde's (D) alleged disclosures regarding the postoperative takings of blood and other samples. Moore (P) alleges that Golde (D) actively concealed his economic interest in Moore's (P) cells. During each of Moore's (P) visits, Golde (D) repeatedly represented to Moore (P) that there was no commercial or financial value to his blood and other bodily substances, and in fact actively discouraged Moore (P) from asking whether there could be any economic or scientific value in the cells. Moore (P) admits in his complaint that Golde (D) disclosed that he and the hospital (D) were "engaged in strictly academic and purely scientific medical research." However, Golde's (D) representation that he had no financial interest in this research became false when he began to investigate and initiate the procedures for acquiring a patent on the cell line developed from Moore's (P) cells. Moore (P) plainly asserts that Golde (D) concealed an economic interest in the postoperative procedures. Therefore, applying the principles already discussed, the allegations state a cause of action for breach of fiduciary duty or lack of informed consent. We thus disagree with the superior court's ruling that Moore (P) had not stated a cause of action. Reversed.

Analysis:

To prevent exploitation of the physician-patient relationship, the law places upon physicians certain duties, including the duty to disclose potential conflicts of interest that might affect the physician's diagnoses or decisions. This is the seminal case in this area. In *Moore* the California Supreme Court held that when a physician has interests extraneous to a patient's health, and those interests might possibly affect the physician's judgment in dealing with the patient, the patient has a right to know about those interests. *Moore* has been accepted by courts throughout the United States and is now the prevailing rule with respect to disclosure of physician research interests.

■ CASE VOCABULARY

LEUKEMIA: A disease that is characterized by an unusual increase in the number of white blood cells in a patient's body tissues and blood.

SPLENECTOMY: The removal of the spleen.

Canterbury v. Spence

(Patient) v. *(Doctor)*

464 F.2d 772 (D.C. Cir. 1972)

TO WIN AN INFORMED CONSENT ACTION A PLAINTIFF MUST SHOW A CAUSAL RELATIONSHIP BETWEEN THE PHYSICIAN'S FAILURE TO DISCLOSE AND THE HARM SUFFERED BY THE PATIENT

■ **INSTANT FACTS** A back-surgery patient sued his doctor and the hospital in which the surgery was performed when he became paralyzed just following the surgery.

■ **BLACK LETTER RULE** A causal connection between nondisclosure and harm to the patient exists only when disclosure of significant risks incidental to treatment would have resulted in a decision against accepting that treatment, as demonstrated by a showing of what a reasonable person would do under similar circumstances.

■ **PROCEDURAL BASIS**

Appeal to the D.C. Circuit Court of Appeals of a district court's decision to grant a directed verdict in favor of a physician and a hospital accused of negligence.

■ **FACTS**

[These are the same facts set forth for this case earlier in the book.] In December of 1958, Canterbury (P) began to experience severe back pain. After other treatments failed, Canterbury (P) approached Dr. Spence (D), a neurosurgeon. Dr. Spence (D) was unable to find anything wrong with Canterbury (P) after an office examination and x-rays, so he ordered a myelogram. The myelogram revealed a "filling defect" in the area of the fourth thoracic vertebrae. Upon making this finding, Dr. Spence (D) told Canterbury (P) that he would have to undergo a laminectomy to correct what he suspected was a ruptured disk. Canterbury (P) did not ask and was not told about the nature of the laminectomy. Nor was he told of its potential risks. Prior to the surgery Dr. Spence (D) also spoke with Canterbury's (P) mother. When she asked about the seriousness of the surgery she was simply told that it was "not any more [serious] than any other operation." She too was not told of the risks inherent in a laminectomy. The surgery revealed some unique problems with Canterbury's (P) back which Dr. Spence (D) attempted to fix. For the first twenty-four hours following the surgery, Canterbury (P) recovered normally. He then suffered a fall, however, and an immediate setback. It is unclear why exactly Canterbury (P) fell, but it was determined that he had been left unattended in a bed without rails. Within a matter of hours after the fall, Canterbury (P) began to have trouble breathing. He also became paralyzed from the waist down. Dr. Spence (D) was rushed to the hospital and performed another surgery to allow the spinal cord more room to pulsate. After the second surgery Canterbury (P) was able to exercise almost-normal control over his lower body muscles, but he was unable to void properly. From that point forward Canterbury (P) had to make frequent visits to a urologist and other specialists, and suffered from continued urinal incontinence and paralysis of the bowels. Canterbury (P) also had difficulty finding work because he needed to remain seated at almost all times and had to be very close to a bathroom. In 1968, approximately nine years after the initial surgery, Canterbury (P) filed suit against Dr. Spence (D) and the Washington Hospital Center in the Federal District Court for the District of Columbia, seeking recovery for pain and suffering, medical expenses, and lost earnings. At the close of Canterbury's (P) case-in-chief both Dr. Spence (D) and the hospital moved for directed verdicts. Both were granted on the ground that Canterbury (P) had not shown that the actions of each defendant were in any way medically responsible for his condition. Canterbury (P) appealed.

■ **ISSUE**

To win an informed consent action, must a patient show a causal link between the physician's nondisclosure and the harm of which the plaintiff complains?

■ **DECISION AND RATIONALE**

(Robinson, J.) Yes. Nonfulfillment of the physician's obligation to disclose alone does not establish liability to a patient. An unrevealed risk that should have been made known must materialize if the omission is to be of any legal consequence. Further, there must be a causal relationship between the physician's failure to adequately disclose material information and that harm. A causal connection exists only when disclosure of significant risks incidental to treatment would have resulted in a decision against it. The patient has no complaint if he would have submitted to the therapy notwithstanding awareness of the risk. The more difficult question is whether the factual issue on causality calls for an objective or subjective determination. Some have assumed that this issue is to be resolved according to whether the fact finder believes the patient's testimony that he would not have agreed to the treatment if he had known of the danger which later ripened into injury. We think this view is unsatisfactory. The objective of the risk-disclosure is preservation of the patient's interest in intelligent self-choice. When, prior to commencement of therapy, the patient is sufficiently informed of the risks and he exercises his choice, it may truly be said that he did exactly what he wanted to do. But when causality is explored at a post-injury trial with a professedly uninformed patient, the question whether he actually would have turned the treatment down if he had known the risks is purely hypothetical. In our view, this method of dealing with the issue of causation places the physician in jeopardy of the patient's hindsight and bitterness. It places the fact finder in the position of deciding whether a speculative answer to a hypothetical question is to be credited. The better approach is to resolve the causality issue on an objective basis: in terms of what a prudent person in the patient's position would have decided if suitably informed of all significant risks. If adequate disclosure could reasonably be expected to have caused that person to decline the treatment, causation is shown. Otherwise it is not. The patient's testimony is relevant, but it would not threaten to dominate the findings. And since that testimony would probably be appraised congruently with the fact finder's belief in its reasonableness, the case for an objective standard is strengthened. Such a standard will ease the fact-finding process and better assure a finding of truth. Reversed.

Analysis:

As is the case with all negligence-based lawsuits, to win an informed consent or nondisclosure lawsuit a patient must demonstrate causation. In this case, that means causation between the physician's failure to disclose and the patient's harm. For example, if a physician fails to disclose that a certain treatment will cause the patient to gain an enormous amount of weight, yet the only adverse result of the treatment is the fact that the patient's blood pressure skyrockets, the patient will not win an informed consent lawsuit against the physician (though other grounds for victory may be available). If, however, the patient does gain weight, causation will be found and an informed consent lawsuit will go to the jury. As this portion of *Canterbury* demonstrates, there are two tests for causation. The first, accepted by the *Canterbury* court, is an objective test. As stated in the court's opinion, the objective test looks to what the reasonable person would do, and not necessarily what the patient would have done had he or she been fully informed. The second test is a subjective test, under which the jury's determination is based wholly on what the plaintiff would have done had he or she been fully informed. Plaintiff testimony is, quite obviously, of much greater importance under the subjective test. *Canterbury* chose to follow the objective test because it was of the view that the subjective test gives more weight to plaintiff testimony than that testimony deserves, and potentially allows for conjecture, hindsight, or bitterness to affect the physician's liability. A different court that accepted the subjective test did so for the following reason: "[T]he totally objective standard . . . denies the individual's right to decide what is to be done with his or her body and may deny the individual the right to base consent on proper information in light of their individual fears, apprehensions, religious beliefs and the like." *Cheung v. Cunningham.* Most jurisdictions have accepted the objective test for causation.

Tisdale v. Pruitt, Jr., M.D.

(Patient) v. (Doctor)

302 S.C. 238, 394 S.E.2d 857 (Ct. App. 1990)

PUNITIVE DAMAGES ARE NOT AVAILABLE IN ALL MEDICAL MALPRACTICE CASES

■ **INSTANT FACTS** A lawsuit was filed when a physician performed a dilation and curettage (D & C) in his office; had the physician looked closely at the patient's chart, he would have discovered that she was not there to have the procedure performed, but only to get a second opinion about its necessity.

■ **BLACK LETTER RULE** In a medical malpractice action, punitive damages are only available when there is evidence of wilful, wanton, or reckless conduct on the part of the physician.

■ PROCEDURAL BASIS

Appeal to the Court of Appeals of South Carolina of a trial court's decision not to instruct a medical malpractice jury on the issue of implied consent.

■ FACTS

When Laurel Tisdale's (P) family physician recommended a dilation and curettage (D & C), her insurance company refused to pay for the procedure until she got a second opinion. The insurance company referred her to Dr. Bert Pruitt (D), with whom Tisdale (P) made an appointment. Prior to being seen by Dr. Pruitt (D), Tisdale (P) filled out an information sheet and informed the receptionist that she was there for a second opinion. Dr. Pruitt's (D) receptionist noted the reason for Tisdale's (P) visit in two places on her chart. Dr. Pruitt (D), by his own admission, did not fully read Tisdale's (P) chart when he went into the examination room to see her. Nor did he talk with Tisdale (P) enough to determine why she was there. As a result, Dr. Pruitt (D) did not give a second opinion, but instead performed a D & C in his office without anesthesia. It was not performed satisfactorily and had to be redone by another doctor at a hospital. Thereafter, Tisdale (P) filed suit against Dr. Pruitt (D) for assault, battery, and negligence. The assault and battery causes of action were barred by the statue of limitations, but the negligence claim was not. It went to the jury without an instruction on implied consent and Tisdale (P) was awarded $5,000 in actual damages and $25,000 in punitive damages. Dr. Pruitt (D) appealed.

■ ISSUE

Are punitive damages available in all medical malpractice lawsuits?

■ DECISION AND RATIONALE

(Littlejohn, J.) No. Under the doctrine of informed consent, a physician planning to perform any medical procedure must disclose to the patient, in the absence of any emergency, the following: (1) the diagnosis, (2) the general nature of the contemplated procedure, (3) the material risks involved, (4) the probability of success associated with the procedure, (5) the prognosis if the procedure is not performed, and (6) the existence of any alternatives. In a letter written to Dr. Murphy, Dr. Pruitt (D) effectively pleads guilty to negligence, recklessness, and willfulness. He wrote: "I am most distressed that I did not realize Mrs. Tisdale was referred to the office ... for a second opinion. Although my receptionist had put this on the chart, I did not notice it .... I do hope that you will pardon my 'goof.' I only wish that Mrs. Tisdale ... had mentioned to me more clearly why she was sent to the office. If she did, it fell on deaf ears." An analysis of Dr. Pruitt's (D) testimony further leaves much to be desired in the way of informing a patient of facts upon which an informed consent can be made. There is testimony that Mrs. Tisdale (P) suffered pain from the procedure without anesthesia; she was deprived of her right to choose the doctor to perform her D & C; in addition, she sustained emotional injury. Both actual and punitive damages are supported by the evidence. We hold that the evidence is not susceptible of the inference that the patient gave informed consent. Accordingly, the trial judge properly declined to charge the law of implied consent. Affirmed.

Analysis:

Punitive damages are not generally available or awarded in the majority of medical malpractice cases. When injury to the patient is caused solely by physician negligence, actual damages will be recoverable but punitive damages will not. Actual damages include lost wages, past and future medical expenses, loss of earning capacity, and pain and suffering. Punitive damages are only available when there is evidence of wilful, wanton, or reckless conduct on the part of the physician. Punitive damages were permitted in *Tisdale* because Dr. Pruitt's (D) failure to look closely at Tisdale's (P) chart or to ask her why she was there was found to be reckless conduct.

■ CASE VOCABULARY

DILATION AND CURETTAGE: A surgical scraping or cleaning of a woman's uterus that is performed with an instrument known as a curette.

Canterbury v. Spence

(Patient) v. *(Doctor)*

464 F.2d 772 (D.C. Cir. 1972)

THERE ARE TWO EXCEPTIONS TO THE GENERAL RULE THAT PHYSICIANS MUST DISCLOSE ALL INFORMATION NECESSARY FOR A PATIENT TO MAKE AN INFORMED CHOICE ABOUT PROPOSED TREATMENT

■ **INSTANT FACTS** A back-surgery patient sued his doctor and the hospital in which the surgery was performed when he became paralyzed just following the surgery.

■ **BLACK LETTER RULE** A physician can treat a patient without making all material disclosures when: (1) the patient is unconscious or otherwise incapable of consenting, and the harm from a failure to treat is imminent and outweighs any harm threatened by the proposed treatment, or (2) the disclosure of the risks poses such a threat of detriment to the patient that it becomes improper from a medical point of view.

■ **PROCEDURAL BASIS**

Appeal to the D.C. Circuit Court of Appeals of a district court's decision to grant a directed verdict in favor of a physician and a hospital accused of negligence.

■ **FACTS**

[These are the same facts as set forth *supra.*] In December of 1958, Canterbury (P) began to experience severe back pain. After other treatments failed, Canterbury (P) approached Dr. Spence (D), a neurosurgeon. Dr. Spence (D) was unable to find anything wrong with Canterbury (P) after an office examination and x-rays, so he ordered a myelogram. The myelogram revealed a "filling defect" in the area of the fourth thoracic vertebrae. Upon making this finding, Dr. Spence (D) told Canterbury (P) that he would have to undergo a laminectomy to correct what he suspected was a ruptured disk. Canterbury (P) did not ask and was not told about the nature of the laminectomy. Nor was he told of its potential risks. Prior to the surgery Dr. Spence (D) also spoke with Canterbury's (P) mother. When she asked about the seriousness of the surgery she was simply told that it was "not any more [serious] than any other operation." She too was not told of the risks inherent in a laminectomy. The surgery revealed some unique problems with Canterbury's (P) back which Dr. Spence (D) attempted to fix. For the first twenty-four hours following the surgery, Canterbury (P) recovered normally. He then suffered a fall, however, and an immediate setback. It is unclear why exactly Canterbury (P) fell, but it was determined that he had been left unattended in a bed without rails. Within a matter of hours after the fall, Canterbury (P) began to have trouble breathing. He also became paralyzed from the waist down. Dr. Spence (D) was rushed to the hospital and performed another surgery to allow the spinal cord more room to pulsate. After the second surgery Canterbury (P) was able to exercise almost-normal control over his lower body muscles, but he was unable to void properly. From that point forward Canterbury (P) had to make frequent visits to a urologist and other specialists, and suffered from continued urinal incontinence and paralysis of the bowels. Canterbury (P) also had difficulty finding work because he needed to remain seated at almost all times and had to be very close to a bathroom. In 1968, approximately nine years after the initial surgery, Canterbury (P) filed suit against Dr. Spence (D) and the Washington Hospital Center in the Federal District Court for the District of Columbia, seeking recovery for pain and suffering, medical expenses, and lost earnings. At the close of Canterbury's (P) case-in-chief both Dr. Spence (D) and the hospital moved for directed verdicts. Both were granted on the ground that Canterbury (P) had not shown that the actions of each defendant were in any way medically responsible for his condition. Canterbury (P) appealed.

■ **ISSUE**

Are there any exceptions to the physician's duty to disclose?

■ **DECISION AND RATIONALE**

(Robinson, J.) Yes. There are two exceptions to the general rule of disclosure. The first comes into play when the patient is unconscious or otherwise incapable of consenting, and the harm from a failure to treat is imminent and outweighs any harm threatened by the proposed treatment. When a genuine emergency arises, the impracticability of conferring with the patient dispenses with the need for it. The physician should attempt to secure a relative's consent if possible, but that is not a prerequisite. The second exception arises when risk-disclosure poses such a threat of detriment to the patient that it becomes improper from a medical point of view. Patients occasionally become so distraught when the material facts are presented to them that the disclosure forecloses a rational decision, complicates or hinders the treatment, or even poses psychological damage to the patient. Where that is so, the physician is armed with a privilege to keep the information from the patient. The critical inquiry is whether the physician responded to a sound medical judgment that communication of the risk information would present a threat to the patient's well-being. And it is important to remember that the privilege to withhold information for therapeutic reasons must be carefully circumscribed, or otherwise be improperly used. Reversed.

Analysis:

The emergency-treatment exception has been recognized by the common law for some time. The difficult part of the emergency-treatment exception is determining when it applies. Certainly if a person is unconscious and needs life saving surgery immediately, such as after a car accident, there is clearly an emergency, no consent can be given, and the exception applies. Other situations, such as when a patient is disoriented, are not so clear. To protect doctors, courts have generally erred on the side of allowing them to perform emergency treatment without consent in these borderline situations. One thing that the emergency-treatment exception cannot do, however, is override a refusal of treatment made by one who is capable of giving consent. More difficult is the second exception enumerated by the *Canterbury* court. "[P]atients occasionally become so ill or emotionally distraught on disclosure as to foreclose a rational decision, or complicate or hinder the treatment, or perhaps even pose psychological damage to the patient." In these situations, a doctor need not disclose information that will make the situation worse.

■ **CASE VOCABULARY**

HYPERTENSION: Abnormally high blood pressure.

Humphers v. First Interstate Bank of Oregon

(Former Patient) v. *(Deceased Doctor's Personal Representative)*

298 Or. 706, 696 P.2d 527 (1985)

A PHYSICIAN'S DUTY TO KEEP MEDICAL AND RELATED INFORMATION ABOUT A PATIENT IN CONFIDENCE IS BEYOND QUESTION

■ **INSTANT FACTS** A woman sued her former doctor when he revealed her identity to a daughter whom she had given up for adoption over twenty years earlier.

■ **BLACK LETTER RULE** An unauthorized and unprivileged disclosure of confidential information obtained in a confidential relationship can give rise to tort damages.

■ **PROCEDURAL BASIS**

Appeal to the Supreme Court of Oregon of an appellate court decision recognizing as actionable two breach of confidentiality and invasion of privacy claims.

■ **FACTS**

In 1959, Ramona Jean Peek (P) gave birth to a daughter. Unmarried, Ramona (P) had her doctor admit her to the hospital under the name of "Mrs. Jean Smith." The baby was delivered and given up for adoption, and the hospital records were sealed. Ramona (P) subsequently remarried and raised a family, becoming Ramona Humphers (P). Only Humphers (P), her husband, and her Doctor, Harry E. Mackey, knew of the birth and adoption. Twenty-one years later, Dawn Kastning, the baby given up for adoption, decided to find her biological mother. Unable to gain access to the confidential hospital and adoption files, Dawn was able to find Dr. Mackey. To assist her in her quest, Dr. Mackey fraudulently wrote a letter claiming that in caring for Humphers (P) he had given her diethylstilbestrol, stating that the possible consequences of that medication made it important for Dawn to find her biological mother. Dawn subsequently found Humphers (P). The return of her daughter caused Humphers (P) significant emotional distress, for which she filed suit against Dr. Mackey's estate (D). (Dr. Mackey had died prior to the filing of the suit.) Humphers (P) filed suit on five different theories: commission of outrageous conduct, breach of physician standard of care, breach of confidential relationship, invasion of privacy, and breach of contract. The trial court dismissed all of the claims, but the Court of Appeals resurrected the breach of confidential relationship and invasion of privacy claims. The case was appealed to the Oregon Supreme Court.

■ **ISSUE**

Does a cause of action arise when a person's former physician reveals the person's identity to a daughter whom she had given up for adoption?

■ **DECISION AND RATIONALE**

(Linde, J.) Yes. Physician liability for the disclosure of confidential patient information is not a new problem. There exists much precedent for damage actions based on unauthorized disclosure of confidential facts, though we know of none involving the disclosure of an adoption. These decisions have not rested on a single legal theory, however, and the question before us is on what grounds does the rule rest. Today we consider the theories of breach of confidential relationship and invasion of privacy, those on which the Court of Appeals has allowed Humphers (P) to proceed. Claims of a breach of privacy and of wrongful disclosure of confidential information, though similar, depend on different premises and cover different ground. Both assert a right to control information, but they differ in important respects. The most important distinction is that only one who holds information in confidence can be charged with a breach of confidence. An oft-debated subject, Dean Prosser and his successors concluded that invasion of privacy is not one tort, but a complex of four torts. They identify four kinds of claims grouped under the privacy tort as, first, appropriation of the plaintiff's name or likeness; second, unreasonable and offensive intrusion upon another's seclusion; third, public disclosure of private facts; and fourth, publicity which places the plaintiff in a false light in the public eye. This court has not adopted all forms of the tort wholesale. The Court of Appeals concluded that the complaint alleges a case of tortious intrusion upon Humphers' (P) seclusion in the sense of an offensive prying into her personal matters that she reasonably had sought to keep private. We do not believe that the theory fits this case. Humphers (P) has a privacy interest in the secrecy of her giving birth to a child and the subsequent adoption. This privacy interest is granted by way of Oregon statutes that close adoption records to inspection without a court order. But as already stated, to identify an interest deserving protection does not suffice to collect damages from anyone who causes injury to that interest. Dr. Mackey helped Dawn Kastning find her biological mother, but we are not prepared to assume that Ms. Kastning became liable for invasion of privacy in seeking her out. Nor would anyone else who knew the facts without an obligation of secrecy commit a tort simply by telling them to Ms. Kastning. Dr. Mackey did not approach Humphers (P) or pry into any personal facts that he did not know. Instead he failed to keep a confidence. If Dr. Mackey incurred liability for his actions, it must result from an obligation of confidentiality beyond any general duty of people at large not to invade one another's privacy. We therefore turn to Humphers'(P) claim that Dr. Mackey's estate (D) is liable for a breach of confidence. An unauthorized and unprivileged disclosure of confidential information obtained in a confidential relationship can give rise to tort damages. In the case of medical professionals, courts have found sources of a non-consensual duty of confidentiality. For example, medical licensing statutes and professional regulations are legal duties imposed as a condition of engaging in the professional practice of medicine. Under these duties, physicians may be legally obliged to report medical information to others for the protection of the patient, other individuals, or the public. Even without such a legal obligation, there may be a privilege to disclose information for the safety of individuals or important to matters of public interest. In other situations, however, a physician's duty to keep medical and related information about a patient in confidence is beyond question. It is imposed by ORS § 677.190(5), which provides for disqualifying or otherwise disciplining a physician for "willfully or negligently divulging a professional secret." ORS § 677.190(5) arguably applies in this case. Even better, however, are the statutes that specifically mandate the secrecy of adoption records. Given these clear legal constraints, there is no privilege to disregard the professional duty imposed by § 677.190(5) solely to satisfy the curiosity of the person who was given up for adoption. Humphers (P) may proceed under her claim of breach of confidentiality. Reversed in part and affirmed in part.

Analysis:

Some courts have held that tort laws prohibiting the unwanted invasion of another's privacy are the source of liability for the unauthorized disclosure of patient information. As the *Humphers* opinion states, however, the Oregon Supreme Court disagrees. In this case, it is state licensing and privilege statutes and rules of medical ethics that are used to impose liability on Dr. Mackey. Another theory that has been used in some states to support the same proposition is breach of contract. Two theories that have failed to gain any support are medical malpractice and defamation. In sum, *Humphers* teaches two important lessons. First, doctors must be careful not to disclose confidential patient information when it is not required by law because a duty of confidentiality exists. And second, there is no uniform theory supporting this rule; instead, courts have applied a number of different theories and set forth a number of different grounds in support of the above rule.

■ CASE VOCABULARY

DIETHYLSTILBESTROL: A synthetic chemical compound used as a source of estrogen that has been found to cause cancer or other birth defects in children if used by their mother during pregnancy.

Doe v. Medlantic Health Care Group, Inc.

(HIV Patient) v. *(Hospital)*

814 A.2d 939 (D.C. Ct. App. 2003)

UTMOST CARE MUST BE USED TO PREVENT DISCLOSURE OF PATIENT INFORMATION

■ **INSTANT FACTS** A hospital employee (D) told Doe's (P) co-workers that Doe (P) was HIV positive.

■ **BLACK LETTER RULE** The tort of breach of a confidential relationship consists of the unconsented, unprivileged disclosure to a third party of nonpublic information learned within a confidential relationship.

■ **PROCEDURAL BASIS**

Appeal from an order granting judgment notwithstanding the verdict.

■ **FACTS**

Doe (P) worked nights for a company that provided janitorial services to the State Department. He had been diagnosed with HIV, but he had not told any of his co-workers about his condition. One of his co-workers, Goldring (D), also worked days as a receptionist at the Employee Health Department at the Washington Hospital Center (WHC) (D). When Doe (P) became ill, he went to the emergency room at WHC (D). He was discharged three days later, but was unable to return to work for two weeks. When he returned to WHC (D) for a follow-up clinic visit, he paid a courtesy call on Goldring (D) at her desk at WHC (D). Goldring (D) asked Doe (P) for the correct spelling of his last name, saying that she wanted to send him a get-well card. Doe (P) told her the spelling, and testified later that he did no think there was anything unusual about her request. Goldring (D) never sent Doe (P) a card.

Before Doe (P) returned to work, Goldring (D) told Fuell, another co-worker, that Doe (P) had HIV or AIDS. Goldring (D) told Fuell that she got her information from "the hospital," and the co-worker knew that Goldring worked at WHC. Within a few days of his conversation with Goldring (D) at the hospital, Doe (P) learned that his co-workers knew of his AIDS diagnosis. Fuell told him that Goldring (D) was telling everybody, but did not say how Goldring (D) obtained the information. Co-workers started teasing Doe (P) and making offensive remarks. He was shunned, stared at, and the object of unwanted attention. Doe (P) contacted WHC (D) to ask if it had a policy on employees who disseminate confidential information. Doe (P) was told that this type of dissemination was against hospital policy and local law. Doe (P) gave WHC (D) Goldring's (D) name and was advised that someone would speak with her.

Approximately one year later, Doe (P) commenced suit against Medlantic (D) and Goldring (D), alleging invasion of privacy and breach of confidential relationship based on WHC's (D) negligence in allowing Goldring (D) access to confidential patient information. The jury found for Doe (P) on the breach of confidential relationship claim, but found for Medlantic (D) on the breach of privacy claim because Goldring's (D) disclosure was not within the scope of her employment (Goldring (D) had been dismissed from the case). The jury specifically found that Doe's (P) action had been commenced within the applicable limitations period. The trial court entered judgment notwithstanding the verdict, overruling the jury's finding on the statute of limitations question. The court held that the limitations period began to run when Fuell told Doe (P) that Goldring (D) was spreading rumors about him. Medlantic (D) also argued that Doe (P) had not made out a *prima facie* case, since there was no evidence that WHC (D) disclosed confidential information.

■ ISSUE

Did Doe (P) make out a *prima facie* case of a breach of a confidential relationship?

■ DECISION AND RATIONALE

(Ruiz, J.) Yes. The tort of breach of a confidential relationship consists of the unconsented, unprivileged disclosure to a third party of nonpublic information learned within a confidential relationship. A hospital is under a duty to observe the utmost caution to protect the confidentiality of patients' medical records, and the evidence in this case is sufficient to permit the jury to find that that duty was breached in this case. The jury was instructed regarding WHC's (D) protocols and was told that it could consider whether those protocols were followed and whether they were successful in preventing unauthorized disclosure.

There was substantial evidence introduced regarding WHC's (D) protocols and the routine failure of employees to comply with those protocols. Former employees of WHC (D) who worked with the medical records testified regarding the departures in practice from the protocols. Employees were given records even if they did not provide information, including the purpose of the request, required by the protocols. The rules were followed less often in the Employee Health Department. Even though employees of that department did not have the authority to ask for charts of persons who were not hospital employees, a person with a hospital badge who asked for a record was given the record, without any verification of whether the record pertained to an employee.

Goldring (D) was the only one of Doe's co-workers who could have had access to Doe's (P) records. She was identified as the source of the rumors about Doe (P), and she asked for the spelling of Doe's (P) name to send him a card, which she never did. There was no evidence produced by WHC (D) to show that someone else accessed Doe's (P) records at the relevant time. Although there was no direct evidence of a breach, there was ample evidence from which the jury could conclude that the duty of confidentiality was breached. Reversed and remanded with instructions to reinstate the jury's verdict.

Analysis:

The excerpt relates to a cross-appeal by Medlantic (D): the court is agreeing with the trial court's rejection of an argument Medlantic (D) did not raise at trial. The appellate court actually reverses the trial court's determination on the statute of limitations issue. The court held that the trial judge erred in not accepting the jury's factual findings on the accrual of the statute of limitations, and whether Doe's (P) delay in commencing his action was reasonable.

Herman v. Kratche

(Patient) v. *(Physician)*

2006 WL 3240680 (Ohio Ct. App. 2006)

HONEST MISTAKE IS NO DEFENSE TO A CLAIM FOR UNAUTHORIZED DISCLOSURE OF CONFIDENTIAL MEDICAL RECORDS

I don't care if it was a mistake,
I still suffered from you telling Mom my secret.

■ **INSTANT FACTS** A clinic disclosed a patient's non-work-related medical records to the patient's employer without her consent.

■ **BLACK LETTER RULE** A healthcare provider can be held liable for the unauthorized disclosure of patient medical records if a fiduciary relationship is breached, causing the patient's damages.

■ **PROCEDURAL BASIS**

On appeal to review a trial court decision dismissing plaintiff's claims on summary judgment.

■ **FACTS**

In March 2003, Herman (P) worked for Nestle USA, Inc. In March and April, she received three non-work-related medical examinations at the Clinic (D) by Dr. Kratche (D). After each of these three examinations, Herman's (P) medical records and other private information were forwarded to a human resources representative at Nestle for purposes of workers' compensation coverage. The Clinic's Administrator admitted that the Clinic (D) made a mistake in sending Herman's (P) non-work-related records to her employer. Herman (P) sued Kratche (D) and the Clinic (D) for unauthorized disclosure, invasion of privacy, and intentional infliction of emotional distress, but the trial court granted the defendants' joint motion for summary judgment on all claims.

■ **ISSUE**

Did the court err in granting judgment in favor of the defendants on Herman's (P) unauthorized disclosure and invasion of privacy claims?

■ **DECISION AND RATIONALE**

(Judge Undisclosed.) Yes. A healthcare provider can be held liable for the unauthorized disclosure of patient medical records if a fiduciary relationship is breached, causing the patient's damages. Under Ohio law, a cause of action exists for the unauthorized disclosure to a third party of nonpublic medical information obtained in the course of the physician-patient relationship. Founded in the duty of confidentiality owed by physician to patient, the tort of unauthorized disclosure ensures the free flow of important medical information without the fear that it will become public knowledge. A physician's breach of this duty of confidentiality amounts to a breach of fiduciary duty. Accordingly, to establish a claim for unauthorized disclosure, a plaintiff must demonstrate that the defendant owed a fiduciary duty, that the defendant breached that duty, and that the plaintiff suffered damage as a result of the breach. Here, because the Clinic (D) is a medical provider, it clearly owes a fiduciary duty of confidentiality, which was clearly breached upon disclosure of Herman's (P) medical records to her employer.

The Clinic (D), however, claims that Herman (P) has suffered no damage from the disclosure because, like itself, her employer owes a duty of confidentiality to Herman (P) and therefore is not a third party. Additionally, the Clinic (D) claims that no damage has been caused because nobody at Nestle read

Herman's (P) medical information. We reject these arguments. First, just because Nestle owes a duty not to disclose Herman's (P) confidential information does not make it an authorized third party to which the Clinic (D) may justifiably disclose confidential information without Herman's (P) consent. Moreover, the record indicates that Nestle's human resources representative read enough of the disclosed medical records to learn that they were not related to Herman's (P) employment. As soon as these records were opened at Nestle, Herman (P) suffered damage from the Clinic's (D) unauthorized disclosure.

The Clinic (D) further argues that it cannot be liable for unauthorized disclosure because, under the Health Insurance Portability and Accountability Act of 1996 ("HIPAA"), both Nestle and the Clinic (D) are in the same "circle of confidentiality" that excuses mistaken disclosures. HIPAA was enacted to protect the privacy of an individual's personal health information by establishing specific regulations for the collection, use, and disclosure of such information by "covered entities," including health plans, healthcare clearinghouses and healthcare providers. But Nestle is not a covered entity as defined by HIPAA and, if it were, nothing in HIPAA justifies unauthorized disclosures among covered entities so as to support the Clinic's (D) "circle of confidentiality" argument. In addition, although HIPAA allows disclosure with the patient's consent, disclosure must be strictly limited to the consent given. Here, although Herman (P) authorized disclosure for "treatment, payment, [and] healthcare operations," the Clinic did not disclose any information for these purposes. Herman (P) maintained private health insurance coverage through which unpaid bills were to be paid, limiting the scope of her consent to disclosure.

Finally, an "unwarranted appropriation or exploitation of one's personality, the publicizing of one's private affairs with which the public has no legitimate concern, or the wrongful intrusion into one's private activities in such a manner as to outrage or cause mental suffering, shame or humiliation to a person of ordinary sensibilities" constitutes a negligent invasion of the right of privacy under Ohio law. Here, once the Clinic (D) mistakenly mailed Herman's (P) private information to Nestle, it intruded into her private life. Likewise, when Herman (P) realized that a Nestle representative had access to these intimate medical details, she was embarrassed, angry, and emotionally distraught, establishing her damages.

Accordingly, the trial court order erred in dismissing the plaintiff's unauthorized disclosure and invasion of privacy claims. Reversed in part.

Analysis:

The Clinic's (D) "circle of confidentiality" argument has some general support in the law, but it has not yet been successfully used in a case involving a HIPAA violation. In general, the "circle of confidentiality" is an important component of a physician's duty of confidentiality, for the circle serves to protect confidential medical records by creating a duty upon all affiliated with a treating physician. If Herman (P) had been treated at the Clinic (D) for work-related injuries, and only those records were disclosed, it is quite possible that Nestle would have fallen within the circle of confidentiality.

■ CASE VOCABULARY

CONFIDENTIALITY: Secrecy; the state of having the dissemination of certain information restricted.

FIDUCIARY RELATIONSHIP: A relationship in which one person is under a duty to act for the benefit of the other on matters within the scope of the relationship. Fiduciary relationships—such as trustee-beneficiary, guardian-ward, agent-principal, and attorney-client—require the highest duty of care. Fiduciary relationships usually arise in one of four situations: (1) when one person places trust in the faithful integrity of another, who as a result gains superiority or influence over the first, (2) when one person assumes control and responsibility over another, (3) when one person has a duty to act for or give advice to another on matters falling within the scope of the relationship, or (4) when there is a specific relationship that has traditionally been recognized as involving fiduciary duties, as with a lawyer and a client or a stockbroker and a customer.

INVASION OF PRIVACY: An unjustified exploitation of one's personality or intrusion into one's personal activity, actionable under tort law and sometimes under constitutional law.

RIGHT OF PRIVACY: The right of a person and the person's property to be free from unwarranted public scrutiny or exposure.

Acosta v. Byrum et al.

(Patient) v. *(Office Manager)*

638 S.E.2d 246 (N.C. Ct. App. 2006)

HIPAA VIOLATIONS MAY GIVE RISE TO CIVIL LIABILITY FOR NEGLIGENCE

You were negligent! You should have known that telling my secrets would result in emotional distress.

■ **INSTANT FACTS** The plaintiff's confidential medical and psychiatric records were impermissibly accessed and disseminated to third parties.

■ **BLACK LETTER RULE** Although HIPAA confers no private right of action, HIPAA requirements may be relied upon to establish the standard of care for a negligence claim.

■ **PROCEDURAL BASIS**

On appeal to review an order dismissing the plaintiff's complaint.

■ **FACTS**

Acosta (P) was a patient of Psychiatric Associates (D) in Ahoskie, North Carolina, which was owned by Dr. Faber (D). Byrum (D) was employed by Psychiatric Associates (D) as its office manager. According to Acosta's (P) complaint, Dr. Faber (D) allowed Byrum (D) to utilize his medical records access number and Byrum (D) used the access number to obtain Acosta's (P) confidential medical and psychiatric records, which Byrum (D) disseminated to third parties. Acosta's (P) complaint alleged that Dr. Faber violated various hospital rules and regulations and HIPAA privacy provisions. The complaint further claimed invasion of privacy and intentional infliction of emotional distress against Byrum (D) and negligent infliction of emotional distress against Dr. Faber (D). Dr. Faber moved to dismiss for failure to state a claim upon which relief can be granted, which motion was granted by the trial court.

■ **ISSUE**

Did Acosta's (P) complaint state a valid claim for negligent infliction of emotional distress?

■ **DECISION AND RATIONALE**

(Judge Undisclosed.) Yes. Although HIPAA confers no private right of action, HIPAA requirements may be relied upon to establish the standard of care for a negligence claim. Acosta (P) did not specifically aver on which of the hospital's rules and regulations and HIPAA privacy provisions she based her cause of action, but the allegations in the complaint sufficiently place the defendants on notice that Acosta (P) intends to rely on these provisions as the standard of care owed by the defendants. Accordingly, Acosta's (P) reliance on HIPAA requirements does not allege an action under the HIPAA statutes, which confers no private right of action, but merely satisfies one of the elements of her negligent infliction of emotional distress claims. Acosta (P) stated a valid claim, and her complaint should not have been dismissed. Reversed.

Analysis:

Although the court is quick to point out that the federal HIPAA statutes do not confer a private remedy for the plaintiff, it did not dismiss the plaintiff's claims. Instead, it permitted the plaintiff's HIPAA-like claim to proceed under a common law negligence theory. In the process, the court recognizes HIPAA's statutory limitations on the disclosure of private information as the standard of care the defendant owed to the plaintiff and determined that the defendant was liable for violating the statute. In essence, the court has allowed a private right of action by allowing the plaintiff to recover for a violation of the statute *if* she could prove private damages as a result.

■ CASE VOCABULARY

NEGLIGENT INFLICTION OF EMOTIONAL DISTRESS: The tort of causing another severe emotional distress through one's negligent conduct. Most courts will allow a plaintiff to recover damages for emotional distress if the defendant's conduct results in physical contact with the plaintiff or, when no contact occurs, if the plaintiff is in the zone of danger.

RIGHT OF ACTION: The right to bring a specific action to court.

STANDARD OF CARE: In the law of negligence, the degree of prudence that a reasonable person should exercise.

CHAPTER FIVE

Liability of Health Care Professionals

Hall v. Hilbun

Instant Facts: In a malpractice suit, the plaintiff presented expert testimony that doctors should follow minimal nationwide standards of care, but this testimony was excluded.

Black Letter Rule: In a medical malpractice suit, any expert witness may testify about procedures which demonstrate the minimal nationwide standard of care among physicians.

Hinlicky v. Dreyfuss

Instant Facts: At trial, the court admitted into evidence a medical algorithm relied upon by a testifying physician in making a medical decision concerning a patient's treatment.

Black Letter Rule: Hearsay evidence is admissible in negligence cases when used as demonstrative evidence to assist the jury in understanding the medical decision-making of a treating physician.

Helling v. Carey

Instant Facts: When a patient sues her ophthalmologists for not administering tests to detect an uncommon eye disease, they contend they are not negligent because the profession does not give such tests routinely.

Black Letter Rule: Doctors may be liable for malpractice if they fail to take reasonable precautions, even if similar specialists routinely do not take those precautions.

Strasel v. Seven Hills OB–GYN Assoc., Inc.

Instant Facts: Strasel (P) experienced panic attacks, anxiety, and emotional distress after her unborn baby underwent an unnecessary medical procedure that placed the baby's health in danger.

Black Letter Rule: A cause of action for the negligent infliction of serious emotional distress may be stated where the plaintiff-bystander reasonably appreciated the peril that took place, whether or not the victim suffered actual physical harm, and, as a result of this cognizance or fear of peril, the plaintiff suffered severe emotional distress.

Wickline v. State

Instant Facts: After a patient on welfare underwent state-funded surgery, the state refused to approve extended hospitalization, and her treating physician did not appeal. After discharge, the patient suffered complications requiring amputation, and now sues the state for negligently denying necessary care.

Black Letter Rule: If the state pays for patients' medical care, it may be liable in malpractice for denying payment for medically-necessary treatment, but only if it unreasonably ignores or overrules the treating physicians' medical judgement.

Chumbler v. McClure

Instant Facts: An accident victim sued his neurologist for prescribing estrogen, an uncommon remedy.

Black Letter Rule: Where multiple schools of thought exist among competent physicians concerning proper treatment for a given ailment, and each is supported by responsible medical authority, it is not malpractice to follow the minority school.

Henderson v. Heyer–Schulte Corp.

Instant Facts: After a surgeon performs a breast implant using the antiquated method of releasing liquid silicone directly into the breast, the patient sues for malpractice.

Black Letter Rule: A course of treatment is negligent if no "reasonable and prudent" doctor would perform it under similar circumstances.

Brook v. St. John's Hickey Memorial Hospital

Instant Facts: When a doctor diagnosing a small child decided to inject a contrast medium into her calf rather than her buttocks, the child sued for injuries.

Black Letter Rule: Reasonable and prudent clinical innovation creates no malpractice liability.

Richardson v. Miller

Instant Facts: Richardson (P) brought a malpractice action against her physician, Dr. Miller (D), and the court refused to allow her to introduce evidence of off-label use of a medication to stop labor.

Black Letter Rule: The labeling or PDR reference of a prescription drug, when introduced with other expert evidence on the standard of care, is admissible evidence on the question of whether the drug presented an unacceptable risk to the patient.

Hardi v. Mezzanotte

Instant Facts: Hardi (D) made a mistaken diagnosis of Mezzanotte's (P) condition and then claimed that her malpractice suit against him was barred by the statute of limitations.

Black Letter Rule: Under the discovery rule, a medical malpractice claim does not accrue until the patient has some knowledge of (1) the injury, (2) the injury's cause in fact, and (3) evidence of wrongdoing on the part of the person responsible.

Ostrowski v. Azzara

Instant Facts: When a diabetic sued a surgeon for a botched surgery, the surgeon contended her smoking and overeating after surgery prevented proper recovery.

Black Letter Rule: In medical malpractice actions, plaintiffs' pre-treatment negligence may reduce/preclude liability under comparative/contributory negligence statutes, but plaintiffs' post-treatment failure to mitigate damages may only reduce the recovery.

Robins v. Garg

Instant Facts: Robins (P) died after consulting with Dr. Garg (D) for many years about her risks of heart disease.

Black Letter Rule: To establish causation in a wrongful death action, the plaintiff must establish that the injury would not have occurred but for the defendant's conduct.

Herskovits v. Group Health Cooperative of Puget Sound

Instant Facts: When a doctor's failure to diagnose a cough as cancer delayed the patient's cancer surgery, the decedent patient's estate sued for "loss of chance."

Black Letter Rule: Negligent medical care providers are liable for "loss of chance" for reducing a patient's probability of recovering, even if the patient's original chance of recovery was less than 50%.

Hall v. Hilbun

(Patient) v. *(Doctor)*

466 So.2d 856 (Miss. 1985)

IN MALPRACTICE SUITS, DUE CARE IS MEASURED BY OBJECTIVE NATIONAL STANDARDS UNDER THE CIRCUMSTANCES

■ **INSTANT FACTS** In a malpractice suit, the plaintiff presented expert testimony that doctors should follow minimal nationwide standards of care, but this testimony was excluded.

■ **BLACK LETTER RULE** In a medical malpractice suit, any expert witness may testify about procedures which demonstrate the minimal nationwide standard of care among physicians.

■ **PROCEDURAL BASIS**

In medical malpractice action for wrongful death, appeal from directed verdict for defendant.

■ **FACTS**

Patient Hall (P) was admitted to the small rural Singing River Hospital for abdominal pain, where she consulted with general surgeon Dr. Glyn Hilbun (D). Dr. Hilbun (D) believed the pain was caused by bowel obstruction, and performed exploratory laparotomy with apparent success. After surgery, Dr. Hilbun (D) waited with Hall (P) for 105 minutes, then completed his shift and went home. Dr. Hilbun (D) did not give any post-operative instructions to Hall (P), her husband, or the nurse, and did not call later to check her condition. Later that night, Hall (P) felt pain and had trouble breathing, and finally died of respiratory failure. Dr. Hilbun (D) was called, but arrived too late. Hall's (P) husband Glenn (collectively "Hall") filed suit against Dr. Hilbun (D) for wrongful death, contending Dr. Hilbun (D) committed malpractice by (i) not checking Hall's (P) status before leaving, and (ii) failing to give appropriate post-operative care instructions to the nursing staff. Hall (P) called 2 witnesses to testify about the proper standards of care. Dr. Hoerr, a retired surgeon, testified that he did not know the standard of care practiced by surgeons in that county, but believed there was a national standard of care. Dr. Hoerr testified that (i) Dr. Hilbun (D) was negligent in not checking on Hall (P) later that evening or delegating the task to another doctor, (ii) Dr. Hilbun (D) was possibly negligent in not giving the nurses instructions to contact him if Hall's (P) condition exceeded certain parameters, and (iii) the nurses negligently failed to contact Dr. Hilbun (D) when complications surfaced. Next, witness Dr. Dohn, a local surgeon, testified that the personnel, equipment, and resources at Singing River Hospital were much inferior to large urban hospitals'. However, at trial, the judge excluded Dr. Hoerr's testimony, apparently holding there was no nationwide standard of medical care about which Hoerr could testify. Afterwards, Dr. Hilbun (D) moved for a directed verdict, contending Hall (P) failed to present a prima facie case of negligence. The court granted Dr. Hilbun's (D) motion. Hall (P) appeals, contending the exclusion of his medical experts' testimony was improper.

■ **ISSUE**

In a medical malpractice suit, may expert witnesses testify about nationwide standards of care for physicians?

■ **DECISION AND RATIONALE**

(Robertson, J.) Yes. In a medical malpractice suit, any expert witness may testify about procedures which demonstrate the minimal nationwide standard of care among physicians. Medical malpractice is

---

legal fault by a physician, which arises from physicians' failure to provide the quality of care required by law. When physicians treat a patient, they bear the obligation to use minimally-sound medical judgement and render minimally-competent care. If the patient sustains injury because of the physician's failure to perform his legal duty, the physician may be liable for damages. However, physicians do not guarantee recovery, and are not liable *per se* for mere [non-negligent] errors or complications. Generally, the test of reasonability has been the "locality rule" [whereby reasonability is dictated by local medical standards]. However, we cannot ignore that there are minimal national standards, since all physicians are taught basically similar procedures in medical schools, residency programs, and medical journals. Thus, each physician is expected to possess and demonstrate such medical knowledge as is reasonably available to minimally competent practitioners of the same specialty throughout the United States. Beyond that, each physician must have a practical working knowledge of available facilities, equipment, personnel (including nurses), and other resources, including those reasonably available through larger hospitals nearby. Each physician, in treating a patient, has a non-delegable duty to render services consistent with that objectively-ascertained minimal competence, throughout every stage of the care process (including examination, diagnosis, treatment, medication, follow-up, etc.). If a physician renders a discretionary medical judgement, he is not liable if it is erroneous, unless it fell below minimal standards. This is because such judgement calls vary between physicians, and should not be punished unless clearly negligent. We recognize that medical customs may vary among medical communities, and hold that, while satisfying the local custom is evidence of due care, it is not conclusive. However, the duty to make adept use of available medical facilities necessarily depends on what facilities are available. Thus, the physician's non-delegable duty of care is this: given the circumstances, each physician has a duty to use his knowledge to treat each patient with all reasonable procedures, with such reasonable diligence, skill, and care as is practiced by minimally-competent physicians of the same specialty throughout the United States, who have available the same general facilities. Where specialized facilities are not available locally but are reasonably accessible in nearby cities, the physician may have a duty to use those facilities where transfer seems reasonably safe and necessary. Next, we turn to the question of who can give expert testimony in malpractice cases. Generally, witnesses may testify as experts if they have the requisite knowledge, skill, experience, and/or education, coupled with independence and lack of bias, to assist the fact-finder with specialized knowledge. Medical malpractice cases generally require expert witnesses to help fact-finders understand the evidence. Generally, the place where a proposed witness practices has no relevance *per se* on his qualifications as an expert. We hold that any qualified medical expert witnesses may express an opinion regarding the duty of care and whether it was met, without making any special showing of additional qualifications. Such witnesses may opine on the conclusions that competent practitioners should reach, or actions they should take, if these witnesses first familiarize themselves with the facilities available (through visiting, hearing others' descriptions, interacting with local doctors, etc.). Here, we find Hall's (D) experts' testimony was excluded improperly; had it been included, Hall (D) might have survived the motion. Reversed and remanded.

Analysis:

This case introduces the topic of medical malpractice and the standard of care for doctors. *Hall* largely rejects the "locality" test, substituting instead a minimum national standard as the mandatory level of care; this is the majority rule. The "locality rule" is sometimes seen as an incentive to attract doctors to rural areas with poor medical resources, with the promise of reduced liability risk. However, it may create bad incentives to permit rural doctors to practice medicine at a lower level than they were trained at. Under the majority approach, doctors are held to objective minimum nationwide standards, though their decisions are to be considered in light of the circumstances (including limited medical facilities and heat-of-the-moment decisions). *Hall* also sets forth the basic rule that malpractice suits must be established by expert testimony that the procedure followed was unreasonable, and this testimony may be given by anyone familiar with that specialty (i.e., by any other practitioner of the same specialty).

■ CASE VOCABULARY

DIRECTED VERDICT: In jury trial, verdict given by a judge, upon his finding the evidence is so overwhelming that no jury could reasonably find otherwise.

LOCALITY RULE: In medical malpractice law, the theory that doctors' standards of care must be determined according to standards in the community where he actually practices. Generally, this theory is *not* accepted as the test of whether a doctor's actions were reasonable.

MALPRACTICE: Tort which occurs when a professional, including a doctor, fails to exercise reasonable care in performing his professional duties, injuring the plaintiff thereby.

RESIDENCY: Doctors' clinical training at a hospital prior to independent practice; akin to an internship.

WRONGFUL DEATH [ACTION]: Tort lawsuit brought *on behalf of the decedent* by the next of kin, against whoever killed him. This lawsuit compensates for the *decedent's* pain and suffering, and represents what the decedent would have received as compensation for the fatal injury, if he could collect it. Here, Hall's husband filed suit on behalf of his wife.

Hinlicky v. Dreyfuss

(Patient's Estate) v. *(Physician)*

6 N.Y.3d 636, 815 N.Y.S.2d 908, 848 N.E.2d 1285 (2006)

ALGORITHMS ESTABLISHING GENERAL PHYSICIAN GUIDELINES ARE ADMISSIBLE IF NOT OFFERED FOR THEIR TRUTH

This is your defense? Let's hope the jurors are smarter than I am.

stus.com

■ **INSTANT FACTS** At trial, the court admitted into evidence a medical algorithm relied upon by a testifying physician in making a medical decision concerning a patient's treatment.

■ **BLACK LETTER RULE** Hearsay evidence is admissible in negligence cases when used as demonstrative evidence to assist the jury in understanding the medical decision-making of a treating physician.

■ **PROCEDURAL BASIS**

On appeal to review an appellate division decision affirming a trial court judgment.

■ **FACTS**

In 1996, Hinlicky (P) underwent a surgical procedure to remove plaque buildup in her carotid artery. Though the surgery was successful, she died of a heart attack 25 days later. The plaintiff's estate brought a medical malpractice suit, contending that the defendants were negligent in failing to obtain a preoperation cardiac evaluation to ensure that Hinlicky's (P) heart could tolerate the procedure.

During the nine-day trial, the jury considered the testimony of three treating physicians and several medical experts for both parties. Dr. Frank (D) testified that he had treated Hinlicky (P) for many years for high blood pressure and other complaints, but none was determined to have been cardiac in nature. In 1996, Hinlicky (P) indicated that her brother and sister had experienced heart problems, prompting Frank's (D) concern about blockage of her carotid arteries. Frank (D) concluded that complaints of decreased vision were likely a result of arterial blockage, and referred her for a surgical evaluation. Hinlicky (P) was then examined by Dr. Dreyfuss (D), who ordered various tests that revealed a seventy- to seventy-five-percent blockage of the carotid artery. He recommended surgery to remove plaque buildup in the artery, but did not order any invasive cardiology workups for Hinlicky (P). Dreyfuss (D) testified that it was his practice not to order such tests unless a patient has previously had heart attacks, open-heart surgery or other heart conditions, which Hinlicky (P) had not. Dr. Ilioff (D), an anesthesiologist treating Hinlicky (P), testified that based on Hinlicky's (P) medical records, charts, and a personal interview and examination of Hinlicky (P), a preoperative cardiac evaluation was not necessary for this type of surgery.

Ilioff (D) based his decision on a set of guidelines published by the American Heart Association (AHA) and the American College of Cardiology (ACC), which contained an algorithm that helped decide which patients could proceed directly to surgery. On cross examination, the defense asked Ilioff (D) for background on the guidelines. Plaintiff's counsel objected that any testimony as to what other physicians have stated or done constituted inadmissible hearsay. The court allowed Ilioff (D) to testify about his use of the algorithm, but not how others use the algorithm in their practices. Ilioff (D) testified that he commonly referenced the algorithm with patients who, like Hinlicky (P), were at risk of coronary disease to determine the need for a cardiac evaluation. When the defense sought to admit the algorithm itself into evidence, plaintiff's counsel again objected to it as hearsay. The trial court admitted the

---

algorithm under the professional reliability exception, finding that the algorithm itself is not determinative of any issue in the case, but rather is a document reasonably relied upon by anesthesiologists that explains Ilioff's (D) decision on the course of treatment taken.

In a battle of expert witnesses, the plaintiff and defendants offered differing views of the algorithm's significance to the standard of care. The plaintiff's expert cardiologist claimed the algorithm merely established general guidelines that are somewhat useful, but that the standard of care required careful consideration of the patient's individual circumstances. The defendants' medical experts, on the other hand, fully embraced the algorithm and supported reliance upon the guidelines in making a medical judgment. Ultimately, the jury found the defendants negligent for failing to order preoperative cardiac evaluations before Hinlicky's (P) surgery. On appeal, the Appellate Division affirmed, finding no error in the trial court's admission of the algorithm into evidence. The algorithm, the appellate division ruled, was not offered for its truth or to establish the standard of care, but rather merely to illustrate a physician's decision-making methodology.

■ ISSUE

Did the trial court err in admitting the algorithm into evidence?

■ DECISION AND RATIONALE

(Judge Undisclosed.) No. Hearsay evidence is admissible in negligence cases when used as demonstrative evidence to assist the jury in understanding the medical decision-making of a treating physician. While scientific works are generally excluded as hearsay when offered for their truth, the algorithm was not offered for its truth. Defense counsel questioned Ilioff (D) about the methodology used in deciding not to refer Hinlicky (P) for preoperative cardiac evaluations, to which Ilioff (D) responded that he had used the algorithm as a clinical guideline. Defense counsel then offered the algorithm not for its truth, but as a demonstrative aid to assist the jury in understanding the witness's testimony. While juries could potentially confuse the demonstrative evidence as the proper standard of care, the plaintiff could have requested a limiting instruction to reduce any confusion. The trial court invited experts for both parties to comment on the importance of the guidelines, and each side generally had no issues with them so long as they were not utilized as a rule for treating all patients in all situations. Accordingly, the trial court correctly admitted the algorithm as demonstrative evidence. Affirmed.

Analysis:

In the ordinary medical malpractice case, the appropriate standard of care is often established by medical expert testimony. If an algorithm, such as that relied upon by Dr. Ilioff (D) here, did constitute the appropriate standard of care, it likely would be introduced through the testimony of an expert practitioner, who would recite the standard under oath to the jury. Because guidelines are only generally applicable depending on the specific needs of the patient, however, courts carefully weigh the prejudicial influence their admission can have on the jury.

■ CASE VOCABULARY

DEMONSTRATIVE EVIDENCE: Physical evidence that one can see and inspect (such as a model or photograph) and that, while of probative value and usually offered to clarify testimony, does not play a direct part in the incident in question.

HEARSAY: Traditionally, testimony that is given by a witness who relates not what he or she knows personally, but what others have said, and that is therefore dependent on the credibility of someone other than the witness. Such testimony is generally inadmissible under the rules of evidence.

Helling v. Carey

(Patient) v. *(Doctor)*

83 Wash.2d 514, 519 P.2d 981 (1974)

DOCTORS MAY BE NEGLIGENT FOR NOT EXCEEDING GENERALLY ACCEPTED STANDARDS

■ **INSTANT FACTS** When a patient sues her ophthalmologists for not administering tests to detect an uncommon eye disease, they contend they are not negligent because the profession does not give such tests routinely.

■ **BLACK LETTER RULE** Doctors may be liable for malpractice if they fail to take reasonable precautions, even if similar specialists routinely do not take those precautions.

■ **PROCEDURAL BASIS**

In medical malpractice suit, appeal from affirmation of judgement for defendant.

■ **FACTS**

Patient Ms. Helling (P) suffered from primary open angle glaucoma, a vision problem which causes excess pressure of the eye fluids, which can damage the eye. The disease has few symptoms, and generally cannot be detected in time to prevent permanent damage unless an eye pressure test detects the condition. However, ophthalmologists do not routinely perform pressure tests for patients under 40, since it is rare among young patients. Helling (P) had consulted with ophthalmologists Drs. Carey (D) and Laughlin (D), who did not perform a pressure test or diagnose her condition until after she lost her peripheral vision permanently. Helling (P) sued Drs. Carey (D) and Laughlin (D), contending they were negligent in not administering the test sooner. The doctors (D) defended, offering expert testimony that ophthalmologists generally do not perform pressure tests for patients under 40 because the disease was rare at that age, unless they suspected the symptoms of glaucoma. At trial, the jury found for the defendants. Helling (P) appealed, but the Washington Court of Appeals affirmed. Helling (P) appeals again, contending ophthalmologists should be required to administer pressure tests, and that the defendant doctors (D) had special knowledge which should have led them to suspect and test for glaucoma.

■ **ISSUE**

In malpractice suits, is a doctor who follows procedures commonly accepted by that specialty deemed non-negligent?

■ **DECISION AND RATIONALE**

(Hunter, J.) No. Doctors may be liable for malpractice if they fail to take reasonable precautions, even if similar specialists routinely do not take those precautions. This a unique case. It is undisputed that the standards of the profession of ophthalmology do not require giving routine pressure tests to persons under age 40, because the risk of glaucoma is so rare in this age group—1 in 250,000. The defendants (D) argue that following the standard of the profession is sufficient to insulate them from negligence liability. However, we find that the 1 person in 250,000 is entitled to the protection essential for timely avoidance of vision loss. The pressure test is simple, relatively inexpensive, and reliable. There is no reason it could not have been given to Helling (P) sooner. Courts must set standards of care based on what should be done, not what is commonly done. Common practice is persuasive, but not determinative. There are precautions so imperative that even their universal disregard will not excuse their omission. Here, we find Drs. Carey (D) and Laughlin (D) should have given the test to Helling (P), and for failing to do so are liable for the partial blindness which they proximately caused. Reversed.

Analysis:

Helling illustrates that judges will occasionally reject customary medical standards, substituting instead their own judgement of what procedures should be followed. While such judicial second-guessing is rare, when it occurs, it may work an injustice on the accused doctors and promulgates standards that are likely to be unreasonable. Presumably, judges have no special insight into what is medically necessary or feasible. The fact that the medical profession as a whole has decided against a test or procedure tends to indicate that it is widely believed to be unnecessary, especially since the decision *not* to perform a procedure is untainted by that doctors' self-interest. Commentators note that procedure in question here is unpopular because it has a high rate of false positives. Consequently, some 99% of those found to have high pressure are required to undergo expensive follow-up testing but turn out not to have glaucoma.

■ CASE VOCABULARY

OPHTHALMOLOGIST: Eye doctor, who prescribes glasses/contact lenses in addition to treating eye complaints.

Strasel v. Seven Hills OB–GYN Assoc., Inc.

(Pregnant Woman) v. *(Physicians)*

170 Ohio App. 3d 98, 866 N.E.2d 48 (2007)

A PLAINTIFF MAY RECOVER DAMAGES FOR HER FEAR OF BIRTH DEFECTS IN HER UNBORN CHILD

You look great, but your mommy was nevertheless traumatized.

stus.com

■ **INSTANT FACTS** Strasel (P) experienced panic attacks, anxiety, and emotional distress after her unborn baby underwent an unnecessary medical procedure that placed the baby's health in danger.

■ **BLACK LETTER RULE** A cause of action for the negligent infliction of serious emotional distress may be stated where the plaintiff-bystander reasonably appreciated the peril that took place, whether or not the victim suffered actual physical harm, and, as a result of this cognizance or fear of peril, the plaintiff suffered severe emotional distress.

■ PROCEDURAL BASIS

On appeal to review a jury verdict for the plaintiff.

■ FACTS

Strasel (P), who was obese and had a history of pregnancy-related irregularities, consulted Seven Hills OB–GYN Associates, Inc. (D) for an initial pregnancy appointment. During her appointment, Strasel (P) underwent a sonogram to determine her due date. The sonogram revealed a sac in Strasel's (P) uterus, but did not detect a heart beat or a fetal pole. Although the sonographer suspected Strasel (P) may not in fact have been pregnant, she noted that Strasel's (P) weight limited the sonographer's view and that a second sonogram was recommended. After reviewing the sonographer's report and sonogram photos, a Seven Hills doctor, Dr. Ortiz (D), noted a gestational sac that appeared not to contain a viable fetus. Despite the sonographer's recommendation of a second sonogram, Dr. Ortiz (D) neither ordered the sonogram nor examined Strasel (P). Instead, he scheduled and performed a dilatation and curettage ("D & C") procedure to remove the contents of Strasel's (P) uterus. Several weeks later, Strasel (P) returned for an examination, which detected a viable thirteen-week-old fetus. She immediately began receiving prenatal care to ensure the health of the baby and address any harmful effects caused by the D & C. Throughout her pregnancy, Strasel (P) suffered panic attacks, anxiety, and emotional distress from the fear that her baby may suffer neurological problems as a result of the D & C. Despite her worries, Strasel (P) gave birth to a healthy baby girl. Nonetheless, she sued Seven Hills (D) and Dr. Ortiz (D) for malpractice and negligent infliction of emotional distress, requesting punitive damages. After an arbitrator awarded Strasel (P) $210,000, the defendants appealed the award to the district court. There, the trial court directed a verdict in the defendants' favor on the punitive damages claim, and the jury awarded Strasel (P) $372,000 in damages.

■ ISSUE

Since Strasel's (P) baby experienced no harm from Dr. Ortiz's (D) D & C procedure, did Strasel (P) state a viable claim for negligent infliction of emotional distress?

■ DECISION AND RATIONALE

(Per Curiam.) Yes. A cause of action for the negligent infliction of serious emotional distress may be stated where the plaintiff-bystander reasonably appreciated the peril that took place, whether or not the victim suffered actual physical harm, and, as a result of this cognizance or fear of peril, the plaintiff suffered severe emotional distress. Strasel's (P) baby was placed in real, actual peril by Dr. Ortiz's negligent conduct, which resulted in Strasel's (P) emotional distress.

Emotional distress claims are unavailable in such cases as when a patient is incorrectly diagnosed with cancer or HIV infection, because, despite the understandable fears held by those patients, there is no actual risk of harm arising from an incorrect diagnosis of cancer or HIV. But here, Strasel (P) stated a viable negligent infliction of emotional distress claim because, although her baby suffered no actual harm as a result of the D & C procedure, she was placed in actual peril, which resulted in Strasel's (P) psychological injuries, and the plaintiff's expert witnesses established that her injuries were proximately caused by her fear for her child's safety. The jury verdict is affirmed.

Analysis:

Negligent infliction of emotional distress claims in the medical context are often difficult to reconcile. As the court indicates, the viability of such claims depends largely on whether a person is placed in actual peril that caused her emotional distress. Often, however, actual peril is not known until sometime after the emotional distress is in fact experienced. One's reasonable fear and anxiety over the existence of potential peril is no less real than the fear and anxiety of the consequences of that same peril.

■ CASE VOCABULARY

NEGLIGENT INFLICTION OF EMOTIONAL DISTRESS: The tort of causing another severe emotional distress through one's negligent conduct. Most courts will allow a plaintiff to recover damages for emotional distress if the defendant's conduct results in physical contact with the plaintiff or, when no contact occurs, if the plaintiff is in the zone of danger.

Wickline v. State

(Patient) v. *(State Insurance Fund)*

192 Cal.App.3d 1630, 239 Cal.Rptr. 810 (1986)

STATE-INSURED PATIENTS MAY SUE STATE FOR DENYING NECESSARY TREATMENT

■ **INSTANT FACTS** After a patient on welfare underwent state-funded surgery, the state refused to approve extended hospitalization, and her treating physician did not appeal. After discharge, the patient suffered complications requiring amputation, and now sues the state for negligently denying necessary care.

■ **BLACK LETTER RULE** If the state pays for patients' medical care, it may be liable in malpractice for denying payment for medically-necessary treatment, but only if it unreasonably ignores or overrules the treating physicians' medical judgement.

■ **PROCEDURAL BASIS**

In medical malpractice action, appeal from judgement for plaintiff.

■ **FACTS**

Ms. Wickline (P) was covered by California's (D) state medical assistance program Medi-Cal (D), which paid poor citizens' medical bills. Wickline (P) was diagnosed with arteriosclerosis. She was examined by Dr. Daniels, a general practitioner, who recommended surgery. Dr. Daniels submitted a treatment authorization request to Medi-Cal (D), asking 10 days' hospitalization. In the hospital, surgeon Dr. Polonsky operated, removing part of Wickline's (P) artery and substituting a synthetic one. However, Wickline (P) developed complications. As Wickline (P) was about to check out, Dr. Polonsky decided it was medically necessary for her to remain there for 8 more days, because he feared a leg infection might develop. Dr. Polonsky sent Medi-Cal (D) a form describing Wickline's (P) condition and requesting an 8-day extension. However, Medi-Cal's (D) consultant/surgeon Dr. Glassman rejected the request, and authorized only a 4-day extension. Drs. Polonsky and Daniels did not appeal, instead writing a discharge order. After discharge, Wickline (P) contracted a leg infection, which later required amputation. Wickline (P) sued Medi-Cal (D) and California (D), contending their agent Dr. Glassman negligently discontinued funding and caused her to be discharged prematurely. At trial, Dr. Polonsky testified (i) Wickline (P) was in stable condition at discharge, (ii) he was aware he could request an extension from Dr. Glassman, but felt it would be denied, (iii) Dr. Glassman violated ordinary medical standards by making medical decisions without either seeing the patient or consulting her doctors, and (iv) had Wickline (P) remained in the hospital, her leg would have been saved. Medi-Cal (D) defended, contending that the decision to discharge was made by Drs. Polonsky and Daniels, and was reasonable. Medi-Cal's (D) expert, Dr. Kaufman, testified he agreed with Dr. Glassman that further hospitalization seemed unnecessary, and that it was routine practice for consultants to make decisions based only on the forms, which was necessary to save time. After trial, the jury found for Wickline (P). California (D) and Medi-Cal (D) appeal.

■ **ISSUE**

If the state pays for medical care, may it be liable in malpractice for denying payment for medically-necessary treatment?

■ DECISION AND RATIONALE

(Rowen, J.) Yes. If the state pays for patients' medical care, it may be liable in malpractice for denying payment for medically-necessary treatment, but only if it unreasonably ignores or overrules the treating physicians' medical judgement. Responding to concerns about escalating health care costs, public and private payors [i.e., HMOs and state Medicare equivalents] experimented with various cost-containment mechanisms, including prospective utilization review. This case appears to be the first attempt to make a health care payor liable for malpractice, and deals with policy issues of profound importance. Thus, we permitted the filing of amicus curiae briefs. Previously, utilization review was done by hospitals' medical staff. It was usually retrospective, meaning that *after* a procedure was done, the payor reviewed the records to decide whether it was medically necessary. If not, the health care provider's claim for payment was denied. The new, prospective utilization review at issue here is designed to prevent unnecessary services, but may have more drastic effects on medical care; while retrospective review denied payment, prospective review denies treatment. Under California's prior case law, Medi-Cal (D) is absolved from negligence liability. We hold it is the treating physician's responsibility to decide the course of treatment, including whether and when to discharge. Here, it is undisputed that, had Drs. Polonsky or Daniels insisted on continued hospitalization, Medi-Cal (D) would have considered the request. Under the then-current *California Administration Code*, "The determination of need for acute care shall be made in accordance with the usual standards of medical practice in the community." Thus, patients harmed by denial of required treatment may recover from everyone responsible, including health care payors. Third-party payors of health care services may be liable when a cost-containment program produces medically-inappropriate decisions, e.g., arbitrarily or unreasonably ignoring/denying physicians' appeal for medical care. However, physicians who comply with payors' limitations without protest bear the ultimate responsibility for their patients' care. Here, Polonsky was intimidated by Medi-Cal (D), but was not powerless to appeal; had he made the medical judgement that Wickline (P) should remain hospitalized, he should have tried to keep her there. Instead, he indicated his medical judgement was that she should be discharged. Medi-Cal (D) was not a party to that decision, and did not override the treating physicians' medical judgement. Thus, Medi-Cal (D) cannot be liable. Further, Medi-Cal's (D) consultant's decision to deny longer hospitalization was reasonable. Reversed.

Analysis:

Wickline examines the effects of prospective utilization review, a procedural safeguard used to curb medical costs by preventing unnecessary treatments. It is commonly used by third-party payors e.g., insurers, HMOs, and Medicare/Medicaid and its state counterparts. But there is widespread concern that such third-party payors may deny funding for necessary treatment, either because they are more concerned with budgets than patients, or because the "gatekeeper" who decides whether to approve payment is unfamiliar with the patient's needs. *Wickline* makes third party payors liable for negligent decisions by their agent gatekeepers. However, it also places on treating physicians a duty to appeal payors' denial of coverage if they feel the requested procedure is medically necessary.

■ CASE VOCABULARY

ARTERIOSCLEROSIS: Hardening of the arteries. Here, the hardening apparently restricted blood flow to Wickline's (D) leg, causing gangrene.

PROSPECTIVE UTILIZATION REVIEW: Procedure used by HMOs and government health care funds, whereby all medical procedures must be pre-approved, generally by a "gatekeeper" physician or bureaucrat employed by the payor. It is used to curb costs by denying unnecessary procedures.

Chumbler v. McClure

(Patient) v. *(Doctor)*

505 F.2d 489 (6th Cir. 1974)

DOCTORS MAY PRESCRIBE UNCOMMON TREATMENT IF SUPPORTED BY RESPECTABLE MINORITY

■ **INSTANT FACTS** An accident victim sued his neurologist for prescribing estrogen, an uncommon remedy.

■ **BLACK LETTER RULE** Where multiple schools of thought exist among competent physicians concerning proper treatment for a given ailment, and each is supported by responsible medical authority, it is not malpractice to follow the minority school.

■ **PROCEDURAL BASIS**

In medical malpractice action, appeal from directed verdict for defendant.

■ **FACTS**

Mr. Chumbler (P) was injured in an explosion. His neurosurgeon Dr. McClure (D) diagnosed his wound as cerebral vascular insufficiency, and prescribed the female hormone estrogen. Apparently, the therapy caused breast enlargement and suppressed Chumbler's (P) libido. Chumbler (P) sued Dr. McClure (D) for malpractice. Dr. McClure (D) defended, contending his treatment did not deviate from accepted medical practice. Expert testimony established Dr. McClure (D) was the only one of nine local neurosurgeons who treated such conditions with estrogen, but that there was no single established treatment method. At trial, the court granted a directed verdict for Dr. McClure (D). Chumbler (P) appeals.

■ **ISSUE**

Is a physician who prescribes an uncommon treatment liable for malpractice?

■ **DECISION AND RATIONALE**

No. Where multiple schools of thought exist among competent physicians concerning proper treatment for a given ailment, and each is supported by responsible medical authority, it is not malpractice to follow the minority school. The evidence adduced at trial below, viewed favorably, is that there is a division of opinion in the medical profession regarding use of estrogen to treat cerebral vascular insufficiency. Dr. McClure (D) was the only local neurosurgeon to use such therapy. But the test for malpractice is not to be determined solely by plebiscite. Affirmed.

Analysis:

Chumbler sets forth the "respectable minority" rule, whereby a remedy is not deemed improper for being the less commonly prescribed, as long as it has sufficient acceptance in the medical community. Such a doctrine is good policy in cases where there is no universally accepted therapy for a given illness, since holding otherwise would allow doctors to follow only one course of treatment—the most popular in the area—without reason to believe it is the best cure. The doctrine allows some experimentation, yet the treatment must be accepted by a sufficient number of physicians that it is considered "respectable," in the court's opinion.

■ **CASE VOCABULARY**

CEREBRAL VASCULAR INSUFFICIENCY: Apparently, a shortage of oxygen reaching the brain.

PLEBISCITE: Election by majority vote. Here, the court means that the most popular treatment is not deemed to be the only correct one.

Henderson v. Heyer-Schulte Corp.

(Patient) v. *(Implant Manufacturer and Doctor)*

600 S.W.2d 844 (Tex. Ct. Civ. App. 1980)

SOME STATES REJECT "RESPECTABLE MINORITY" DOCTRINE IN FAVOR OF "REASONABLE AND PRUDENT" PHYSICIAN TEST

■ **INSTANT FACTS** After a surgeon performs a breast implant using the antiquated method of releasing liquid silicone directly into the breast, the patient sues for malpractice.

■ **BLACK LETTER RULE** A course of treatment is negligent if no "reasonable and prudent" doctor would perform it under similar circumstances.

■ **PROCEDURAL BASIS**

In medical malpractice action, appeal from judgement for defendant.

■ **FACTS**

Ms. Henderson (P) underwent a breast implant, performed by surgeon Dr. Rothenberg (D). In doing so, Dr. Rothenberg (D) intentionally injected silicone gel directly into the breast by slitting the silicone sacs. This technique was once in common use, but at the time was not recognized or accepted. [Modern surgeons now insert sealed silicone or saline pouches into the breast, after researchers found that free silicone causes breast cancer and infection.] Because of this, Henderson (P) developed disfiguring breast infections. Henderson (P) sued Dr. Rothenberg (D) for malpractice (and also Heyer-Schulte Corp. (D), which apparently manufactured the silicone). At trial, the judge instructed the jury that plastic surgeons recognized more than 1 method of inserting implants. Based on this, the jury found for Dr. Rothenberg (D). Henderson (P) appeals.

■ **ISSUE**

Is a doctor who performs a procedure which is no longer commonly accepted liable for malpractice?

■ **DECISION AND RATIONALE**

No. A course of treatment is negligent if no "reasonable and prudent" doctor would perform it under similar circumstances. Here, the jury instructions given were improper. Under Texas caselaw, when a plaintiff attacks the surgical procedure selected by the doctor as malpractice, the doctor is not liable if the treatment was one that a reasonable and prudent doctor would undertake in similar circumstances. Texas courts rejected the "respectable minority" and "considerable number" rules. Here, the jury instructions given failed to ask the jury to consider whether the procedure was reasonable or prudent. However, this error was harmless, as Henderson (P) has not proven the "rupture method" employed was no longer in use by reasonable plastic surgeons. Affirmed.

Analysis:

As this case demonstrates, some states reject the "respectable minority" rule in favor of other means of analysis. Here, it is unclear whether the "reasonable and prudent" physician test is stricter or more lenient than the "respectable minority" doctrine. The standard here could merely amount to an objective determination by the fact-finder as to whether the procedure was "reasonable and prudent." However, if the same procedure is utilized by a sufficiently large number of doctors, jurors would be hard pressed to decide that no reasonable doctor would use it.

Brook v. St. John's Hickey Memorial Hospital

(Patient) v. *(Doctor)*

269 Ind. 270, 380 N.E.2d 72 (1978)

REASONABLE CLINICAL INNOVATION IS NOT MALPRACTICE

■ **INSTANT FACTS** When a doctor diagnosing a small child decided to inject a contrast medium into her calf rather than her buttocks, the child sued for injuries.

■ **BLACK LETTER RULE** Reasonable and prudent clinical innovation creates no malpractice liability.

■ **PROCEDURAL BASIS**

In medical malpractice action, appeal from appellate reversal of judgement for defendants.

■ **FACTS**

Tracy Lynn Brook (P), age 2, was taken to St. John's Hickey Memorial Hospital ("Hospital") (D) with a possible urological disorder. To diagnose, Brook (P) would require an X-ray, which required her to be injected with a contrast medium. Radiologist Dr. Fischer (D) injected the contrast medium into Brook's (P) calves, which was unusual. The medium's manufacturer's package insert advised injecting into the buttocks. No other doctor had injected into the calf, though apparently others had targeted the thighs instead. Afterwards, Brook's (P) Achilles tendon [between the calf and heel] shortened, making walking difficult. The shortening may have been caused by trauma, like an injection to the calf. Brook (P) sued Dr. Fischer (D) and Hospital (D) for malpractice. At trial, Brook (P) requested a jury instruction that doctors should not try untested experimental procedures on patients, but the judge refused the instruction, finding no evidence Dr. Fischer (D) experimented. After trial, the court held for the defendants. Brook (P) appeals, contending the doctor was negligent in choosing a procedure which was not specifically recommended by the medical community, and that his deviation amounted to a medical experiment. On appeal, the Court of Appeals reversed, holding Dr. Fischer's (D) choice of procedure could be deemed an experiment. The defendants appeal.

■ **ISSUE**

Does a doctor's discretionary deviation from ordinary medical procedures amount to unauthorized "medical experimentation"?

■ **DECISION AND RATIONALE**

(Hunter, J.) No. Reasonable and prudent clinical innovation creates no malpractice liability. The Court of Appeals was incorrect in finding Dr. Fischer's (D) choice of the calves as an injection point may have amounted to a medical experiment. The record shows Dr. Fischer (D) had compelling professional reasons for choosing the calf. First, he read medical journals cautioning against injecting the medium into small children's buttocks, and other articles cautioning against the thighs. He chose the calves as the next largest muscle mass away from the trunk, to avoid damaging the sciatic nerve. Second, he had previously injected children's calves successfully. He also never heard anything proscribing the calf muscles as an injection site. Therapeutic innovation is permissible to avoid serious consequences, since practicing medicine requires innovation and judgement calls. A physician is presumed to have the knowledge and skill necessary to use some innovation to fit a case's circumstances. Thus, Dr. Fischer's (D) injection was reasonably and prudently calculated to accomplish the intended diagnosis, and was not a medical experiment. Reversed.

Analysis:

The "clinical innovation" rule seems oddly inconsistent with the "competing schools" and "respectable minority" rules, since an "innovative" medical procedure is by definition one not accepted by any school of thought. The doctrine seems to move the analysis back to whether the procedure was reasonable under the circumstances; if so, it is not malpractice, even if no one else has adopted that approach. Policy dictates that doctors should be allowed to exercise their judgement in adapting treatments to situational requirements, especially if conventional treatment is ineffective or impractical under the circumstances. However, this case illustrates that innovation may cause greater harm than good, and it may be difficult to draw the line between desirable "innovation" and offensive "medical experimentation."

■ CASE VOCABULARY

CONTRAST MEDIUM: Injectable dye, sometimes used to make blood vessels show up better on scans, such as x-rays.

Richardson v. Miller

(Patient) v. *(Physician)*

44 S.W. 3d 1 (Tenn. Ct. App. 2000)

EVIDENCE OF A DRUG'S APPROVED USES MAY BE ADMITTED ON THE QUESTION OF WHETHER THE DRUG WAS APPROPRIATE FOR THE PATIENT

Bring me some terbutaline-- I'm brewing a potion to halt premature labor.

But that's an off-label use!

stus.com

■ **INSTANT FACTS** Richardson (P) brought a malpractice action against her physician, Dr. Miller (D), and the court refused to allow her to introduce evidence of off-label use of a medication to stop labor.

■ **BLACK LETTER RULE** The labeling or PDR reference of a prescription drug, when introduced with other expert evidence on the standard of care, is admissible evidence on the question of whether the drug presented an unacceptable risk to the patient.

■ **PROCEDURAL BASIS**

Appeal from a judgment in favor of Dr. Miller (D).

■ **FACTS**

Dr. Miller (D) was a physician providing prenatal care to Richardson (P), who was pregnant with her first child. A few weeks after Richardson (P) learned she was pregnant, she complained of shortness of breath and chest pains, and Miller (D) referred her to a cardiologist. The cardiologist found nothing abnormal with Richardson's (P) heart, and recommended no change in her care.

In June 1993, when Richardson (P) was approximately thirty-five weeks pregnant, she was admitted to a hospital in labor. Miller (D) was concerned about complications from the premature labor and birth, and ordered bed rest and hydration for Richardson (P). When the labor did not stop on its own, Miller (D) tried to halt the labor by giving Richardson (P) medication to stop her uterine contractions. Miller (D) first prescribed magnesium sulfate, and when that was not successful, he prescribed terbutaline. Terbutaline had been approved by the FDA for treatment of bronchial asthma, but was also widely used for tocolysis, the process of delaying or inhibiting labor. Richardson (P) received two oral doses of terbutaline, but after she woke up with severe chest pains, she refused a third dose.

When Miller (D) learned that Richardson (P) refused further oral doses of terbutaline, he suggested using a pump to infuse smaller doses of terbutaline into Richardson's (P) system. Richardson (P) may not have known that the pump would be administering the same drug as she had refused, but she did understand she would be receiving a drug to retard her labor. Richardson (P) also understood that Millard's (P) plan was to stabilize her and send her home with the pump in place until her pregnancy was full term. Miller (D) had little experience with terbutaline infusion pumps, so he directed a nurse to arrange for a pump. The nurse was directed to Tokos Medical Corporation (D), a supplier of medical equipment. Tokos (D) arranged to supply a pump and sent a nurse to the hospital with the pump. The nurse from Tokos (D) did not confer with Miller (D), but reviewed Richardson's (P) records and instructed the hospital staff on the use of the pump and the dosage Richardson (P) would receive.

Richardson's (P) labor contractions slowed down and then stopped. All of her vital signs were normal around the time the contractions ceased. Then Richardson's (P) sister visited her and told her that her mother's dog had died. Richardson (P) became upset and experienced pain in her chest, arm, jaw, and head. She said she was having a heart attack. The nursing staff disconnected her from the pump and transferred her to another unit. An electrocardiogram confirmed that she had suffered a heart attack.

That night, Richardson (P) gave birth to a healthy baby boy. A few days later, she had open-heart by-pass surgery, and she was discharge after recuperating for several days.

Richardson (P) and her husband (P) brought a malpractice action against Miller (D) and Tokos (D). The Richardsons (P) claimed Miller (D) was negligent for continuing to have terbutaline administered after Richardson (P) experienced chest pains, and by electing to administer the drug by using a pump. They claimed Tokos (D) acted negligently by failing to inform Miller (D) that Richardson (P) was not a good candidate for a pump, and by failing to insist on an electrocardiogram before Richardson (P) was started on the pump. Richardson's (P) medical insurer intervened to collect reimbursement for the medical expenses it paid. Miller (D) made a motion *in limine* to exclude reference at trial to off-label use of terbutaline taken from the drug's package insert, the Physician's Desk Reference (PDR), and deposition testimony from an expert witness. The motion to exclude references to off-label usage was granted. The jury returned a verdict for defendants Miller (D) and Tokos (D).

■ ISSUE

Should the trial court have admitted evidence of the off-label use of terbutaline?

■ DECISION AND RATIONALE

(Koch, Jr., J.) Yes. The labeling or PDR reference of a prescription drug, when introduced with other expert evidence on the standard of care, is admissible evidence on the question of whether the drug presented an unacceptable risk to the patient. Off-label use of a prescription medication is a neutral term, and refers to a situation in which a patient uses a medication or device in a manner that varies from the FDA-approved use of the device or drug. FDA approval of a device or drug considers only the use or uses for which the manufacturer has conducted safety and efficacy studies. After the FDA determines that a new drug is safe and effective, the FDA and the manufacturer negotiate the language to be included in the drug's labeling. The labeling submitted by the manufacturer must be limited to the intended use of the drug. Manufacturers are neither required nor expected to submit language covering all possible uses of the drug. The labeling is intended to ensure that the promotional literature for a drug contains accurate information regarding the approved uses and known risks of the drug. Labeling will not be approved by the FDA if it contains instructions about uses other than those for which the drug has been shown to be safe and effective.

The labeling approved by the FDA includes the package inserts that accompany the drug. The same information is included in the PDR, an encyclopedia of medications provided annually to all practicing physicians. The labeling, package inserts, and PDR references are the primary ways of ensuring a drug's safe use. In fact, package inserts and the PDR are the most frequently consulted sources of information on the use of prescription drugs.

After approval of a drug, the manufacturer and the FDA continue to collect both positive and negative information regarding the efficacy and safety of the drug. If off-label use is widespread, the FDA is obligated to investigate it. The manufacturer may not market or promote the drug for off-label use unless the manufacturer submits the drug for a series of clinical trials similar to those required for initial approval. Manufacturers frequently do not request approval for a new use unless the change in labeling will result in increased profits.

A lack of approval for a particular use does not mean that use is either disapproved or improper. Physicians are free to use approved devices or drugs in any way they believe will best serve their patients. The FDA recognizes the prevalence of off-label use, and off-label use is an integral part of contemporary medical practice. Legislatures have passed laws to forbid medical insurers from declining to pay for off-label prescriptions, and courts have recognized the legitimacy of off-label prescriptions. On the other hand, because of the FDA's restrictions on the dissemination of information about off-label usage, physicians do not have the same information concerning use, dosage, and method of administration as they do for approved uses. Physicians who prescribe a device or drug for off-label use have a responsibility to be well-informed about the drug or device. This information must come from sources other than product labeling, and must be up-to-date and reliable.

Virtually every court that has addressed the admissibility of labeling or PDR references has held that this evidence is admissible with regard to the standard of care for the use and administration of the drug. The great weight of authority is that this evidence must be accompanied by other expert evidence regarding the standard of care. Tennessee law requires that the standard of care to be established is the recognized standard of professional practice in the profession and specialty of the defendant in the community in which the defendant practices. This standard requires expert testimony. The labeling and PDR references are not, in themselves, sufficient evidence regarding the standard of care for several reasons. Allowing the labeling or PDR reference alone to establish the standard of care would allow drug manufacturers, rather than the medical profession, to determine the standard. It was not intended that the labeling or references should establish a standard of care. In addition, the public may not be able to understand the labeling or references without the aid of expert testimony. Finally, the labeling and references cannot be cross-examined.

The medical evidence indicates that the safety and efficacy of terbutaline administered with an infusion pump for tocolysis was being debated at the time it was administered to Richardson (P), and continues to be debated. Warnings against the intramuscular use of terbutaline for tocolysis began appearing in the early 1980s. Despite these warnings, the off-label use continued. The infusion pump came into use in the mid–1980s. Terbutaline became the most commonly used drug for tocolysis, despite the manufacturer's warnings, after a competing drug was removed from the market. The FDA invited manufacturers to submit applications to have terbutaline approved for tocolysis, but the manufacturers declined to do so. The debate about the safety and efficacy of terbutaline continued, and in 1997, the FDA issued a letter to the medical community expressing concerns about the safety of administering terbutaline by a continuous pump. The warning was renewed in 1999.

The off-label use of drugs is widespread and not inherently inappropriate. There are, however, documented instances where an accepted off-label use has been harmful. Off-label use may constitute negligence if the decision to use a drug off-label is sufficiently careless, imprudent, or unprofessional. In this case, the evidence of terbutaline's off-label use was relevant to the breach of the standard of care. Reversed.

Analysis:

The inherent risk of off-label usage is that the information about the usage may not be complete. The FDA-approved labeling and PDR references of a drug do not only tell about the known efficacy of the drug, but also warn of the known dangers of a drug. These warnings will help a physician determine if a drug is appropriate for an individual patient, not just whether it has been shown to be effective to treat the patient's condition. Information about off-label use comes with no assurances of reliability or completeness, and so will not always be as helpful to the physician in evaluating a drug's use in a given situation.

Hardi v. Mezzanotte

(Physician) v. *(Patient)*

818 A.2d 974 (D.C. Ct. App. 2003)

THE STATUTE OF LIMITATIONS FOR MEDICAL MALPRACTICE BEGINS TO RUN WHEN NEGLIGENCE IS DISCOVERED

■ **INSTANT FACTS** Hardi (D) made a mistaken diagnosis of Mezzanotte's (P) condition and then claimed that her malpractice suit against him was barred by the statute of limitations.

■ **BLACK LETTER RULE** Under the discovery rule, a medical malpractice claim does not accrue until the patient has some knowledge of (1) the injury, (2) the injury's cause in fact, and (3) evidence of wrongdoing on the part of the person responsible.

■ **PROCEDURAL BASIS**

Appeal from a verdict entered after a bench trial.

■ **FACTS**

Mezzanotte (P) was treated for diverticulitis in 1990. In January and February 1994, she suspected a recurrence of diverticulitis and sought treatment from Hardi (D). Hardi (D) was aware of Mezzanotte's (P) history of diverticulitis, but he diagnosed her condition as a gynecological problem and referred her to a gynecologist. The condition Hardi (D) detected could have been either diverticulitis or a gynecological problem, but Hardi (D) did not note that alternate diagnosis on Mezzanotte's (P) chart. The gynecologist ran tests, but could not determine whether Mezzanotte's (P) condition was diverticulitis or gynecological. Further tests were recommended.

Hardi (D) attempted to perform exploratory procedures on Mezzanotte (P) but was unable to do so because of obstructions in her digestive system. Hardi (D) discussed with a radiologist the possibility that the obstructions were caused by diverticulitis rather than cancer in her reproductive organs. Mezzanotte's (P) condition continued to deteriorate. She was admitted to the hospital for emergency surgery, and on March 8, 1994, her reproductive organs were removed. After the surgery, Mezzanotte's (P) husband was informed that she did not have cancer, but diverticulitis. The surgery caused additional complications, and Mezzanotte (P) was forced to have four additional surgeries over the next two years.

Mezzanotte (P) commenced a medical malpractice action against Hardi (D) on March 6, 1997. Hardi (D) claimed that her action was barred by the three year statute of limitations, because the last date any misdiagnosis could have happened was March 2, 1994, the date of Mezzanotte's (P) last pre-surgical treatment.

■ **ISSUE**

Did Mezzanotte's (P) claim accrue on the last date of pre-surgical treatment, such that it was barred by the statute of limitations?

■ **DECISION AND RATIONALE**

(Wagner, C.J.) No. Under the discovery rule, a medical malpractice claim does not accrue until the patient has some knowledge of the injury, of the injury's cause in fact, and of evidence of wrongdoing on the part of the person responsible. The discovery rule is applied when the fact of the tortious conduct and the resulting injury are not readily apparent.

Hardi (D) argues that Mezzanotte (P) had actual knowledge of her injury, because she went to Hardi (D) for a suspected recurrence of diverticulitis and she knew that he did not treat her for that condition. This argument would charge Mezzanotte (P) with knowledge that Hardi (D) did not have. Hardi (D) diagnosed her condition as gynecological, and her diverticulitis was discovered only after emergency surgery for a ruptured colon. Mezzanotte (P) was relying on Hardi's (D) skill and knowledge. Generally, patients do not have the knowledge to determine that a physician was negligent. Patients who seek medical care are not responsible for diagnosing their own condition.

There is no evidence that Mezzanotte (P) knew or should have known the cause of her injury before March 8, 1994. The trial court correctly granted partial summary judgment on this issue. Affirmed.

Analysis:

Although the discovery rule may create its own set of problems, one could argue that it has a solid base in elementary tort principles. If a person has suffered no detectable harm as a result of a negligent act, there is no basis for bringing a lawsuit. A plaintiff may not base a claim entirely on an error that may, in the future, cause some problems; although damages may be awarded for potential future harm, potential future harm cannot be the only basis of a plaintiff's claim. If the negligence has not been discovered, there is, arguably, no claim.

■ CASE VOCABULARY

DISCOVERY RULE: The rule that a limitations period does not begin to run until the plaintiff discovers (or reasonably should have discovered) the injury giving rise to the claim. The discovery rule usually applies to injuries that are inherently difficult to detect such as those resulting from medical malpractice.

OCCURRENCE RULE: The rule that a limitations period begins to run when the alleged wrongful act or omission occurs, rather than when the plaintiff discovers the injury. This rule applies to most breach-of-contract claims.

Ostrowski v. Azzara

(Patient) v. *(Doctor)*

111 N.J. 429, 545 A.2d 148 (1988)

PATIENTS' PRE-TREATMENT CARELESSNESS MAY REDUCE OR PRECLUDE DAMAGES, AND POST-TREATMENT NEGLIGENCE MAY REDUCE DAMAGES

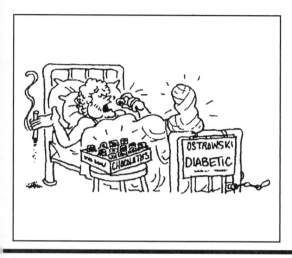

■ **INSTANT FACTS** When a diabetic sued a surgeon for a botched surgery, the surgeon contended her smoking and overeating after surgery prevented proper recovery.

■ **BLACK LETTER RULE** In medical malpractice actions, plaintiffs' pretreatment negligence may reduce/preclude liability under comparative/contributory negligence statutes, but plaintiffs' post-treatment failure to mitigate damages may only reduce the recovery.

■ **PROCEDURAL BASIS**

In medical malpractice action, appeal from judgement for defendant.

■ **FACTS**

Diabetic Ms. Ostrowski (P) consulted podiatrist (foot specialist) Dr. (Ms.) Azzara (D) about a sore toe. Dr. Azzara (D) decided to remove part of the toenail. Dr. Azzara (D) instructed Ostrowski (P) to maintain a low sugar level to avoid diabetes-related complications. Apparently, Ostrowski (P) continued smoking and failed to maintain her diet, which aggravated her diabetes. Later, Dr. Azzara (D) removed the toenail, but Ostrowski's (P) diabetes inhibited healing. Consequently, Ostrowski (P) required 3 follow-up operations to restore blood flow to the toe. Ostrowski (P) sued Dr. Azzara (D) for malpractice. At trial, Dr. Azzara (D) presented Ostrowski's (P) *post*-surgery health habits as evidence of comparative negligence. The jury denied Ostrowski (P) any recovery, apportioning her fault at 51% (and finding Dr. Azzara (D) was 49% negligent in operating without considering the consequences of diabetes). On appeal, the Appellate Division affirmed. Ostrowski (P) appeals again.

■ **ISSUE**

In a medical malpractice action, may a plaintiff-patient's lifestyle be introduced as evidence of comparative negligence?

■ **DECISION AND RATIONALE**

(O'Hern, J.) Yes. In medical malpractice actions, plaintiffs' pre-treatment negligence may reduce/preclude liability under comparative/contributory negligence statutes, but plaintiffs' post-treatment failure to mitigate damages may only reduce the recovery. This case interweaves several strands of doctrine. Comparative negligence is a legislative amelioration of common-law contributory negligence, allowing recovery by a plaintiff who was less at fault than the defendant. Contributory and comparative negligence doctrines consider the plaintiff's carelessness *before* the defendant's wrong. The "avoidable consequences" doctrine bars plaintiffs who are negligent *after* the tort from recovering damages which could have been avoided by exercising ordinary care. However, a counterweight to "avoidable consequences" is the "particularly susceptible victim" doctrine, familiarly expressed as "the defendant must take plaintiff as he finds him.'" But under the related "preexisting condition" doctrine, when defendants' negligence aggravates a plaintiff's existing condition, the defendant is liable only for the additional aggravation, not the original condition. Finally, the element of "proximate cuase" generally allows recovery only for foreseeable harm. To avoid confusion, we note that "contributory negligence" bars recovery for the plaintiff's negligence *before* the defendant's negligent act, while "avoidable consequences" disallows some recovery for the plaintiff's negligent acts *after* the tort. In other words, avoidable plaintiff's *post*-tort conduct should not preclude recovery for injuries proximately caused by defendants' negligence. In such cases, jury instructions may express "mitigation of damages" as a percentage of fault which reduces recoverable damages, as long as the jury is made to understand that "avoidable consequences" will not bar all recovery if the defendant's conduct was a substantial factor without which the ultimate injury would not have arisen. Generally, once a plaintiff proves the defendant's acts contributed to the injury, the defendant should bear the burden of demonstrating what percentage of the injury was due to pre-existing condition, and how the plaintiff was negligent in not mitigating damages. But patient-plaintiffs' pretreatment lifestyles or health habits are not to be considered as evidence of contributory/comparative negligence, because society has not yet imposed a normative life-style, and because policy may require that doctors have a special responsibility toward diseased patients. Here, we approve the jury instruction that post-treatment mitigation (or lack thereof) may be expressed as a percentage representing Ostrowski's (P) fault, but find the judge should also have explained that this percentage is relevant only to disallowing some (avoidable) damages, not to denying all recovery based on greater comparative fault. Also, the judge should have explained that Dr. Azzara (D) bears the burden of proving her treatment did not aggravate Ostrowski's (P) pre-existing condition, and of quantifying the avoidable damages which Ostrowski (P) failed to mitigate. Finally, the court should have carefully scrutinized the evidence to see if there was sound basis for the assertion that Ostrowski's (P) post-treatment conduct indeed increased damages, before submitting the issue to the jury. Reversed and remanded.

Analysis:

The defense of failure to mitigate damages is usually raised when the plaintiff fails to follow the doctor's post-treatment instructions. Many courts also recognize the defense of contributory/comparative negligence where the plaintiff performs some specific negligent act before seeking treatment (e.g., misrepresenting his medical condition to the treating physician, electing unnecessary surgery despite warnings, etc.). However, the tactic of classifying the plaintiff-patient's long-term lifestyle as constituting comparative/contributory negligence is uncommon and generally rejected by courts, as here. The policy concern is that, since the effects of lifestyle on most diseases are unclear, it would be unfair to let defendants make unsupported claims, blaming the plaintiff for his disease or for the ineffectiveness of treatment.

■ CASE VOCABULARY

AMELIORATION: Improvement; reform.

COMPARATIVE NEGLIGENCE: Later tort doctrine where patients whose own negligence contrubted to their injury may still recover from negligent defendants, but have their recovery reduced by their percentage of fault. "Pure" comparative negligence allows partial recovery as long as the plaintiff is less than 100% responsible. However, under the "modified" comparative negligence at issue here, negligent plaintiffs cannot recover from any defendant whose percentage of fault is less than those unforeseeable consequence of the defendant's carelessness.

Robins v. Garg

(Patient's Estate) v. *(Physician)*

276 Mich. App. 351, 741 N.W.2d 49 (2007)

DIFFERING INTERPRETATIONS OF UNDISPUTED FACTS SUFFICE TO CREATE A QUESTION OF FACT FOR THE JURY

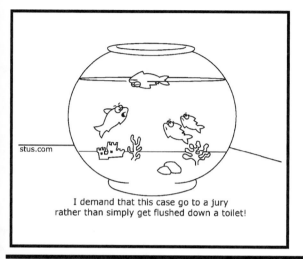

I demand that this case go to a jury rather than simply get flushed down a toilet!

■ **INSTANT FACTS** Robins (P) died after consulting with Dr. Garg (D) for many years about her risks of heart disease.

■ **BLACK LETTER RULE** To establish causation in a wrongful death action, the plaintiff must establish that the injury would not have occurred but for the defendant's conduct.

■ **PROCEDURAL BASIS**

On appeal to review a trial court decision granting the defendant's motion for summary disposition.

■ **FACTS**

Robins (P) first sought treatment from Dr. Garg (D) in 1986, at which time Garg (D) noted that Robins (P) was at risk for heart disease due to a family history of heart disease, high cholesterol, and a history of smoking. Although he did not refer Robins (P) to a cardiologist, Garg (D) ordered her to undergo testing to determine her cholesterol level. A year later, in 1987, Garg (D) diagnosed Robins (P) with asthma, but did not order any additional testing for heart disease. Robins (P) continued to see Garg (D) as needed for many years until, in 1998, Garg (D) once again tested Robins' (P) cholesterol levels. Noting that Robins' (P) cholesterol levels were high, Garg (D) prescribed various medications, which Robins (P) did not take regularly as prescribed. Finally, in 2001, Robins (P) came to see Garg (D) with pain in her chest and back. While preparing for an electrocardiogram at Garg's (D) clinic, Robins (P) went into cardiac arrest and stopped breathing. Garg (D) unsuccessfully attempted to resuscitate her, and Robins (P) died. In the medical malpractice suit that followed, the trial court granted Garg's (D) motion for summary disposition, find that the plaintiff failed to show genuine issues of material fact concerning the cause of death.

■ **ISSUE**

Did the plaintiff present sufficient factual evidence to establish a genuine issue of material fact as to the cause of death?

■ **DECISION AND RATIONALE**

(Judge Undisclosed.) Yes. To establish causation in a wrongful death action, the plaintiff must establish that the injury would not have occurred but for the defendant's conduct. In a medical malpractice claim, the plaintiff bears the burden of proving that the defendant's conduct was the proximate cause of her injuries. To do so, she must prove both cause in fact and legal causation. "Generally, an act or omission is a cause in fact of an injury only if the injury could not have occurred without (or 'but for') that act or omission." When the evidence presented allows a reasonable inference of causation—that it is more likely than not that the injury arose from the defendant's conduct—summary disposition is inappropriate.

Here, the medical examiner testified in his deposition that the cause of death was asthma complicated by myocardial infarction. While not disagreeing with the medical examiner's factual findings, the plaintiff's expert opined that Robins (P) died of a myocardial infarction. This theory of causation is not impermissibly speculative and sufficiently creates a question of fact regarding whether Robins' (P) heart condition caused her death. The trial court erred in granting Garg's (D) motion for summary disposition. Reversed.

Analysis:

It must be noted that the court's decision was made on a motion for summary disposition and not after the evidence has been presented. At the summary disposition stage, the plaintiff need not dispose of all possible causes of her injuries; she must come forth with evidence that, if supported by the facts provided, allows a jury to find that the defendant's conduct caused her injuries. To succeed in the case, however, the plaintiff must generally show by a preponderance of the evidence that her theory of causation is more likely than not to have occurred.

■ CASE VOCABULARY

BUT–FOR CAUSE: The cause without which the event could not have occurred.

CAUSATION: The causing or producing of an effect.

MALPRACTICE: An instance of negligence or incompetence on the part of a professional.

PROXIMATE CAUSE: A cause that is legally sufficient to result in liability. A cause that directly produces an event and without which the event would not have occurred.

Herskovits v. Group Health Cooperative of Puget Sound

(Patient) v. *(Hospital and Doctor)*

99 Wash.2d 609, 664 P.2d 474 (1983)

PATIENT MAY SUE FOR A MALPRACTICE WHICH REDUCES HIS CHANCE OF LIVING

■ **INSTANT FACTS** When a doctor's failure to diagnose a cough as cancer delayed the patient's cancer surgery, the decedent patient's estate sued for "loss of chance."

■ **BLACK LETTER RULE** Negligent medical care providers are liable for "loss of chance" for reducing a patient's probability of recovering, even if the patient's original chance of recovery was less than 50%.

■ PROCEDURAL BASIS

In medical malpractice action, appeal from summary judgement for defendant.

■ FACTS

Mr. Herskovits (P) consulted Dr. Spencer (D) of Group Health Cooperative of Puget Sound ("Group Health") (D) about lung pain and coughing. Dr. Spencer (D) negligently failed to diagnose the problem as cancer, and prescribed cough medicine. About 7 months later, Herskovits (P) consulted one Dr. Ostrow, who identified the lung cancer. Herskovits (P) had his lung removed, but died 20 months later at age 60. Dr. Ostrow gave expert testimony that Dr. Spencer's misdiagnosis was negligent, and testified that (i) Herskovits' (P) chance of surviving 5 more years with a correct diagnosis was 39%, and (ii) his chance of surviving 5 years by the time he was diagnosed correctly had fallen to 25%. Herskovits's (P) estate (P) sued Dr. Spencer (D) and Group Health (D) for "loss of chance," alleging their misdiagnosis reduced Herskovits' (P) chance of 5-year survival by 14%. Dr. Spencer (D) and Group Health (D) defended, contending (i) they could not have prevented Herskovits' (P) death within several years, and (ii) claims for "loss of chance" cannot be maintained without proving the patient would "probably" have survived but for the malpractice (i.e., that the patient must have had at least a 51% chance of survival). At trial, the court dismissed. Herskovits (P) appeals.

■ ISSUE

Are negligent medical care providers liable for reducing a patient's probability of recovering if the patient's original chance of recovery was under 50%?

■ DECISION AND RATIONALE

(Dore, J.) Yes. Negligent medical care providers are liable for "loss of chance" for reducing a patient's probability of recovering, even if the patient's original chance of recovery was less than 50%. For this appeal, we accept the parties' stipulations that Dr. Spencer (D) was negligent in diagnosing Herskovits (P), that misdiagnosis proximately caused a 14% reduction in his chance of survival, and that he had less than a 50% chance of survival at all times. *Restatement (Second) of Torts § 323(a)* applies, but this court has never previously considered whether a reduction in the chances of survival is proof of proximate cause sufficient to take the issue to the jury. Some other courts allow this, emphasizing that defendants who deprived the decedent of a "significant" chance to recover should not be allowed to speculate that result was inevitable. Others disallow suit unless plaintiffs prove the defendants' negligence was *more likely than not* the cause of harm. We adopt the first approach, that defendants' reduction of a decedent's chance of survival is sufficient evidence of probable cause. Deciding otherwise would release doctors from any liability whenever the patient had less than a 50% chance of survival, regardless of how flagrant their negligence. There is no danger of the jury speculating if the evidence includes percentage probabilities. [No, but the percentages generated by expert witnesses are usually pretty speculative.] Here, Dr. Spencer (D) and Group Health (D) may be sued for loss of chance. However, loss of chance does not make defendants liable for all damages caused by the victim's death, only those caused directly by premature death (e.g., lost earnings, additional medical expenses, etc.). Reversed.

■ CONCURRENCE

(Pearson, J.) I concur, because I am persuaded by scholarly commentary that the "all or nothing rule" (which allows recovery only if the decedent had over 50% chance of survival) is arbitrary, and denies recovery for demonstrable harm. The damages should be 14% of the compensable value of Herskovits' (P) remaining life.

■ DISSENT

(Brachtenbach, J.) Here, I would dismiss because Herskovits (P) failed to prove proximate causation. Here, the statistical evidence presented is mere speculation and conjecture. There is no proof the defendants' negligence caused Herskovits' (P) death, and little credible evidence that, had he been diagnosed properly, he could have been treated sufficiently to survive much longer.

Analysis:

Most jurisdictions recognize claims for "loss of chance," where the defendant doctor's malpractice reduced the possibility of the patient surviving. But even such jurisdictions are split on whether to apply the "pure" lost chance rule or the "all or nothing rule," whereby decedents who had less than fifty percent chance of being helped by the original treatment cannot sue. In theory, *if* expert testimony could accurately establish the percentage of reduction in survival chances, then all proven reductions should be compensable, and the "all or nothing" rule is arbitrary. However, in practice, it seems difficult to establish an objective percentage of loss of chance. Thus, it seems the "all or nothing" rule evolved as a check on the "loss of chance" doctrine's potentially sweeping liability.

CHAPTER SIX

Liability of Health Care Institutions

Grimm v. Summit County Children Servs. Bd.

Instant Facts: Hospital employees failed to report their articulable suspicions that a minor patient was or could be a victim of child abuse and the child sued.

Black Letter Rule: A hospital is vicariously liable for the negligence of its employees.

Scott v. SSM Heathcare St. Louis

Instant Facts: Koch, a principal in a partnership that contracted with SSM Healthcare St. Louis (D) to provide radiology services, negligently diagnosed a patient at the hospital, causing severe injuries.

Black Letter Rule: "An independent contractor is one who contracts with another to do something for him but is neither controlled by the other nor subject to the other's control with respect to his physical conduct in the performance of the undertaking."

Burless v. West Virginia University Hospitals, Inc.

Instant Facts: Burless (P) and Pritt (P) brought suit against West Virginia University Hospitals (WVUH) (D), and the court entered summary judgment in favor of WVUH (D), finding that the physicians who allegedly committed malpractice were not its employees or agents.

Black Letter Rule: A hospital will be liable for a physician's negligence under a theory of apparent agency if the hospital either acted or failed to act in such a manner as to cause a reasonable person to believe that the physician was an agent of the hospital and the patient relied on the apparent agency.

Washington v. Washington Hospital Center

Instant Facts: When a patient becomes comatose from failure to supply oxygen during surgery, she sues the hospital for failing to install breathing monitors.

Black Letter Rule: In negligence actions predicated on medical malpractice, plaintiffs must prove (i) the applicable standard of care, (ii) defendants' deviation from that standard, and (iii) a causal relationship between that deviation and the injury.

Muse v. Charter Hospital of Winston–Salem, Inc.

Instant Facts: When a hospital's policy required patients' discharge after their insurance expired, a discharged suicidal boy overdosed after discharge.

Black Letter Rule: Hospitals have a duty to avoid discharging patients in violation of their attendant doctors' medical judgement.

Darling v. Charleston Community Memorial Hospital

Instant Facts: When treatment for a teen's broken leg stops circulation and requires amputation, the patient sues the hospital for failing to supervise the doctor.

Black Letter Rule: Hospitals may be liable for failing to prevent staffers' malpractice.

Thompson v. Nason

Instant Facts: When a car accident victim suffers paralysis caused by excessive anticoagulants, she sues the hospital for failing to supervise her attendant doctor.

Black Letter Rule: Hospitals are liable for "corporate negligence" for failing to supervise affiliated doctors' treatment.

Carter v. Hucks–Folliss

Instant Facts: Despite failing the board certification exam three times, the defendant hospital renewed Dr. Hucks–Folliss's (D) hospital privileges.

Black Letter Rule: Hospitals owe a duty of care to their patients to ascertain that a physician is qualified to perform surgery before granting that physician the privilege of conducting surgery in the hospital.

Larson v. Wasemiller

Instant Facts: Larson (P) brought an action against St. Francis Medical Center (D), alleging that it had negligently credentialed Wasemiller (D).

Black Letter Rule: A common-law cause of action for negligent credentialing does exist, and is not precluded by the peer-review statute.

Kadlec Med. Ctr. v. Lakeview Anesthesia Assoc.

Instant Facts: The defendant healthcare provider failed to disclose that it terminated an anesthesiologist for suspected drug abuse when questioned by the anesthesiologist's prospective employer.

Black Letter Rule: A claim for negligent misrepresentation requires that (1) the defendant, in the course of its business or other matters in which it had a pecuniary interest, supplied false information; (2) the defendant had a legal duty to supply correct information to the plaintiff; (3) the defendant breached its duty, which can result from omission as well as affirmative misrepresentation; and (4) the plaintiff suffered damages or pecuniary loss as a result of its justifiable reliance upon the omission or affirmative misrepresentation.

Petrovich v. Share Health Plan of Illinois, Inc.

Instant Facts: A woman is suing her HMO under agency principles for the negligence of its participating physicians in failing to discover her oral cancer in a timely manner.

Black Letter Rule: An HMO may be held vicariously liable for the negligence of its independent-contractor physicians under both the doctrines of apparent authority and implied authority.

Pagarigan v. Aetna U.S. Healthcare of California, Inc.

Instant Facts: Pagarigan's children (P) alleged that their mother died due to the wrongdoing of Aetna (D), her HMO.

Black Letter Rule: An HMO that contracts out coverage decisions and the responsibility for patient care owes enrollees a duty of due care when choosing providers and in making contracts with those providers.

Shannon v. McNulty

Instant Facts: A woman sued her HMO and her doctor after she experienced all the symptoms of pre-term labor, but her doctor told her she was not in labor, and as a result she lost her baby.

Black Letter Rule: An HMO may, under the right circumstances, be held corporately liable for a breach of duty which causes harm to its subscribers.

Brannan v. Northwest Permanente, P.C.

Instant Facts: A patient sought disclosure of her physician's compensation structure in order to demonstrate a financial incentive not to refer her for diagnostic testing.

Black Letter Rule: A defendant's motive for acting is irrelevant to whether he breached the standard of care owed in a negligence case.

Grimm v. Summit County Children Servs. Bd.

(Patient) v. *(Public Agency)*
2006 WL 1329689 (Ohio Ct. App. 2006)

VIOLATION OF A STATUTORY OBLIGATION TO REPORT CHILD ABUSE CONSTITUTES NEGLIGENCE PER SE

My name IS Grimm, but my life ain't no fairy tale.

stus.com

■ **INSTANT FACTS** Hospital employees failed to report their articulable suspicions that a minor patient was or could be a victim of child abuse and the child sued.

■ **BLACK LETTER RULE** A hospital is vicariously liable for the negligence of its employees.

■ **PROCEDURAL BASIS**

On appeal to review a jury verdict for the plaintiff.

■ **FACTS**

Grimm (P) sued Summa Health System (D), Akron City Hospital (D), the Summit County Child Services Board (D), and others for negligence. Grimm (P), a minor, claimed that the defendants each breached their duty to report known or suspected child abuse committed by Grimm's (P) stepfather. Grimm's (P) stepfather had been convicted of raping Grimm (P) and was the father of her child, was present in the delivery room when the child was born, and was present in Grimm's (P) hospital room when she was undressed and breastfeeding. After trial, a jury awarded Grimm (P) $224,000 in damages, holding Summa Health System (D) liable for its employees' failure to report suspected child abuse as required by state statute.

■ **ISSUE**

Is a hospital vicariously liable for the conduct of its employees when such conduct constitutes negligence per se?

■ **DECISION AND RATIONALE**

(Judge Undisclosed.) Yes. A hospital is vicariously liable for the negligence of its employees. In negligence cases, the plaintiff must establish a duty, a breach of duty, causation, and damages. When the conduct challenged constitutes a statutory violation, however, the reasonable person standard of care is supplanted by the statutory duty, a violation of which constitutes negligence per se. But negligence per se is not liability per se. First, to assert negligence per se, a plaintiff must demonstrate that she is among the class of individuals that the statute is designed to protect. Moreover, a plaintiff still must prove that she suffered damages that were caused by the defendant's statutory violation.

Here, the child abuse reporting statute requires healthcare professionals to immediately report any known or suspected child abuse. Because Grimm (P) is a minor, she is among the class intended to be protected by the statute. Likewise, the evidence suggests that Summa's (D) employees had cognizable factual suspicions that Grimm (P) was or could be an abused child. While no expert witness was called to establish that the facts known to the employees sufficed to raise their suspicions, such matters are appropriately left to the common knowledge and experience of lay jurors. Given the articulable suspicions, Summa's (D) employees were negligent per se. Consequently, because Summa (D) maintained control over its employees' actions, it is liable for their failure to report suspected child abuse under the doctrine of respondeat superior.

Analysis:

Most child abuse statutes create exceptions to the physician-patient privilege so that a physician cannot be held liable for disclosing confidential information obtained from a patient when reporting known or suspected child abuse. While these statutes are designed to protect children, this waiver of the duty of confidentiality arguably undermines the free flow of information crucial to medical treatment of children suffering abuse. More often than not, however, reports of child abuse come from suspicions derived from examinations rather than from admissions by child patients.

■ CASE VOCABULARY

NEGLIGENCE PER SE: Negligence established as a matter of law, so that the breach of the duty is not a jury question. Negligence per se usually arises from a statutory violation.

RESPONDEAT SUPERIOR: The doctrine holding an employer or principal liable for the employee's or agent's wrongful acts committed within the scope of employment or agency.

VICARIOUS LIABILITY: Liability that a supervisory party (such as an employer) bears for the actionable conduct of a subordinate or associate (such as an employee) because of the relationship between the two parties.

Scott v. SSM Heathcare St. Louis

(Patient) v. *(Healthcare Provider)*

70 S.W.3d 560 (Mo. Ct. App. 2002)

HOSPITALS MAY "CONTROL" PHYSICIANS EVEN THOUGH THEY CANNOT DICTATE THE TREATMENT GIVEN TO PATIENTS

■ **INSTANT FACTS** Koch, a principal in a partnership that contracted with SSM Healthcare St. Louis (D) to provide radiology services, negligently diagnosed a patient at the hospital, causing severe injuries.

■ **BLACK LETTER RULE** "An independent contractor is one who contracts with another to do something for him but is neither controlled by the other nor subject to the other's control with respect to his physical conduct in the performance of the undertaking."

■ **PROCEDURAL BASIS**

On appeal to review a judgment for the plaintiff.

■ **FACTS**

Scott (P) was involved in a minor car accident and was treated at SSM Healthcare St. Louis ("the Hospital") (D) for minor injuries and was released. Two days later, Scott (P) returned complaining of a severe headache. The emergency room physician examined Scott (P) and requested a CT scan of his head. The Hospital (D) had contracted with RIC to perform radiology services. Dr. Koch, an RIC partner, reviewed the CT scan results and determined they were normal. Scott (P) was diagnosed with a mild concussion and sent home. Two days later, Scott (P) collapsed at home, unable to use the right side of his body. He was rushed to Barnes Hospital, where a spinal tap and CT scan showed a brain infection that had caused swelling in his brain. Scott (P) underwent several surgeries and was comatose for several weeks. Scott (P) filed medical malpractice claims against the Hospital (D) and its doctors and RIC and its employees, including Koch. The claims against RIC and Koch were settled, and the case went to trial against the Hospital (D). After the court determined that the treating physicians were negligent, a jury held the Hospital (D) liable for Koch's negligence.

■ **ISSUE**

Did the court err in presenting the issue of Koch's agency to the jury?

■ **DECISION AND RATIONALE**

(Judge Undisclosed.) No. "An independent contractor is one who contracts with another to do something for him but is neither controlled by the other nor subject to the other's control with respect to his physical conduct in the performance of the undertaking." One who employs an independent contractor is generally not vicariously liable for the contractor's negligence as he is for his employees' negligence under the doctrine of respondeat superior. Whether one is an agent of another is a question of fact to be determined by a jury.

A principal-agent relationship is established by a showing of two elements. First, the principal must expressly or impliedly consent to the agent's acting on his behalf. Second, the agent must be subject to the principal's control. The right of control is often the defining element in hospital-physician scenarios. Here, the evidence presented was sufficient to submit the agency issue to the jury. Although the Hospital (D) offered evidence that it engaged Koch by a written contract in which RIC agreed to provide radiology services, that RIC was a partnership in which Koch was a partner, that the Hospital (D) did not employ Koch, and that the Hospital (D) neither set Koch's hours nor billed patients directly for RIC's radiology services, strong conflicting evidence was offered. Specifically, the evidence showed that the Hospital (D) established the acceptable medical standards governing radiology services provided at the Hospital (D), the Hospital (D) determined whether Koch had the necessary qualifications to provide services at the Hospital (D), and the Hospital (D) had the right to require Koch to submit reports regarding radiological services rendered. Additionally, the Hospital (D) set the prices for Koch's services, which could not be changed without the Hospital's (D) consent, and required Koch to be an active member of the Hospital's (D) staff. Finally, the Hospital (D) required Koch to maintain liability insurance, had the right to terminate him if it became dissatisfied with Koch's services, and provided all office space and equipment used by Koch in rendering his services. This evidence, along with RIC's long history of providing radiologists working at the Hospital (D), sufficiently justifies the jury's conclusion that Koch was the Hospital's (D) agent. The mere fact that Koch was permitted and expected to utilize his professional experience in making medical judgments does not diminish the Hospital's (D) right of control. Affirmed.

Analysis:

The court references the ten factors listed by the Restatement (Second) of Agency § 220(2) that are often looked to in determining whether a person is a servant or an independent contractor. Those ten factors are: (1) the extent of control that, by the agreement, the master may exercise over the details of the work; (2) whether or not the one employed is engaged in a distinct occupation or business; (3) the kind of occupation, with reference to whether, in the locality, the work is usually done under the direction of the employer or by a specialist without supervision; (4) the skill required in the particular occupation; (5) whether the employer or the workman supplies the instrumentalities, tools, and the place of work for the person doing the work; (6) the length of time for which the person is employed; (7) the method of payment, whether by the time or by the job; (8) whether or not the work is a part of the regular business of the employer; (9) whether or not the parties believe they are creating the relation of master and servant; and (10) whether the principal is or is not in business.

■ CASE VOCABULARY

AGENT: One who is authorized to act for or in place of another; a representative.

CONTROL: The direct or indirect power to direct the management and policies of a person or entity, whether through ownership of voting securities, by contract, or otherwise; the power or authority to manage, direct, or oversee.

INDEPENDENT CONTRACTOR: One who is hired to undertake a specific project but who is left free to do the assigned work and to choose the method for accomplishing it.

PRINCIPAL: One who authorizes another to act on his or her behalf as an agent.

RESPONDEAT SUPERIOR: The doctrine holding an employer or principal liable for the employee's or agent's wrongful acts committed within the scope of employment or agency.

VICARIOUS LIABILITY: Liability that a supervisory party (such as an employer) bears for the actionable conduct of a subordinate or associate (such as an employee) because of the relationship between the two parties.

Burless v. West Virginia University Hospitals, Inc.

(Patient) v. *(Hospital)*

215 W.Va. 765, 601 S.E. 2d 85 (2004)

HOSPITALS MAY BE LIABLE FOR ACTS OF PHYSCIANS IF APPARENT AGENCY IS CREATED

Yes, I'm a doctor. And yes I work at the hospital. But why would you think I work for the hospital?

stus.com

■ **INSTANT FACTS** Burless (P) and Pritt (P) brought suit against West Virginia University Hospitals (WVUH) (D), and the court entered summary judgment in favor of WVUH (D), finding that the physicians who allegedly committed malpractice were not its employees or agents.

■ **BLACK LETTER RULE** A hospital will be liable for a physician's negligence under a theory of apparent agency if the hospital either acted or failed to act in such a manner as to cause a reasonable person to believe that the physician was an agent of the hospital and the patient relied on the apparent agency.

■ **PROCEDURAL BASIS**

Appeals from orders granting summary judgment.

■ **FACTS**

Burless (P) and Pritt (P) gave birth to children at West Virginia University Hospital (D). Both of them signed consent forms that stated that they each understood that "the faculty physicians and resident physicians who provide treatment" were not employees of the hospital (D). Burless (P) alleged that the doctors and WVUH (D) were negligent in failing to monitor her labor and delivery. She claimed that this negligence caused her child to suffer severe mental, neurological, and psychological injuries.

Pritt (P) received prenatal care and treatment for an ovarian cyst at WVUH (D). Surgery was performed to remove the cyst, and fluid leaked into her pelvic cavity, which was not treated. Pritt (P) developed an abdominal infection, which caused premature labor. Pritt (P) alleged that premature birth caused her child to suffer mental, neurological, and psychological injuries.

Burless (P) and Pritt (P) claimed vicarious liability on the part of WVUH (D), based in part on a theory of apparent agency. WVUH (D) moved for summary judgment, claiming that there was no apparent agency relationship between WVUH (D) and the physicians. Summary judgment was granted in both cases.

■ **ISSUE**

Can a hospital be held liable for physician malpractice on a theory of apparent agency?

■ **DECISION AND RATIONALE**

(Davis, J.) Yes. A hospital will be liable for a physician's negligence under a theory of apparent agency if the hospital either acted or failed to act in such a manner as to cause a reasonable person to believe that the physician was an agent of the hospital and the patient relied on the apparent agency. The first portion of the test focuses on the actions or inaction of a hospital. Usually, it is satisfied when a hospital holds itself out as a "provider of care." Courts have held that it is not necessary that a hospital make any express representations. A hospital will be found to be a provider of care unless it gave "contrary notice." The "contrary notice" generally is a disclaimer. If meaningful written notice is provided to a patient, and that notice is acknowledged by the patient, a hospital will be able to avoid liability. Liability will not attach on a theory of apparent agency when the patient knew, or reasonably should have known, that the treating physician was an independent contractor. Failure to provide meaningful written notice may constitute a failure to take action that would allow a reasonable person to believe that a particular doctor is an agent of the hospital. If, however, the disclaimer unambiguously explains the independent contractor status of physicians, then, absent any overt acts to the contrary, the disclaimer will suffice to immunize the hospital from liability. In the instant cases, the disclaimer was not sufficient. The disclaimer referred to "faculty physicians" and "resident physicians." It presupposes that a patient is able to distinguish between faculty, resident, and any other physicians practicing at WVUH (D). For this disclaimer to be effective, a patient would have to inquire as to the employment status of each person treating him or her. Such a requirement would be absurd.

The reliance part of the apparent agency inquiry is subjective, and depends on the patient's subjective belief. Reliance is established when a patient looks to the hospital, rather than an individual physician, for treatment. This factor focuses on the patient's belief that the hospital was providing care, but it also looks at the reasonableness of that belief. This determination is made by considering the totality of the circumstances, including any special knowledge the patient may have regarding the relationship between the physician and the hospital. Burless (P) and Pritt (P) both presented evidence indicating that they believed that the physicians treating them were employees of WVUH (D). They established genuine issues of material fact on the question of their reliance on the apparent agency relationship between WVUH (D) and the physicians, so summary judgment was improper. Reversed and remanded.

Analysis:

The test for apparent agency has been made very easy by this case. Virtually any hospital will be found to hold itself out as providing care, and many patients will be able to show that they came to the hospital for treatment instead of singling out a particular physician. Hospitals will have to prove that their disclaimers are sufficient, but given the many different relationships between hospitals and those who provide care in those hospitals, a truly effective disclaimer may be difficult to create. Note that the court stated that a patient's actual knowledge of the relationship between a physician and a hospital would be taken into account in deciding the reliance question. This could allow hospitals to shift the task of making a disclaimer to the physicians, perhaps as a condition of having privileges at a hospital.

■ CASE VOCABULARY

APPARENT AGENT: A person who reasonably appears to have authority to act for another, regardless of whether actual authority has been conferred.

Washington v. Washington Hospital Center

(Hospital Patient) v. *(Hospital)*
579 A.2d 177 (D.C. Ct. App. 1990)

HOSPITALS MAY BE DIRECTLY LIABLE FOR THEIR OWN NEGLIGENCE

■ **INSTANT FACTS** When a patient becomes comatose from failure to supply oxygen during surgery, she sues the hospital for failing to install breathing monitors.

■ **BLACK LETTER RULE** In negligence actions predicated on medical malpractice, plaintiffs must prove (i) the applicable standard of care, (ii) defendants' deviation from that standard, and (iii) a causal relationship between that deviation and the injury.

■ PROCEDURAL BASIS

In medical malpractice action, appeal from verdict for plaintiff.

■ FACTS

Patient Ms. Thompson (P) underwent an abortion at Washington Hospital Center ("Hospital") (D), attended by Dr. Bobrow (D), anesthesiologist Dr. Walker ("Anesthesiologist") (D), and nurse-anesthetist Adler ("Nurse") (D). Allegedly, Nurse (D) inserted a breathing tube into Thompson's (P) throat rather than her lungs, so she didn't receive oxygen. Anesthesiologist (D) supervised the insertion. Dr. Bobrow (D) began the procedure, and reported to Nurse (D) that the patient's (P) blood was dark, indicating insufficient oxygen. Nurse (D) checked the patient's (P) vitals and found them stable. Thompson (P), deprived of oxygen, suffered cardiac arrest and permanent brain damage, rendering her essentially permanently comatose. Thompson's (P) representatives (P) sued for malpractice, alleging that (i) Anesthesiologist (D) and Nurse (D) misplaced the breathing tube, (ii) Dr. Bobrow (D) failed to detect the improper intubation, and (iii) Hospital (D) was negligent in not providing anesthesiologists with a carbon dioxide monitor which could have detected the oxygen deprivation in time to prevent damage. At trial, Thompson's (P) expert witness Dr. Steen opined that Hospital (D) should have provided carbon dioxide monitors, noting they were available "in many other hospitals," and that some medical journals "encouraged" using them. However, the witness admitted these recommendations were non-binding, and there was no nationwide requirement. Also, Hospital's (D) chief anesthesiologist Dr. Murray opined there was no standard of care relating to carbon dioxide monitors, but had earlier requested such monitors as necessary "to meet the national standard of care." After trial, the jury found for Thompson (P) against Hospital (D). Hospital (D) moved for judgement n.o.v., contending expert Dr. Steen's testimony was insufficient to prove the standard of care.

■ ISSUE

May a hospital be found liable for malpractice for failing to provide equipment which was just gaining popular acceptance?

■ DECISION AND RATIONALE

(Farrell, J.) Yes. In negligence actions predicated on medical malpractice, plaintiffs must prove (i) the applicable standard of care, (ii) defendants' deviation from that standard, and (iii) a causal relationship between that deviation and the injury. Generally, the "standard of care" is "the ... action that a reasonably prudent [professional] with the defendant's specialty would have taken under . . . similar circumstances." For hospitals, this court rejects the "locality" rule in favor of a national standard. Here, the question is whether Dr. Steen's evidence would allow reasonable jurors to find a reasonably prudent hospital situated similarly to Hospital (D) at the time, operating on national standards, would have supplied a carbon dioxide monitor for a similar surgery. We conclude Steen's opinion, combined with other evidence, was sufficient to create an issue for the jury on whether monitors were required of prudent hospitals. On that evidence, reasonable jurors could find the then-prevalent standard of care required Hospital (D) to supply monitors. We need not decide whether Steen's testimony was sufficiently grounded in fact to actually establish the standard of care. Affirmed.

Analysis:

Washington highlights the obvious rule that hospitals may themselves be negligent, and thus may be liable for negligence separate from that of the attendant doctors, e.g., for negligently maintaining facilities/equipment; negligent hiring, retention, or supervision; etc. Plaintiffs seeking to prove a hospital's negligence must prove the same elements as for negligence or malpractice: the standard of care, negligence, and causation. The standard of care is almost always established by doctors' expert testimony, and most jurisdictions require proof of prevailing nationwide standards rather than local practice norms. While the standard of care is a factual question for the jury, judges have considerable discretion is deciding whether to allow any given testimony as reliable. The issue of negligence is almost always a jury question.

■ CASE VOCABULARY

"LOCALITY" RULE: In medical malpractice law, the minority view that the standard of care for medical procedures be determined with reference to the local practice in the area where the defendant doctor practices.

"NATIONAL [STANDARD]" RULE: In contrast, the majority view that the standard of care should be dictated by a nationwide minimal standard of competence, which practitioners in any locality are expected to meet or exceed.

Muse v. Charter Hospital of Winston-Salem, Inc.

(Hospital Patient) v. *(Hospital)*

117 N.C. App. 468, 542 S.E.2d 589 (1995)

HOSPITALS MAY HAVE DUTY TO CONTINUE TREATING INSOLVENT PATIENTS

■ **INSTANT FACTS** When a hospital's policy required patients' discharge after their insurance expired, a discharged suicidal boy overdosed after discharge.

■ **BLACK LETTER RULE** Hospitals have a duty to avoid discharging patients in violation of their attendant doctors' medical judgement.

■ **PROCEDURAL BASIS**

In wrongful death action, appeal from verdict for plaintiff.

■ **FACTS**

Muse (P), age 16, was admitted to Charter Hospital of Winston-Salem, Inc. (D) for depression and suicidal thoughts. Treatment proved difficult. Charter Hospital's (D) policy was to discharge patients once their medical insurance expired. As Muse's (P) insurance was about to expire, Charter Hospital's (D) attendant psychiatrist Dr. Barnhill asked that Muse (P) be allowed to stay an extra 2 days to perform a blood test to determine the proper dosage for antidepressants. Muse's (P) parents promised to sign promissory notes for the extra cost, but Charter Hospital (D) refused. Soon after discharge, Muse (P) overdosed on antidepressants and died. Muse's (P) parents (P) sued Charter Hospital (D) for wrongful death, contending Charter Hospital (D) was negligent in instituting a mandatory-discharge policy which interfered with treating physicians' medical judgement. At trial, the judge instructed the jury, "A hospital is under a duty not to have policies ... which operate in a way that interferes with the ability of a physician to exercise his medical judgement." After trial, the jury found for Muse (P), awarding compensatory damages of $1M and $6M in punitive damages for "willful and wanton" acts. Charter Hospital (D) appeals, contending this theory of negligence is not accepted, and that there was no evidence of wantonness.

■ **ISSUE**

Is a hospital liable for discharging a patient whose insurance expired, if his treating physician recommended additional treatment?

■ **DECISION AND RATIONALE**

(Lewis, J.) Yes. Hospitals have a duty to avoid discharging patients in violation of their attendant doctors' medical judgement. North Carolina's Supreme Court recognizes that hospitals owe a duty of care to patients. Previously, this court held hospitals owe patients a duty to obey treating doctors' reasonable instructions. Another recognized duty is to make reasonable efforts to monitor treatments administered by affiliated doctors. After these holdings, it seems axiomatic that hospitals have a duty not to institute policies which interfere with doctors' medical judgement. Applied here, this means Charter Hospital (D) had a duty not to institute a policy which discharged Muse (D) when his insurance expired, if discharge interfered with Dr. Barnhill's medical judgement. Here, there was sufficient evidence Charter Hospital (D) actually followed such a discharge policy, since it was widely discussed

---

as patients' insurance was expiring. Next, Charter Hospital (D) contends there was no evidence of willful or wanton conduct, but we find otherwise. Judgement affirmed, but remanded to recompute punitive damages.

Analysis:

Muse illustrates a controversial new trend in delimiting hospitals' duties: some courts will hold hospitals liable for discharging patients prematurely when their treating physicians' medical judgment calls for continued care. Obviously, this is only a problem when the patient is unable to pay for necessary care, and it strays dangerously close to requiring hospitals to provide needy patients with free or subsidized care. However, this duty-to-treat is still the minority rule for now.

Darling v. Charleston Community Memorial Hospital

(Hospital Patient) v. *(Hospital)*

33 Ill.2d 326, 211 N.E.2d 253 (1965)

HOSPITALS MAY BE LIABLE FOR IMPROPER SUPERVISION

■ **INSTANT FACTS** When treatment for a teen's broken leg stops circulation and requires amputation, the patient sues the hospital for failing to supervise the doctor.

■ **BLACK LETTER RULE** Hospitals may be liable for failing to prevent staffers' malpractice.

■ **PROCEDURAL BASIS**

In medical malpractice action, appeal from appellate affirmation of verdict for plaintiff.

■ **FACTS**

Darling (P) broke his leg playing football and was taken to Charleston Community Memorial Hospital (D) and treated by Dr. Alexander (D). Dr. Alexander (D) bound Darling's (P) leg in a cast, which apparently interfered with his circulation. Later, Darling's (P) protruding toes swelled and darkened. After treatment was unsuccessful, Darling's (P) leg was amputated. Darling's (P) father, as "next friend," sued Dr. Alexander (D) for malpractice. He also sued Charleston Hospital (D) and staffers (D) for negligently supervising Dr. Alexander (D), contending the proper procedure was to check Darling's (P) toe circulation regularly, and that no one at Charleston Hospital (D) required Dr. Alexander (D) to do so. [Darling's (P) suggestion at trial was that the elderly Dr. Alexander (D) used outdated methods, and that Charleston Hospital (D) never required him to keep current.] As evidence, Darling (P) contended Charleston Hospital's (D) bylaws and customs define its standard of care. Dr. Alexander (D) settled before trial. At trial, the jury returned a verdict against Charleston Hospital (D) for $140K. On appeal, the Fourth Circuit affirmed. Charleston Hospital (D) appeals.

■ **ISSUE**

Is a hospital liable for not preventing an affiliated doctor's negligence?

■ **DECISION AND RATIONALE**

Yes. Hospitals may be liable for failing to prevent staffers' malpractice. The issue is whether the proper standard of care here is embodied by the community standard, state hospital regulations, and/or Charleston Hospital's (D) own bylaws. Community custom is relevant, but not conclusive, because it illustrates what is feasible, suggests knowledge that defendant hospitals should possess, and warns courts if they are about to require higher standards than are currently common. A particular hospital's regulations, standards, and bylaws are equivalent to custom evidence. Hospitals are responsible for the treatment administered by their affiliated staff, under *Bing v. Thunig* and state statutes. At trial, Darling (P) submitted to the jury claims including evidence that Charleston Hospital (D) employed insufficient nursing staff and failed to require doctors to consult with specialists in emergencies. The jury verdict is supportable on either ground, and the evidence presented would let the jury conclude reasonably that Charleston Hospital's (D) nurses failed to test circulation regularly, failed to alert Dr. Alexander (D), and neglected to inform Dr. Alexander's (D) superiors. Affirmed.

Analysis:

Darling illustrates the basic rule that hospitals have a duty to prevent affiliated doctors'/staffers' malpractice. Hospitals may violate this duty when (1) they have no procedural safeguards against malpractice, (2) existing safeguards are unreasonable, or (3) existing safeguards are not followed by staffers. One difficulty in the rule arises when the chief treating physician is negligent. In such cases, the staffers that may be in a position to prevent the negligence are often nurses or other lesser-trained personnel, who either may not know enough to recognize the error, or else may be reluctant to second-guess their supervising doctor (or report him to superior doctors) and risk hurting their careers.

■ **CASE VOCABULARY**

NEXT FRIEND: Nominal "plaintiff" who sues on behalf of an underage plaintiff. Here, Darling (P) was a minor, so his father sued in his name as "next friend."

Thompson v. Nason

(Patient) v. *(Hospital)*

527 Pa. 330, 591 A.2d 703 (1991)

STATES ARE ADOPTING CORPORATE LIABILITY FOR HOSPITALS

■ **INSTANT FACTS** When a car accident victim suffers paralysis caused by excessive anticoagulants, she sues the hospital for failing to supervise her attendant doctor.

■ **BLACK LETTER RULE** Hospitals are liable for "corporate negligence" for failing to supervise affiliated doctors' treatment.

■ **PROCEDURAL BASIS**

In medical malpractice action, appeal from denial of summary judgement for defendant, on allocatur.

■ **FACTS**

Car accident victim Ms. Thompson (P) was taken to Nason Hospital (D) with injuries to her head and leg. Thompson (P) was treated by general practitioner Dr. Schultz (D), who had staff privileges, at the request of regular staffers. In treating Thompson (P), Dr. Schultz consulted with several specialists. Thompson (P) was left partially paralyzed, allegedly because Nason Hospital's (D) staffers (D) administered too much anticoagulant (to stop blood clotting), which caused blood to accumulate in her brain. Thompson (P) sued Dr. Schultz (D) for malpractice, and Nason Hospital (D) for failing to supervise him or require him to consult with specialists more frequently. Nason Hospital (D) defended, contending it had no duty to supervise independent contractors' treatments. At trial, Nason Hospital (D) moved for summary judgement on the claims predicated on corporate liability, but the court denied it. Nason Hospital (D) appeals the order, contending Pennsylvania courts never recognized such a claim. The appellate court granted allocatur to the Pennsylvania Supreme Court.

■ **ISSUE**

In Pennsylvania, may a hospital be liable for "corporate negligence" for failing to supervise an affiliated doctor's treatment?

■ **DECISION AND RATIONALE**

(Zappala, J.) Yes. In Pennsylvania, hospitals are liable for "corporate negligence" for failing to supervise affiliated doctors' treatment. The issue is whether the Superior Court erred in adopting a theory of corporate liability for hospitals, which is a case of first impression in Pennsylvania. Previously, hospitals enjoyed absolute immunity from tort liability, as "charitable" organizations. Later, hospital immunity was eliminated as hospitals evolved into sophisticated corporations operating for profit, with a comprehensive supervisory structure. Courts allowed hospitals to be sued on several negligence theories, including respondeat superior, ostensible agency, and corporate negligence. "Corporate negligence" doctrine makes hospitals liable for failing to uphold the proper standard of care owed to patients, which is to ensure patients' well-being while at the hospital. This doctrine creates a nondelegable duty which the hospital owes directly to patients, allowing injured patients to sue hospitals directly without proving doctors' negligence. Hospitals' duties are fourfold: (i) to use reasonable care in maintaining safe and adequate facilities and equipment, (ii) to select and retain only competent doctors, (iii) to oversee all medical practitioners on its premises, and (iv) to formulate, adopt, and enforce adequate policies to ensure quality care. Notably, for hospitals to be charged with negligence, they must have had actual or constructive knowledge of the defect, and their negligence must have been a "substantial factor" in harming the patient. We now affirm the lower court's adoption of "corporate negligence" to hospitals, noting it is an emerging trend in other jurisdictions too. Here, Nason Hospital (D) argues it did not become aware of any exceptional circumstances in Thompson's (P) treatment which justified intervention, and that it could not realistically conduct daily review and supervision of each doctor's medical judgement. However, it is established that hospital staffers and employees have a duty to recognize abnormalities in patients' treatment and condition, and report them. If the attendant doctor is informed of such abnormalities but fails to act, the hospital staffers or employees must report this to hospital authorities so that appropriate action might be taken. When there is a failure to report changes in patients' condition or to question physicians' unusual orders, then if the patient is injured as a result, the hospital is liable for negligence. Here, there is sufficient evidence of negligence to raise a material issue. Order affirmed.

Analysis:

Originally "corporate liability" applied to large corporations that employed large supervisory staffs, which made it appropriate to require them to actually supervise their agents to ensure due care. This theory can also be extended to hospitals, which now adopt a semi-corporate structure and are often capable of supervising doctors' treatments to weed out negligence. The application of corporate liability eliminates contentious issues about whether the hospital could exercise sufficient control over nominal "independent contractors" to classify them as "employees," since corporate liability makes hospitals liable for employees and contractors alike.

■ CASE VOCABULARY

ALLOCATUR: Lower court's referral of legally-important cases to the state's highest court, usually to decide novel legal issues. Here, the court below was hesitant to adopt "corporate liability" as the law of Pennsylvania when that state had never previously recognized such a theory, so it allocated the issue directly to the Pennsylvania Supreme Court.

CORPORATE LIABILITY: Doctrine that a business is responsible for monitoring employees' and contractors' work to prevent them from committing negligent torts. Under it, the business is jointly and severally liable for agents' torts if it knew/should have known of the negative conduct and failed to prevent it, even if the agent is an independent contractor.

STAFF PRIVILEGES: Independent doctor's contractual right to bring private patients to the hospital to use its facilities. Here, Dr. Schultz (D) was not regularly employed by the Nason Hospital (D), but merely had a contract permitting him to use its facilities from time to time. He was apparently conscripted to treat Thompson (P) by nurses, because the regular emergency room doctor was occupied.

Carter v. Hucks–Folliss

(Patient) v. *(Physician)*

131 N.C. App. 145, 505 S.E.2d 177 (1998)

A HOSPITAL SHOULD CONSIDER A DOCTOR'S BOARD CERTIFICATION STATUS WHEN GRANTING HOSPITAL PRIVILEGES

Hospital management is here to make sure we're "board certified" evil geniuses.

stus.com

■ **INSTANT FACTS** Despite failing the board certification exam three times, the defendant hospital renewed Dr. Hucks–Folliss's (D) hospital privileges.

■ **BLACK LETTER RULE** Hospitals owe a duty of care to their patients to ascertain that a physician is qualified to perform surgery before granting that physician the privilege of conducting surgery in the hospital.

■ **PROCEDURAL BASIS**

On appeal to review a trial court decision granting summary judgment.

■ **FACTS**

Dr. Hucks–Folliss (D) performed neck surgery on Carter (P) in 1993 at Moore Regional Hospital (D). Hucks–Folliss (D) had been a neurosurgeon on the hospital medical staff since 1975 but had never been board certified and failed his certification exam three times. Moore Regional (D) reviewed Hucks–Folliss's credentials (D) every two years to renew his hospital privileges. When Hucks–Folliss (D) was last reviewed in 1992, Moore Regional (D) had implemented credentialing and re-credentialing standards promulgated by the Joint Commission on Accreditation of Healthcare Organizations (JCAHO), which call for a hospital to consider board certification in its decision. At his last review, Hucks–Folliss (D) completed an application admitting he was not board certified and acknowledging that he had failed the certification exam three times. No other inquiry appears to have been made into Hucks–Folliss's (D) certification, and the hospital renewed his privileges. The plaintiff sued the hospital, alleging it was negligent in re-certifying Hucks–Folliss (D) as a hospital neurosurgeon without considering his certification status as required by JCAHO standards. The trial court granted the defendant's motion for summary judgment.

■ **ISSUE**

Did the plaintiff raise a genuine issue of fact as to the defendant's negligence by re-certifying Hucks–Folliss (D)?

■ **DECISION AND RATIONALE**

(Greene, J.) Yes. Hospitals owe a duty of care to their patients to ascertain that a physician is qualified to perform surgery before granting that physician the privilege of conducting surgery in the hospital. Failure of a JCAHO-accredited hospital to comply with JCAHO standards is some evidence that the hospital breached its duty of care. Here, Moore Regional (D) agreed to comply with the standards established by JCAHO, one of which is to consider board certification when determining hospital privileges. Despite Hucks–Folliss's (D) disclosure of his certification status on his application, it does not appear that the hospital gave it any weight in granting or denying Hucks–Folliss's (D) hospital privileges. At the very least, the plaintiffs' expert witnesses' testimony created a genuine issue of material fact. Reversed and remanded.

Analysis:

Negligent credentialing claims are relatively new creatures in American law. In the past, hospitals were not generally held liable for the actions of non-employee physicians offering services on their premises. Unlike medical malpractice claims, however, negligent credentialing claims do not seek to hold hospitals vicariously liable for the actions of the treating physician, who is the proper defendant in a malpractice suit, but rather hold these hospitals directly liable for their negligence in allowing an unqualified physician to render medical services to their patients.

Larson v. Wasemiller

(Patient) v. *(Surgeon)*
738 N.W. 2d 300 (Minn. 2007)

HOSPITALS MAY BE LIABLE FOR NEGLIGENTLY GIVING CREDENTIALS TO PHYSICIANS

Sure, we'll grant you surgery privileges at the hospital.

Terrific!

St. Francis Medical Center

stus.com

■ **INSTANT FACTS** Larson (P) brought an action against St. Francis Medical Center (D), alleging that it had negligently credentialed Wasemiller (D).

■ **BLACK LETTER RULE** A common-law cause of action for negligent credentialing does exist, and is not precluded by the peer-review statute.

■ PROCEDURAL BASIS

Appeal from an order reversing a denial of a motion to dismiss.

■ FACTS

Wasemiller (D) performed gastric bypass surgery on Larson (P). The surgery was performed at St. Francis Medical Center (D). Complications developed, and Larson (P) had to undergo further surgery to correct the complications. She was hospitalized for over two months.

Larson (P) brought a medical malpractice action against Wasemiller (D). Her action also alleged that St. Francis (D) was negligent in credentialing Wasemiller (D). The credentialing process usually does not create an employer-employee relationship between the physician and the hospital, but allows the physician access to the hospital facilities. The process also imposes certain professional standards. St. Francis (D) moved to dismiss for failure to state a claim, but the trial court denied the motion, holding that Minnesota law recognizes a claim for negligent credentialing. The trial court, however, certified the question of whether a valid claim could be made for negligent credentialing to the Minnesota Court of Appeals. The trial court also certified the question of whether the statute that provides for confidentiality of peer-review processes granted immunity to hospitals for negligent credentialing. The appellate court held that there was no common-law cause of action for negligent credentialing. The court also held that the statutes do not grant immunity for negligent credentialing, but liability is limited by statute to liability for actions not made in the reasonable belief that such actions are warranted, based on facts known to the hospital at the time the actions were taken. Larson (P) appealed only the appellate court's holding that there was no common-law action for negligent credentialing.

■ ISSUE

Is there a common-law action against a hospital for negligently credentialing a physician?

■ DECISION AND RATIONALE

(Hanson, J.) Yes. A common-law cause of action for negligent credentialing does exist, and is not precluded by the peer-review statute. The statute that provides immunity to peer-review organizations provides for immunity only when the organization acts in the reasonable belief that its action is warranted by facts known after reasonable efforts to ascertain the facts upon which the action is taken. The language implies that an action would lie if an action is not reasonably based on facts that were known or that could have been known by reasonable efforts. The statute, although phrased in the negative, contemplates the existence of a cause of action. It does not create a cause of action, but it does not preclude one.

The court will look at four factors in deciding whether to recognize a common-law tort. The first factor is whether the tort is inherent in, or an extension of, a common-law right. Negligent credentialing is not grounded in vicarious liability, but is grounded in a hospital's duty to use reasonable care in providing care to patients. Minnesota law recognizes that hospitals have a duty to protect patients from harm caused by third parties. A hospital's duty is analogous to the duty to protect in the innkeeper/guest and common carrier/passenger relationships. In addition, a claim for negligent credentialing is analogous to the generally recognized torts of negligent hiring of an employee and negligent selection of an independent contractor. Negligent credentialing is thus inherent in and the natural extension of well-established common law rights.

The second factor is whether a majority of common law jurisdictions recognize the tort. The tort of negligent credentialing is recognized in at least twenty-seven states, and only two states that have considered the claim have rejected it. Some courts have recognized the tort as simply the application of common law negligence principles. Others have held that the tort is an extension of previous decisions that hospitals have a duty to exercise ordinary care and attention for the safety of their patients. Still other courts have held that negligent credentialing is the natural extension of the torts of negligent hiring, or negligent selection of an independent contractor.

The third factor is whether recognition of the tort would create tension with other applicable laws. St. Francis (D) argued that a claim for negligent credentialing would conflict with the confidentiality and limited liability provisions of Minnesota statutes. The confidentiality provisions make confidential data and information acquired by a review organization. Negligence may, however, be shown on the basis of what the organization should have known. In addition, the data and information are not confidential if they were obtained from original sources instead of from the review organization. The law would prevent hospitals from disclosing the fact that certain information was considered by a review committee, but that same information could be introduced if it came from the original source. This law may benefit the hospital, since the hospital knows what information it considered and may choose to emphasize the information that most strongly supports its decision. The limited liability provision of the statute provides that no action will lie against a peer review organization if its actions were reasonably based on facts that were known after making reasonable efforts to ascertain the facts. This language does limit liability, but it does not foreclose an action. It does not raise the standard of proof, but merely codifies the common law standard of negligence.

The fourth and final factor is whether the tension created with other laws is outweighed by the importance of additional protections granted by the recognition of the tort. The purpose of the peer-review statute is to improve the quality of healthcare by granting protection to medical review organizations, and to encourage the medical profession to police its own activities with minimal judicial interference. These policy goals are addressed adequately by the preclusion of access to confidential peer review materials. We recognize that a claim of negligent credentialing raises questions about the necessity of a bifurcated trial, to prevent the evidence that is relevant to the credentialing process from being considered as a part of a malpractice claim. In addition, questions are raised regarding the scope of the confidentiality provisions of the peer review statute. There is also the question here of whether a plaintiff must first prove the physician's negligence before the hospital may be liable for negligent credentialing. These are trial management questions, and are best left to the trial judge. Reversed and remanded.

■ CONCURRENCE

(Anderson, J.) Peer review statutes may not be fulfilling their intended purpose of improving patient care. Physicians are often reluctant to participate in the peer review panel, and have little motivation to participate aggressively and meaningfully. Even the qualified immunity provided by statute does little to encourage effective participation in the process.

Analysis:

An action for negligent credentialing raises numerous questions about the plaintiff's proof. The most basic one is, what is negligence in the context of reviewing credentials? Failure to do a basic investigation of a physician's credentials or past record might qualify as negligence, but the plaintiff is still left with the burden of proving that the negligence was a cause of his or her injuries. Causation might be easily proven in the case of a physician with a long and persistent history of errors or malfeasance, but may be harder to show in other circumstances (for example, if a peer-review committee did not do a check of credentials).

■ CASE VOCABULARY

PEER–REVIEW PRIVILEGE: A privilege that protects from disclosure the proceedings and reports of a medical facility's peer-review committee, which reviews and oversees the patient care and medical services provided by the staff.

Kadlec Med. Ctr. v. Lakeview Anesthesia Assoc.

(Employer) v. *(Anesthesiologists' Association)*

2005 WL 1309153 (E.D. La. 2005)

HOSPITALS MAY FACE LIABILITY FOR FAILING TO DISCLOSE A FORMER ANESTHESIOLOGIST'S SUSPECTED DRUG ABUSE

This seemed a lot more glamorous when I was a renowned anesthesiologist.

stus.com

■ **INSTANT FACTS** The defendant healthcare provider failed to disclose that it terminated an anesthesiologist for suspected drug abuse when questioned by the anesthesiologist's prospective employer.

■ **BLACK LETTER RULE** A claim for negligent misrepresentation requires that (1) the defendant, in the course of its business or other matters in which it had a pecuniary interest, supplied false information; (2) the defendant had a legal duty to supply correct information to the plaintiff; (3) the defendant breached its duty, which can result from omission as well as affirmative misrepresentation; and (4) the plaintiff suffered damages or pecuniary loss as a result of its justifiable reliance upon the omission or affirmative misrepresentation.

■ **PROCEDURAL BASIS**

District court consideration of the defendant's motion for summary judgment.

■ **FACTS**

From 1997 to 2001, Dr. Berry was an anesthesiologist at LRMC (D) and, ultimately, a shareholder of Lakeview Anesthesia Associates (D), along with Drs. Dennis, Preu, Boldone, and Parr. In 2000, LRMC (D) conducted an audit of Berry's narcotic medication records and noted discrepancies in his withdrawal records with regard to the drug Demerol. In March 2001, Berry did not respond to hospital pages while working at LRMC (D) and was found sleeping in a chair in an apparently sedated state. Berry was immediately terminated due to this incident and the earlier suspicions that he had diverted Demerol to his own use. Later that year, Berry sought employment at Kadlec Medical Center (P). Kadlec (P) sent LRMC (D) a letter requesting information on Berry's competence as an anesthesiologist and a candid evaluation of his "training, continuing clinical performance, skill, and judgment, interpersonal skills and ability to perform the privileges requested." Kadlec (P) supplied a questionnaire to assist in LRMC's (D) response. LRMC (D) did not complete the questionnaire and, in response to the letter, offered only that Berry was on its staff from 1997 through March 2001 and that its standard business practice did not allow for any additional information due to the large number of inquiries received. Kadlec (P) retained Berry's services as an anesthesiologist in October 2001. About a year later, Berry performed a tubal ligation procedure under the influence of drugs, causing the patient extensive brain damage. In the resulting malpractice case, Kadlec (P) learned that Berry had been terminated by LRMC (D) with cause. Kadlec (P) settled the malpractice suit and filed this action against LRMC (D) and others for negligent misrepresentation, intentional misrepresentation, strict responsibility misrepresentation, and negligence. LRMC (D) moved for summary judgment, arguing that Kadlec (P) failed to establish an element of its misrepresentation claims.

■ **ISSUE**

Did LRMC (D) have sufficient pecuniary interest in the omission of Berry's employment history to sustain plaintiff's misrepresentation claims?

■ DECISION AND RATIONALE

(Judge Undisclosed.) Yes. Louisiana law follows the Restatement (Second) of Torts § 552(1), which provides that a claim for negligent misrepresentation requires that (1) the defendant, in the course of its business or other matters in which it had a pecuniary interest, supplied false information; (2) the defendant had a legal duty to supply correct information to the plaintiff; (3) the defendant breached its duty, which can result from omission as well as affirmative misrepresentation; and (4) the plaintiff suffered damages or pecuniary loss as a result of its justifiable reliance upon the omission or affirmative misrepresentation. Likewise, intentional misrepresentation requires a misrepresentation of material fact made with intent to deceive, and causing justifiable reliance with resultant injury.

Here, the court concluded that LRMC (D) had adequate pecuniary interest in the omitted information. Had LRMC (D) disclosed Berry's termination for suspected drug abuse, it may have faced defamation or other claims from Berry. Additionally, a failure to respond to such inquiries from other healthcare providers could complicate LRMC's (D) future recruiting and credentialing efforts, because of potential denial of reciprocal physician inquiries and the professional reputation that it withholds such information with respect to its departing employees. Moreover, disclosure of its suspicions about Berry's drug abuse could lead to malpractice actions from past LRMC (D) patients. LRMC (D) had adequate pecuniary interest to conceal Berry's employment history. Motion denied.

Analysis:

In a portion of the court's decision that has been omitted from the case book, the court offers an interesting discussion of LRMC's (D) duty to provide any information in response to Kadlec's (P) inquiry. Under Louisiana law, those in a "special relationship" have a duty to disclose material facts to one another. Based on this requirement, the court determined that "policy considerations weigh heavily in favor of imposing a duty to disclose information related to a doctor's adverse employment history that risks death or bodily injury to future patients." Based on this special relationship, not only must LRMC (D) provide full, accurate information in response to Kadlec's (P) request, but its stated policy of withholding such requests appears to violate public policy.

■ CASE VOCABULARY

NEGLIGENT MISREPRESENTATION: A careless or inadvertent false statement in circumstances where care should have been taken.

FRAUD: A knowing misrepresentation of the truth or concealment of a material fact to induce another to act to his or her detriment; a misrepresentation made recklessly without belief in its truth to induce another person to act; unconscionable dealing, especially in contract law; the unfair use of the power arising out of one of the parties' relative positions and resulting in an unconscionable bargain.

Petrovich v. Share Health Plan of Illinois, Inc.

(Oral Cancer Patient) v. (Negligent HMO)

188 Ill.2d 17, 241 Ill.Dec. 627, 719 N.E.2d 756 (1999)

AGENCY LAW PROVIDES A MEANS BY WHICH AN HMO MAY BE HELD VICARIOUSLY LIABLE FOR THE NEGLIGENCE OF ITS INDEPENDENT-CONTRACTOR PHYSICIANS

■ **INSTANT FACTS** A woman is suing her HMO under agency principles for the negligence of its participating physicians in failing to discover her oral cancer in a timely manner.

■ **BLACK LETTER RULE** An HMO may be held vicariously liable for the negligence of its independent-contractor physicians under both the doctrines of apparent authority and implied authority.

■ **FACTS**

In 1989, Petrovich's (P) employer provided health care coverage to its employees by selecting Share (D), an HMO, and enrolling its employees therein. Petrovich (P) selected Dr. Kowalski from Share's list of participating physicians, and began seeing her in August 1989. In September of 1990, Petrovich (P) saw Dr. Kowalski because she was experiencing persistent pain in the right sides of her mouth, tongue, throat and face. She also complained of a foul mucus in her mouth. Dr. Kowalski referred her to two other physicians who had contracts with Share (D): Dr. Slavick, a neurologist, and Dr. Friedman, an ear, nose and throat specialist. Dr. Friedman recommended that Petrovich (P) have an MRI test or a CT scan performed. Dr. Kowalski, however, informed Petrovich (P) that Share (D) would not allow those tests, and instead gave Dr. Friedman a copy of an old MRI test result. Nonetheless, Dr. Kowalski later ordered an updated MRI. However, this test failed to image the right side of Petrovich's (P) tongue area as directed by Dr. Friedman. When Dr. Kowalski met with Petrovich, she stated that the MRI showed no abnormality. Petrovich's (P) pain persisted. In April or May of 1991, Petrovich saw Dr. Friedman for the third time. On June 7, 1991, Dr, Friedman performed multiple biopsies on the right side of the base of Petrovich's (P) tongue and surrounding tissues. The biopsy results revealed squamous cell carcinoma, a cancer. Later that month, Dr. Friedman operated on Petrovich (P) to remove the cancer. He removed part of the base of her tongue, and portions of her palate, pharynx and jaw bone. After the surgery, Petrovich (P) underwent radiation treatments and rehabilitation. Petrovich (P) subsequently brought this medical malpractice action against Share (D), Dr. Kowalski and others. Dr. Friedman was not a named party defendant. Her complaint alleges that both Dr. Kowalski and Dr. Friedman were negligent in failing to disclose the cancer in a timely manner, and that Share (D) is vicariously liable for their negligence under agency principles.

■ **ISSUE**

May an HMO be held vicariously liable for the negligence of its independent-contractor physicians under agency law?

■ **DECISION AND RATIONALE**

(Bilandic, J.) Yes. We have never addressed a question of whether an HMO may be held liable for medical malpractice. Share (D) asserts that holding HMOs liable for medical malpractice will cause health care costs to increase and make health care inaccessible to large numbers of people. Share (D) suggests that, with this consideration in mind, we should impose only narrow, or limited, forms of liability on HMOs. We disagree with Share (D) that the cost-containment role of HMOs entitles them to special consideration. The principle that organizations are accountable for their tortious actions and those of their agents is fundamental to our justice system. There is no exception to this principle for HMOs. Moreover, HMO accountability is essential to counterbalance the HMO goal of cost-containment. To the extent that HMOs are profit-making entities, accountability is also needed to counterbalance the inherent drive to achieve a large and ever-increasing profit margin. Market forces alone are insufficient to cure the deleterious effects of managed care in the health care industry. Courts, therefore, should not be so hesitant to apply well-settled legal theories of liability to HMOs where the facts so warrant and where justice so requires. This appeal concerns whether Share (D) may be held vicariously liable under agency law for the negligence of its independent-contractor physicians. We must determine whether Share (D) was properly awarded summary judgment on the ground that Drs. Kowalski and Friedman were not acting as Share's (D) agents in their treatment of Petrovich (P). Petrovich (P) argues that Share (D) is not entitled to summary judgment on this record. She asserts that genuine issues of material fact exist as to whether Drs. Kowalski and Friedman were acting within Share's (D) apparent authority, implied authority or both. As a general rule, no vicarious liability exists for the actions of independent contractors. Vicarious liability may nevertheless be imposed for the actions of independent contractors where an agency relationship is established under either the doctrine of apparent authority or the doctrine of implied authority. We now hold that the apparent authority doctrine may also be used to impose vicarious liability on HMOs. To establish apparent authority against an HMO for physician malpractice, the patient must prove (1) that the HMO held itself out as the provider of health care, without informing the patient that the care is given by independent contractors, and (2) that the patient justifiably relied upon the conduct of the HMO by looking to the HMO to provide health care services, rather than to a specific physician. Apparent agency is a question of fact. That is, whether a person has notice of a physician's status as an independent contractor, or is put on notice by the circumstances, is a question of fact. In this case, Petrovich (P) testified that she did not recall receiving the subscriber certificate, which states that Share (D) physicians are independent contractors. Share (D) responded that it customarily provides members with this information. Share (D) has never claimed to know whether Share (D) actually provided Petrovich (P) with this information. Thus, a question of fact exists as to whether Share (D) gave this information to Petrovich (P). If this information was not provided to Petrovich (P), it cannot be used to defeat her apparent agency claim. Evidence in the record supports Petrovich's (P) contentions that Share (D) held itself out to its members as the provider of health care, and that Petrovich (P) was not aware that her physicians were independent contractors. Notably, Petrovich (P) stated that, at the time that she received treatment, Petrovich (P) believed that Drs. Kowalski and Friedman were Share (D) employees. Petrovich (P) was not aware of the type of relationship that her physicians had with Share (D). We hold that the testimony by Petrovich (P) supports the conclusion that Share (D) held itself out to Petrovich (P) as the provider of her health care, without informing her that the care was actually provided by independent contractors. Therefore, a triable issue of fact exists as to the holding-out element. A plaintiff must also prove the element of "justifiable reliance" to establish apparent authority against an HMO for physician malpractice. This means that the plaintiff acted in reliance upon the conduct of the HMO or its agent, consistent with ordinary care and prudence. Share (D) maintains that Petrovich (P) cannot establish the justifiable reliance element because she did not select Share (D). We reject Share's (D) argument. Where a person has no choice but to enroll with a single HMO and does not rely upon a specific physician, then that person is likewise relying upon the HMO to provide health care. In the present case, the record discloses facts sufficient to raise the reasonable inference that Petrovich (P) relied upon Share (D) to provide her health care services. In conclusion, as set forth above, Petrovich (D) has presented sufficient evidence to support justifiable reliance, as well as a holding out by Share (D). Share (D), therefore, is not entitled to summary judgment against Petrovich's (P) claim of apparent authority. We now address whether the implied authority doctrine may be used against HMOs to negate a physician's status as an independent contractor. Petrovich (P) contends that her physicians' status as independent contractors should be negated, and she asserts that Share (D) actively interfered with her physicians' medical decision-making by designing and executing its capitation method and "quality assurance" programs. Petrovich (P) also points to Share's (D) referral system as evidence of control. Petrovich (P) submits that Share's (D) capitation method of compensating its medical groups is a form of control because it financially punishes physicians for ordering certain medical treatment. She maintains that a reasonable inference to be drawn from Share's (D) capitation method of compensation is that Share (D) provides financial disincentives to its primary care physicians in order to discourage them from ordering the medical care that they deem appropriate. Petrovich (P) argues that this is an example of Share's (D) influence and control over the medical judgment of its physicians. Share (D) counters that its capitation method of compensation cannot be used as evidence of control here because Dr. Kowalski is paid the same salary every month. We disagree with Share (D) that this fact makes Share's (D) capitation system irrelevant to our inquiry. Whether control was actually exercised is not dispositive in this context. Rather, the right to control the alleged agent is the proper query, even where that right is not exercised. We conclude that Petrovich (P) has presented adequate evidence to entitle her to a trial on the issue of implied authority. All the facts and circumstances before us, if proven at trial, raise the reasonable inference that Share (D) exerted such sufficient control over Drs. Kowalski and Friedman so as to negate their status as independent contractors. Share (D), therefore, is not entitled to summary judgment against Petrovich's (P) claim of implied authority. In conclusion, an HMO may be held vicariously liable for the negligence of its independent-contractor physicians under both the doctrines of apparent authority and implied authority. Petrovich (P) here is entitled to a trial on both doctrines. The circuit court therefore erred in awarding summary judgment to Share (D). The appellate court's judgment, which reversed the circuit court's judgment and remanded the cause to the circuit court for further proceedings, is affirmed.

Analysis:

This appeal came before the court amidst great changes in the relationships among physicians, patients, and those entities paying for medical care. Traditionally, physicians treated patients on demand, while insurers merely paid the physicians their fee for the services provided. Today, managed care organizations (MCOs) have stepped into the insurer's shoes, and often attempt to reduce the price and quantity of health care services provided to patients through a system of health care cost containment. Under the doctrine of apparent authority, a principal will be bound not only by the authority that it actually gives to another, but also by the authority that it appears to give. The doctrine functions like an estoppel. When the principal creates the appearance of authority, a court will not hear the principal's denials of agency to the prejudice of an innocent third party, who has been led to reasonably rely upon the agency and is harmed as a result. Vicarious liability under the apparent authority doctrine will not attach, however, if the patient knew or should have known that the physician providing treatment is an independent contractor.

■ CASE VOCABULARY

APPARENT AUTHORITY: A principal will be bound not only by the authority that it actually gives to another, but also by the authority that it appears to give.

ESTOPPEL: The party is prevented by his own acts from claiming a right to the detriment of the other party who was entitled to rely on such conduct and has acted accordingly.

IMPLIED AUTHORITY: Actual authority, circumstantially proved.

RESPONDEAT SUPERIOR: A principal is liable for certain acts of his agent.

VICARIOUS LIABILITY: The imposition of liability on one person for the actionable conduct of another, based solely on a relationship between the two persons.

Pagarigan v. Aetna U.S. Healthcare of California, Inc.

(Decedent's Children) v. (HMO)

2005 WL 2742807 (Cal. Ct. App. 2005)

HMOS MAY BE HELD LIABLE FOR NEGLIGENT SELECTION OF PROVIDERS

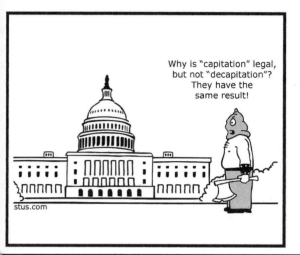

■ **INSTANT FACTS** Pagarigan's children (P) alleged that their mother died due to the wrongdoing of Aetna (D), her HMO.

■ **BLACK LETTER RULE** An HMO that contracts out coverage decisions and the responsibility for patient care owes enrollees a duty of due care when choosing providers and in making contracts with those providers.

■ **PROCEDURAL BASIS**

Appeal from an order sustaining a demurrer.

■ **FACTS**

Pagarigan (P) enrolled in an HMO operated by Aetna in 1995, and remained a member until her death in June 2000. In January 2000, she suffered a severe stroke. As a member of the Aetna (D) HMO, she was assigned to the Magnolia Gardens nursing home and placed under the care of Dr. Buttleman. While at Magnolia Gardens, Pagarigan (P) allegedly became malnourished and dehydrated, and developed sores and infections. Dr. Buttleman delayed ordering Pagarigan (P) removed to an acute care hospital for several months, until it was too late to help her. Pagarigan's children (P) alleged that the delay was for economic reasons: as long as Pagarigan (P) was at Magnolia Gardens, her costs were covered by the state's medical insurance plan, but if she transferred to an acute care hospital, Aetna (D) would be responsible for her costs.

Although Aetna (D) called its plan an HMO, it differed from the traditional HMO model in that it did not employ doctors or own hospitals. Aetna (D) used an arrangement called a capitation. Aetna (D) agreed to pay a management firm a certain amount per year for each enrollee Aetna (D) assigned to that firm. The firm received the same amount for a particular person regardless of how much or how little that person's medical care cost. Pagarigan's children (P) alleged that Aetna (D) thereby created economic incentives to deny treatment, or to supply substandard treatment. Pagarigan's children (P) also alleged that Aetna's (D) failure to disclose the capitation system amounted to fraud. They further argued that Aetna's (D) marketing materials contained misrepresentations and false promises that amounted to fraud. The trial court sustained Aetna's (D) demurrer to the complaint.

■ **ISSUE**

May an HMO be liable for substandard care provided by its contractors?

■ **DECISION AND RATIONALE**

(By the Court) Yes. An HMO that contracts out coverage decisions and the responsibility for patient care owes enrollees a duty of due care when choosing providers and in making contracts with those providers. This duty is inherent in the common law. The Legislature confirmed this common-law duty by enacting Cal. Civ. Code § 3428. That statute, which was enacted after Pagarigan's (P) death, provides that a healthcare service plan "shall have a duty of ordinary care to arrange for the provision of

---

medically necessary healthcare service to its subscribers and enrollees." The statute also provides for liability for harm caused by the failure to exercise that care. The duty of care is breached by the selection of a deficient provider, or one known to be prone to malpractice. Likewise, the duty is breached if the contract terms with a provider foreseeably increase the likelihood that the provider will offer substandard services that will injure enrollees. The most critical contractual term here is the level of the capitation payment. A plan will breach its duty if the capitation payments are set so low that the provider must provide substandard services or deny medically necessary services in order to survive.

Capitation itself is not improper, and has been endorsed by the Legislature. It is true that the system creates incentives to underinvest in healthcare services, just as a fee-for-services plan creates incentives to overinvest. These incentives are inherent in the capitation system, which has been approved by the federal and state governments. Capitation alone cannot be the basis for a negligence action, but the manner in which the capitation is carried out may be. Pagarigan's children (P) must show not only that their mother's care was substandard, but that Aetna (D) knew or should have known of the deficiencies. It is not a violation of an HMO's duty of care for a provider to make an erroneous decision on an enrollee's care. It is another thing for an HMO to contract with a provider that is improperly managed, inadequately staffed, or provided with insufficient funding to care for patients.

Pagarigan's children (P) cannot, however, base a claim for constructive fraud on the failure of Aetna (D) to disclose the capitation arrangement. They do not allege a failure when it would have been reasonable to expect disclosure; namely, when their mother decided to enroll. Instead, they allege a failure to disclose when treatment options were considered. These allegations are insufficient to show fraud. Aetna's (D) claim that there was no fiduciary duty is doubtful, but the claim fails for lack of a sufficient factual allegation. Finally, Pagarigan's children (P) have not made out a sufficient claim that Aetna's (D) marketing materials were fraudulent. The trial court sustained a demurrer to this part of the complaint, saying that the marketing materials were mere "puffery," and could not be the basis for a fraud claim. While it is possible that marketing materials could be the basis for a fraud claim, the allegations made by Pagarigan's children (P) were neither specific nor substantive enough to state a claim for fraud. The alleged misrepresentations are so vague that they do not even rise to the level of "puffery." Reversed and remanded with instructions to sustain the demurrer with leave to amend the complaint.

Analysis:

There is a definite tension between the interest insurers (and society at large) have in containing expenditures for medical care and the duty to provide at least adequate medical care. Although there should be no disincentives to providing reasonably priced medical services, that does not mean substandard services should be tolerated in the interests of saving money. Usually, the threat of tort liability (if not professionalism concerns) for those providing care directly to the patients will dictate that the tension be resolved in favor of providing adequate care even if not profitable.

■ CASE VOCABULARY

DEMURRER: A pleading stating that although the facts alleged in a complaint may be true, they are insufficient for the plaintiff to state a claim for relief and the for the defendant to frame an answer. In most jurisdictions, such a pleading is now termed a *motion to dismiss,* but the demurrer is still used in a few states, including California, Nebraska, and Pennsylvania.

Shannon v. McNulty

(Parents) v. *(Pre-Natal Care Provider)*

718 A.2d 828 (Pa. Super. 1998)

THE THEORY OF CORPORATE LIABILITY CREATES A NONDELEGABLE DUTY WHICH A HOSPITAL OWES A PATIENT

■ **INSTANT FACTS** A woman sued her HMO and her doctor after she experienced all the symptoms of pre-term labor, but her doctor told her she was not in labor, and as a result she lost her baby.

■ **BLACK LETTER RULE** An HMO may, under the right circumstances, be held corporately liable for a breach of duty which causes harm to its subscribers.

■ **PROCEDURAL BASIS**

Appeal from the trial court's grant of the defendant's motion for a compulsory nonsuit against the plaintiff.

■ **FACTS**

Mrs. Shannon (P) was a subscriber of the HealthAmerica HMO (D) when she became pregnant for the first time. HealthAmerica (D) gave her a list of six OB/GYN doctors from which she selected Dr. McNulty (D). Her HealthAmerica membership card instructed her to contact either her doctor or HealthAmerica (D) in the event she had any medical questions or emergency medical conditions. She saw McNulty (D) monthly but also called the HealthAmerica (D) phone line a number of times for advice and to schedule appointments. She called Dr. McNulty (D) on October 2, 1992 with complaints of abdominal pain. Three days later, the doctor examined her for five minutes and told her the pain was the result of a fibroid uterus, prescribed rest and took her off of work for one week. He did no testing to confirm his diagnosis and did not advise her of the symptoms of pre-term labor. She next called McNulty's (D) office on October 7 and again on the 8th and 9th, because her abdominal pain was continuing, she had back pain, was constipated and could not sleep. She asked Dr. McNulty (D) if she could be in pre-term labor because her symptoms were similar to those described in a reference book she had on labor. She told McNulty (D) her pains were irregular and about ten minutes apart. Dr. McNulty (D) told her she was not in labor, and she testified that he was becoming impatient with her. On October 10th, she called HealthAmerica's emergency phone line and told them about her severe irregular abdominal pain, back pain, and that she thought she might be in pre-term labor. The triage nurse advised her to call Dr. McNulty (D) again. Mrs. Shannon did not, because she did not feel he would help her. She called the HealthAmerica triage line again the next day, and said her symptoms were getting worse and Dr. McNulty was not responding. The nurse again advised her to call Dr. McNulty, so she did. McNulty (D) was again short with her and angry, and insisted that she was not in pre-term labor. She again called the HealthAmerica (D) phone service, and one of the in-house physicians told her to go to West Penn Hospital to get her back examined. She drove an hour to the hospital, passing three other hospitals on the way. Later that night, at West Penn, she delivered a one and one-half pound baby who died two days later due to his severe prematurity. The Shannons' (P) expert, Dr. Warner, testified that HealthAmerica (D), through its triage nurses, deviated from the standard of care by not immediately referring Mrs. Shannon (P) to a physician or hospital for a cervical exam and fetal stress test. As with Dr. McNulty (D), these precautions would have led to her labor being detected and increased the baby's chances of survival. The Shannons (P) brought this medical malpractice action, claiming that Dr. McNulty (D) was negligent for failing to timely diagnose and treat signs of pre-term labor, and HealthAmerica (D) was vicariously liable for the negligence of its nursing staff in failing to respond to Mrs. Shannon's (P) complaints by timely referring her to an appropriate physician or hospital for diagnosis and treatment of her pre-term labor. The Shannons (P) also alleged HealthAmerica (D) was corporately liable for its negligent supervision of Dr. McNulty's (D) care and its lack of appropriate procedures and protocols when dispensing telephonic medical advice to subscribers. The case went to a trial before a jury, and at the close of the Shannons' (P) case, HealthAmerica (D) moved for a compulsory nonsuit. The trial court denied the motion. HealthAmerica (D) then proceeded to put on its case by calling two of its triage nurses. The court then recessed for the day. The following morning, the court, sua sponte, reconsidered HealthAmerica's (D) motion, and granted the nonsuit. The Shannons (P) filed timely post trial motions seeking to have the nonsuit removed. After denial of such motions, this appeal followed.

■ ISSUE

May an HMO be held corporately liable for a breach of duty which causes harm to its subscribers?

■ DECISION AND RATIONALE

(Melvin, J.) Yes. The theory of corporate liability as it relates to hospitals was first adopted in this Commonwealth in the case of *Thompson v. Nason Hospital.* Our supreme court upheld a direct theory of liability against the hospital. Corporate negligence is a doctrine under which the hospital is liable if it fails to uphold the proper standard of care owed the patient, which is to ensure the patient's well-being while at the hospital. This theory of liability creates a nondelegable duty which the hospital owes directly to a patient. Therefore, an injured party does not have to rely on and establish the negligence of a third party. The court in *Thompson* set forth four general areas of corporate liability: (1) A duty to use reasonable care in the maintenance of safe and adequate facilities and equipment; (2) A duty to select and retain only competent physicians; (3) A duty to oversee all persons who practice medicine within its walls as to patient care; (4) A duty to formulate, adopt and enforce adequate rules and policies to ensure quality care for patients. Viewing the evidence in the light most favorable to the Shannons (P) as the non-moving party, our examination of the instant record leads us to the conclusion that the Shannons (P) presented sufficient evidence to establish a prima facie case of corporate liability pursuant to the third duty set forth in *Thompson.* However, due to the different entities involved (i.e. hospital vs. HMO), this determination does not end our inquiry. HealthAmerica (D) argues that the *Thompson* duties are not applicable to an HMO. We disagree. Where the HMO is providing health care services rather than just merely providing money to pay for services, their conduct should be subject to scrutiny. We see no reason why the duties applicable to hospitals should not be equally applied to an HMO when that HMO is performing the same or similar functions as a hospital. When a benefits provider, be it an insurer or a managed care organization, interjects itself into the rendering of medical decisions affecting a subscriber's care it must do so in a medically reasonable manner. Here, HealthAmerica (D) provided a phone service for emergency care staffed by triage nurses. Hence, it was under a duty to oversee that the dispensing of advice by those nurses would be performed in a medically reasonable manner. Accordingly, we find that HMOs may, under the right circumstances, be held corporately liable for a breach of any of the *Thompson* duties which causes harm to its subscribers.

Analysis:

Generally, in a medical malpractice case, the plaintiff must establish: (1) a duty owed by the health care provider to the patient; (2) a breach of that duty; (3) that the breach was the proximate cause of, or a substantial factor in, bringing about the harm suffered by the patient; and (4) damages suffered by the patient that were a direct result of that harm. Moreover, except where it is obvious, the plaintiff must present expert testimony that the health care provider's conduct deviated from an accepted standard of care, and that such deviation was the proximate cause of the harm suffered. In adopting the *Thompson* doctrine of corporate liability, the court recognized the corporate hospital's role in the total health care of its patients. Likewise, this Court recognized the central role played by HMOs in the total health care of its subscribers.

■ CASE VOCABULARY

PRIMA FACIE CASE: Sufficient evidence in a case to get the plaintiff past a motion for a directed verdict in a jury case, or a motion to dismiss in a nonjury case.

SUA SPONTE: Of its own will or motion.

Brannan v. Northwest Permanente, P.C.

(Patient) v. *(Healthcare Provider)*

2006 WL 2794881 (W.D. Wash. 2006)

A PHYSICIAN'S COMPENSATION HISTORY IS IRRELEVANT TO A PATIENT'S NEGLIGENCE CASE

The court said my HMO doesn't have to show me my doctor's compesation contract because it's not "relevant". I say the fact they're hiding it <u>proves</u> it's relevant.

■ **INSTANT FACTS** A patient sought disclosure of her physician's compensation structure in order to demonstrate a financial incentive not to refer her for diagnostic testing.

■ **BLACK LETTER RULE** A defendant's motive for acting is irrelevant to whether he breached the standard of care owed in a negligence case.

■ PROCEDURAL BASIS

District court consideration of the plaintiff's motion to compel production of documents.

■ FACTS

In a negligence action, Brannan (P) deposed her primary physician, Dr. Lin, about the terms of his employment with Kaiser Permanente (D). Seeking to establish that Kaiser Permanente (D), like many HMOs, provided a financial incentive to its physicians to refrain from making referrals and ordering diagnostic tests, Brannan (P) sought production of Lin's employment compensation contract and other documents that pertained to any bonuses or incentives paid to Lin. The defendants opposed disclosure, arguing that whether Lin had a motive for referring or testing Brannan (P) is not relevant to whether Lin breached the standard of care.

■ ISSUE

In a medical malpractice action, is a patient entitled to discovery of a treating physician's employment contract and bonus structure to determine a motive?

■ DECISION AND RATIONALE

(Judge Undisclosed.) No. A defendant's motive for acting is irrelevant to whether he breached the standard of care owed in a negligence case. Here, Lin's employment contract and incentive package is irrelevant to the issues of the case and is unlikely to lead to discoverable material. A medical malpractice case is just like any other negligence case. The fundamental question that must be determined is whether the defendant deviated from the professional standard of care owed to the patient. The reason or motive for his deviation is immaterial, so long as the deviation is in fact proven by the evidence. Motion denied.

Analysis:

In some instances, a physician's compensation structure may be relevant to the facts and issues of the case, perhaps where intent is an issue. However, in a medical malpractice case like this, where a plaintiff merely alleges a deviation from the applicable standard of care, it matters not *why* a physician acted so long as the plaintiff proves that he did in fact act as alleged, and that a reasonable physician would act differently under similar circumstances.

■ CASE VOCABULARY

MALPRACTICE: An instance of negligence or incompetence on the part of a professional.

MOTION TO COMPEL DISCOVERY: A party's request that the court force the party's opponent to respond to the party's discovery request (as to answer interrogatories or produce documents).

NEGLIGENCE: The failure to exercise the standard of care that a reasonably prudent person would have exercised in a similar situation; any conduct that falls below the legal standard established to protect others against unreasonable risk of harm, except for conduct that is intentionally, wantonly, or willfully disregardful of others' rights.

CHAPTER EIGHT

Access to Health Care: The Obligation to Provide Care

Ricks v. Budge

Instant Facts: Ricks (P) was being treated for a hand ailment when, in an emergency situation, Budge (D) refused to treat because Ricks' (P) bill was delinquent.

Black Letter Rule: Once a physician-patient relationship is commenced, the physician has a duty to continue treatment until (1) the ailment has been fully treated, (2) the patient discharges the physician, or (3) the physician withdraws after giving the patient reasonable notice so as to enable the patient to secure other medical attention.

Childs v. Weis

Instant Facts: Childs (P) was in labor but turned away from Weis' (D) clinic. Childs (P) ended up giving birth in a car while on the way to another physician. The baby lived about twelve hours.

Black Letter Rule: A physician owes no legal duty to a patient unless there exists a contract between them, either express or implied, giving rise to a physician-patient relationship.

Williams v. United States

Instant Facts: White (P) was denied emergency care at a hospital operated by the Public Health Service (D) because he was not Native American.

Black Letter Rule: State anti-discrimination laws and regulations do not create a cause of action against a hospital that refuses to provide care for racial reasons.

Baber v. Hospital Corporation of America

Instant Facts: Brenda Baber was taken to the hospital for an emergency condition. While there she fell and, unknown to staff, fractured her skull. She died some time later after being transferred twice.

Black Letter Rule: 1) EMTALA does not permit private suits for damages against attending physicians. 2) EMTALA requires that before transfer a patient be given an appropriate medical screening that comports with the hospital's standard screening procedure given the condition of the patient. 3) EMTALA requires a hospital to stabilize a patient before transfer only if it has actual knowledge of an emergency medical condition.

Bragdon v. Abbott

Instant Facts: Bragdon (D), a dentist, refused to treat Abbot (P) in the dental clinic because Abbot (P) is HIV positive.

Black Letter Rule: 1) HIV positive status is a physical impairment that affects a major life activity from the time of infection and is thus considered a disability under the Americans with Disabilities Act. 2) Health care providers may not refuse treatment to HIV positive patients on the basis of their infection unless it poses a direct threat to the health or safety of others and there are not any reasonable precautions that would remove the threat.

Howe v. Hull

Instant Facts: Mr. Charon (P), infected with HIV, went to the hospital experiencing a reaction to an antibiotic. Dr. Hull (D), the on-call physician, refused to admit Mr. Charon (P), possibly because of his HIV positive status.

Black Letter Rule: 1) The ADA prohibits hospitals from refusing treatment to an individual based, to any extent, on the individual's disability. 2) The Federal Rehabilitation Act (FRA) prohibits hospitals from refusing treatment based solely on an individual's disability.

Ricks v. Budge

(Hand Patient) v. *(Group of Physicians)*

91 Utah 307, 64 P.2d 208 (1937)

ONCE A DOCTOR-PATIENT RELATIONSHIP IS COMMENCED, THERE EXISTS A DUTY TO CARE FOR THE PATIENT UNTIL THE RELATIONSHIP IS PROPERLY TERMINATED

■ **INSTANT FACTS** Ricks (P) was being treated for a hand ailment when, in an emergency situation, Budge (D) refused to treat because Ricks' (P) bill was delinquent.

■ **BLACK LETTER RULE** Once a physician-patient relationship is commenced, the physician has a duty to continue treatment until (1) the ailment has been fully treated, (2) the patient discharges the physician, or (3) the physician withdraws after giving the patient reasonable notice so as to enable the patient to secure other medical attention.

■ FACTS

Ricks (P) was being treated by Budge (D) (a group of related doctors practicing together) for a hand aliment. Ricks (P) left the hospital on March 15th, after his initial treatment. Budge (D) advised him to return for further treatment at once if his finger showed any signs of getting worse at any time. On the morning of March 17th, Ricks (P) phoned Budge (D) and explained that his hand was getting worse. Budge (D) told Ricks (P) to come to his office. Ricks (P) arrived at 2 p.m. and was examined by Budge (D) who told Ricks (P): "You have got to go back to the hospital." After Ricks (P) went to the hospital Budge (D) arrived and told Ricks (P) that he would receive no treatment until he paid up his accounts. Ricks (P) was unable to do so and Budge (D) refused to treat. After being given some help moving, Ricks (P) left the hospital and made the short journey a few blocks away to Cache Valley Hospital. When Ricks (P) arrived, his hand was swollen with fluid oozing from it and required immediate surgery. About two weeks after arriving at this hospital it became necessary for Ricks (P) to have his middle finger amputated. Ricks (P) remained under the care of Cache Valley Hospital for about a month. In defense of the malpractice suit filed by Ricks (P), Budge (D) maintains (1) that there was no contract of employment between the parties and in the absence of such contract Budge (D) was not obligated to proceed with treatment, (2) that if a contract had existed, there was no evidence that the refusal to treat resulted in any damage to Ricks (P).

■ ISSUE

Does a doctor have a duty to treat a patient in the absence of a contract of employment between the parties?

■ DECISION AND RATIONALE

(Ephraim, J.) Yes. Under this evidence it cannot be said that the relation of physician and patient did not exist on March 17th. It had never been terminated after being commenced on March 11th. Indeed, once Budge (D) began treatment of Ricks (P) there was an ongoing duty of care. Even were this not so, once Ricks (P) came to Budge's (D) office on March 17th and was examined and directed to proceed immediately to the hospital for further treatment, a physician-patient relationship existed. This cannot be seriously questioned. The law is well settled that a physician, upon undertaking a case, is under a duty, in the absence of an agreement limiting the service, of continuing his attention, after the first operation or first treatment, so long as the case requires attention. This obligation to continue care can be terminated only by the cessation of the necessity which gave rise to the relationship [read: patient is cured], or by the discharge of the physician by the patient, or by the withdrawal from the case by the physician after giving the patient reasonable notice so as to enable the patient to secure other medical attention. As to Budge's (D) assertion regarding proof of damages, this is a question for the jury, not the court.

■ CONCURRENCE AND DISSENT

(Folland, J.) The theory that Ricks (P) alleged in his complaint is that there was no continued relationship from the first employment but that a new relationship was entered into. I do not think a new contract was entered into during Ricks' (P) March 17th visit to the clinic. As soon as Budge (D) reached the hospital where Ricks (P) had been directed to go, he opened negotiations with Ricks (P) that might have resulted in a new contract, but this did not occur because Ricks (P) decided to seek attention elsewhere. Ricks (P) made no suggestion as to how the situation could be worked out and Budge (D) had a right to refuse to incur the expenses of the newly needed treatment without some sort of arrangement for payment. Even if there was a continuing relationship stemming from the first one or two treatments, Budge (D) had a right, with proper notice, to discontinue the relationship. Ricks (P) had ample time to find another treatment alternative in a short time, which he did. I am satisfied from my reading of the record that no injury or damage flowed from the delay occasioned by Ricks (P) leaving the Budge Hospital and going to Cache Valley Hospital.

Analysis:

Is there any valid reason why Ricks' (P) attorney (assuming he was represented) would not assert that the physician-patient relationship began at the time of the first consultation/treatment, rather than asserting that it was ended and subsequently began anew? Technically, Justice Folland is correct. Because Ricks (P) did not assert an ongoing relationship, the court could not rely on such a foundation to sustain the malpractice claim. It is a good thing for Ricks (P) that the court found an alternative theory to hold that a relationship did exist on March 17. If such was the case, and Ricks (P) had been turned away the day he phoned Budge (D) regarding the worsening of his hand, then the case may have turned out differently. Had this come to pass, Ricks' (P) attorney would have been vulnerable to a malpractice claim himself. Justice Folland would have held that a new physician-patient relationship was not formed on March 17. His reasoning rests on contract theory. There are certainly special considerations, however, when an individual in dire peril of life or limb is seeking emergency medical attention. One does not have the luxury of dickering with the doctor under such circumstances.

Childs v. Weis

(Pregnant Woman) v. *(Physician)*

440 S.W.2d 104 (Tex. Ct. Civ. App. 1969)

AN EXPRESS OR IMPLIED CONTRACT BETWEEN A PATIENT AND PHYSICIAN IS REQUIRED TO FORM A PHYSICIAN-PATIENT RELATIONSHIP

■ **INSTANT FACTS** Childs (P) was in labor but turned away from Weis' (D) clinic. Childs (P) ended up giving birth in a car while on the way to another physician. The baby lived about twelve hours.

■ **BLACK LETTER RULE** A physician owes no legal duty to a patient unless there exists a contract between them, either express or implied, giving rise to a physician-patient relationship.

■ **PROCEDURAL BASIS**

Appeal to the Court of Civil Appeals after the trial court granted summary judgment in favor of Weis (D).

■ **FACTS**

In November 1966, Daisy Childs (P), a resident of Dallas County, was about seven months pregnant. Childs (P) was visiting in Lone Oak, Texas. At about 2 a.m. Childs (P) went to the Greenville Hospital emergency room and stated that she was bleeding and had labor pains. The nurse examined Childs (P) and stated she would call the doctor. According to Childs (P), the nurse returned and stated "that the Dr. said that I would have to go to my doctor in Dallas. I stated to [the nurse] that I'm not going to make it to Dallas. [The nurse] stated that I was just starting into labor and that I would make it." About an hour after being turned away by the hospital, Childs (P) had the baby while in a car traveling to medical facilities in Sulphur Springs. The baby lived about twelve hours. Dr. Weis (D) never examined Childs (P), never spoke to her, and never agreed to or consented to the examination or treatment of Childs (P). Weis (P) stated that on the day in question he received a phone call from a nurse in the emergency room who told him that there was "a negro girl in the emergency room having a 'bloody show' and some 'labor pains.'" That the nurse advised him that Childs (P) was visiting the area and her regular doctor lived in Garland, Texas. Weis (P) asserts that he told the nurse over the phone "to have the girl call her doctor in Garland and see what he wanted her to do" and that is the last he heard of the matter.

■ **ISSUE**

Does a physician owe a duty of care to a patient absent some sort of contract, either express or implied, that gives rise to a physician-patient relationship?

■ **DECISION AND RATIONALE**

(Williams, J.) No. It is unquestionably the law that the relationship of physician and patient depends upon a contract, either express or implied. A physician cannot be held liable for arbitrarily refusing to respond to a call of a person even urgently in need of medical attention, provided that the relation of physician and patient does not exist at the time the patient presents herself for treatment. Here there is an entire absence of evidence of contract, either express or implied, which would create a physician-patient relationship between Weis (D) and Childs (P). Under these circumstances, Weis (D) was under

---

no duty whatsoever to examine or treat Childs (P). Weis' (D) actions in telling Childs (P) to call her doctor in Garland were not only reasonable, but completely within the bounds of professional ethics. Weis' (D) statement to the nurse over the phone did not amount to an acceptance of the case. While the nurse may not have relayed in perfect form everything said by Weis (D), such words were uttered by the nurse and cannot be used to make a contract between Weis (D) and Childs (P). Affirmed.

Analysis:

When an individual comes to an emergency room, it is expected that emergency medical attention will be rendered. It can be looked at as a sort of standing offer to the community at large. The act of showing up at the emergency room is acceptance of the offer. A person who suffers loss because of a refusal to treat should be able to recompense that loss under contract theory. Another way to fashion a remedy would be to hold that an emergency room is by its existence a promise of the availability of emergency medical care to anyone in need of that care. When a patient relies on this promise by seeking such care and suffers loss, the hospital can be held liable on promissory estoppel theory. In *Childs*, one is left with a strong suspicion, given the place and the times, that Childs' (P) race played a part in her being turned away. Modern anti-discrimination laws would quite probably proscribe Weis' (D) behavior, but whether they would allow for a private cause of action depends on the particular statutes.

■ CASE VOCABULARY

ESTOPPEL: A legal theory holding that a promise made for no consideration will still be binding if (1) the promisor intends the promise to induce reliance (or should reasonably expect it to), (2) the promise is actually relied on by the promisee, and (3) failure to enforce the promise will cause a detriment or injury to the promisee.

Williams v. United States

(Administrator of Estate) v. *(Hospital Operator)*

242 F.3d 169 (4th Cir. 2001)

NO PRIVATE RIGHT OF ACTION EXISTS FOR DISCRIMINATION IN MEDICAL CARE

■ **INSTANT FACTS** White (P) was denied emergency care at a hospital operated by the Public Health Service (D) because he was not Native American.

■ **BLACK LETTER RULE** State anti-discrimination laws and regulations do not create a cause of action against a hospital that refuses to provide care for racial reasons.

■ PROCEDURAL BASIS

Appeal from an order dismissing an action.

■ FACTS

White (P) became short of breath and started showing signs of respiratory distress. He went to the emergency room of a Native American hospital operated by the United States Public Health Service (D). Hospital employees refused to treat him or to refill his oxygen tank because White (P) was not Native American. The federal law that funded the hospital prohibits treating non-Indians, although hospitals were allowed but not required to provide emergency care to non-Indians. *See* 25 U.S.C. § 1680c. Hospital staff referred White (P) to another hospital, approximately ten miles away. When White (P) arrived at that hospital, he was in extreme respiratory distress and he died the next day.

Williams (P) brought suit on behalf of White (P), claiming that White's (P) death was caused by the refusal to provide care and the delay of access to medical care. The United States (D) moved for dismissal of the complaint, and the motion was granted.

■ ISSUE

Does Williams (P) have a cause of action against the hospital for refusal to treat him based on his non-Indian race?

■ DECISION AND RATIONALE

(Niemeyer, J.) No. State anti-discrimination laws and regulations do not create a cause of action against a hospital that refuses to provide care for racial reasons. Williams (P) cites two state laws and one state regulation that prohibit racial discrimination in providing medical treatment. None of those laws or regulations creates a private right of action. Any enforcement action under those laws belongs to the appropriate state agency.

The duties imposed by law are narrower than the duties imposed by morality. If the allegations of the complaint are true, White's (P) life could have been saved by simple obedience to a moral command. Affirmed.

Analysis:

The Indian Health Service was created to honor treaty commitments to provide health care to various native tribes. Unfortunately, the hospitals and clinics are chronically underfunded—on some reservations, residents say that emergency care is not available unless a person is near death. The statute that allows IHS hospitals to provide emergency care to non-Indians says that factors to be considered include whether providing care to non-Indians will divert resources from Indians, and whether emergency care is available nearby. Note that in this case there was another emergency room ten miles away.

Baber v. Hospital Corporation of America

(Decedent's Brother) v. *(Parent Corporation)*

977 F.2d 872 (4th Cir. 1992)

THE EMERGENCY MEDICAL TREATMENT AND ACTIVE LABOR ACT (EMTALA) DOES NOT PROVIDE FOR A PRIVATE ACTION AGAINST A PHYSICIAN

■ **INSTANT FACTS** Brenda Baber was taken to the hospital for an emergency condition. While there she fell and, unknown to staff, fractured her skull. She died some time later after being transferred twice.

■ **BLACK LETTER RULE** 1) EMTALA does not permit private suits for damages against attending physicians. 2) EMTALA requires that before transfer a patient be given an appropriate medical screening that comports with the hospital's standard screening procedure given the condition of the patient. 3) EMTALA requires a hospital to stabilize a patient before transfer only if it has actual knowledge of an emergency medical condition.

■ **PROCEDURAL BASIS**

Appeal to the federal circuit court of appeals after the district court granted summary judgment in favor of defendants.

■ **FACTS**

Brenda Baber (decedent), accompanied by her brother, Barry Baber (Baber) (P), sought treatment at Raleigh General Hospital (RGH) at 10:40 p.m. on August 5, 1987. Decedent was nauseated, agitated, and thought she might be pregnant. Decedent had stopped taking her anti-psychosis medications and had been drinking heavily. Dr. Kline, the attending physician, ran several tests on decedent and examined her central nervous system, lungs, cardiovascular system and abdomen. While waiting for the test results, decedent continuously paced around the emergency department. Decedent was given medication to calm her, but these did not initially work. While roaming around the department decedent convulsed and fell, striking her head upon a table and lacerating her scalp. Decedent quickly regained consciousness and her laceration was sutured. Decedent did experience some anxiety, disorientation, restlessness, and speech problems, which Dr. Kline concluded were caused by her pre-existing psychiatric problems and alcohol withdrawal. Dr. Kline discussed decedent's condition with her psychiatrist, Dr. Whelan, who concluded her behavior was compatible with her serious psychotic and chronic mental illness. Both doctors were concerned about decedent's seizure in the emergency department and agreed she needed further treatment in a psychiatric ward. RGH did not have such a ward so decedent was transferred to Beckley Appalachian Regional Hospital (BARH). Baber (P) was informed of this plan and neither objected nor consented, but simply requested that decedent be given an x-ray because of the blow to her head when she fell. Dr. Kline did not conclude decedent had a serious head injury so the transfer was ordered. On August 6, decedent was admitted directly into the BARH psych ward where she was restrained and checked on every fifteen minutes but was not given an extensive neurological exam. At the 3:45 a.m. check, decedent was discovered having a grand mal seizure, Decedent was taken to the BARH emergency department and given a CT scan which revealed a fractured skull and a subdural hematoma. Decedent was transferred back to RGH where she could receive more adequate treatment. Upon decedent's arrival back at RGH at 7:00 a.m. she was comatose. Decedent died later that day, apparently as a result of an intracerebrovascular rupture. Baber (P) asserts three violations of the Emergency Medical Treatment and Active Labor Act (EMTALA or the Act) by Dr. Kline, RGH, and its parent corporation: (1) Failure to provide decedent with an "appropriate medical screening examination;" (2) Failure to stabilize decedent's "emergency medical condition;" and (3) Transferring decedent to BARH without first providing stabilizing treatment. The district court treated Defendant Hospital Corporation of America's (HCA)(D) 12(b)(6) motion as a motion for summary judgment and granted it.

■ ISSUE

1) Does EMTALA provide for a private cause of action for damages against an individual physician? 2) Does EMTALA require that an "appropriate medical screening" comport with national standards? 3) Does a hospital violate the EMTALA by transferring a patient when it should have known of the patient's emergency medical condition, but did not have actual knowledge of such condition?

■ DECISION AND RATIONALE

(Williams, CJ.) 1) No. 2) No. 3) No. Baber (P) first asserts that the EMTALA was violated when decedent was not given an "appropriate medical screening." It is urged that we construe the EMTALA as requiring a medical screening to satisfy a national standard of care in order to be "appropriate." The Act does not define "appropriate medical screening examination." The plain language of the statute requires a hospital to develop a screening procedure designed to identify such critical conditions that exist in symptomatic patients and to apply that screening procedure uniformly to all patients with similar complaints. This does not, and cannot, guarantee that all diagnoses will be correct as a result of this screening. The statutory language clearly indicates that EMTALA does not impose a national standard of care. It only requires a hospital to provide a screening exam that is "appropriate" and "within the capability of the hospital's emergency department," including "routinely available" ancillary services. This standard will of necessity be individualized for each hospital because different hospitals have different capabilities. Had Congress wanted a uniform standard it could have clearly specified such a standard. Using this standard of EMTALA we must next determine whether there is any genuine issue of material fact regarding whether RGH provided decedent a medical screening exam that differed from its standard procedure. Baber (P) has offered no evidence of disparate treatment. Instead, it is claimed that Dr. Kline did not do enough to accurately diagnose decedent's condition or to treat her injury. However, accuracy and adequacy are not the critical questions. What is the correct question is whether the hospital deviated from its evaluation procedures that would normally be performed. Dr. Kline's actions did not differ from the standard set by the hospital. While Dr, Kline's assessment and judgment may have been erroneous and not within acceptable standards of medical care, he did perform a screening exam that was not so substandard as to amount to no examination. Therefore, the district court properly granted summary judgment on the medical screening issue. Baber (P) also claims that decedent was inappropriately transferred. EMTALA's transfer requirements do not apply unless the hospital actually determines that there is an emergency medical condition; that is, it had actual knowledge of such condition. If this determination is made the patient must first be stabilized before being transferred. Baber (P) urges us to adopt a standard that would impose liability if the hospital failed to stabilize the patient when it knew or should have known of the emergency medical condition. The plain language of the statute clearly rejects this assertion by stating that the requirement exists only when an "individual ... comes to hospital and the hospital determines that the individual has an emergency medical condition." Baber (P) failed to present any evidence that the hospital had actual knowledge of decedent's emergency medical condition. On the other hand, Dr. Kline stated in his affidavit that decedent's condition was stable prior to transfer and that he did not believe she was suffering from an emergency medical condition. We therefore hold that the district court correctly granted summary judgment on Baber's (P) claim that decedent was transferred in violation of EMTALA. Affirmed.

Analysis:

The Emergency Medical Treatment and Labor Act was passed in order to try and stem the increasing prevalence in the early 1980s of a practice called "patient dumping." Patient dumping was the transfer of patients from private hospitals to public hospitals because the patients did not have the means to pay their medical bills. The vast majority of patients dumped were uninsured. While transferring patients is not normally a problem, many of the patients dumped were not in a condition to withstand being transferred. Hence the EMTALA requirement that all patients be given an "appropriate medical screening" before being transferred. While the Act does allow for private damages suits against hospitals, it does not allow such suits against individual physicians. Only the Department of Health and Human Services may bring an action against an individual physician. The Act applies only to those hospitals that accept Medicare reimbursement and operate an emergency room.

Bragdon v. Abbott

(Dentist) v. *(HIV Patient)*

524 U.S. 624, 118 S.Ct. 2196 (1998)

THE AMERICANS WITH DISABILITIES ACT PREVENTS DISCRIMINATION AGAINST PERSONS WHO ARE HIV POSITIVE UNLESS IT WOULD POSE A DIRECT THREAT TO THE HEALTH OR SAFETY OF OTHERS

■ **INSTANT FACTS** Bragdon (D), a dentist, refused to treat Abbot (P) in the dental clinic because Abbot (P) is HIV positive.

■ **BLACK LETTER RULE** 1) HIV positive status is a physical impairment that affects a major life activity from the time of infection and is thus considered a disability under the Americans with Disabilities Act. 2) Health care providers may not refuse treatment to HIV positive patients on the basis of their infection unless it poses a direct threat to the health or safety of others and there are not any reasonable precautions that would remove the threat.

■ **PROCEDURAL BASIS**

Certification to the U.S. Supreme Court after the Circuit Court of Appeals affirmed the ruling of the trial court granting summary judgment to Abbot (P). Bragdon is the petitioner at this level.

■ **FACTS**

Sidney Abbot (P) was infected with HIV in 1986. On September 16, 1994 (before the infection had manifested its most serious symptoms), Abbot (P) went to the dental office of Bragdon (D) for a routine appointment. Bragdon (D) discovered that Abbot (P) had a cavity that needed filling and informed Abbot (P) that his policy did not allow filling cavities of HIV positive patients in the clinic. Bragdon (D) offered to perform the work at a hospital with no added fee for his services, though Abbot (P) would be responsible for the costs of using the hospital's facilities. Abbot (P) sued Bragdon (D) under § 302 of the Americans with Disabilities Act (ADA), alleging discrimination on the basis of her disability. § 302 bars discrimination by any place of public accommodation "on the basis of disability." A later subchapter excuses a failure to treat or allow participation where "the individual poses a direct threat to the health or safety of others." The District Court entered summary judgment for Abbot (P), and the Circuit Court affirmed.

■ **ISSUE**

1) Is HIV positive status an affliction that constitutes a disability under the ADA? 2) May an individual with a qualifying disability under the ADA be refused the opportunity for treatment or other participation where such participation would pose a direct threat to the health or safety of others even in the face of all reasonable precautions?

■ **DECISION AND RATIONALE**

(Kennedy, J.) 1) Yes. 2) Yes. The ADA defines "disability" as: (a) a physical or mental impairment that substantially limits one or more of the major life activities of such individual .... [The Court states that the ADA's definition of a disability is drawn from the Rehabilitation Act (FRA) and is intended to provide at least as much protection as the definition of handicap in the FRA.] Our first step is to decide if Abbott's (R) HIV status constitutes a physical impairment. HIV infection falls within the general definition of physical impairment as set forth by the Department of Health, Education, and Welfare (HEW) in the regulations interpreting the FRA. In light of the immediacy with which HIV begins to damage the infected person's white blood cells and the severity of the disease, we hold it is an impairment from the moment of infection. For the impairment to be covered under the ADA it must affect a major life activity. Abbot (P) claims that her HIV infection placed a substantial limitation on her ability to reproduce and to bear children. The question thus becomes: is reproduction a major life activity? We have little difficulty concluding that it is. The plain meaning of the word "major" denotes comparative importance and suggests that the touchstone in the inquiry is the activity's significance. Reproduction being central to the life process itself, it falls well within the phrase "major life activity." Now we must determine whether Abbott's (R) physical impairment was a substantial limit on the major life activity she asserts. Abbott's (R) infection substantially limited her ability to reproduce in two independent ways. First, a woman infected with HIV who tries to conceive a child imposes on the man a significant risk of becoming infected. Second, an infected woman risks infecting her child during gestation and childbirth. Because such conception and childbirth are so dangerous to the public health, this meets the definition of a substantial limitation and we thus hold that HIV infection is a qualifying disability under the ADA. We now turn to the issue of whether a private health care provider must perform invasive procedures on an infectious patient in his office, should courts defer to the health care provider's professional judgment, as long as it is reasonable in light of then-current medical knowledge. This issue assumes that the provider's assessment of the objective facts was reasonable. Notwithstanding the protections of the ADA, Ragdon (P) could have refused to treat Abbot (P) if her infectious condition "posed a direct threat to the health or safety of others." The ADA defines a direct threat to be "a significant risk to the health or safety of others that cannot be eliminated by a modification of policies, practices, procedures, or by the provision of auxiliary aids or services." As a health care professional, Bragdon (D) had the duty to assess the risk of infection based on the objective, scientific information available to him and others in his profession. Bragdon's (P) belief that a significant risk existed, even if maintained in good faith, would not relieve him from liability. In assessing the reasonableness Bragdon's (P) actions, the views of public health authorities are of special weight and authority. These views are not conclusive, however. We are concerned that the Court of Appeals may have placed mistaken reliance upon two sources. The Court of Appeals relied on the CDC Dentistry Guidelines and the 1991 American Dental Association Policy on HIV. This evidence is not definitive. They set out the CDC's recommendation that the universal precautions are the best way to combat the risk of HIV transmission. They do not assess the level of risk. Also, without more information on the manner in which the American Dental Association formulated its HIV policy, we are unable to determine the policy's value in evaluating whether Bragdon's (P) assessment of the risk was reasonable as a matter of law. There are also reasons to doubt whether Bragdon (D) advanced evidence sufficient to raise a triable issue of fact on the significance of the risk. Bragdon (D) first asserts that the use of high-speed drills and surface cooling with water created a risk of airborne HIV transmission. A study supporting this position was cited, but the expert witness formed his opinion based on the absence of contrary evidence, not on positive data. Scientific evidence and expert testimony must have traceable, analytical basis in objective fact before it may be considered on summary judgment. Bragdon's (P) also asserts as support that as of September 1994, CDC had identified seven dental workers with possible occupational transmission of HIV. It is unclear whether these workers contracted HIV on the job, however. It is unclear on this record whether this information was available to Bragdon (D) in September 1994. They may have provided more support for Bragdon's (P) position. We conclude the proper course is to give the Court of Appeals an opportunity to apply our foregoing analysis to see if it would change its conclusion that Bragdon (D) presented neither objective evidence nor a triable issue of fact on the question of risk. Remanded for further consideration.

■ CONCURRENCE

(Stevens, J.) I don't believe Bragdon (D) has sustained his burden of providing evidence sufficient to raise a triable issue of fact on the significance of the risk posed by treating Abbot (P) in his office. I join the opinion even though I would prefer an outright affirmance.

■ **CONCURRENCE**

(Ginsburg, J.) I am completely satisfied that Abbott's (R) condition meets the statutory and regulatory definitions of the ADA. I further agree, given the importance of the issue to healthcare workers, that it is wise to remand this case in order to ensure a fully informed determination whether Abbott's (R) disease posed a significant risk that could not be eliminated by a change in policies and/or procedures.

■ **CONCURRENCE AND DISSENT**

(Rehnquist, C.J.) There is not a shred of evidence indicating that, prior to becoming infected, Abbott's (R) major life activities included reproduction, assuming that reproduction is a major life activity. There is absolutely no evidence that, absent the HIV, Abbot (P) would have had or was even considering having children. But even aside from the facts of this particular case, the Court is simply wrong in concluding as a general matter that reproduction is a "major life activity." Fundamental importance of the sort attached to reproduction is not the common thread linking the statute's listed activities. The common thread is rather that the activities are repetitively performed and essential in the day-to-day existence of a normally functioning individual. They are quite different from the series of activities leading to the birth of a child. Even if I agreed that reproduction is a major life activity, I do not agree that an asymptomatic HIV infection "substantially limits" that activity. There is no support in language, logic, or our case law for the proposition that such voluntary choices constitute a "limit" on one's own life activities. I also take issue with the Court's giving more deference to the reports of public health agencies. I am aware of no provision of law or judicial practice that would require or permit courts to give some scientific views more credence than others simply because they have been endorsed by a politically appointed public health authority. Finally, given the "severity of the risk" involved here, *i.e.*, near certain death, and the fact that no public health authority had outlined a protocol for *eliminating* this risk in the context of routine dental treatment, it seems likely that Bragdon (D) can establish that it was objectively reasonable for him to conclude that treating Abbot (P) in his office posed a "direct threat" to his safety.

■ **CONCURRENCE AND DISSENT**

(O'Connor, J.) I agree with The Chief Justice that Abbot (P) has failed to establish that her asymptomatic HIV status substantially limited one or more of her major life activities. Giving birth is not the same as the representative major life activities of all persons—"caring for one's self, performing manual tasks, walking, seeing, hearing, speaking, breathing, learning, and working"—listed in regulations relevant to the ADA. I also agree that the Court of Appeals failed to properly determine whether Abbott's (R) condition posed a direct threat. According, I agree that a remand is necessary on that issue.

Analysis:

The Americans with Disabilities Act prohibits discrimination based on a person's disability, either real or perceived, that substantially affects one or more of that individual's major life activities. As *Bragdon* illustrates, whether an activity is "a major life activity" can often be a very contentious issue. Here the Court decides that reproduction is a major life activity. Did it make the correct ruling? Should the Court promulgate criteria to be used in assessing the likelihood of a woman becoming pregnant in the future? Chief Justice Rehnquist may have raised some eyebrows when he suggested that a woman with asymptomatic HIV is still fully capable of having a child, and thus not "substantially limit[ed]" in such activity.

Howe v. Hull

(Patient's Partner) v. *(On-Call Physician)*

874 F.Supp. 779 (N.D. Ohio 1994)

THE AMERICANS WITH DISABILITIES ACT PROHIBITS A HOSPITAL FROM DENYING TREATMENT DUE TO A DISABILITY

■ **INSTANT FACTS** Mr. Charon (P), infected with HIV, went to the hospital experiencing a reaction to an antibiotic. Dr. Hull (D), the on-call physician, refused to admit Mr. Charon (P), possibly because of his HIV positive status.

■ **BLACK LETTER RULE** 1) The ADA prohibits hospitals from refusing treatment to an individual based, to any extent, on the individual's disability. 2) The Federal Rehabilitation Act (FRA) prohibits hospitals from refusing treatment based solely on an individual's disability.

■ **PROCEDURAL BASIS**

This is an action brought in the federal district court with jurisdiction founded on federal questions under the ADA, FRA, and EMTALA, in which Defendant Howe has moved for summary judgment.

■ **FACTS**

Charon (P) and Howe (P) were traveling through Ohio while on vacation. Charon (P) was HIV-positive. Charon (P) had taken a floxin tablet for the first time that morning. Floxin is a prescription antibiotic. Within two hours of taking the tablet, Charon (P) began experiencing fever, headache, nausea, joint pain and redness of the skin. Charon (P) and Howe (P) sought medical attention at the Fremont Memorial Hospital (FMH) emergency room where Dr. Mark Reardon was on duty. Dr. Reardon testified that Charon (P) was suffering from a severe drug reaction and that the diagnosis was probably Toxic Epidermal Necrolysis (TEN). This diagnosis was recorded in Charon (P)'s record. Dr. Reardon determined that Charon (P) "definitely needed to be admitted" to FMH. It was required that Charon (P) be admitted by the on-call physician, Dr. Hull (D). Dr. Reardon spoke with Dr. Hull (D) by phone and told him that he wanted to admit Charon (P), who was HIV-positive and suffering from a non-HIV related severe drug reaction. Dr. Hull (D) inquired neither into Charon (P)'s physical condition nor vital signs, nor did he ask about the possibility of TEN. During this conversation Dr. Hull (D) told Dr. Reardon that "if you get an AIDS patient in the hospital, you will never get him out," and directed that Charon (P) be sent to the AIDS program at the Medical College of Ohio (MCO). After speaking with Dr. Hull (D), Dr. Reardon told Charon (P) and Howe (P) that "I'm sure you've dealth with this before." Dr. Reardon also stated that "You have to understand, this is a small community, and the admitting doctor does not feel comfortable admitting [Charon (P)]." Charon (P) was not admitted and instead transferred to MCO. It is disputed whether Charon (P) was stabilized prior to the transfer.

■ **ISSUE**

1) Does the Americans with Disabilities Act (ADA) prohibit a medical facility from refusing to treat a patient based in any way on the patient's HIV-positive status? 2) Does the Federal Rehabilitation Act (FRA) prohibit a medical facility from refusing to treat a patient based solely on the patient's HIV-positive status?

■ DECISION AND RATIONALE

(Potter, Sr. J.) 1) Yes. 2) Yes. No matter the reason for FMH's transfer of Charon (P), it did not violate the Emergency Medical Transfer and Active Labor Act (EMTALA) so long as Charon (P) was stabilized prior to transfer. The initial inquiry then focuses on whether Charon (P) was stabilized before transfer. A medical expert testified that he did not agree that there was no material deterioration of Charon's (P) condition during transfer and that there was a "50/50 chance" of such deterioration at the time of transfer. He further testified that he would have been uncomfortable transferring Charon (P). Given these and other factors, a jury could reasonably conclude that the TEN diagnosis was a fabrication or ad hoc justification for Charon's (P) transfer. Dr. Hull's (D) statements about AIDS patients could cause a jury to believe the sole reason for transfer was Charon's (P) HIV status. Also, if the jury found that Charon's (P) actual diagnosis was a non-AIDS-related drug reaction, it could reasonably find that FMH transferred Charon (P), while he was unstable, without providing him necessary medical care. The motion for summary judgment on the EMTALA claim is therefore denied. We now turn to Howe's (P) ADA and FRA claims. Discrimination can take the form of the denial of the opportunity to receive medical treatment based upon a disability. To establish a prima facie case under the FRA a plaintiff must show (a) the plaintiff has a disability; (b) plaintiff was otherwise qualified to participate in the program; (c) defendants discriminated against plaintiff solely on the basis of the disability; and (d) the program received federal funding. As we have already stated, a reasonable jury could conclude that the TEN diagnosis was a pretext and that Charon (P) was denied treatment solely because of his disability. Summary judgment on the FRA claim is therefore denied. Dr. Hull (D) and FMH argue that the "solely on the basis of" standard that appears in the FRA should be imported into the ADA as well. It is conspicuous that Congress used the word "solely" in the FRA, but not in the ADA. This fact militates in favor of not importing the "solely" requirement into the ADA. It is thus quite clear that use of this language was a purposeful act of Congress and not a drafting error. The inquiry under the ADA, then, is whether Howe (D), despite the articulated reasons for the transfer, improperly considered Charon's (P) HIV-positive status in refusing to admit and treat Charon (P). The Court finds that Howe (P) has presented sufficient evidence to preclude a grant of summary judgment on these claims.

Analysis:

There has been much consternation and several law review articles written on the subject of whether the "solely" standard of the FRA should be read into the ADA as well. The vast majority of the circuit courts that have taken a position on what standard the ADA requires hold that the "solely" standard of the Rehabilitation Act is correct. For example, in *Keys v. Joseph Beth Booksellers, Inc.*, the Sixth Circuit stated that the third element needed for an ADA complaint to survive summary judgment is that the plaintiff "was discriminated against solely because of his disability." The court does so after quoting the ADA's prohibition of discrimination against an employee "because of [a] disability," and without referring to the Rehabilitation Act. As the *Howe* court illustrates, however, there are several courts that rely on the fact that Congress obviously knew how to use the word "solely," and its failure to do so in the ADA is a strong indication that the "solely" standard is inappropriate in ADA cases.

CHAPTER NINE

Private Health Insurance and Managed Care: State Regulation and Liability

Lubeznik v. HealthChicago, Inc.

Instant Facts: A cancer patient's insurance company denied her coverage for special treatments, claiming that it was "experimental" and, therefore, not a covered benefit under her insurance policy.

Black Letter Rule: Where an insurer seeks to deny insurance coverage based on an exclusionary clause contained in an insurance policy, the clause must be clear and free from doubt; any doubts with respect to coverage are resolved in favor of the insured.

Colonial Life Insurance Company of America v. Curiale

Instant Facts: The Superintendent of Insurance (D) promulgated two regulations establishing a shared risk pool system which the plaintiff challenged as exceeding the Superintendent's (D) authority.

Black Letter Rule: It is constitutional for states to require insurance companies to assume equal risks by requiring payments into a pool.

Lubeznik v. HealthChicago, Inc.

(*Cancer Patient*) v. (*Insurance Company*)

268 Ill.App.3d 953, 206 Ill.Dec. 9, 644 N.E.2d 777 (1994)

COVERAGE PROVISIONS IN AN INSURANCE CONTRACT ARE TO BE LIBERALLY CONSTRUED IN FAVOR OF THE INSURED TO PROVIDE THE BROADEST POSSIBLE COVERAGE

■ **INSTANT FACTS** A cancer patient's insurance company denied her coverage for special treatments, claiming that it was "experimental" and, therefore, not a covered benefit under her insurance policy.

■ **BLACK LETTER RULE** Where an insurer seeks to deny insurance coverage based on an exclusionary clause contained in an insurance policy, the clause must be clear and free from doubt; any doubts with respect to coverage are resolved in favor of the insured.

■ **PROCEDURAL BASIS**

Appeal from the trial court's judgment in favor of the plaintiff.

■ **FACTS**

In November 1988, Lubeznik (P) was diagnosed with Stage III ovarian cancer. At the time of her diagnosis, the cancer had spread through her abdomen and liver and she had a 20% survival rate over the next five years. In June 1991, Lubeznik (P) was referred to Dr. Stiff at Loyola University Medical Center. Dr. Stiff was to determine the prospect of treating Lubeznik (P) with HDCT/ABMT, a state of the art treatment for leukemia and Hodgkin's disease for many years. It began to be used in the late 1980s for women who were in the late stages of breast cancer. On October 28, 1991, Dr. Stiff contacted HealthChicago (D) requesting that it pre-certify (agree in advance to pay for the treatment) Lubeznik (P) for the HDCT/ABMT. Her insurance policy required her to get pre-certified before receiving elective treatment, procedures and therapies. Dr. Mathy, HealthChicago's (D) medical director, told Dr. Stiff that the ABMT/HDCT was not a covered benefit under Lubeznik's (P) insurance policy because the treatment was considered experimental. The policy provided that "[e]xperimental medical, surgical, or other procedures as determed by the [Insurance] Plan in conjunction with appropriate medical tehnology assessment bodies" are excluded. On October 31, 1991, Lubeznik (P) filed a two-count complaint against HealthChicago (D) and Loyola, seeking injunctions for pre-certification and admission without a deposit. Both HealthChicago (D) and Loyola filed motions to dismiss the complaint, and subsequently, Lubeznik (P) took a voluntary non-suit against Loyola. The trial court denied the motion to dismiss, and after a hearing issued an injunction against HealthChicago (D) ruling that the ABMT/HDCT is not an experimental therapy for ovarian cancer. HealthChicago (D) then filed this appeal.

■ **ISSUE**

Did the trial court err in determining that the plaintiff's treatment was covered by her policy and was not an excluded benefit as an experimental treatment?

■ DECISION AND RATIONALE

(Johnson, J.) No. Where an insurer seeks to deny insurance coverage based on an exclusionary clause contained in an insurance policy, the clause must be clear and free from doubt. This is so because all doubts with respect to coverage are resolved in favor of the insured. After carefully reviewing the evidence, we agree that the trial court properly determined the HDCT/ABMT to be a covered benefit under Lubeznik's (P) insurance policy. We disagree with HealthChicago's (D) contention that the exclusionary language was clear and unambiguous. We note that Lubeznik's (P) insurance policy does not define the phrase "appropriate medical technology boards." The plain language of the policy does not indicate who will determine whether a certain medical board is appropriate. Thus, the phrase, without more, gives rise to a genuine uncertainty about which medical boards are considered appropriate and how and by whom the determination is made. Additionally, we must note that even if the exclusionary language did apply, HealthChicago (D) failed to follow the terms of the insurance policy. Lubeznik's insurance policy excludes from coverage medical and surgical procedures that are considered experimental by HealthChicago (D) "in conjunction with appropriate technology assessment bodies." At the hearing, Dr. Mathy testified that upon learning of Lubeznik's (P) pre-certification request, he had already determined that the HDCT/ABMT was experimental prior to receiving or reviewing any information from the medical assessment boards. Given our careful review of the evidence, including HealthChicago's (D) admitted disregard for the terms of the insurance policy, we hold that the trial court did not err in ruling that the requested treatment was a covered benefit under the policy. Lastly, HealthChicago (D) claims that the trial court improperly granted the mandatory injunction because Lubeznik (P) failed to meet the requirements for an injunction to issue. An injunction may be granted only after the plaintiff establishes that (1) a lawful right exists; (2) irreparable injury will result if the injunction is not granted; and (3) his or her remedy at law is inadequate. Dr. Stiff testified that the HDCT/ABMT was an effective treatment for Lubeznik (P) and offered her a "very high chance of a complete disappearance of her disease." In addition, when asked during direct examination to give a prognosis of Lubeznik's (P) condition, Dr. Stiff stated that [without the treatment] she "has a fatal illness with a zero percent to one percent chance of being alive at five years, let alone alive and disease free." Given the evidence presented at the hearing, including Dr. Stiff's testimony, we agree that Lubeznik (P) showed that she would suffer irreparable harm without the treatment. Therefore, we hold that the trial court did not abuse its discretion in granting the requested injunctive relief.

Analysis:

Courts have traditionally viewed insurance contracts as adhesion contracts and interpreted them under the doctrine of contra proferentum. This has made it difficult for insurance companies to control their exposure to risk through general clauses that refuse payment for care that is not "medically necessary" or that is "experimental." Usually, when such clauses are litigated, as in this case, the treating physician testifies that care is standard and is urgently necessary, and the insurer's medical director testifies that the care is experimental or unnecessary. So the question for the court becomes who to believe. As the court mentioned here, coverage provisions in an insurance contract are to be liberally construed in favor of the insured to provide the broadest possible coverage. In determining whether a certain provision in an insurance contract is applicable, a trial court must first determine whether the specific provision is ambiguous. A provision that is clear or unambiguous must be applied as written. When a provision is ambiguous, its language must be construed in favor of the insured.

■ CASE VOCABULARY

ADHESION CONTRACT: A contract with basically a "take it or leave it" basis, where the weaker party has no realistic choice as to its terms.

ANSWER INSTANTER: An immediate response to the pleadings, usually within 24 hours.

DOCTRINE OF CONTRA PROFERENTUM: Contrary to the way contracts *should* be entered (e.g. meaningful choice on the part of all parties to the contract).

INJUNCTION: A court order prohibiting someone from doing some specified act or commanding someone to undo some wrong or injury.

Colonial Life Insurance Company of America v. Curiale

(Insurance Company) v. *(Superintendent of Insurance)*

205 A.D.2d 58, 617 N.Y.S.2d 377 (1994)

A STATE MAY REQUIRE HEALTH INSURANCE COMPANIES TO POOL FUNDS AND SHARE RISKS

■ **INSTANT FACTS** The Superintendent of Insurance (D) promulgated two regulations establishing a shared risk pool system which the plaintiff challenged as exceeding the Superintendent's (D) authority.

■ **BLACK LETTER RULE** It is constitutional for states to require insurance companies to assume equal risks by requiring payments into a pool.

■ **PROCEDURAL BASIS**

Cross-appeals by both parties from the adverse portions of the court's judgment.

■ **FACTS**

Colonial Life (P) is a commercial insurance company which issues small group health insurance policies. It challenged two regulations promulgated by the Superintendent of Insurance (D) to implement chapter 501 of the Laws of 1992. Chapter 501 requires a commercial insurer to employ "community rating" and to offer "open enrollment" for any insurance policies issued. The new law was to spread the risk among more people and provide greater rate stability. The Superintendent (D) was directed to promulgate regulations designed to protect insurers writing policies from claim fluctuations and "unexpected significant shifts in the number of persons insured." Pursuant thereto, the Superintendent (D) promulgated 11 NYCRR parts 360 and 361 which implemented what he deemed a statutory directive that insurers be required to share the risk of high-cost claims by establishing a pool system which compares the risk of insurers in seven regions of the State. After these comparisons were made, insurers with worse than average demographic factors would get money from regional pooling funds, while insurers with better than average factors would pay money into these pooling funds. Colonial Life (P) commenced this proceeding seeking to have 11 NYCRR parts 360 and 361 invalidated. The court dismissed the petition to the extent that it challenged part 361, but granted the petition with respect to part 360. Both parties have cross-appealed from the adverse portions of the judgment.

■ **ISSUE**

Is it constitutional for the State to require insurance companies to assume equal risks by requiring payments into a pool?

■ **DECISION AND RATIONALE**

(Peters, J.) Yes. The Superintendent of Insurance's interpretation of the Insurance Law provisions is entitled to great deference because of his special competence and expertise with respect to the insurance industry unless such interpretation is irrational or contrary to the clear wording of a statutory provision. Colonial Life (P) contends that 11 NYCRR part 361 imposes an unconstitutional tax, gives State money to private organizations and takes property without just compensation. Our review indicates that the Legislature intended pool payments be mandatory and that those payments consist of the amounts necessary to permit sharing or equalization of the risk of high cost claims. Having chosen to require such payments, the Legislature could therefore delegate the responsibility to the Superintendent (D) to collect such amounts. We find that such pool contributions are a valid exercise of the Legislature's power to regulate and as the enactment intended to regulate rather than generate revenue it is not a tax. We find, as did the Supreme Court, that Colonial Life (P) cannot support its contention that it has a constitutionally protected interest in maintaining a healthier than average risk pool. The Supreme Court invalidated 11 NYCRR part 360, holding that it exceeded the scope of the authority delegated to the Superintendent by chapter 501. Should the Superintendent's regulation be permitted to stand, it would run counter to the legislative directive that the implementing regulations shall not require any insurer to enter any line of business as a condition of continuing in any other line o business. Hence, as the Supreme Court reasoned, since an administrative agency may not promulgate a regulation that adds a requirement that does not exist under the statute, we affirm the Supreme Court's determination to annul this provision. Thus the judgment of the Supreme Court is affirmed in its entirety.

Analysis:

By manipulating coverage, imposing cost-sharing obligations, and marketing selectively, as well as by creating "association" plans or using other devices that allow small group or individual plans to masquerade as large group plans, insurers can still often control the risk to which they are exposed, allowing them on the one hand to remain prosperous, but on the other hand, to continue to exclude high-risk individuals. To a considerable degree, however, the effects that small group reforms might have had on insurers or insureds has been masked by a dramatic growth of managed care in small group markets, which has held down increases in premiums that reforms might otherwise have caused

■ CASE VOCABULARY

COMMUNITY RATING: Requires the insurer to base the policy premium on the experience of the entire pool of risks covered by that policy without regard to age, sex, health status or occupation.

OPEN ENROLLMENT: Provides that any individual or small group applying for health insurance must be accepted for any coverage offered by the insurer.

CHAPTER TEN

Regulation of Insurance and Managed Care: The Federal Role

Rush Prudential HMO, Inc. v. Moran

Instant Facts: Moran (P) sought independent review of Rush's (D) denial of benefits pursuant to a state law, and Rush (D) claimed that ERISA preempted the state law claim.

Black Letter Rule: ERISA does not preempt a state insurance regulatory scheme that does not provide a new cause of action under state law and that does not authorize a new form of ultimate relief.

Retail Industry Leaders Association v. Fielder

Instant Facts: The State of Maryland (D) enacted legislation requiring large employers to pay a certain percentage of their payroll toward health insurance costs of employees, and the Retail Industry Leaders (P) claimed the law was preempted by ERISA.

Black Letter Rule: A state law is preempted by ERISA if it directly regulates or effectively mandates some part of the structure or administration of employers' ERISA plans.

Pegram v. Herdrich

Instant Facts: An HMO and its physician are sued for medical malpractice and charged with a breach of an ERISA fiduciary duty, after a patient complaining of abdominal pain and showing noticeable inflammation is injured, due the physician's decision to have the patient wait eight more days for proper treatment at a facility staffed by the HMO.

Black Letter Rule: Mixed eligibility and treatment decisions by HMO physicians are not fiduciary decisions under ERISA.

Aetna Health, Inc. v. Davila

Instant Facts: Davila (P) brought suit in state court against Aetna (D) for failure to exercise ordinary care in handling coverage decisions, and Aetna (D) sought to remove the case to federal court.

Black Letter Rule: All actions brought for the denial of benefits by an ERISA-regulated benefit plan fall within the scope of, and are preempted by, ERISA.

Doe v. Group Hospitalization & Medical Services

Instant Facts: A patient diagnosed with a rare form of blood cancer sues a health care plan for its denial of benefits for cancer treatment, made pursuant to an amendment in the patient's insurance contract, claiming that the health care plan improperly amended the contract, and that regardless, the contract language as amended did not exclude coverage for the treatment.

Black Letter Rule: Where an administrator or fiduciary is operating under a conflict of interest, courts should review the merits of a plan interpretation to determine whether it is consistent with that of a fiduciary free of the conflict.

Winslow v. IDS Life Insurance Co.

Instant Facts: An individual currently treated for mild depression, files an action against an insurance company under the ADA and the state's human rights act, after the insurance company denied the individual coverage based on their policy which categorically denies long-term disability insurance to those being treated for mental or nervous conditions.

Black Letter Rule: The categorical denial of access to insurance coverage to a class of disabled individuals is a violation of the ADA.

Rush Prudential HMO, Inc. v. Moran

(Health Insurer) v. *(Insured)*

536 U.S. 355, 122 S.Ct. 2151, 153 L.Ed.2d 375 (2002)

ERISA DOES NOT PREEMPT STATE STATUTES THAT REQUIRE REVIEWING MEDICAL NECESSITY DETERMINATIONS

■ **INSTANT FACTS** Moran (P) sought independent review of Rush's (D) denial of benefits pursuant to a state law, and Rush (D) claimed that ERISA preempted the state law claim.

■ **BLACK LETTER RULE** ERISA does not preempt a state insurance regulatory scheme that does not provide a new cause of action under state law and that does not authorize a new form of ultimate relief.

■ **PROCEDURAL BASIS**

Appeal from an order of the Seventh Circuit Court of Appeals, reversing a trial court's denial of Moran's (P) claim.

■ **FACTS**

Moran (P) was a beneficiary under a health insurance plan administered by Rush Prudential (D). On the recommendation of her physician, she sought a particular treatment for her shoulder, but was told that Rush (D) would not pay for that treatment because it was not "medically necessary." Moran (P) made a written demand for an independent medical review of her claim, as authorized by the Illinois HMO Act. Rush (D) did not provide the independent review, and Moran (P) brought suit in state court to compel the review. Moran (P) had the requested surgery at her own expense while her suit was pending. She submitted a claim for reimbursement, which Rush (D) denied. Rush (D) removed the case to federal court, arguing that Moran's (P) cause of action was completely preempted by ERISA. The federal court remanded the case back to state court, concluding that Moran's (P) claim was not completely preempted by ERISA, because the request for an independent review would not require interpretation of an ERISA plan. The state court ordered Rush to submit to review by an independent physician.

The reviewer determined that the surgery was medically necessary, but Rush (D) refused to concede and continued to deny the claim. Moran (P) amended her complaint to seek reimbursement, and Rush (D) again removed the case to federal court, arguing that the suit was now a claim for ERISA benefits and was therefore preempted by the civil enforcement provisions in ERISA. The federal court treated Moran's (P) claim as a claim under ERISA and held that ERISA preempted the Illinois independent review statute. Moran's (P) claim was denied. The Seventh Circuit Court of Appeals reversed the trial court.

■ **ISSUE**

Does ERISA preempt the Illinois independent medical review statute?

■ **DECISION AND RATIONALE**

(Souter, J.) No. ERISA does not preempt a state regulatory scheme that does not provide a new cause of action under state law and that does not authorize a new form of ultimate relief. Although ERISA expressly preempts state laws that relate to employee benefit plans, ERISA also contains a saving

---

clause that says that state insurance, banking, or securities laws are not preempted. The independent review statute is saved from preemption only because it regulates insurance.

State regulation of insurance will be preempted if the regulation allows the participants in a plan to obtain remedies not available under ERISA. The case of *Pilot Life Ins. Co. v. Dedeaux,* 481 U.S. 41 (1987), rejected common-law tort and contract claims brought by an ERISA plan participant. The Court went on to hold that Congress intended a federal common law of rights and obligations to develop under ERISA, without embellishment by independent state remedies. Rush (D) argues that the independent review statute creates a form of binding arbitration that would supplant the judicial review provisions of ERISA.

The independent review statute does not create a new remedy. Independent review under the statute may well settle the fate of a benefit claim. Nevertheless, the independent review statute does not enlarge the claim beyond the benefits authorized by ERISA. Although the reviewer's determination as to what is "medically necessary" under the contract would presumably replace the determination by the HMO, the relief that is ultimately available would still be the same relief authorized by ERISA in a suit for benefits. Minor procedural disuniformities are the inevitable result of the congressional decision to allow state regulation of insurance.

A state could provide for a type of review that would be so much like an adjudication that it would run afoul of the bar in *Pilot Life.* Rush (D) and the dissent argue that the Illinois independent review statute does that by imposing an alternate scheme for arbitration that goes against the congressional purpose of confining adjudication to the courts. The Illinois statute resembles an arbitration provision to the extent that an independent reviewer considers disputes about the meaning of the contract and receives "evidence." On the other hand, the reviewer is not given a free-ranging power to construe contract terms, but is limited to construing only the term "medical necessity." The independent examiner must be a physician with credentials similar to the primary care physician and is expected to render independent medical judgment. The review thus looks less like arbitration, and more like a practice of obtaining another medical opinion. Obtaining another opinion is far removed from an enforcement scheme.

Rush (D) also argues that the review statute clashes with a substantive rule providing a deferential standard of review for benefit denials. ERISA does not require any particular standard of review, however. The law requires only that plan beneficiaries have some mechanism for internal review of a benefit denial. The standard of review employed is simply a matter of plan design or the drafting of an HMO contract. The Illinois statute prohibits designing an insurance contract to provide unfettered discretion to the insurer. ERISA's enforcement scheme is not implicated at all.

Illinois has chosen to regulate insurance as one way of regulating the practice of medicine. Regulating insurance tied to what is medically necessary is probably inseparable from enforcing the quintessentially state-law standards of reasonable medical care. Affirmed.

■ DISSENT

(Thomas, J.) The Illinois independent review statute cannot be characterized as anything other than an alternative state-law remedy or vehicle for seeking benefits. The statute comes into play only if there is a dispute about an entitlement to benefits. As a binding decision on the merits of a controversy, the statutory review resembles nothing so much as an arbitration. The majority is wrong to characterize the review as nothing more than obtaining a second medical opinion. A second medical opinion is just that—an opinion. A determination under the review statute is a conclusive determination with respect to the award of benefits. Independent review provisions make it more likely that HMOs will have to subsidize the beneficiaries' treatment of choice, making it harder to control costs, and thus making it harder for employers to provide medical coverage to their employees.

Analysis:

Whether a particular treatment is medically necessary is not addressed by the statute, but is defined by the HMO contract. The contract at issue in this case contained a detailed definition of whether a treatment would be considered medically necessary, so that the issue for review was an interpretation of that contractual provision. The surgery Moran (P) wanted is described in detail in the opinion of the court of appeals. *See Moran v. Rush Prudential HMO, Inc.,* 230 F.3d 959 (7th Cir. 2000). Briefly, it was a more complex version of the nerve reconstruction surgery that would have been approved by Rush (D) for her condition.

■ CASE VOCABULARY

ERISA: Employee Retirement Income Security Act. A federal statute that regulates private pension plans and employee benefit plans and that established the Pension Benefit Guaranty Corporation.

HMO: Health Maintenance Organization. A group of participating health care providers that furnish medical services to enrolled members of a group health-insurance plan.

Retail Industry Leaders Association v. Fielder

(Employers' Association) v. *(State Secretary of Labor, Licensing, and Regulation)*

475 F.3d 180 (4th Cir. 2007)

STATE LAWS REQUIRING EMPLOYERS TO PAY HEALTH INSURANCE COSTS ARE PREEMPTED BY ERISA

"Do unto others" is preempted by ERISA?!?

stus.com

■ **INSTANT FACTS** The State of Maryland (D) enacted legislation requiring large employers to pay a certain percentage of their payroll toward health insurance costs of employees, and the Retail Industry Leaders (P) claimed the law was preempted by ERISA.

■ **BLACK LETTER RULE** A state law is preempted by ERISA if it directly regulates or effectively mandates some part of the structure or administration of employers' ERISA plans.

■ **PROCEDURAL BASIS**

Appeal from an order enjoining enforcement of a state law.

■ **FACTS**

In 2006, the State of Maryland (D) enacted the Fair Share Healthcare Fund Act. The law required employers with 10,000 or more Maryland employees to spend at least eight percent of their payrolls on employees' health insurance costs. As an alternative, employers could pay the amount their healthcare spending falls short of the eight percent minimum into a state fund that would be used to support the Maryland Medical Assistance Program. The Maryland law was passed after the General Assembly heard testimony about the rising costs of the Maryland Medical Assistance Program. The General Assembly directed its attention particularly to Wal–Mart (P), because of claims that Wal–Mart (P) provided substandard healthcare benefits to its employees, and that many of its employees ended up in state-sponsored public health programs. Wal–Mart (P) provided health coverage to approximately forty-five percent of its total workforce. The Fair Share Act was in fact crafted to cover just Wal–Mart (P). Of the four employers in Maryland with at least 10,000 employees, only Wal–Mart (P) fell short of the minimum spending threshold. The General Assembly assumed that Wal–Mart (P) would increase its healthcare spending, rather than make payments to the state. Wal–Mart (P) and the Retail Industry Leaders (P) claimed that the Fair Share Act was preempted by ERISA.

■ **ISSUE**

Is the Maryland Fair Share Act preempted by ERISA?

■ **DECISION AND RATIONALE**

(Niemeyer, J.) Yes. A state law is preempted by ERISA if it directly regulates or effectively mandates some part of the structure or administration of employers' ERISA plans. The only rational choice employers have under the Fair Share Act is to restructure their healthcare plans to meet the minimum spending threshold. The Act thus has an "obvious connection" with employee benefit plans, because it effectively mandates that employers structure their plans to provide a certain level of benefits. The Act is therefore preempted by ERISA.

The important question in the instant case is whether Congress would have intended that the Fair Share Act be preempted. To make this determination, the court should look at the objectives of ERISA, as well as the nature of the effect the law would have on ERISA plans. The primary objective of ERISA is to provide a uniform regulatory regime over employee benefit plans. The provisions of ERISA that preempt state laws aim to minimize the burdens of complying with different state and federal regulatory requirements and to reduce the "tailoring" of plans and employer conduct to each jurisdiction. A state law relates to an ERISA plan if it has a "connection with or reference to" such a plan.

The State of Maryland (D) argues that the Fair Share Act is intended to collect funds for the Medical Assistance Program. The core provision of the Act, however, aims at requiring covered employers to provide medical benefits to employees. This provision will force employers to structure their recordkeeping and benefit spending to comply with the Act. The Act would disrupt employers' uniform administration of benefit plans. The problem would likely arise in other states, as other state and local governments adopt spending mandates that would clash with the Fair Share Act. If these laws were permitted to stand, Wal–Mart would have to tailor its healthcare benefit plans to each specific state, and to specific counties and cities.

Maryland (D) also argues that the Act is not mandatory, and therefore does not have a connection with employee benefit plans because employers have two options to avoid increasing benefits. An employer may increase healthcare spending on employees in ways that do not qualify as ERISA plans, or employers may refuse to increase benefits and pay the state the amount by which their spending falls short of eight percent. Increasing spending in ways that do not constitute an ERISA plan is not a meaningful option. Health Savings Accounts, one example of non-ERISA spending, are not always an option. Not all employees are eligible to establish accounts, and, even if an employee is eligible, accounts must be established voluntarily by the employee. The narrow circumstances under which an employer would not be forced to increase spending on healthcare plans only reinforces the conclusion that the effect of the Act would be to mandate spending increases. In fact, Wal–Mart (P) averred that it would increase healthcare spending rather than pay Maryland (D). Affirmed.

■ DISSENT

(Michael, J.) The Maryland law does not require a covered employer to make a choice that has an impact on an employee benefit plan. An employer can comply with the law either by increasing payments for health insurance or by paying assessments into a special fund. There is no preference for one method of support. The law is not preempted by ERISA.

Analysis:

The legislative history of the Act, which emphasized Wal–Mart (D) and its record on providing healthcare benefits to its employees, provides support for the majority's finding that the Fair Share Act concerned ERISA plans. Although the statute gave employers options other than those specifically relating to ERISA plans, the court dismisses those other options. The discussion emphasizes ERISA benefit plans as the only "rational" choice, probably because the legislature assumed that was the option employers would take.

■ CASE VOCABULARY

ERISA: Employee Retirement Income Security Act.

PREEMPTION: The principle (derived from the Supremacy Clause) that a federal law can supersede or supplant any inconsistent state law or regulation.

Pegram v. Herdrich

(Patient) v. *(Physician and HMO)*

530 U.S. 211, 120 S.Ct. 2143, 147 L.Ed2d 164 (2000)

MIXED ELIGIBILITY/TREATMENT DECISIONS ARE NOT ACTS OF PLAN ADMINISTRATION THAT "RELATE TO" ERISA

■ **INSTANT FACTS** An HMO and its physician are sued for medical malpractice and charged with a breach of an ERISA fiduciary duty, after a patient complaining of abdominal pain and showing noticeable inflammation is injured, due the physician's decision to have the patient wait eight more days for proper treatment at a facility staffed by the HMO.

■ **BLACK LETTER RULE** Mixed eligibility and treatment decisions by HMO physicians are not fiduciary decisions under ERISA.

■ **PROCEDURAL BASIS**

Certification to the United States Supreme Court, of a judgment by the Court of Appeals reversing the District Courts grant of motion to dismiss for failure to state a claim.

■ **FACTS**

Carle Clinic Association, P.C., Health Alliance Medical Plans Inc., and Carle Health Insurance Management Co., Inc (collectively Carle) (D2) function as a health maintenance organization (HMO) organized for profit. Lori Pegram (Dr. Pegram) (D1), a Carle (D2) physician, examined Cynthia Herdrich (Herdrich) (P), who was covered by Carle (D2) through her husband's employer, State Farm Insurance. Herdrich (P) complained of pain in the midline area of her groin, and six days later, Dr. Pegram (D1) discovered a six by eight centimeter inflamed mass in Herdrich's (P) abdomen. Despite the noticeable inflammation, Dr. Pegram (D1) did not order an ultrasound diagnostic procedure at a local hospital, but instead decided to have Herdrich (P) wait eight more days for an ultrasound to be performed at a facility staffed by Carle more than 50 miles away. Before the eight days were over, Herdrich's (P) appendix ruptured, causing peritonitis. Herdrich (P) sued Dr. Pegram (D1) and Carle (D2) in state court for medical malpractice, and later added two counts charging state-law fraud. Dr. Pegram (D1) and Carle (D2) responded that ERISA preempted the new counts, and removed the case to federal court. The District Court granted their motion for summary judgment on the second fraud count, but granted Herdrich (P) leave to amend the one remaining. Herdrich (P) did this by alleging that the provision of medical services under the terms of the Carle (D2) HMO organization, rewarding its physician owners for limiting medical care, entailed an inherent or anticipatory breach of an ERISA fiduciary duty, since these terms created an incentive to make decisions in the physicians' self interest rather than the exclusive interest of plan participants. Herdrich (P) sought relief under *29 U.S.C. § 1109(a)* [which generally states that a fiduciary of a plan who breaches his or her duties, shall be personally liable to make good to such plan any losses to the plan resulting from each such breach, to restore to such plan any profits of such fiduciary which have been made through use of assets of the plan by the fiduciary, and shall be subject to such other equitable or remedial relief as the court may deem appropriate]. Carle (D2) moved to dismiss the ERISA count for failure to state a claim upon which relief can be granted, and the District Court, agreeing that Carle (D2) was not involved in these events as an ERISA fiduciary, granted the motion. After prevailing on the original malpractice counts and receiving $35,000 for injuries, Herdrich (P) appealed the dismissal of the ERISA claim. The Court of Appeals reversed, holding that incentives can rise to the level of breach where, as pleaded here, the fiduciary trust between plan participants and plan fiduciaries no longer exists. Therefore, Carle (D2) was acting as a fiduciary when its physicians made the challenged decisions and that Herdrich's (P) allegations were sufficient to state a claim. Carle (D2) appeals.

■ ISSUE

Are mixed eligibility and treatment decisions by HMO physicians, fiduciary decisions under ERISA?

■ DECISION AND RATIONALE

(Souter, J.) No. Traditionally, medical care in the United States has been provided on a "fee-for-service" basis, allowing a physician to bill the patient for the services provided, or if there is insurance and the doctor is willing, bill the insurance company for the patient's care. In this system, a physician's financial incentive is to provide more care, not less, so long as payment is forthcoming. The check on this incentive is a physician's obligation to exercise reasonable medical skill and judgment in the patient's interest. By the late 1960's insurers and others developed new models for health-care delivery, including HMOs, which consisted of the receipt of a fixed fee for each patient enrolled. The HMO thus assumes the financial risk of providing the benefits promised, keeping the money if the patient never gets sick, but then being responsible for the treatment agreed upon even if its cost exceeds the participant's premium. Like other risk-bearing organizations, HMOs take steps to control costs by, for example, scrutinizing services against the contractual provisions to make sure that a request for care falls within the scope of covered circumstances. Their physicians are generally given guidelines about the appropriate levels of care, and commonly require utilization review (where a decision maker other than the treating physician reviews a treatment decision) and approval in advance for many types of care, keyed to standards of medical necessity or the reasonableness of a proposed treatment. These measures are commonly complemented by specific financial incentives to physicians, rewarding them for decreasing utilization of health-care services, and penalizing them for what may be found to be excessive treatment. Thus in an HMO system, a physician's financial interest lies in providing less care, not more, and the check for this influence is the professional obligation to provide covered services with a reasonable degree of skill and judgment in the patient's interest. No matter the form of medical organization, the adequacy of professional obligation to counter financial self-interest has been challenged. While fee-for service physicians were thought to be providing unnecessary or useless service, it is argued that HMOs often ignore the individual needs of a patient in order to improve the HMO's bottom line.

Herdrich (P) focuses on the Carle (D) scheme's provision for a "year-end distribution" to the HMO's physician owners, arguing that this incentive device of annually paying physician owners the profit resulting from their own decisions rationing care can distinguish Carle's (D) organization from HMOs generally, so that reviewing Carle's (D) decision under a fiduciary standard would not open the door to like claims about other HMO structures. Although it is true here that the relationship between sparing medical treatment and physician reward is not subtle, no HMO organization could survive without some incentive connecting physician reward with treatment rationing, since inducement to ration care goes to the very point of any HMO scheme, and necessarily raises some risks while reducing others. Any legal principle purporting to draw a line between good and bad HMOs would embody a judgment about socially acceptable medical risks. A judgment of this sort would necessarily turn on facts to which the court does not have ready access to, and thus such complicated factfinding and debatable social judgment is better handled through the legislative process. Therefore, we assume that the decision listed in the complaint cannot be subject to a claim that they violate fiduciary standards unless all such decisions by all HMOs acting through their owner or employee physicians are to be judged by the same standard and subject to the same claim. Turning now to the requirements of ERISA, we see that a fiduciary must be someone acting in the capacity of a manager, administrator, or financial adviser to a "plan," and accordingly, Herdrich's (P) ERISA count charges Carle (D2) with a breach of fiduciary duty in discharging its obligation under the State Farm medical plan. The fiduciary function addressed by Herdrich's (P) ERISA count is the exercise of discretionary authority or responsibility in the administration of an ERISA plan. Although Carle (D2) is not an ERISA fiduciary merely because it administers or exercises discretionary authority over its own HMO business, it may still be a fiduciary if it administers the plan. Under ERISA, fiduciaries shall discharge their duties with respect to a plan solely in the interest of the participants and beneficiaries. The responsibilities are derived from the common law of trusts, under which fiduciaries are charged with a duty of loyalty to guarantee a beneficiaries' interests, and must exclude all selfish interest and all consideration of the interests of third persons. Here however, the analogy between ERISA fiduciary and common law trustee becomes problematic, since the trustee at common law characteristically wears only his fiduciary hat when he takes action to affect a beneficiary, whereas the trustee under ERISA may wear different hats. However, under ERISA, an administrator is a fiduciary only to the extent that he acts in such a capacity in relation to a plan. Therefore, the threshold question is not whether the actions of some person employed to provide services under a plan adversely affected a plan beneficiary's interest, but whether that person was acting as a fiduciary when taking the action subject to complaint. Here, Herdrich (P) does not point to a particular act by any Carle (D2) physician owner as a breach, nor complain about Pegram's (D1) actions. What she does claim is that Carle (D2), acting through its physician owners, breached its duty to act solely in the interest of beneficiaries by making decisions affecting medical treatment while influenced by the terms of the Carle (D2) HMO "profit" scheme. She emphasizes the threat to fiduciary responsibility in the Carle (D2) scheme's feature of a year-end distribution to the physicians of profit derived from the spread between subscription income and expenses of care and administration. The specific payout detail of the plan was a feature that the employer as plan sponsor was free to adopt without breach of any fiduciary duty under ERISA, since an employer's decision about the content of a plan are not themselves fiduciary acts. The nub of the claim, then, is that when State Farm contracted with Carle (D2), Carle (D2) became a fiduciary under the plan, acting through its physicians. At once, Carle (D2) as fiduciary administrator was subject to such influence from the year-end payout provision that its fiduciary capacity was necessarily compromised, and its readiness to act amounted to anticipatory breach of fiduciary obligation. The pleadings must be parsed very carefully to understand what acts by physician owners acting on Carle's (D2) behalf are alleged to be fiduciary in nature. It helps to keep two sorts of arguably administrative acts in mind. The first are called pure "eligibility decisions", which turn on the plan's coverage of a particular condition or medical procedure for its treatment. "Treatment decisions" on the other hand are choices about how to go about diagnosing and treating a patient's condition. These decisions are often inextricable from one another not merely because, under a scheme like Carle's (D2), treatment and eligibility decisions are made by the same person, but because most coverage questions are not simple yes-or-no questions, but rather when-and-how questions. Physicians must generally decide what to do in particular cases. In practical terms, eligibility decisions cannot be untangled from physicians' judgments about reasonable medical treatment, and in the case before us, Dr. Pegram's (D1) decision was one of that sort. The closest Herdrich's (P) ERISA count comes to stating a claim for a pure, unmixed eligibility decision is her general allegation that Carle (D2) determines which claims are covered under the Plan and to what extent. This vague statement, difficult to interpret in isolation, is given content by the other elements of the complaint, all of which refer to decisions thoroughly mixed with medical judgment. We believe that Congress did not intend any HMO to be treated as a fiduciary to the extent that it makes mixed eligibility decisions acting through its physicians. First, we doubt that Congress would ever have thought of a mixed eligibility decision as fiduciary in nature. Such decisions by an HMO acting through its physicians have only a limited resemblance to the usual business of traditional trustees. While traditional trustees administer a medical trust by paying out money to buy medical care, physicians making mixed eligibility decisions consume the money as well. Furthermore, private trustees do not make treatment judgments, whereas treatment judgments are what physicians reaching mixed decisions do by definition. The setting bears no more resemblance to trust departments than a decision to operate turns on the factors controlling the amount of a quarterly income distribution. Therefore, it is questionable whether Congress would have had mixed eligibility decisions in mind when it provided that decisions administering a plan were fiduciary in nature. Second, our doubt turns into conviction when we consider the consequences that would follow from Herdrich's (P) contrary view. Recovery would be warranted simply upon a showing that the profit incentive to ration care would generally affect mixed decisions, in derogation of the fiduciary standard to act solely in the interest of the patient without possibility of conflict. Although Herdrich (P) is vague about the mechanism of relief, it seems clear that she seeks the return of profit from the pockets of the Carle(D2) HMO owners, with the money to be given to the plan for the benefit of the participant. Since the provision for profit is what makes the HMO a proprietary organization, her remedy in effect would be nothing less than elimination of the for-profit HMO. Although, we are in no position to tell whether and to what extent nonprofit HMO schemes would ultimately survive the recognition of Herdrich's (P) theory, it is enough to recognize that the judiciary has no warrant to precipitate the upheaval that would follow a refusal to dismiss Herdrich's (P) ERISA claim. This would be acting contrary to congressional policy that has, for over 27 years, promoted the formation of HMO practices. A second possible consequence of applying this standard, would flow from the difficulty of extending it to a particular mixed decision. While the fiduciary is obliged to act exclusively in the interest of the beneficiary, this translates into no rule readily applicable to HMO decisions. While the incentive of the HMO physician is to give treatment sparingly, imposing a fiduciary obligation upon him would not lead to a simple default rule of say, whenever there is disagreement the physician should treat aggressively. After all, HMOs came into being because some groups of physicians consistently provided more aggressive treatment than others in similar circumstances. Nor would it be possible to translate fiduciary duty into a standard that would allow recovery from an HMO whenever a mixed decision influenced by the HMO's financial incentive resulted in a bad outcome for the patient. It would be so easy to allege and find an economic influence when sparing care did not lead to a well patient, that any such standard in practice would allow a factfinder to convert an HMO into guarantor of recovery. Although the Court of Appeals tried to confine the fiduciary breach to cases where "the sole purpose" of delaying or withholding treatment was to increase the physician's financial rewards, this attempt entails erroneous corruption of fiduciary obligation and would simply lead to further difficulties that we think fatal. Whether under the Court of Appeals' rule or a straight standard of undivided loyalty, the defense of any HMO would be that its physician did not act out of financial interest but for good medical reasons, which would require reference to standards of reasonableness and customary medical practice in like circumstances. Thus, every claim of fiduciary breach by an HMO physician making a mixed decision would boil down to a malpractice claim, requiring the application of law already available in state courts, and do nothing more than bring the same claim into a federal court under federal-question jurisdiction. Furthermore, not only would an HMO be liable as a fiduciary in the first instance for its own breach of fiduciary duty committed through its physicians, but the physician employee would also be subject to liability as a fiduciary on the same basic analysis that charge the HMO. Hence the physician would also be subject to suit in federal court applying an ERISA standard of reasonable medical skill, which would raise a puzzling issue of preemption. Federal fiduciary law applying a malpractice standard would seem to be a prescription for preemption of state malpractice law, since the new ERISA cause of action would cover the subject of state-law malpractice claims. Although we could struggle with this problem, we find nothing to be gained by opening the federal courthouse doors for a fiduciary malpractice claim. We hold that mixed eligibility and treatment decisions by HMO physicians are not fiduciary decisions under ERISA. Reversed.

Analysis:

Here, the Court concluded that Congress did not consider that ERISA would open federal court doors to fiduciary malpractice claims. Therefore, the Court objected to extending the reach of federal fiduciary law to medical malpractice, on the grounds that it would duplicate and possibly preempt state law. Although this case does not directly address the issue of preemption, it seems to have significantly narrowed the reach of ERISA preemption, since mixed eligibility and treatment decisions describe the medical administrative decisions made everyday. It seems that so long as medical judgments are involved, a claim may be found not to "relate to" ERISA. Thus, this case has allowed many courts to find ways around ERISA preemption.

■ CASE VOCABULARY

FIDUCIARY DUTY: A duty to act in good faith, to act with complete loyalty, and to exercise the highest standard of care when administering a health a care plan for the benefit of a beneficiary or plan participant.

Aetna Health, Inc. v. Davila

(HMO) v. *(Insured)*

542 U.S. 200 (2004)

___

ERISA PREEMPTS ALL STATE ACTIONS FOR DENIAL OF BENEFITS

___

All I want for Christmas is compensation for my health plan's denial of benefits.

Sorry, even Santa is preempted by ERISA.

stus.com

■ **INSTANT FACTS** Davila (P) brought suit in state court against Aetna (D) for failure to exercise ordinary care in handling coverage decisions, and Aetna (D) sought to remove the case to federal court.

■ **BLACK LETTER RULE** All actions brought for the denial of benefits by an ERISA-regulated benefit plan fall within the scope of, and are preempted by, ERISA.

___

■ **PROCEDURAL BASIS**

Appeal from an order reversing dismissals of complaints with prejudice.

■ **FACTS**

Davila (P) was a participant in an ERISA-regulated employee benefit plan administered by Aetna (D), and Calad (P) was a beneficiary of a plan administered by CIGNA Healthcare (D). Both Davila (P) and Calad (D) brought actions against their plans for injuries allegedly sustained by the denial of treatment. Davila (P) claimed that Aetna (D) refused to pay for Vioxx, prescribed by his physician for arthritis pain. Davila (P) did not contest this decision or pay for Vioxx himself and seek reimbursement. Instead, Davila (P) took Naprosyn, which allegedly caused a severe reaction that required hospitalization and extensive treatment. Calad (P) underwent surgery and was discharged from the hospital against the recommendation of her physician, because CIGNA (D) determined that she did not meet the criteria for an extended hospital stay. Calad (P) experienced complications from her surgery allegedly caused by her early discharge, and had to return to the hospital.

Davila (P) and Calad (P) brought suit against their respective plans under the Texas Healthcare Liability Act, Tex. Civ. Prac. & Rem. Code §§ 88.001—88.003. The suits alleged a failure to exercise ordinary care in making healthcare treatment decisions. Aetna (D) and CIGNA (D) removed the cases to federal district court, claiming that Davila's (P) and Calad's (P) causes of action were within the scope of, and preempted by, ERISA. The district courts agreed, and refused to remand the cases to state court. Davila (P) and Calad (P) refused to amend their complaints to state explicit ERISA claims, so their complaints were dismissed with prejudice. The Fifth Circuit Court of Appeals reversed, holding that the suits were not contract claims or suits for reimbursement for benefits denied, but were claims for tort damages.

■ **ISSUE**

Does ERISA preempt all actions against regulated benefit plans?

■ **DECISION AND RATIONALE**

(Thomas, J.) Yes. All actions brought for the denial of benefits by an ERISA-regulated benefit plan fall within the scope of, and are preempted by, ERISA. It does not matter that claims might be labeled "tort claims" rather than contract claims. Courts will look to the substance of the claim, rather than the label given to them.

The purpose of ERISA is to provide a uniform regulatory scheme for employee benefit plans. The regulatory scheme includes an integrated enforcement mechanism that is essential to the congressional purpose of creating a comprehensive statute to regulate employee benefit plans. Any state-law cause of action that duplicates, supplements, or supplants the civil enforcement remedy in ERISA conflicts with the congressional intent to make the remedies in ERISA exclusive and is thus preempted. The preemption provisions of ERISA operate to convert a state common law complaint into one that sets out a federal cause of action.

The civil enforcement provisions of ERISA give a participant or beneficiary in a plan the right to bring suit to recover benefits that have been denied. A participant or beneficiary may also bring suit to "enforce his rights ... or to clarify his rights to future benefits under the plan." It follows that a suit brought that complains of a denial of medical coverage to an individual entitled to such coverage only because of the terms of an ERISA-regulated plan, where no legal duty other than ERISA or the plan terms have been violated, is a suit within the scope of ERISA. In the instant case, Davila (P) and Calad (P) are complaining only about the denial of coverage promised under the terms of ERISA-regulated benefit plans.

Davila (P) and Calad (P) claim that their lawsuits allege violations of legal duties that are independent of ERISA. Their suits were brought under the Texas Healthcare Liability Act, and allege a violation of the duty of care created by that statute. In the context of the instant case, however, the duties imposed by Texas law do not arise independently of ERISA or the plan terms. The liability of a plan for denial of coverage depends on whether the plan itself provides coverage. The Texas law does not create a duty to provide treatment not covered by the plan, so there can be no liability unless treatment is covered by the plan. Interpretation of the terms of the plans is an essential part of Davila's (P) and Calad's (P) claims, and liability would exist only because of the administration of ERISA-regulated health plans. The potential liability of Aetna (D) or CIGNA (D) derives entirely from rights and obligations established by the plans, so the Texas causes of action are not entirely independent of the federally regulated plan. Calling the claims tort claims, or basing them on a state law, cannot put the action outside the preemptive scope of ERISA. ERISA does not preempt only duplicative state law causes of action, because allowing actions that supplement ERISA's remedies would undermine the exclusive civil enforcement mechanism established by Congress.

Davila (P) and Calad (P) also argue that their actions are not preempted because the Texas Healthcare Liability Act is a state law regulating insurance, exempted from preemption by the terms of ERISA. The existence of a comprehensive regulatory scheme shows an overpowering federal policy that determines the interpretation of the exemption from preemption. Allowing Davila (P) and Calad (P) to proceed with their state law claims would pose an obstacle to the purposes and objectives of Congress. Under ordinary preemption principles, even a state law that regulates insurance will be preempted if it provides a way to assert a claim for benefits outside of, or in addition to, ERISA's regulatory scheme.

The case of *Pegram v. Herdrich,* 530 U.S. 211 (2000), does not help Davila (P) and Calad (P). In that case, the plaintiff sued her physician-owned-and-operated medical plan for medical malpractice and for breach of an ERISA fiduciary duty. There, the treating physician also determined eligibility for benefits, so that treatment and the determination of benefits were "inextricably mixed." Mixed eligibility decisions are not fiduciary in nature, since they are not the type of fiduciary decisions commonly made by plan administrators. Reversed and remanded.

Analysis:

In her concurrence, Justice Ginsburg agreed with the result reached by the majority, but stated that the broad interpretation of ERISA's preemption of state law created a "regulatory vacuum," since few federal remedies are provided to substitute for preempted state law remedies. She, along with Justice Breyer, called on Congress either to revise ERISA or to provide added remedies. There have been legislative proposals to add additional remedies to ERISA, or to repeal or modify the preemption provisions, but to date none of these efforts has been particularly successful.

Doe v. Group Hospitalization & Medical Services

(Cancer Patient) v. *(Health Insurance Administrator)*

3 F.3d 80 (4th Cir. 1993)

A FIDUCIARY'S ROLE AS A DECISION-MAKER IN APPROVING BENEFITS UNDER A PLAN, IS HELD TO LIE IN CONFLICT WITH ITS PROFIT-MAKING ROLE AS A BUSINESS

■ **INSTANT FACTS** A patient diagnosed with a rare form of blood cancer sues a health care plan for its denial of benefits for cancer treatment, made pursuant to an amendment in the patient's insurance contract, claiming that the health care plan improperly amended the contract, and that regardless, the contract language as amended did not exclude coverage for the treatment.

■ **BLACK LETTER RULE** Where an administrator or fiduciary is operating under a conflict of interest, courts should review the merits of a plan interpretation to determine whether it is consistent with that of a fiduciary free of the conflict.

■ **PROCEDURAL BASIS**

Appeal to the United States Court of Appeals, of a decision by the district court granting defendant's cross-motions for summary judgment.

■ **FACTS**

John Doe (Doe) (P), a 59-year-old law partner of Firm Doe (P2), was diagnosed in late 1991 with multiple myeloma, a rare and fatal form of blood cancer. Dr. Kenneth C. Anderson (Dr. Anderson) prescribed a treatment that involved an initial course of chemotherapy to reduce the percentage of tumor cells, and a subsequent high-dose chemotherapy, radiation therapy, and an autologous bone marrow transplant. The total cost of the treatment was estimated at $100,000, and was described by Dr. Anderson as Doe's (P) only chance of long-term survival. Doe (P) and Firm Doe (P2) sought health insurance benefits for the treatment from Group Hospitalization and Medical Services, Inc., doing business as Blue Cross and Blue Shield of the National Capital Area (Blue Cross) (D). Blue Cross (D) insured and administered Firm Doe's (P2) employee welfare benefit plan pursuant to a group insurance contract entered into on January 1, 1989. On November 30, 1990, the contract was amended by a letter to Firm Doe (P2). Relying on language in the amendments that excludes benefits for bone marrow transplants undergone in treating multiple myeloma and "related" services and supplies, Blue Cross (D), in a letter sent to Dr. Anderson on March 30, 1992, denied the benefits. Doe (P) and Firm Doe (P2) immediately filed suit under § 502 of the Employee Retirement Income Security Act (ERISA), claiming that Blue Cross (D) denied benefits based solely upon improperly adopted amendments to the group insurance contract and that regardless, the contract language as amended did not exclude coverage for the treatment. The district court entered judgment for Blue Cross (D) on their cross-motions for summary judgment, holding that Blue Cross (D) properly denied coverage based on the Group Contract and its amendments. Doe (P) appeals.

■ **ISSUE**

Is a plan administrator's decision to deny benefits to a participant afforded deferential review when the administrator is operating under a conflict of interest?

■ DECISION AND RATIONALE

(Niemeyer, J.) No. Where an administrator or fiduciary is operating under a conflict of interest, courts should review the merits of a plan interpretation to determine whether it is consistent with that of a fiduciary free of the conflict. The November 30 letter was a form letter sent to all administrators of Blue Cross (D) group insurance contracts, addressing changes to no less than eight separate aspects of coverage. Included was the section "Organ Transplant" that incorporated the language in question. Doe (P) and Firm Doe (P2) contend first, that the amendments were ineffective because it was not adopted in accordance with the contract's specified periods for making amendments. However, we find that the amendment was effective because Blue Cross (D) had provided 30-day notice of the change in accordance with the contract. Doe (P) also argues that regardless, the language of the amendment misled the Firm Does (P2) and its employees about the nature of the changes. Specifically, they argue that the section headed "Organ Transplants" purports to "clarify" the types of transplants covered, but in fact narrows the coverage since before the amendments, transplants were simply not addressed and were therefore presumptively covered so long as they were not excluded under some other provision. Thus, Doe (P) argues that Blue Cross (D) failed to disclose the intended effect of the limitation for organ transplants, downplaying the significance of the letter, and failing to put Firm Doe (P2) on notice of an amendment. We find this argument unpersuasive. Health care benefits provided in an employee benefit plan are not vested benefits, and may be modified or withdrawn by the employer at any time, provided that the changes are made in compliance with ERISA and the terms of the plan. Firm Doe (P2) established its benefit plan through a contract with Blue Cross (D), accepting the provision that "benefits, provisions, terms, or conditions," could be changed upon timely notice. We believe that the November 30 letter provided sufficient notice that benefits under the contract were being changed. It states that the letter is an "update" of the terms of the contract, and outlines the changes for specific coverages. Moreover, evidence was presented that Firm Doe (P2) relied on the changes in connection with other coverages, and it continued to pay under the contract without objection. Furthermore, the amendment was circulated well before Doe (P) showed any symptoms or was diagnosed with cancer. Doe (P) contends that regardless, the language of their group insurance contract with Blue Cross (D) does not provide a basis for the insurance company's decision to deny Doe (P) of benefits. Court actions challenging the denial of benefits under *20 U.S.C § 1132(a)(1)(b)* are subject to a standard for review derived from principles of trust law, and announced in *Firestone Tire and Rubber Co. v. Bruch.* There the court observed that in reviewing the actions of a fiduciary who has been given discretionary powers to determine eligibility for benefits and to construe the language of an ERISA plan, deference must be shown and the fiduciary's action will be reviewed only for abuse. If discretionary authority is not provided, denials of claims are to be reviewed de novo. However, the Supreme court in *Firestone* went on to recognize that a conflict of interest could lower the level of deference to be applied to a discretionary decision by a fiduciary. In the instant case, Blue Cross (D) asserts that because it has been given discretionary authority to review claims, determine eligibility, and construe contract terms, our review of its decision to deny Doe (P) benefits is only for abuse of discretion. As stated in the November 30, 1990 letter of amendment, Blue Cross (D) has full power and discretionary authority to control and mange the operation and administration of the contract, subject only to the participant's rights to review and appeal under the contract. Furthermore, the letter states that Blue Cross (D) shall have all powers necessary to accomplish these purposes in accordance with the terms of the contract. Therefore, we agree that the express terms of the group insurance contract gives Blue Cross (D) discretion to the extent it claims. Doe (P) contends that Blue Cross (D), however, operated under a conflict of interest, and that therefore, no deference to its discretion is warranted. They note that ERISA imposes on fiduciaries a duty of loyalty to act with respect to a plan solely in the interest of providing benefits and defraying reasonable expenses. Apparently, Blue Cross (D) is compensated by a fixed premium, which is used to pay claims, and there is no evidence that it has a mechanism to collect from the employer retrospectively for unexpected liabilities. It therefore bears the financial risk for claims made beyond the actuarial norm. Since each time Blue Cross (D) approves a payment of benefits, the money comes out of its own pocket, Doe (D) and Firm Doe (P2) argue that Blue Cross' fiduciary role as decision-maker in approving benefits under the plan therefore lies in conflict with its profit-making role as a business. Undoubtedly, Blue Cross' (D) profit from the insurance contract depends on whether the claim allowed exceeds the assumed risk used to calculate premiums. To the extent that Blue Cross (D) has discretion to avoid paying claims, it thereby promotes the potential for its own profit. This type of conflict flows inherently form the nature of the relationship entered into by the parties and is common where employers contract with insurance companies to provide and administer health care benefits to employees through group insurance contracts. Thus, we must alter our standard of review and hold that when a fiduciary exercises discretion in interpreting a disputed term of the contract where one interpretation will further the financial interests of the fiduciary, we will not act as deferentially as would otherwise be appropriate. We will review the merits of the interpretation to determine whether it is consistent with an exercise of discretion by a fiduciary acting free of the interests that conflict with those of the beneficiaries. Turning to the case at bar, the treatment of blood cancer by chemotherapy and radiation is accordingly clearly covered by the contract. As amended, the contract provides that an autologous bone marrow transplant for multiple myeloma and services and supplies for or related to the transplant are excluded from the plan's coverage. Blue Cross (D) argues that high dose chemotherapy and radiation treatments are excluded because without the autologous bone marrow transplants, the high-dose chemotherapy could not be performed. We believe such an argument misdirects the analysis required for determining the scope of coverage and fails to accommodate harmoniously all provisions of the contract. The bone marrow transplant is not the procedure designed to treat the cancer. The first question to be asked, therefore, is whether the cancer treating procedure is covered by the contract and as we noted, we have found it is. While Blue Cross (D) is well within its rights to exclude coverage for the ancillary bone marrow transplant procedure, the exclusion should not, in the absence of clear language, be construed to withdraw coverage explicitly granted elsewhere in the contract. Additionally, in determining whether a decision has been made solely for the benefit of the participant, we may take into account the principle that in making a reasonable decision, ambiguity acts against the drafting party, especially when the contract is a form provided by the insurer rather than one negotiated between the parties. Therefore, because Blue Cross' (D) discretionary interpretation to the contrary is not entitled to the deference we might otherwise accord, we will construe the contract for the benefit of its beneficiaries and enforce the coverage provided by Part 3 of the group insurance contract and not otherwise explicitly excluded. Affirmed in part, reversed in part, and remanded for further proceedings.

Analysis:

As mentioned in this case, the bodies of law that define ERISA are derived from trust law and classic contract law. Unlike state insurance regulations, which are generally driven by a concern for access rights, ERISA does not compel employers to provide health insurance, but instead entitles participants to sue in federal court when, for instance, a plan administrator wrongfully withholds benefits under 29 U.S.C.A. § 1132(a)(1) (ERISA § 502(a)). ERISA authorizes a review of an administrator's decision, rather than a suit against an administrator as a defendant who has allegedly wronged the claimant. The lower courts are sharply divided in their approach to determining what constitutes a conflict of interest, and what effects a conflict of interest has on the level of review. On one end of the spectrum some courts hold that if a substantial conflict of interest is found, the fiduciary's decision is afforded little deference, or even presumptively void. Courts at the other end of the spectrum insist that conflicts of interests are rarely a problem, because of market competition (i.e., repeated denials will result in a bad reputation and lower competitiveness). Courts in the middle take a conflict of interest into consideration only if a substantial conflict of interest can be shown, that in fact caused a breach in the fiduciary's duty and motivated an improper decision.

Winslow v. IDS Life Insurance Co.

(Disabled Individual) v. *(Long-Term Disability Insurance Provider)*

29 F.Supp.2d. 557 (D. Minn. 1998).

REFUSAL TO PROVIDE HEALTH INSURANCE ON THE BASIS OF A DISABILITY FOUND VIOLATIVE OF THE ADA

■ **INSTANT FACTS** An individual currently treated for mild depression, files an action against an insurance company under the ADA and the state's human rights act, after the insurance company denied the individual coverage based on their policy which categorically denies long-term disability insurance to those being treated for mental or nervous conditions.

■ **BLACK LETTER RULE** The categorical denial of access to insurance coverage to a class of disabled individuals is a violation of the ADA.

■ **PROCEDURAL BASIS**

Filing of a motion for summary judgment of a claim for the denial of long-term disability insurance to the United States District Court.

■ **FACTS**

On October 27, 1994, Susan Winslow (Winslow) (P) applied to IDS Life Insurance Co. (IDS) (D) for standard long-term disability insurance or alternatively, long-term disability insurance with a rider excluding coverage for periods of disability due to her mental health condition. On the application, Winslow (P) indicated that she had been treated for dysthymia or mild depression within the past year and was currently taking an anti-depressant. IDS (D) refused both requests based on its policy of denying long-term disability insurance to applicants who report having received treatment for a mental or nervous condition, regardless of seriousness, within twelve months prior to application. IDS asserts that its policy is based on industry-wide claims experience and actuarial data that indicates that the highest number of payments are made for depression-related claims. Winslow (P) contends that the IDS (D) policy differs from that in the Paul Revere Underwriting Manual, a manual used by IDS (D) in making other underwriting decisions, which does not require automatic rejection of applicants with current histories of mental or nervous conditions, but instead provides for a long-term disability insurance policy with a longer exclusion period. In November 1994, Winslow (P) received notice of the denial and requested reconsideration, asserting that she had never been hospitalized or missed work due to he mental health condition. She also provided corroborative letters from two psychiatrists from whom she had received treatment, affirming that Winslow (P) suffered only mild symptoms, which did not manifest themselves in work situations. After IDS (D) reaffirmed the denial, Winslow (P) filed an action for declaratory and injunctive relief, and for damages under the Americans with Disabilities Act (ADA), and the Minnesota Human Rights Act (MHRA). IDS (D) files a motion for summary judgment.

■ **ISSUE**

Does the exclusion of a class of disabled from an insurance plan violate the ADA?

■ DECISION AND RATIONALE

(Davis, J.) Yes. The categorical denial of access to insurance coverage to a class of disabled individuals is a violation of the ADA. In order to defeat summary judgment, Winslow (P) must demonstrate that she is a person with a disability under the ADA, and thus covered by the ADA. The ADA defines "disability" as a physical or mental impairment, a record of such impairment, or as Winslow (P) claims, being regarded as having a physical or metal impairment that substantially limits one or more of the major life activities of such individual, such as the future ability to work. It is undisputed that work is a "major life activity," which if substantially limited or regarded as such, qualifies as "disabled" under the ADA. As a matter of law, we find that when IDS (D) denied Winslow's (P) application for long-term disability insurance based on depression and anxiety, IDS (D) implicitly considered her to be "impaired" and likely unable to perform either a class of jobs or a broad range of jobs in various classes in the future. IDS (D) asserts that regardless, Winslow (P) has failed to show that IDS (D) regarded her as disabled at the time it denied her application for long-term disability, as required by the ADA. We have previously held that the distinction between present and future limitations is not dispositive, finding that the "regarded as" definition of disability seeks to eradicate discrimination based on irrational fear as well as prejudice. Fear refers not to actual present conditions, but to anticipated future consequences, and the perception of impairment is included by Congress within the definition of disabled to combat the effects of archaic attitudes, erroneous perception, and myths that operate to the disadvantage of persons with or regarded as having disabilities. Therefore, we hold that the purpose of the ADA requires that ADA protection extend to cover the perception of possible future disability. With respect to the applicability of the ADA to insurance polices, we first turn to Title III of the ADA [which provides that no individual shall be discriminated against on the basis of disability in the full and equal enjoyment of the goods, services, facilities, privileges, advantages, or accommodation of any place of public accommodation by any person who owns, leases, or operates a place of public accommodation]. The question here, is whether "public accommodations" are limited to actual physical structures or whether the ADA prohibits more than physical impediments to public accommodations for the disabled. This issue has so far only been decided by the First and Sixth Circuits, which have split on the matter. The Sixth circuit concluded that the plain meaning of the statutory language is that places of public accommodation are limited to physical places open to public access, while the First Circuit concluded that "public accommodation" is not limited to actual physical structures. The California District Court, in following this conclusion, added that the limited interpretation of public accommodation adopted by the Sixth Circuit, would contravene the broadly stated purpose of the ADA to provide a clear and comprehensive national mandate for the elimination of discrimination against individuals with disabilities. By restricting "public accommodation" to include only physical structure, the protection under the ADA for individuals with mental disabilities would be virtually negated, absent circumstances in which a physical structure denied access to the mentally impaired. What is especially relevant is the ADA statutory language that would be rendered irrelevant if Title III were held only to apply to physical access to public structures, including the provision that prohibits the imposition or application of eligibility criteria that screen out an individual with a disability, unless such criteria can be shown relevant, and those that prohibit failure to make reasonable modification in policies, practices or procedure when necessary to provide equal treatment to individuals with disabilities. Also rendered unnecessary is the provision for injunctive relief, which includes requiring the modification of policy. Furthermore, the "Safe Harbor" provision of Title III [which states that subchapters I through III of this chapter and Title IV of this Act shall not be construed to prohibit or restrict an insurer, hospital or medical service company, HMO, or any agent, or entity that administers benefit plans, or similar organization from underwriting risks, classifying risks, or administering such risks that are based on or not inconsistent with State law], supports the conclusion of a growing number of districts, that that ADA applies to the provision of insurance policies. Courts have concluded that the "Safe Harbor" provision would be superfluous if insurers could never be liable under Title III for conduct such as discriminatory denial of insurance coverage. Accordingly, the DOJ in its legislative history of the ADA, also interprets Title III as prohibiting differential treatment of individuals with disabilities in insurance offered by public accommodations unless the differences are justified. Therefore we find that Title III of the ADA is applicable to insurance policies and not limited to access to actual physical structures. IDS (D) argues that the McCarran-Ferguson Act (the Act) precludes application of the ADA to insurance policies because Title III is not intended to regulate the business of private insurance carriers. The Act bars the application of a federal statute if: 1) the statute does not specifically relate to the business of insurance, 2) a state statute has been enacted for the purpose of regulating the business of insurance, and 3) the federal statute would invalidate, impair, or supersede state statute. Two fundamental provisions of the ADA that specifically relate to the business of insurance include the "subterfuge" provision, which prohibits the use of the Safe Harbor provision to evade the purpose of Title III, and the inclusion of an insurance office as an entity considered a public accommodation for the purposes of Title III. The McCarran-Ferguson Act is a form of inverse preemption, and thus principles defining when state remedies conflict with federal law are pertinent in deciding when federal rules invalidate, impair, or supersede state rules. Duplication is not conflict however, and as a general rule, state and federal rules that are substantively identical but differ in penalty do not conflict with or displace one another. Therefore, we find that the McCarran-Ferguson Act does not invalidate, impair, or supersede the relevant Minnesota statutes and does not bar Winslow's (P) ADA claims. Turning to the Safe Harbor provision as mentioned above, the risk underwriting engaged in by insurance companies must be based on or not inconsistent with state law. The subterfuge provision provides however, that even if an insurer's practices are consistent with applicable state law, they can still violate the ADA if a plaintiff demonstrates that the insurance policies are a subterfuge to evade the purposes of the ADA. Thus, the Court must perform a two-part analysis to determine whether the IDS (D) policies in question violate the Safe Harbor provision of the ADA. Generally, under Minnesota law, making or permitting the rejection of an individual's application for accident or health insurance coverage on the basis of a disability, shall constitute an unfair method of competition and an unfair and deceptive act or practice, unless the claims experience and actuarial projections and other data establish significant and substantial differences in class rates because of the disability. Also under Minnesota law, life or health insurance companies are prohibited from engaging in any selection or underwriting process unless the company establishes beforehand substantial data, actuarial projections, or claims experience which support the underwriting standard used. By presenting specific industry data, IDS (D) asserts that it has presented sufficient justification for its eligibility criteria, and therefore has not violated state law. Winslow (P) counters by arguing that IDS (D) fails to demonstrate that individuals receiving treatment for mental or nervous conditions at or near the time of application for insurance are more likely to file claims under their insurance. Furthermore, Winslow (P) asserts that the Paul Revere Underwriting Manual includes various impairments and establishes procedures for processing applications from individuals with such impairments, without recommending total denial of insurance for such applicants. Thus, Winslow (P) claims that a genuine issue of material fact exists as to whether IDS' (D) long-term disability insurance eligibility criteria conforms to sound actuarial principles, claims experience, or substantial data as required by Minnesota law. We agree and deny summary judgment on this matter. We need not pass on the issue as to whether the criteria is a subterfuge of the ADA. We now turn to Winslow's (P) claim that IDS's (D) policy violates the ADA. Courts have found that broad-based distinctions that distinguish between mental and physical health conditions do not qualify as illicit disability-based distinctions under the ADA, since the ADA is only applicable to discrimination between disabled and non-disabled persons, not discrimination among disabled. The aforementioned cases and the EEOC Interim Guidance, however, address disability-based discrimination among the disabled that affect the quality and extent of coverage offered to one class of disabled as compared to another, and do not address the categorical denial of access to insurance coverage to a class of disabled individuals. When courts have addressed the exclusion of a class of disabled from an insurance plan, they have found such exclusions violative of the ADA. Legislative history further supports the proposition that while disability-based distinctions in an insurance policy's terms are permissible under the ADA, a policy to deny insurance coverage categorically to mentally disabled is unacceptable. We find that since IDS's (D) policy denies the aforementioned individuals access to insurance coverage, the policy is founded on a disability-based discrimination violative of the ADA. We also hold that IDS's (D) denial violated the Minnesota Human Rights Act.

Analysis:

many believed that the ADA would limit the ability of employers and insurers to vary the terms and conditions of insurance coverage on the basis of medical condition. To the contrary, many recent cases have indicated that the impact of the ADA will be limited. First, there is a significant disagreement as to when and whether the ADA applies to insurance policies, rather than solely to physical structures. Second, several courts have found that the ADA only prohibits dissimilar treatment between disabled and non-disabled persons. Therefore, disability-based discrimination among the disabled that affects the quality and extent of coverage offered to one class of disabled as compared to another is permissible under the ADA. Third, several courts have read the "safe harbor" provision broadly, protecting insurer practices that are not found to be a subterfuge to evade the purposes of the ADA. And finally, some courts are reluctant to find that Congress meant to turn over the job of regulating insurance underwriting practices to federal courts, based on the McCarran-Ferguson Act.

■ CASE VOCABULARY

DISABILITY: Having a physical or mental impairment that substantially limits one or more of the major life activities of an individual, having a record of such impairment, or being regarded as having such an impairment.

CHAPTER ELEVEN

Public Health Care Programs: Medicare and Medicaid

Bellevue Hospital Center v. Leavitt

Instant Facts: The Department of Health and Human Services (D) was directed by Congress to calculate hospital wages for Medicare reimbursement purposes using all wage and hour data available, but a rule was promulgated that relied on only ten percent of the data.

Black Letter Rule: When assessing the propriety of agency action, if Congress has directly addressed the precise question at issue, the inquiry is over; if there is silence or ambiguity on an issue, the agency has discretion as to how it implements a statute, and the court's inquiry is limited to whether the construction is reasonable.

Shalala v. Illinois Council on Long Term Care, Inc.

Instant Facts: An association of nursing homes seeks to challenge in federal court certain Medicare-related regulations under the Constitution and various statutes, but the regulations first require the issues to be dealt with through administrative review.

Black Letter Rule: 42 U.S.C. § 405(h) requires all actions arising under the Medicare laws and regulations, including challenges to the regulations themselves, to be brought administratively before being brought in federal court unless such a requirement would mean total preclusion of review.

Lankford v. Sherman

Instant Facts: Lankford (P) and the other plaintiffs sought a preliminary injunction against a state Medicaid regulation, alleging that the regulation violated the comparability and reasonableness requirements of the Medicaid law.

Black Letter Rule: Medicaid is a voluntary federal/state program, and a state that elects to participate in the program is bound by the requirements of federal law and regulations.

Westside Mothers v. Haveman

Instant Facts: Westside Mothers (P) brought an action to compel Haveman (D) to comply with Medicaid mandates, but the suit was dismissed.

Black Letter Rule: Medicaid is not merely a contract, it is a federal law that may be enforced by a private right of action brought under 42 U.S.C. § 1983.

Bellevue Hospital Center v. Leavitt

(*Hospital*) v. (*Secretary of Health and Human Services*)

443 F.3d 163 (2d Cir. 2006)

THE MEDICARE ACT DOES NOT GRANT UNLIMITED DISCRETION WHEN MAKING REGULATIONS

■ **INSTANT FACTS** The Department of Health and Human Services (D) was directed by Congress to calculate hospital wages for Medicare reimbursement purposes using all wage and hour data available, but a rule was promulgated that relied on only ten percent of the data.

■ **BLACK LETTER RULE** When assessing the propriety of agency action, if Congress has directly addressed the precise question at issue, the inquiry is over; if there is silence or ambiguity on an issue, the agency has discretion as to how it implements a statute, and the court's inquiry is limited to whether the construction is reasonable.

■ **PROCEDURAL BASIS**

Appeal from an order on a challenge to an administrative regulation.

■ **FACTS**

The Medicare program, administered by the Department of Health and Human Services (D), is required by statute to reimburse hospitals for services provided by paying fixed rates for different categories of services. The payments are divided into non-labor-related costs and labor-related costs. Labor-related costs are adjusted to reflect the different costs for labor in different geographic areas. The Secretary of Health and Human Services (D) is required to compute a wage factor for each hospital in an area at least annually, and that factor must reflect the relative wage factor in the area.

The Secretary (D) grouped hospitals into geographic areas according to the Metropolitan Statistical Areas (MSAs) developed by the Office of Management and Budget. The Center for Medicare and Medicaid Services (CMS) (D), part of the Department of Health and Human Services (D), acknowledged that the MSAs were an unsatisfactory grouping for determining hospital wage rates. The MSAs continued to be used, however, in the absence of a better methodology. In 2000, Congress directed the Secretary (D) to refine its surveys of hospital wages by controlling for differences in the occupational mixes of hospitals. Every three years, the Secretary (D) was to collect data on hospital occupational mixes, and measure the earnings and hours of employment by occupational category, except for labor-related costs incurred in furnishing skilled nursing services. The collection of data and the measurement of earnings were to be completed no later than September 30, 2003, "for application beginning October 1, 2004."

The final notice of the intent to collect data was not published until September 19, 2003. In 2004, the Secretary (D) issued a final rule regarding labor-related costs. The CMS (D) stated that it lacked full confidence in the data for several reasons, so the occupational mix adjustment would be applied to only ten percent of the wage index. The next year, the CMS (D) used largely the same data, and, because it still lacked confidence in the data, applied the adjustment to only ten percent of the index.

■ **ISSUE**

Were the methods used to compute the wage index lawful?

■ DECISION AND RATIONALE

(Katzmann, J.) No. When assessing the propriety of agency action, if Congress has directly addressed the precise question at issue, the inquiry is over; if there is silence or ambiguity on an issue, the agency has discretion as to how it implements the statute, and the court's inquiry is limited to whether the construction is reasonable. This is the test set forth in *Chevron U.S.A. Inc. v. Natural Resources Defense Council,* 467 U.S. 837 (1984). If an agency's action was authorized by statute, the court asks whether the action was arbitrary, capricious, or an abuse of discretion, or unsupported by substantial evidence.

The use of MSAs to determine geographic areas was reasonable. The statute does not define the term "geographic area," so the CMS (D) has discretion in how to interpret the term. MSAs are "geographic areas," and they provide a pool of hospitals large enough to allow averaging. At the same time, they are small enough so that wages in each MSA will bear some similarity. Furthermore, CMS (D) has used the MSAs for more than twenty years without any action form Congress suggesting disapproval. The use of MSAs is also not arbitrary or capricious. It is rational and permissible for an agency to adopt an already extant measure that uses objective criteria rather than assuming the task of creating its own measure.

The Secretary (D) has interpreted the requirement that the data collection be completed for application beginning October 1, 2004 as imposing an obligation only to "begin" applying the adjustment on that date. Bellevue Hospital Center (P), and the district court, interpret that language as requiring full implementation of the adjustment on October 1, 2004. Both interpretations are incorrect. The statute requires application of the adjustment in full on October 1, 2004. Congress is not required to use the words "in full" when directing the implementation of a program. A requirement of application "begin-ning on" a certain date is not a grant of discretion to apply whatever limited portion of the adjustment the Secretary (D) believes appropriate. There is no ambiguity on this point, so the Secretary's interpretation receives no deference.

The Secretary's (D) actions are also arbitrary and capricious. No justification is given for implementation of ten percent, rather than some other fraction, of the data. No explanation has been given for the failure to comply with the requirement that the collection of data and the measurement be completed by September 30, 2003. When the data gathered proved inadequate, the Secretary (D) simply stated an intent to do better next time.

The district court ordered the Secretary to apply the occupational mix adjustment in full based on the data already collected. Application of the adjustment with the flawed data would not only result in irrational policy, but would contravene Congress's purpose in setting up the schedule. The Secretary (D) is therefore ordered to return to the first step and collect data that are sufficiently robust to permit application of the occupational mix adjustment. The Medicare Act does not give the Secretary of Health and Human Services authority to consider data in a manner not permitted by statute when making regulations. Affirmed as modified.

Analysis:

The Center for Medicare and Medicaid Services (CMS) (D) is the division of the U.S. Department of Health and Human Services (D) with far-reaching impact on all healthcare in the United States. It is the agency that oversees Medicare and federal/state healthcare programs such as Medicaid and the State Children's Health Insurance Program (or SCHIP). CMS (D) also sets quality standards for nursing homes and clinical laboratories. It is easy to see how allowing CMS (D) unfettered discretion in implementing its programs could result in a *de facto* restructuring of healthcare that is outside of any congressional authorization. The court's opinion in this case essentially states an obvious point: executive agencies must operate according to the limits set out by Congress.

Shalala v. Illinois Council on Long Term Care, Inc.

(Cabinet Secretary) v. (Nursing Home Association)

529 U.S. 1, 120 S.Ct. 1084 (2000)

LEGAL CHALLENGES TO THE MEDICARE REGULATIONS MUST FIRST BE MADE THROUGH THE CHANNLES PROVIDED UNDER THE MEDICARE STATUTE

■ **INSTANT FACTS** An association of nursing homes seeks to challenge in federal court certain Medicare-related regulations under the Constitution and various statutes, but the regulations first require the issues to be dealt with through administrative review.

■ **BLACK LETTER RULE** 42 U.S.C. § 405(h) requires all actions arising under the Medicare laws and regulations, including challenges to the regulations themselves, to be brought administratively before being brought in federal court unless such a requirement would mean total preclusion of review.

■ PROCEDURAL BASIS

Certification to the U.S. Supreme Court after the Circuit Court of Appeals reversed the district court's decision barring suit due to claim preclusion under the doctrines of ripeness and exhaustion.

■ FACTS

The Illinois Council on Long Term Care, Inc. (Association)(P), an association of nursing homes, sued the Secretary of Health and Human Services (Secretary) (D) in federal district court claiming that certain Medicare-related regulations violated various statutes and the Constitution. The Association invoked federal question jurisdiction under 28 U.S.C. § 1331 [remember your civ pro?]. The District Court dismissed the action for lack of jurisdiction because, it was held, a set of special statutory provisions creates a separate, virtually exclusive, system of administrative and judicial review for Medicare claims; specifically 42 U.S.C. § 405(h), which provides that "[n]o action to recover on any claim" arising under the Medicare laws shall be "brought under section 1331 of title 28." The Court of Appeals reversed.

■ ISSUE

May a challenge of Medicare-related regulations be brought in the first instance in the federal courts pursuant to federal question jurisdiction under 28 U.S.C. § 1331, before exhausting the special administrative and judicial review promulgated under the Medicare system?

■ DECISION AND RATIONALE

(Breyer, J.) No. The Medicare Act Part A requires nursing homes, in order to receive reimbursement, to enter into a provider agreement with the Secretary (D) and comply with numerous statutory and regulatory requirements. The regulations at issue focus on the imposition of sanctions or remedies upon nursing homes that fail to comply. The Association's (P) complaint filed in district court attacked the regulations as violative of the Constitution and various statutes. The complaint does not include any challenges to any Medicare coverage decisions. In dismissing the complaint, the District Court relied upon § 405(h) as interpreted by this Court in *Weinberger v. Salfi*, and *Heckler v. Ringer*. The Court of Appeals reversed and held that a later case, *Bowen v. Michigan Academy of Family Physicians* controlled. The second sentence of § 405(h) says that "[n]o findings of fact or decision of the

[Secretary] shall be reviewed by any person, tribunal, or governmental agency except as herein provided." Its third sentence, at issue here, says that "[n]o action against the United States, the [Secretary], or any officer or employee thereof shall be brought under section 1331 or 1346 of title 28 to recover on any claim arising under this subchapter." The scope of the language "to recover on any claim arising under" is, if read alone, uncertain. Those words clearly apply in the typical benefits case, where an individual seeks benefits and is denied. But does the statute's bar apply when someone challenges the lawfulness of a policy, regulation, or statute that might later bar recovery of that benefit, or authorize the imposition of sanctions or penalties? The cases relied on by the District Court, *Salfi* and *Ringer*, clearly bar this § 1331 suit. In *Salfi*, plaintiffs, on behalf of themselves and a class of individuals, brought a § 1331 action challenging the constitutionality of a statutory provision that, if valid, would deny them social security benefits. We held that § 405(h) barred such an action. In *Ringer*, four individuals brought a § 1331 action challenging the lawfulness of a reimbursement denial, and, in part, the agency's procedures. Relief sought was not an order for payment, but a simple declaration invalidating the agency's procedures. Once again, we held that § 405(h) barred such an action. The bar reaches beyond ordinary administrative law principles of "ripeness" and "exhaustion of administrative remedies," doctrines that normally require channeling a legal challenge through the agency. These doctrines have exceptions though, such as when early review is necessary because the legal question is "fit" for resolution and delay means hardship, or when exhaustion would be futile. The required channeling of claims and challenges through the agency assures greater overall efficiency of the agency, at the occasional price of individual, delay-related hardship. We disagree with the Court of Appeals holding that *Michigan Academy* modified our earlier rulings in *Salfi* and *Ringer*. In *Michigan Academy*, we held a § 1331 challenge valid without the usual administrative review because § 405(g) was silent as to the review of a challenge to Medicare Part B amount determination methodology. Such silence meant that no review was available unless a § 1331 suit was allowed in the first instance. Thus it is more plausible to read *Michigan Academy* as holding that § 1395ii [statute that applies § 405(h) to the Medicare Act] does not apply § 405(h) where doing so would not simply channel review through the agency, but would mean no review at all. This follows through with the distinction we have drawn in the past between total preclusion of review and postponement of review. The Association's (P) argument that *Michigan Academy* does apply because it cannot obtain any review at all unless § 1331 judicial review can be had is unconvincing. At a minimum, this matter must be presented to the agency prior to seeking review in a federal court. This the Association (P) has not done. Reversed.

Analysis:

In this case the Association (P) is attempting to challenge the Secretary's (D) ability to impose sanctions upon nursing homes that do not meet the standards set forth by the Secretary (D). The regulations allowing for the imposition of such sanctions are promulgated by the Secretary (D) herself, the same person who, through delegation, is set to rule on challenges to the regulations. This is analogous to a system of law where the judge, jury, and prosecutor are all one and the same individual. While this may seem like a system lacking in due process, it does have valid policy reasons for its existence, many of which the Court discussed. When the individual(s) challenging a Medicare policy or benefits ruling does not receive satisfaction within the agency, judicial review in the federal courts becomes an option. This is the doctrine of exhaustion the Court mentions in its opinion.

■ CASE VOCABULARY

EXHAUSTION: The doctrine that requires any administrative remedies provided for by statute to be utilized before resorting to judicial remedies.

RIPENESS: The doctrine holding that a case may not be heard until the facts necessary for an informed ruling have been fully developed.

Lankford v. Sherman

(*Medicaid Recipients*) v. (*Director of Department of Social Services*)

451 F.3d 496 (8th Cir. 2006)

STATES THAT PARTICIPATE IN MEDICAID MUST FOLLOW FEDERAL REQUIREMENTS

We don't want to play with our little sister.

Sorry, boys. If I help pay for your equipment, then you have to let all your siblings play ball.

stus.com

■ **INSTANT FACTS** Lankford (P) and the other plaintiffs sought a preliminary injunction against a state Medicaid regulation, alleging that the regulation violated the comparability and reasonableness requirements of the Medicaid law.

■ **BLACK LETTER RULE** Medicaid is a voluntary federal/state program, and a state that elects to participate in the program is bound by the requirements of federal law and regulations.

■ PROCEDURAL BASIS

Appeal from an order denying a preliminary injunction.

■ FACTS

Lankford (P) and other disabled adults (P) received medically prescribed durable medical equipment through the Medicaid program administered by the Missouri Department of Social Services (D). Lankford (P) and the others claimed that this equipment was necessary for their medical care and independence. In 2005, the Missouri General Assembly passed a statute that eliminated coverage for durable medical equipment as a covered Medicaid service, except for Medicaid recipients who were blind or pregnant, or for needy children and those recipients who received home healthcare services.

Lankford (P) and the others brought an action for an injunction against the enforcement of regulations implementing the law, arguing that the state (D) could not provide durable medical equipment benefits to blind adult Medicaid recipients unless the benefits were provided to all adult Medicaid recipients. Lankford (P) claimed that the new regulations violated the federal comparability standards, which require that state Medicaid programs provide equal benefits to all categorically needy recipients. Lankford (P) also claimed that the regulations conflicted with the federal requirements that require reasonable standards for the determination of the extent of benefits that meet Medicaid's basic objectives.

The district court found that the regulation was consistent with the comparability requirement, because the State (D) had applied for a federal waiver from the comparability requirements. The district court also found that the new regulation was consistent with the Medicaid Act, and it therefore denied a preliminary injunction.

■ ISSUE

Was the state regulation consistent with the Medicaid Act so that it could be enforced?

■ DECISION AND RATIONALE

(Benton, J.) No. Medicaid is a voluntary federal/state program, and a state that elects to participate in the program is bound by the requirements of federal law and regulations. State regulation of Medicaid programs is not expressly preempted or displaced by federal law, but state law is preempted to the extent that it actually conflicts with federal law. Federal regulations implement the reasonable standards

---

requirements, and Missouri's (D) failure to provide Medicaid coverage for non-experimental, medically necessary services within a covered Medicaid category is *per se* unreasonable and inconsistent with the stated goals of Medicaid.

Missouri (D) covers some durable medical equipment, and so cannot arbitrarily decide which items of durable medical equipment to reimburse. Missouri (D) argued that pre-approved lists of covered equipment are a permitted utilization control, but, according to the Center for Medicare–Medicaid Services of the Department of Health and Human Services (CMS), the list must include specific criteria for coverage, and must also have a mechanism to request reimbursement for non-covered, medically necessary items. These requirements are not set out explicitly in the Medicaid regulations, but the CMS's interpretation of the regulations is entitled to considerable deference. Missouri (D) claims that the regulations allow a means for receiving non-covered services: recipients who receive home healthcare services will receive necessary items of durable medical equipment, or recipients may seek reimbursement through an established exceptions process. Lankford (P) and the other plaintiffs claim that they are not eligible for home healthcare services, and that the exceptions process does not provide them with an adequate mechanism to obtain non-covered items. The regulation appears unreasonable, based on the present record. The regulation does not, however, violate any established federal right, and so the reasonableness requirement cannot be enforced through a civil rights action brought under 42 U.S.C. § 1983. The statutory language that creates the reasonableness requirement—42 U.S.C. § 1396(a)(17)—does not show a congressional intent to create an individually enforceable federal right.

The regulation is not, however, invalid under the comparability analysis. During the pendency of the appeal, Missouri's (D) request for a waiver was denied, and Missouri (D) deleted the part of its Medicaid plan that called for federal funding for the provision of durable medical equipment to the blind. Since federal funding is not received for this program, the comparability requirement is not implicated. Reversed and remanded.

Analysis:

The court noted briefly that the district court did not discuss the reasonableness requirement. In portions of the court's opinion not included in the excerpt, the court stated that the district court looked only at the comparability requirement, and found that the waiver application meant that Lankford (P) was unlikely to succeed on the merits (although the court stated that, if the waiver were denied, additional items of durable medical equipment could not be provided to blind adults unless they were provided to all adults). The district court also held that the other options for obtaining durable medical equipment indicated that there was no irreparable harm. The appellate court's remand directed the district court to consider all of the factors to be weighed in considering a request for a preliminary injunction, including the public interest, and the balancing of the harm suffered by the movant against the harm sustained by others if the injunction were granted. On remand, the court granted Lankford's (P) motion for a preliminary injunction. *See Lankford v. Sherman,* No. 05–4285–CV–C–DW, 2007 WL 689749 (W.D. Mo. Mar. 2, 2007).

■ CASE VOCABULARY

INJUNCTION: court order commanding or preventing an action. To get an injunction, the complainant must show that there is no plain, adequate, and complete remedy at law and that an irreparable injury will result unless the relief is granted.

MEDICAID: A cooperative federal/state program that pays for medical expenses for those who cannot afford private medical services. The program is authorized under the Social Security Act.

PRELIMINARY INJUNCTION: A temporary injunction issued before or during trial to prevent an irreparable injury from occurring before the court has a chance to decide the case. A preliminary injunction will be issued only after the defendant receives notice and an opportunity to be heard.

Westside Mothers v. Haveman

(Medicaid Recipients) v. *(Director of Department of Community Health)*

289 F.3d 852 (6th Cir. 2002)

MEDICAID MANDATES MAY BE ENFORCED BY A PRIVATE ACTION

■ **INSTANT FACTS** Westside Mothers (P) brought an action to compel Haveman (D) to comply with Medicaid mandates, but the suit was dismissed.

■ **BLACK LETTER RULE** Medicaid is not merely a contract, it is a federal law that may be enforced by a private right of action brought under 42 U.S.C. § 1983.

■ **PROCEDURAL BASIS**

Appeal from an order dismissing Westside Mothers' (P) action.

■ **FACTS**

Westside Mothers (P) brought an action to compel Haveman (D) to comply with statutes that required the provision of certain medical services. The district court dismissed the action on Haveman's (D) motion. The district court held that Medicaid was only a contract between the states and the federal government, and that spending-power programs such as Medicaid were not supreme law of the land. The court also held that it lacked jurisdiction because the real party in interest was Michigan, which possessed sovereign immunity; that the case of *Ex Parte Young,* 209 U.S. 123 (1908), was unavailable to circumvent sovereign immunity; and that even if that case were available, 42 U.S.C. § 1983 does not create a cause of action to enforce the statutory requirements in question.

■ **ISSUE**

May Westside Mothers (P) bring their action to enforce the statutory mandates of Medicaid?

■ **DECISION AND RATIONALE**

(Merritt, J.) Yes. Medicaid is not merely a contract, it is a federal law that may be enforced by a private right of action brought under 42 U.S.C. § 1983. To find that Medicaid was a contract, the court drew on language in the cases of *Pennhurst State School and Hospital v. Halderman,* 451 U.S. 1 (1981) and *Blessing v. Freestone,* 520 U.S. 329 (1997). Those cases do not, however, hold that Medicaid is a contract. Instead, the term "contract" is used metaphorically. Medicaid is described as being "much in the nature of a contract." The Supreme Court has held that Medicaid requirements are not merely contractual provisions, but are binding laws.

There is no authority for the proposition that laws made under the spending power are not supreme law. The argument that Medicaid is merely a contract has been rejected. Programs set up under the spending power are supreme law even though Congress does not have the power to force the states to participate. Congress has the power to place conditions on a state's receipt of federal funds.

The exceptions to sovereign immunity set out in *Ex Parte Young* are available to Westside Mothers (P). Under the doctrine of that case, a suit that claims a state official's actions violate the constitution or federal law is not deemed a suit against the state, as long as the state official is the named defendant and the relief sought is only equitable and prospective. The district court held that *Ex Parte Young* did not apply for four reasons. The first is that the doctrine applies only to enforce the laws that are the supreme law of the land. As noted above, Medicaid is part of the supreme law of the land. The second reason is that under *Young,* a court has no power to interfere with an officer's discretionary functions. An officer, however, has no discretion to violate the law. The third reason given by the court is that the state is the real party in interest. This reasoning is based in part on the theory that Medicaid is a contract; however, as noted above, Medicaid is more than a contract. The reasoning is also based on a claim that Haveman (D) and the other named defendants are not alleged personally to have violated the law, but the complaint clearly sets out that the defendants are being sued for the failure to provide services "as required by federal law." The fourth reason given by the district court is that *Young* does not apply when Congress has set out a detailed remedial scheme for the enforcement of a statutorily created right. There is no detailed remedial scheme: Congress cuts off funds to states not in compliance. *Ex Parte Young* applies to this case.

The district court should have used the test set out in *Wilder v. Virginia Hospital Association,* 496 U.S. 498 (1990), before dismissing Westside Mothers' (P) claim under 42 U.S.C. § 1983. Under that case, a statute creates an enforceable right if it was intended to benefit the plaintiff, if it sets out a binding obligation on a unit of government and not just a congressional preference, and if the interests asserted are not vague and amorphous. All three conditions are met. The statutory provisions clearly are meant to benefit children eligible to receive the services, the statute says those services "shall" be furnished, and the specific services to be provided are set out in detail. Congress did not explicitly foreclose a suit under § 1983, and no alternative remedy has been provided. Reversed.

Analysis:

The alternative to allowing suits forcing compliance with Medicaid requirements is a fairly draconian one: funding is cut off until the state comes into compliance. The extreme nature of the remedy means that is less likely to be used, and so is less credible as a threat. On the other hand, injunctive relief is tailored narrowly to meet the specific violation and does not necessarily jeopardize the continuity of the entire program. The threat of an injunction may not be much of a deterrent, but it does provide a more effective remedy for a violation.

■ CASE VOCABULARY

MEDICAID: A cooperative federal-state program that pays for medical expenses for those who cannot afford private medical services. The program is authorized under the Social Security Act.

SPENDING POWER: The power granted to a governmental body to spend public funds; especially, the congressional power to spend money for the payment of debt and provision of the common defense and general welfare of the United States. U.S. Const. art. I, § 8, cl. 1.

SUPREME LAW OF THE LAND: The U.S. Constitution, acts of Congress made according to the U.S. Constitution, and U.S. treaties.

CHAPTER TWELVE

Professional Relationships in Health Care Enterprises

Sokol v. Akron General Medical Center

Instant Facts: When a hospital limited a cardiac surgeon's staff privileges for having a higher-than-expected patient mortality rate, he demanded reinstatement, claiming the decision was arbitrary.

Black Letter Rule: Hospitals have broad discretion in limiting staff privileges, and courts cannot overturn their decisions absent abuse of discretion.

Mateo–Woodburn v. Fresno Community Hospital

Instant Facts: When a hospital switched its anesthesiology department from a chaotic "open staff" policy to restricted staff privileges, dissenting doctors sue.

Black Letter Rule: Hospitals may adopt a general policy of restricted staff privileges, dismiss some doctors without a hearing, and require remaining doctors to adopt a standard contract, as long as the policy is rational and non-discriminatory.

Mahan v. Avera St. Luke's

Instant Facts: Avera St. Luke's (D) barred any new physicians from seeking staff privileges at the hospital, and Mahan (P) claimed breach of contract.

Black Letter Rule: The medical staff of a hospital has no authority over any corporate decisions, unless such authority is explicitly granted in the corporate bylaws.

Potvin v. Metropolitan Life Ins. Co.

Instant Facts: After an insurer delisted a gynecologist from its preferred provider network under a contract permitting termination without cause, the gynecologist sued to require a hearing, contending the delisting made it impossible to secure alternative work.

Black Letter Rule: If a managed care organization wishes to delist a physician from its preferred provider network, it must provide a rational reason and fair procedure if it possesses market power sufficient that the delisting would impair a competent physician's ability to practice medicine in a particular geographic area.

Wright v. Shriners Hospital for Crippled Children

Instant Facts: An at-will nurse, fired for reporting poor patient care and administration, sues for retaliatory discharge.

Black Letter Rule: Hospitals may fire at-will employees who report poor patient care, unless they are required to report such incidents by statute.

Oakwood Healthcare, Inc.

Instant Facts: Oakwood Healthcare (P) contested the inclusion of charge nurses in a bargaining unit, claiming that charge nurses were "supervisors," outside the coverage of the National Labor Relations Act (NLRA).

Black Letter Rule: The question of whether an employee is a "supervisor" depends on whether the employee spends a regular and substantial portion of his or her work time exercising any of the statutory supervisory functions in the interest of the employer, and whether the exercise of those functions requires the use of independent judgment.

New York University Medical Center and Association of Staff Psychiatrists, Bellevue Psychiatric Hospital

Instant Facts: When an unofficial psychiatric labor group's leaders are fired for refusing longer work hours, they contend they were fired illegally for "concerted" labor activities.

Black Letter Rule: Employees engaged in "concerted" labor activities are protected from retaliatory firing by the National Labor Relations Act, even if they are not part of a recognized union.

Estate of Mauro v. Borgess Medical Center

Instant Facts: When a hospital fires an HIV-positive surgical technician, he sues for employment discrimination, contending the risk of transmission is insignificant.

Black Letter Rule: Hospitals may fire infected health care workers who pose a "direct threat" or "significant risk" of serious infection.

Sokol v. Akron General Medical Center

(Staff Physician) v. *(Hospital)*

173 F.3d 1026 (6th Cir. 1999)

HOSPITALS ENJOY BROAD DISCRETION IN GRANTING/REVOKING STAFF PRIVILEGES

■ **INSTANT FACTS** When a hospital limited a cardiac surgeon's staff privileges for having a higher-than-expected patient mortality rate, he demanded reinstatement, claiming the decision was arbitrary.

■ **BLACK LETTER RULE** Hospitals have broad discretion in limiting staff privileges, and courts cannot overturn their decisions absent abuse of discretion.

■ **PROCEDURAL BASIS**

In action seeking injunction (to reinstate staff privileges), appeal from judgement for plaintiff.

■ **FACTS**

Dr. Sokol (P) was a cardiac surgeon with staff privileges at Akron General Medical Center (D). Akron General (D) began investigating the high mortality rate among Sokol's (P) patients, finding his patients had a 12.09% chance of dying during heart bypass surgery, compared with the "predicted" mortality rate of 3.65%. Akron General's (D) staff complained of the finding, and pursuant to staff bylaws, Akron General (D) appointed an Investigatory Committee to investigate Sokol (P). The Investigatory Committee found the high death rate was caused by Sokol's (P) "poor case selection" (operating on risky patients) and insufficient protection against heart attacks. Sokol (P) protested, contending the high mortality rate was inevitable because he operated on high-risk patients, that the "predicted" mortality rate was arbitrary, and that he made no errors in surgery. The Investigatory Committee curtailed Sokol's (P) staff privileges, requiring independent approval of his surgery decisions, barring him from emergency surgery, and requiring continuing oversight. Under Akron General's (D) bylaws, whenever a staffer's staff privileges are restricted, he must be given notice which specifies "what action was taken or proposed . . . and the reasons," and is allowed to appeal to a Hearing Committee. Sokol (P) appealed, and the Hearing Committee recommended Akron General (D) restore Sokol's (P) staff privileges. The medical staff refused. Sokol (P) appealed again to Akron General's (D) board pursuant to bylaws, but it affirmed. Finally, Sokol (P) sued Akron General (D) for an injunction reinstating his staff privileges. At trial, the magistrate judge held for Sokol (P), ordering Akron General (D) to restore his privileges. Akron General (D) appeals.

■ **ISSUE**

May a hospital revoke staff privileges on finding the physician had a higher-than-expected patient mortality rate?

■ **DECISION AND RATIONALE**

(Norris, J.) Yes. Hospitals have broad discretion in limiting staff privileges, and courts cannot overturn their decisions absent abuse of discretion. Under Ohio law, private hospitals are accorded broad discretion in determining who will enjoy medical staff privileges. Courts should not interfere with this discretion "unless the hospital . . . acted in an arbitrary, capricious or unreasonable manner or . . . has abused its discretion." However, hospitals must provide "procedural due process ... in adopting" "reasonable, nondiscriminatory criteria for the privilege of practicing" surgery in the hospital. Under Ohio law, a fair procedure requires an appeals process and "meaningful notice of adverse actions and the ... reasons." Akron General's (D) bylaws provide for no heightened requirements. Here, Akron General (D) sent Sokol (P) a letter notifying him of the initial decision, included minutes of the Medical Council's meeting, indicated the Investigatory Committee's findings and recommendations, stated "the ... percentage of deaths in Dr. Sokol's population was excessively high compared with published national statistics and other local surgeons," and offered as reasons poor case selection and problems in preventing heart attacks. At trial, the magistrate judge found this notice insufficient because it failed to provide Sokol (P) with specific cases of poor case selection or inappropriate safeguards against heart attacks. However, we find such specific notice was not required, and the notice given was adequate. Had Akron General (D) restricted Sokol's (P) rights just because it determined he had poor case selection or insufficient safeguards, then perhaps it would have been required to provide specific patients' cases. However, Akron General (D) was concerned *broadly* that too many of Sokol's (P) patients died; for reasons including *but not limited to* case selection and heart attack. [Huh? By that reasoning, if the hospital had accused him of 2 specific problems, it would have to provide concrete evidence of both. But since it accused him of 2 specific problems plus other *undisclosed* indiscretions, it need not provide any evidence or explain the hidden reasons behind its decision.] Thus, Sokol (P) received the notice required. It is not for us to decide whether the Investigatory Committee's statistical comparison was correct, since Akron General (D) was well within its broad discretion in basing its decisions on statistical overviews rather than case-by-case analyses. Next, the magistrate judge ruled Akron General's (D) decision was arbitrary, because it lacked a fixed mortality rate with which to compare Sokol's (P) mortality rate. We disagree, since a hospital must be allowed to set a standard initially, else it could never take corrective action. However, the standard set must be nondiscriminatory, meaning Akron General (D) would have to limit the privileges of other physicians whose mortality rate exceeded Sokol's (P). While Sokol (P) presents evidence showing Akron General's (D) decision was assailable, under Ohio law, hospitals' boards have broad discretion in dispensing staff privileges, and a board is within its discretion as long as its decision is supported by any evidence. Here, the statistical study constitutes evidence, so we cannot conclude Akron General (D) abused its discretion. Reversed.

■ DISSENT

(Merritt) Sokol (P) was treated unfairly. Akron General (D) never cited a single instance where Sokol (P) made a mistake, not one. The only group of independent medical experts—the Hearing Committee—exonerated him completely.

Analysis:

Sokol highlights the principle that hospitals enjoy broad discretion in granting, limiting, and revoking staff physicians' privileges. While judicial appeal is permitted, courts review such cases using a deferential "abuse of discretion" standard. Akron General's (D) methodology—using statistical analysis of a physician's medical outcomes to presume negligence—is still new and controversial, but represents a growing trend. However, the common law requires hospitals to institute "fair" procedures under the "fundamental fairness" doctrine applicable to private associations. Further procedural guidelines are mandated by the Joint Commission on Healthcare Organizations (JCAHO) and some states' statutes.

■ CASE VOCABULARY

STAFF PRIVILEGES: Independent doctors' contractual right to admit their own private patients to an affiliated hospital for treatment using the hospital's facilities.

Mateo-Woodburn v. Fresno Community Hospital

(Hospital-Affiliated Doctors) v. *(Hospital)*

221 Cal.App.3d 1169, 270 Cal.Rptr. 894 (1990)

HOSPITALS MAY ADOPT A POLICY LIMITING STAFF PRIVILEGES

■ **INSTANT FACTS** When a hospital switched its anesthesiology department from a chaotic "open staff" policy to restricted staff privileges, dissenting doctors sue.

■ **BLACK LETTER RULE** Hospitals may adopt a general policy of restricted staff privileges, dismiss some doctors without a hearing, and require remaining doctors to adopt a standard contract, as long as the policy is rational and non-discriminatory.

■ **PROCEDURAL BASIS**

In contract/tort action, appeal from judgement for defendant.

■ **FACTS**

Fresno Community Hospital ("FCH") (D) previously operated its anesthesiology department as an "open staff," meaning all participating physicians enjoyed staff privileges. The anesthesiologists competed among themselves via a system which allowed each, on a rotating basis, to participate in the most lucrative operations. This competition provided bad incentives: anesthesiologists undertook the more difficult and lucrative operations regardless of their ability, refused Medicaid patients, left the hospital without notifying anyone, and hated each other. Consequently, the Medical Staff determined to find a more effecient system than "open" staffing. The Medical Staff chose to appoint a director of anesthesiology and allow him to subcontract with selected anesthesiologists, effectively forming a set "closed" staff. The Medical Staff chose Dr. Haas [, apparently an outsider,] and his personal corporation as director, and contracted with him to provide anesthesiology services. Haas offered the anesthesiologists a form contract, which allowed Haas to grant staff privileges to selected anesthesiologists, bar others from FCH (D), and set standard fees, and required accepting anesthesiologists to waive hearing rights guaranteed by FCH's (D) bylaws. Several anesthesiologists, including Dr. Mateo-Woodburn (P), refused to sign the contract, protesting it required them to surrender their vested right to practice anesthesiology at FCH (D), provided no due process before termination, forced signatories to stop practicing at other hospitals except by Haas' permission, imposed unreasonable control over signatories' finances and practice, and failed to provide tenure. [In other words, it prevented them from continuing on as oligopolistic robber barons.] These non-signatories (P) sued FCH (D), contending its restructuring plan was illegal.

■ **ISSUE**

May a hospital institute a system of restricted staff privileges?

■ **DECISION AND RATIONALE**

(Brown, J.) Yes. Hospitals may adopt a general policy of restricted staff privileges, dismiss some doctors without a hearing, and require remaining doctors to adopt a standard contract, as long as the policy is rational and non-discriminatory. This result is mandated by numerous prior cases. When hospitals adopt such a policy, some doctors may be divested of their vested rights to practice. If this divestiture results from a generally-applicable rule or policy (rather than individual doctors' fault), it may be done without a hearing, since a doctor's elimination by reason of departmental reorganization will not reflect upon his professional qualifications or impair future employment. If a hospital's policy change is lawful, the terms of any contract offered to doctors are deemed part of that policy decision, and courts will not interfere with such contracts unless they are substantially irrational or discriminatory. Here, the district court found the change was lawful, and the contract was not unreasonable in light of the prior lack of discipline and scheduling. We agree. Plaintiffs contend the reorganization could not take place without amending the bylaws, and that FCH (D) unlawfully delegated to Haas the medical staff's authority to appoint staffers, but we find the changes did not affect medical staffers' fundamental rights or qualifications. Thus, we conclude FCH's (D) reorganization was proper, and that the plaintiffs' privileges were not terminated unlawfully. Affirmed.

Analysis:

Mateo-Woodburn stands for the proposition that hospitals may adopt a policy granting staff privileges to selected doctors only. The anesthesiologists here raise the claim that FCH's (D) bylaws provide that individual doctors cannot be terminated, or stripped of privileges, without a hearing. This provision, standard among hospital bylaws, serves to protect doctors from unjustified dismissal, which impairs their ability to get work elsewhere. However, the court here held this provision is not implicated when multiple doctors are dismissed as part of a general reorganization, since this carries no shame. This holding has become the majority approach.

Mahan v. Avera St. Luke's

(Orthopedic Surgeon) v. *(Hospital)*

621 N.W.2d 150 (S.D. 2001)

MEDICAL STAFF MEMBERS HAVE NO INHERENT AUTHORITY TO MAKE BUSINESS DECISIONS

Thank you for choosing Avera St. Luke's for your orthopedic spine surgery. We know you have a choice in who cuts you open.

stus.com

■ **INSTANT FACTS** Avera St. Luke's (D) barred any new physicians from seeking staff privileges at the hospital, and Mahan (P) claimed breach of contract.

■ **BLACK LETTER RULE** The medical staff of a hospital has no authority over any corporate decisions, unless such authority is explicitly granted in the corporate bylaws.

■ **PROCEDURAL BASIS**

Appeal from an order granting summary judgment and entering a mandatory permanent injunction against Avera (D).

■ **FACTS**

Avera St. Luke's (D), a hospital, sought to recruit either two neurosurgeons or two spine-trained orthopedic surgeons. During the recruitment process, Avera (D) learned that most neurosurgeons would not be interested in the position if there were already an orthopedic spine surgeon practicing in the area. This was due to the small size of the community and the neurosurgeon's probable need to supplement his or her income by performing back and spine surgery. Applicants doubted whether the community could support both a neurosurgeon and an orthopedic spine surgeon. Avera was successful in recruiting a neurosurgeon.

At roughly the same time, Orthopedic Surgery Specialists (OSS) (P), a group of orthopedic surgeons in the community, decided to build a day surgery center that would directly compete with Avera (D). During the first seven months of the day surgery's operation, Avera (D) lost 1,000 hours of operating room usage. In response, the Avera (D) board passed two resolutions. The first resolution closed Avera's medical staff to physicians for three certain surgical procedures. The second closed the staff to applicants for orthopedic surgery privileges, except for the two surgeons being recruited. In making its decision, the board specifically determined that the closures were in the best interests of the community. The board's decision did not affect those surgeons who already had privileges at Avera (D), including the physicians at OSS (P).

A few months later, OSS (P) recruited Mahan (P), a spine-trained orthopedic surgeon who practiced in the area of orthopedic surgery. Mahan (P) was told that Avera (D) had been closed to orthopedic surgery privileges, but Mahan (P) began practicing with OSS (P) anyway. Mahan (P) applied for staff privileges at Avera (D) at least twice, and was turned down both times. Mahan (P) and OSS (P) brought an action against Avera (D), alleging breach of the staff bylaws. The parties made cross-motions for summary judgment, and the court granted the motions of Mahan (P) and OSS (P).

■ **ISSUE**

Did the closure of staff privileges breach a contract with ODD (P) or Mahan (P)?

■ **DECISION AND RATIONALE**

(Gilbertson, J.) No. The medical staff of a hospital has no authority over any corporate decisions, unless such authority is explicitly granted in the corporate bylaws. The powers set out in the staff bylaws are derived entirely from, and must be authorized by, the corporate bylaws. The bylaws of Avera (D) give the board the exclusive authority to make business decisions without consulting the medical staff. The medical staff is given the authority to make recommendations regarding the professional competence of staff members and employees, and is also given the power to organize under bylaws, subject to the approval of the board, as well as the authority to ensure appropriate care to Avera's (D) patients. Nowhere was the staff explicitly authorized to make business decisions.

The trial court based its decision on the "spirit of the bylaws taken as a whole." This turns the corporate structure of Avera (D) upside down. When the board made its decision to close the medical staff, it was acting within its powers. The authority to manage Avera (D) includes the authority to make decisions on how to operate individual departments to serve the corporation's interests in the best manner. Unprofitable yet essential services cannot be offered unless there is a financial offset from the more profitable services, such as neurosurgery. The board has the power to attempt to insure Avera's (D) economic survival. Any allegations that the board breached its implied duty of good faith must fail.

Mahan (P) and OSS (P) had standing to bring their action. The decision of the Avera (D) board resulted in an economic hardship for OSS (P) and Mahan (P). However, there was no breach of contract. Reversed.

Analysis:

The provision of health care is a business, and economic factors often drive decisions on the delivery of that care. Avera (D) made a business decision to close staff privileges; however, that economic decision was driven or prompted by a desire to recruit medical staff sufficient to insure continuous neurosurgical coverage. Note that Avera (D) is described as the only full service hospital in a ninety-mile radius. Any competition in providing services in such a community is necessarily going to become fierce.

Potvin v. Metropolitan Life Ins. Co.

(Former Preferred Provider) v. *(Insurer/Managed Care Organization)*

22 Cal.4th 1060, 95 Cal.Rptr.2d 496, 997 P.2d 1153 (2000)

INFLUENTIAL MANAGED CARE ORGANIZATIONS WISHING TO DELIST PREFERRED PROVIDER PHYSICIAN MUST FOLLOW FAIR PROCEDURE

■ **INSTANT FACTS** After an insurer delisted a gynecologist from its preferred provider network under a contract permitting termination without cause, the gynecologist sued to require a hearing, contending the delisting made it impossible to secure alternative work.

■ **BLACK LETTER RULE** If a managed care organization wishes to delist a physician from its preferred provider network, it must provide a rational reason and fair procedure if it possesses market power sufficient that the delisting would impair a competent physician's ability to practice medicine in a particular geographic area.

■ **PROCEDURAL BASIS**

In contract action seeking injunction, appeal from reversal of summary judgement for defendant.

■ **FACTS**

Metropolitan Life Ins. Co. ("MetLife") (D) contracted with obstetrician-gynecologist Dr. Potvin (P), making him a "preferred provider" for treating MetLife (D)'s insureds. The contract created no agency or employment relationship, allowed Potvin (P) to contract with others, and allowed termination by either party "at any time, with or without cause, by giving … 30 days prior written notice." Later, MetLife (D) "delisted" Potvin (P), terminating his contract. When Potvin (P) requested a reason, MetLife (D) refused to provide one, maintaining it could terminate without cause. When Potvin (P) asked again, MetLife (D) said his "delistment … was related to the fact that [he] did not meet [its] … retention standard for malpractice history." MetLife's (D) policy was not to hire/retain any physician with over two malpractice suits, or who paid over $50K for such claims. When hired, Potvin (P) had had four prior malpractice lawsuits, and settled one for $713K. [Apparently, MetLife (D) changed its standards after hiring Potvin (P), making him ineligible.] Potvin (P) requested a hearing, but MetLife (D) failed to respond. Potvin (P) found the delisting devastated his practice, especially since he was required to report his delisting, which caused other insurers/managed care entities to reject him, physician groups to deny him credentialing, and MetLife's (D) other preferred providers to withhold referrals. Potvin (P) sued MetLife (D), contending (i) his contract implied a common law right to fair procedures, (ii) his "without cause" termination violated California's statutory right to peer review, and (iii) the contract's "no cause" termination clause should be voided because it violates public policy. At trial, MetLife (D) moved for summary judgement, which was granted. On appeal, the Court of Appeal reversed, finding the common law right to fair procedure required MetLife (D) to give Potvin (P) notice of the grounds and opportunity to be heard, but finding the California statute requiring peer review before removal was inapplicable to preferred provider contracts. MetLife (D) appeals.

■ **ISSUE**

May a managed care organization delist a preferred provider physician without cause if its contract so permits?

■ DECISION AND RATIONALE

(Kennard, J.) No. If a managed care organization wishes to delist a physician from its preferred provider network, it must provide a rational reason and fair procedure if it possesses market power sufficient that the delisting would impair a competent physician's ability to practice medicine in a particular geographic area. When insureds' medical services are provided through the tripartite relationship between an insurance company, insureds, and the physicians comprising its preferred provider network, then a great public interest is at stake. Another public interest is affected when insurance companies, with fiduciary obligations to its insureds, maintain a list of preferred provider physicians. The modern health care revolution, which made health care more affordable and available through managed care entities, also had the practical effect that patients are less free to choose their own doctors. However, managed care's effect on the public interest does not necessarily mean insurers wishing to delist doctors as preferred providers must comply with the common law right to fair procedure, unless the insurer possesses power so substantial that delisting significantly impairs the ability of a competent physician to practice medicine in a particular geographic area, thus affecting an important, substantial economic interest. Here, Potvin's (P) alleged effects of his delisting, if proven, might establish that MetLife (D) wielded economic power sufficient to require fair procedure. Also, Potvin's (P) amici curiae, the American Medical Association and California Medical Association, assert that a few large managed care organizations hold substantial economic power over physicians and patients, and that it is practically necessary for physicians to participate in their managed care arrangement to practice profitably. Insurers obligated to provide fair procedures may still exercise sound business judgement when establishing removal standards, as long as removal is "both substantively rational and procedurally fair." While the contract here waives the right to fair procedure in its "termination without cause" provision, we are loathe to enforce contract provisions offensive to public policy, and void this provision. Affirmed.

■ CONCURRENCE

(George, J.) [Omitted From Casebook.]

■ DISSENT

(Brown, J.) Delisting a physician from a preferred provider network does not impair his ability to practice medicine, but merely limits his income, which should not be protected by law. Insurers should be free to exercise their business judgement, by restricting preferred providers to those with superior malpractice histories, in order to control costs. Further, there is no reason to void the "termination without cause" provision.

Analysis:

Managed care organizations try to offer affordable insurance by cutting the cost of medical care, by exerting market leverage on both the supply (doctors) and demand (insureds). On the demand side, managed care organizations will limit or deny unnecessary medical procedures. On the supply side, they drive hard bargains with individual physicians. As *Potvin*'s dicta notes, such insurers and organizations are able to wield vast market power, because they control the referrals of many thousands of patients in an area. Thus, if a physician is delisted by one such organization, and this delisting effectively blacklists him from working as a preferred provider for any managed care organization, then he is effectively shut out from seeing a vast number of potential patients.

■ CASE VOCABULARY

MANAGED CARE [ORGANIZATION]: System/organization which attempts to provide insureds with cheaper medical insurance/care by cutting costs, through various methods. Typically, the organization limits costs by disallowing insureds from demanding unnecessary medical procedures, and also by negotiating reduced fees with doctors.

PREFERRED PROVIDER [NETWORK]: Doctor(s) chosen by a managed care organization for referral of its insureds. Typically, when an insured needs medical treatment, the managed care organization attempts to send the insured to a participating preferred provider, if one is reasonably available.

Wright v. Shriners Hospital for Crippled Children

(Nurse) v. *(Employer)*

412 Mass. 469, 589 N.E.2d 1241 (1992)

AT-WILL EMPLOYEES MAY BE DISCHARGED FOR REPORTING VIOLATIONS

■ **INSTANT FACTS** An at-will nurse, fired for reporting poor patient care and administration, sues for retaliatory discharge.

■ **BLACK LETTER RULE** Hospitals may fire at-will employees who report poor patient care, unless they are required to report such incidents by statute.

■ FACTS

Nurse Ms. Wright (P) worked at Shriners Hospital for Crippled Children (D), an independent branch of the national headquarters. Later, Wright (D) was promoted to assistant director of nursing. At all times, Wright (D) was employed "at-will." Wright's (D) predecessor wrote a complaint to the national headquarters shortly before leaving, leading the headquarters to send an inspection team to Shriners Hospital (D). Shriners Hospital's (D) administrator Russo believed Wright (D) sent the letter. When the inspectors arrived, Wright (D) told them about friction and communication problems between the doctors, nurses, and administrators, resulting in inconsistent procedures and poor patient care. As a result of the report, the home office made more inspections. Russo fired Wright (D) for "patient care issues that had arisen as a result of the surveys." [Savor the irony.] Wright (D) sued Shriners Hospital (D), contending the retaliatory firing was illegal because it violated public policy. At trial, the jury returned a verdict for Wright (D) for $100K. Shriners Hospital (D) moved for judgement notwithstanding the verdict, which was denied. Shriners Hospital (D) appeals.

■ ISSUE

May a hospital fire an at-will employee for reporting poor administration and patient care to its home office?

■ DECISION AND RATIONALE

(O'Connor, J.) Yes. Hospitals may fire at-will employees who report poor patient care, unless they are required to report such incidents by statute. Generally, "employment at will is terminable by either the employee or the employer without notice, for almost any reason or for no reason at all." However, we recognize exceptions when the termination is contrary to well-defined public policy. Thus, "redress is available for employees who are terminated for asserting a legally-guaranteed right (e.g., filing workers' compensation claims), for doing what the law requires (e.g., serving on a jury), or for refusing to do that which the law forbids (e.g., committing perjury)." Here, the trial court found that Shriners Hospital's (D) firing of Wright (D) violated public policy, since Shriners Hospital's (D) ethics code required nurses to report patient care issues, and based on "various state laws ... requiring reporting of patient abuse." However, we find no public policy was violated. We hesitate to declare that a private professional organization's ethical code can be a source of public policy. Further, we are unaware of any state law directly applicable to Wright (D), or any statute expressing a legislative policy encouraging nurses to make internal reports. Wright (D) urges us to adopt as a source of public policy a regulation promulgated by the Board of Registration in Nursing, which includes the responsibility to "collaborate, communicate and cooperate as appropriate with other health care providers to ensure quality and continuity of care." But we decline to recognize a professional regulation as a source of public policy. Even if we did, it is doubtful the regulation required Wright (D) to report problems to the survey team. Further, Wright's (D) report was an internal matter, and we previously noted that "internal matters . . . could not be the basis of a public policy exception to the at-will rule." Reversed.

■ **DISSENT**

(Liacos, J.) I disagree with the majority's conclusion that a hospital violates no public policy in firing employees for alerting supervisors to matters detracting from good patient care. The majority, in demanding a statutory basis for public policy, relinquishes to the legislature its role in shaping common law. This State's public policy should protect and encourage hospital employees to report perceived detriments to patient care, so such problems may be addressed. That employers may deter employees from reporting problems (for fear of losing their jobs) inhibits good patient care and offends the public interest.

Analysis:

Wright represents the majority of states' construction of the at-will employment public policy exception, except that many states will accept employers' internal ethics codes as iterations of public policy. The public policy exception, so powerful in principle, can be a disappointment in practice. Courts are inconsistent in applying it to whistleblowers, even within a single jurisdiction, so that some employees receive compensation, while others are denied recovery on seemingly indistinguishable facts. To counteract this situation, some state and federal statutes protect whistleblowers, but again courts restrict their effectiveness by construing them narrowly.

■ **CASE VOCABULARY**

AT-WILL EMPLOYMENT: Employment relation where the employee neither serves for a fixed term, nor has a contract requiring termination be "for cause" only. Under such "at-will," employment, employees may be fired (or may leave) without cause or notice.

Oakwood Healthcare, Inc.

(Employer of Nurses)

348 N.L.R.B. (2006)

SUPERVISORY EMPLOYEES USE INDEPENDENT JUDGMENT IN PERFORMING THEIR JOBS

I thought they called the us "supervisors" because of our hard work, but actually they just wanted to hurt the labor union.

■ **INSTANT FACTS** Oakwood Healthcare (P) contested the inclusion of charge nurses in a bargaining unit, claiming that charge nurses were "supervisors," outside the coverage of the National Labor Relations Act (NLRA).

■ **BLACK LETTER RULE** The question of whether an employee is a "supervisor" depends on whether the employee spends a regular and substantial portion of his or her work time exercising any of the statutory supervisory functions in the interest of the employer, and whether the exercise of those functions requires the use of independent judgment.

■ PROCEDURAL BASIS

Review of a decision and direction of election.

■ FACTS

Oakwood Healthcare (P) challenged a decision that its charge nurses be included in a bargaining unit. Charge nurses are nurses who are responsible for overseeing patient care units. They assign other nurses, nursing assistants, technicians, and paramedics to patients. Charge nurses also monitor patients, meet with doctors and patients' family members, and follow up on unusual incidents. Charge nurses may take on patient loads as well, but those who do often take less than a full compliment of patients.

Twelve nurses were designated as permanent charge nurses. Other nurses took turns rotating into the charge nurse position and, in some patient care units, other nurses took over as charge nurses when the permanent charge nurses were off. The rotation might be set by higher-level managers, or it might be worked out by the nurses themselves. Some of the nurses employed by Oakwood (P) did not work as charge nurses—some by choice, some due to the parts of the hospital in which they worked, and some because they were new employees. Oakwood (P) argued that all charge nurses should be excluded from the bargaining unit as supervisors, while the union (D) argued that the charge nurses should be included.

■ ISSUE

Were all of the charge nurses "supervisors," such that, pursuant to the NLRA, they could not be included in the bargaining unit?

■ DECISION AND RATIONALE

(By the Board.) No. The question of whether an employee is a "supervisor" depends on whether the employee spends a regular and substantial portion of his or her work time exercising any of the statutory supervisory functions in the interest of the employer, and whether the exercise of those functions requires the use of independent judgment. "Independent judgment" is determined by the *degree* of discretion exercised, not the *kind* of discretion. Independent judgment involves acting, or effectively recommending action, free of the control of others and forming an opinion or evaluation by discerning and comparing data. Judgment is not independent if it is dictated or controlled by detailed instructions, whether those instructions are set out in company policies or rules, verbal instructions, or a collective bargaining agreement. Company policies do not eliminate independent judgment if the policies allow for discretionary choices.

Supervisory functions are set out in § 2(11) of the NLRA, 29 U.S.C. § 152(11). Those functions are the authority to hire, transfer, suspend, lay off, recall, promote, discharge, assign, reward, or discipline other employees, or responsibly to direct them, or to adjust their grievances, or effectively to recommend such action, if in connection with the foregoing the exercise of such authority is not of a merely routine or clerical nature. . . .

Oakwood (P) claims that the charge nurses responsibly direct the nursing staff by instructing the staff to perform certain tasks. Oakwood (P) has not demonstrated that the charge nurses meet this standard. "Responsible direction" means that the person directing the action is accountable for the performance of the task by the other employee. The person who directs the action has the authority to take corrective action, if necessary. That person may suffer adverse consequences if the task is not performed properly, or if corrective action is not taken. There is no evidence here that the charge nurses are subject to discipline or other adverse action if other staff members do not adequately perform their assigned tasks.

The term "assign" refers to designating a time or a place for an employee to work, or giving significant overall duties to other employees. In the instant case, it includes a charge nurse's responsibility to assign nurses and aides to particular patients. Designating a particular employee as the person who will regularly administer medications to a patient or group of patients is an assignment. Directing a nurse to immediately give a sedative to a particular patient is not an assignment. In this case, in the emergency room, charge nurses assign employees to certain locations, but these locations are rotated by the staff members themselves. In areas of the hospital other than the emergency room, however, charge nurses assign staff members to particular locations and give them significant overall tasks. The assignments made by the charge nurses determine an employee's required work during a shift, which has a material effect on the terms and conditions of employment. Assignments are made based upon the charge nurses' assessments of patients' conditions and needs, and on the abilities of the employees. This shows that the assignments—except in the emergency room—are based on the independent judgment of the charge nurses. Oakwood's (P) written policy does not eliminate a significant discretionary component involved in making assignments. On the other hand, no such judgment is involved in the emergency room assignments.

A "regular" portion of an employee's work time has been found when an employee exercises supervisory functions for at least ten to fifteen percent of his or her work time. The evidence on regularity for the nurses who are not permanently employed as charge nurses is superficial. There is no established pattern or predictable schedule for the rotating charge nurses. Therefore, only the permanent charge nurses will be considered supervisors. Reversed.

Analysis:

A "unit" or "bargaining unit," as the term is used in the NLRA, is the group of employees designated as "appropriate" to select an agent for collective bargaining. 29 U.S.C. § 159(a). Although the union (D) lost its argument that all charge nurses should be included in the bargaining unit, Oakwood's (P) victory was not a large one. Of the 181 staff registered nurses employed by Oakwood (P), only twelve were excluded from the bargaining unit. A decision that the nurses who were not permanent charge nurses were also supervisors would have resulted in a much smaller and, presumably, less powerful bargaining unit, since only recent hires, or those who worked in some specialized areas or chose not to be charge nurses, would not have been excluded.

■ CASE VOCABULARY

BARGAINING UNIT: A group of employees authorized to engage in collective bargaining on behalf of all the employees of a company or an industry sector.

COLLECTIVE BARGAINING AGREEMENT: A contract between an employer and a labor union regulating employment conditions, wages, benefits, and grievances.

NATIONAL LABOR RELATIONS ACT: A federal statute regulating the relations between employers and employees and establishing the National Labor Relations Board. 29 USCA §§ 151–169. The statute is also known as the Wagner Act of 1935. It was amended by the Taft–Hartley Act of 1947 and the Landrum–Griffin Act of 1959.

NATIONAL LABOR RELATIONS BOARD: An independent five-member federal board created to prevent and remedy unfair labor practices and to safeguard employees' rights to organize into labor unions. The board hears complaints of unfair labor practices and issues orders that can be reviewed or enforced by a U.S. court of appeals. The agency was created by the National Labor Relations Act of 1935.

New York University Medical Center and Association of Staff Psychiatrists, Bellevue Psychiatric Hospital

(Employee Group) v. *(Employer)*

324 NLRB No. 139 (1997)

NATIONAL LABOR RELATIONS ACT PROTECTS ALL EMPLOYEES ENGAGED IN "CONCERTED" LABOR ACTIVITIES

■ **INSTANT FACTS** When an unofficial psychiatric labor group's leaders are fired for refusing longer work hours, they contend they were fired illegally for "concerted" labor activities.

■ **BLACK LETTER RULE** Employees engaged in "concerted" labor activities are protected from retaliatory firing by the *National Labor Relations Act,* even if they are not part of a recognized union.

■ **PROCEDURAL BASIS**

Administrative hearing on wrongful discharge claim.

■ **FACTS**

At Bellevue Psychiatric Hospital ("Bellevue" or "HHC," after the name of its corporate management) (D), employee psychiatrists formed an Association of Staff Psychiatrists ("Association") (P) to negotiate grievances with HHC (D). Association (P) was not the psychiatrists' official union, since Bellevue (D) had a previously-defined staff psychiatrists' "unit" (union). Specifically, the grievances arose under Bellevue's (D) unofficial "9 to 3" policy, whereby staff psychologists actually worked from 9 A.M. to 3 P.M., instead of the 40 hours required under their contract. At a meeting, HHC's (D) representative Dr. Trujillo announced that HHC (D), facing financial problems, would require staff psychiatrists to work at least 35 hours per week, suspending the "9 to 3" policy. [Slavedrivers!] Association's (P) elected representative Dr. (Ms.) Mahon (P) objected, suggesting HHC's (D) physician-administrators help with clinical care. Trujillo refused to recognize Association (P) as a bargaining unit, and threatened to "punish" Association (P) and Mahon (P). Later, HHC (D) fired 6 of Association (P)'s senior executives, citing budget reductions. Association (P) and the fired physicians (P) sued HHC (D), contending it illegally threatened employees with layoffs and fired the workers in retaliation for protected "concerted" activities, in violation of the *National Labor Relations Act §§ 8(a)(1)* and *8(a)(3).* HHC (D) defends, contending the terminations were a good faith response to budget cuts.

■ **ISSUE**

Can an employer fire employees for participating in collective bargaining outside of the official union?

■ **DECISION AND RATIONALE**

No. Employees engaged in "concerted" labor activities are protected from retaliatory firing by the *National Labor Relations Act,* even if they are not part of a recognized union. The evidence shows the Association of Staff Psychiatrists (D) is a "labor organization" under the *National Labor Relations Act.* But it is not a "union," because Bellevue's (D) staff psychologists (D) already have a previously-defined "unit" to deal with HHC (D) on matters such as salaries, working hours and conditions, and grievances. This union has elected officials, a dues-paying membership, and a record of bargaining with HHC (D).

It is undisputed HHC (D) faced a budget cut of $2M. [Among the ten doctors terminated were 6 members of Association's (P) executive committee. The evidence shows each was competent.] The evidence also shows Association (P) and its member psychiatrists engaged in concerted actions to protest HHC's (D) announced work hour changes, and that HHC (D) was aware of such activities. The record is replete with evidence of Dr. Trujillo's animosity toward Association (P) and its executive board (P), and his statements were obviously threats rather than warnings. I am persuaded that a motivating factor in the discharge of the 6 psychiatrists (P) was HHC's (D) animus toward Association (P) and its members' protected concerted activities, including their open opposition to changing the "9 to 3" schedule. Thus, the burden shifts to the employer to establish it would have taken the same action even absent the protected concerted action. Here, HHC (D) failed to prove this. Judgement for plaintiffs.

Analysis:

This case illustrates that employees engaged in "concerted" (union-related) activities may be protected from retaliatory termination by the National Labor Relations Act, even if the employees are not part of a NLRB-certified "union." Here, the Association (P) is protected as a "labor organization," even though it is unofficial and has fewer members than required to form a "union." Other cases have extended the NLRA's protections to even individuals who oppose the employer, somehow finding that they were engaged in "concerted action."

■ CASE VOCABULARY

UNION: Employee organization certified by the National Labor Relations Board as representing a majority of a given employer's workers. The union engages in collective bargaining with the employer on behalf of members. Here, Association (P) was not the official union of Bellevue psychiatrists.

"UNIT": Under the *National Labor Relations Act,* a discrete group of employees empowered to collectively bargain on behalf of members. Under the *NLRA,* one employer's employees can only organize into a limited number of "units," whose members must have a common job and interests.

Estate of Mauro v. Borgess Medical Center

(HIV-Positive Medical Technician) v. *(Employer)*

137 F.3d 398 (6th Cir. 1998)

HOSPITALS MAY FIRE HEALTH CARE EMPLOYEES WHOSE HIV INFECTION POSES SIGNIFICANT RISKS

■ **INSTANT FACTS** When a hospital fires an HIV-positive surgical technician, he sues for employment discrimination, contending the risk of transmission is insignificant.

■ **BLACK LETTER RULE** Hospitals may fire infected health care workers who pose a "direct threat" or "significant risk" of serious infection.

■ **PROCEDURAL BASIS**

In employment discrimination action, appeal from summary judgement for defendant.

■ **FACTS**

Mauro (P) was employed at Borgess Medical Center ("Borgess") (D) as a surgical technician, which required him to reach into patients' open wounds during surgery and adjust/cut stitches. Mauro (P) contracted HIV, which came to the attention of Borgess (D). Borgess (D), concerned about the risk of HIV transmission to patients, tried to accommodate Mauro (P) by offering him an alternative position without patient contact, but Mauro (P) refused. Borgess (D) fired Mauro (P). Mauro (P) sued Borgess (D) for employment discrimination, under the Americans with Disabilities Act and Rehabilitation Act [which prohibit refusing to hire otherwise-qualified handicapped applicants]. At trial, Borgess (D) moved for summary judgement. The judge granted summary judgement for Borgess (D), finding Mauro's (P) HIV was a direct threat to others' safety and could not be eliminated by reasonable accommodation. Mauro (P) appeals, contending he posed virtually no risk to patients.

■ **ISSUE**

May a hospital fire an HIV-positive surgical technician?

■ **DECISION AND RATIONALE**

(Gibson) Yes. Hospitals may fire infected health care workers who pose a "direct threat" or "significant risk" of serious infection. Rehabilitation Act § 504 provides that otherwise-qualified handicapped individuals cannot be excluded from any program receiving federal financial assistance [i.e., a publicly-funded hospital], solely by reason of his handicap. Congress' intent was to protect disabled individuals "from deprivations based on prejudice, stereotypes, or unfounded fear, while giving appropriate weight to such legitimate concerns ... as avoiding exposing others to significant health and safety risks." School Board of Nassau County v. Arline. Arline noted the handicapped are especially vulnerable to irrational fear of contagiousness, and that the *Act* aimed to replace reflexive reactions with reasonable and medically-sound criteria. Plaintiffs under the Rehabilitation Act must establish they are "otherwise qualified" to do the job, meaning able to perform the job's "essential functions." In situations involving persons with contagious diseases, the inquiry should also consider whether the individual poses "a significant risk of communicating the disease to others in the workplace." The Americans with Disabilities Act provides that qualified disabled individuals cannot be excluded from participation in public entities [i.e., employment in public hospitals]. Plaintiffs must show they are "otherwise qualified" for the job, meaning they can perform the job's essential functions. However, individuals are not deemed "qualified" if they pose a "direct threat" to others' health or safety which cannot be eliminated by reasonable accommodation. The Americans with Disabilities Act's "direct threat" standard is similar to the Rehabilitation Act's "significant risk" standard. Here, the combined issue is whether Mauro's (P) activities as a surgical technician pose a direct threat or significant risk to others' health or safety. *Arline* laid down 4 factors to consider: (i) the risk's nature (how the disease is transmitted), (ii) the risk's duration (how long carriers are infectious), (iii) the risk's severity (potential harm to third parties), and (iv) the probability the disease will be transmitted and will cause varying degrees of harm. Neither law requires the elimination of all risk, so an insignificant risk is not grounds for termination. Similarly, EEOC guidelines provide that employers may not deny employment merely because of a slightly increased risk. Here, the parties agree Mauro's (P) risk was significant in nature, duration, and severity. Mauro (P) argues that, because the probability of transmission was slight, it overwhelmed the other 3 factors. *Arline* instructs courts, in determining whether employees pose a "significant risk" or "direct threat," to defer to "the reasonable medical judgements of public health officials." Here, one such official group—the Centers for Disease Control ("CDC")—found the risk of HIV transmission from infected health care workers to patients is very small, and thus recommended most HIV-positive health care workers continue performing most surgical procedures, while following safety precautions. However, the CDC distinguishes "exposure-prone procedures" with greater risk of skin-piercing injury, and does not recommend that HIV-positive workers perform those. We defer to the CDC's recommendations. However, we note the CDC does not specify which procedures are "exposure-prone." Here, Mauro (P) admits that skin-piercing is possible for surgical technicians, and previously happened to him twice. Thus, Mauro's (P) work is "exposure prone," and the district court did not err in finding Mauro (P) posed a direct threat to others' health and safety. Affirmed.

■ DISSENT

(Boggs) Since reasonable minds can differ on the degree of risk posed by HIV-positive surgical technicians, the question should be submitted to the jury. To decide this, jurors should receive more information about specific probabilities that Mauro (P) would transmit HIV to others.

Analysis:

This opinion recounts the anti-discrimination laws applicable to hospital workers, with the focus on the acute modern problem of HIV infection. It relies heavily on the pivotal Supreme Court case of *School Board of Nassau County v. Arline,* which first analyzed how Rehabilitation Act § 504 applies to employees with transmissible diseases. *Arline* found that employees with physically impairing and contagious diseases (namely, a tubercular teacher) are "handicapped," and thus protected against discriminatory termination. Later federal cases applied the same standard to HIV infection. In practice, courts tackling the issue of HIV-infected health care workers must decide whether the risk of individual workers infecting others is large enough to be "significant" or a "direct threat," considering the individual's position and duties and his personal safety record.

■ CASE VOCABULARY

REASONABLE ACCOMMODATION: Under the Americans with Disabilities Act, larger employers are required to provide disabled workers with "reasonable accommodations" (e.g., facilities, special equipment, etc.) which would enable them to work on par with able employees. Reasonableness is usually analyzed in terms of cost. Here, Borgess (D) concluded there was no way to eliminate the risk of Mauro (P) infecting others while retaining him as a full-service medical technician, though it attempted to accommodate him by transferring him to a job handling tools and equipment.

CHAPTER THIRTEEN

The Structure of the Health Care Enterprise

Stern v. Lucy Webb Hayes National Training School for Deaconesses and Missionaries

Instant Facts: When a charitable hospital's investigation revealed its trustees had "invested" its money into their affiliated banks' low-interest-bearing accounts, patients sued as a class for breach of fiduciary duties.

Black Letter Rule: Charitable hospitals' "trustee"-directors are in breach of their fiduciary duties to manage their hospital's financial affairs if (i) while assigned to a Board committee assigned financial/investment responsibility, they fail to use due diligence in supervising those employees responsible for day-to-day financial/investment decisions, or (ii) they knowingly permit the hospital to enter business transactions with themselves or their affiliated entities without disclosing their interest and any significant reasons why the transaction might not be in the hospital's best interests, or (iii) they participated actively in any decision to transact business with themselves or their affiliated entities, or (iv) they otherwise failed to perform their duties honestly, in good faith, and with reasonable care.

In re Caremark International Inc. Derivative Litigation

Instant Facts: When a corporation charged with health care bribery is forced to pay $250 million and promise better management in a settlement with government agencies, angry shareholders request the court reject the settlement and permit them to sue the directors for negligently permitting the bribery.

Black Letter Rule: Corporate directors have a duty to make good faith efforts to institute a corporate monitoring system they believe will alert them of material events, but are not liable if the system fails to detect wrongdoing.

Manhattan Eye, Ear and Throat Hospital v. Spitzer

Instant Facts: Manhattan Eye, Ear and Throat Hospital (MEETH) (P) brought a petition for approval of a sale of its assets.

Black Letter Rule: In order to obtain judicial approval of a sale of all or substantially all of a non-profit corporation's assets, the board must show that the consideration and terms of the transaction are fair and that the purposes of the corporation will be promoted.

Berlin v. Sarah Bush Lincoln Health Center

Instant Facts: A corporate hospital's employee doctor, wishing to escape his non-competition covenant, claims the hospital's hiring of doctors constitutes unauthorized medical practice by the hospital.

Black Letter Rule: While the "corporate practice of medicine" doctrine prevents corporations from providing medical services, it exempts licensed corporate hospitals.

Utah County v. Intermountain Health Care, Inc.

Instant Facts: A wealthy nonprofit hospital applies for property tax exemption as a "charity."

Black Letter Rule: Hospitals seeking "charitable" tax treatment must provide services below cost or reduce government burdens.

IHC Health Plans, Inc. v. Commissioner of Internal Revenue

Instant Facts: The Tax Court denied IHC's (P) request for tax-exempt status.

Black Letter Rule: An organization will not be considered charitable unless it is operated primarily to serve a public rather than a private interest.

IHC Health Plans, Inc. v. Commissioner of Internal Revenue

Instant Facts: The Tax Court denied IHC's (P) request for tax-exempt status.

Black Letter Rule: An organization that is not itself tax-exempt may become tax-exempt if it operates solely to provide goods or services to an exempt organization that are essential to the operation of that exempt organization.

Redlands Surgical Services v. Commissioner of Internal Revenue

Instant Facts: When a tax-exempt nonprofit hospital entered a joint venture with a for-profit hospital, the IRS denied the joint venture tax exemption.

Black Letter Rule: Tax-exempt nonprofit hospitals may jointly venture with for-profit entities, but the joint venture is not tax exempt unless the joint venture is controlled by the nonprofit and is obligated to pursue charitable objectives exclusively.

Stern v. Lucy Webb Hayes National Training School for Deaconesses and Missionaries

(Hospital Patients, as Class) v. *(Charitable Hospital)*

381 F.Supp. 1003 (D.D.C. 1974)

CHARITABLE HOSPITAL'S TRUSTEES HAVE FIDUCIARY DUTIES TO PREVENT FINANCIAL MISMANAGEMENT

■ **INSTANT FACTS** When a charitable hospital's investigation revealed its trustees had "invested" its money into their affiliated banks' low-interest-bearing accounts, patients sued as a class for breach of fiduciary duties.

■ **BLACK LETTER RULE** Charitable hospitals' "trustee"-directors are in breach of their fiduciary duties to manage their hospital's financial affairs if (i) while assigned to a Board committee assigned financial/investment responsibility, they fail to use due diligence in supervising those employees responsible for day-to-day financial/investment decisions, or (ii) they knowingly permit the hospital to enter business transactions with themselves or their affiliated entities without disclosing their interest and any significant reasons why the transaction might not be in the hospital's best interests, or (iii) they participated actively in any decision to transact business with themselves or their affiliated entities, or (iv) they otherwise failed to perform their duties honestly, in good faith, and with reasonable care.

■ **PROCEDURAL BASIS**

Derivative class action, seeking damages and injunctive relief.

■ **FACTS**

Charitable corporation Lucy Webb Hayes National Training School for Deaconesses and Missionaries ("School") (D) built an affiliated Sibley Memorial Hospital ("Hospital") (D) (collectively, "School-Hospital"). Under School-Hospital's (D) by-laws, its finances were to be managed by the Board of Trustees (D), with an interim Executive Committee to open bank accounts, a supervisory Finance Committee to oversee the cash and budget, and an Investment Committee to supervise investments. In fact, School-Hospital's (D) finances were handled by trustees (D) Orem (D) and Ernst (D). Orem (D) and Ernst (D) dominated School-Hospital's (D) business affairs, commanding the Board and dissolving the committees. After Orem (D) died, Ernst (D) continued handing School-Hospital's (D) finances. When other Trustees (D) expressed concern, Ernst (D) ignored them. Later, Ernst (D) died. Afterwards, it was revealed much of School-Hospital's (D) assets were parked in no-/low-interest-bearing accounts at various Banks (D), which were affiliated with Ernst (D), Orem (D), and several other Trustees (D). [No wonder it's a not-for-profit hospital.] School-Hospital's (D) Patients, as a class, sued School-Hospital (D), those Trustees (D), and those Banks (D) for breaching their fiduciary duties of care and loyalty, by conspiring to enrich the affiliated Banks (D) [by "lending" the Banks (D) huge sums at little or no interest], at the expense of School-Hospital (D) and its Patients (P). School-Hospital (D) and Trustees (D) defend, contending there was no duty to avoid self-dealing.

■ **ISSUE**

Does a corporate non-profit hospital's trustees have a fiduciary duty to avoid self-dealing transactions in managing the hospital's finances?

■ DECISION AND RATIONALE

(Gesell, J.) Yes. Charitable hospitals' "trustee"-directors are in breach of their fiduciary duties to manage their hospital's financial affairs if (i) while assigned to a Board committee assigned financial/investment responsibility, they fail to use due diligence in supervising those employees responsible for day-to-day financial/investment decisions, or (ii) they knowingly permit the hospital to enter business transactions with themselves or their affiliated entities without disclosing their interest and any significant reasons why the transaction might not be in the hospital's best interests, or (iii) they participated actively in any decision to transact business with themselves or their affiliated entities, or (iv) they otherwise failed to perform their duties honestly, in good faith, and with reasonable care. First, we find the Patients (P) failed to prove a conspiracy between the Trustees (D) and/or Banks (D). Though the facts alleged do not establish conspiracy, they may still allege mismanagement, nonmanagement, or self-dealing. In determining charitable corporations' directors' liability, most jurisdictions apply corporate law rather than trust law, since charitable directors' functions are indistinguishable from their corporate counterparts'. Corporate directors and charitable trustees are both liable for losses caused by their negligent mismanagement of assets. However, the standard of care is different; trustees are liable for "mere" negligence, while some jurisdictions hold directors must have committed "gross" or heightened negligence to be liable. However, the District of Columbia's case law holds charitable trustees liable for ordinary negligence. Third, trustees have an affirmative duty to maximize trust income by prudent investment; this duty is non-delegable. *Restatement (Second) of Trusts § 171.* In contrast, corporate directors may delegate their investment responsibilities, but must continue exercising general supervision over those delegates' activities. For charitable corporations, charitable trustees should be permitted to delegate investment decisions to a committee of board members, so long as all directors assume responsibility for supervising such committees by scrutinizing their work periodically. However, no director may abdicate his supervisory role totally, e.g., by failing to acquire information necessary to supervise investment policy, or regularly skipping policy meetings. When a director's failure to supervise permits others' negligent mismanagement, that director has committed an independent wrong against the corporation, separate from respondeat superior or constructive notice. Finally, we turn to the alleged self-dealing. Under District of Columbia law, trustees/directors are not barred absolutely from placing controlled funds into banks with interlocking directorships. But such transactions will be subjected to the closest scrutiny to determine whether they breached the duty of loyalty. E.g., trustees'/corporate directors' deliberate conspiracy to enrich the interlocking bank at the expense of the trust/corporation constitutes a breach of loyalty, and renders conspirators liable for any losses. For charitable corporate trustees, most courts apply the less-stringent "gross negligence" rule. Some jurisdictions also require that directors disclose their interlocking responsibilities and refrain from influencing corporate decisions to transact business with any company in which they have significant interest/control. Thus, a charitable hospital's "trustee" (director) is in default of his fiduciary duty to manage his hospital's financial affairs if (i) while assigned to a Board committee empowered by the by-laws with financial or investment responsibility, he fails to use due diligence in supervising employees responsible for day-to-day financial/investment decisions, or (ii) he knowingly permits the hospital to enter business transactions with himself or his affiliated entity without disclosing his interest and any significant reasons why the transaction might not be in the hospital's best interests, or (iii) he participated actively in any decision to transact business with himself or his affiliated entity, or (iv) he otherwise failed to perform his duties honestly, in good faith, and with reasonable care. Applying these standards here, we find all the Trustees (D) breached their fiduciary duties to supervise School-Hospital's (D) investments, because they were elected to the Investment Committee but never called a meeting in 10 years, and failed to even review School-Hospital's (D) annual audit reports. There was frequent self-dealing among the Trustees (D) and Banks (D) which was never pointed out, though it seems the Trustees (D) were generally aware of each others' affiliations with various Banks (D), and most such transactions were minor. Legally, it is irrelevant that many such transactions caused no measurable injury to School-Hospital (D), though the Court may consider this in fashioning appropriate relief. [As for relief here, we grant an injunction that (i) School-Hospital's (D) committees and officers draft and present to its Board a written policy governing School-Hospital's (D) investments, funds, and cash, (ii) the Board establish a procedure for periodic review of investments and finances, and (iii) that each Trustee (D) disclose fully his affiliation with any financial institutions doing business with School-Hospital (D). We decline to remove any of the Trustees (D), or impose personal liability here.] Trustees' management of non-profit charitable hospitals imposes severe obligations on them. Such charitable hospitals are not regulated by public authorities, have no duty to file financial reports, and have self-perpetuating Boards. Patients lack meaningful participation in such hospitals' affairs, since the hospital deals with the large insurers who pay the patients' bills. Obviously, over time, new trustees will join such hospitals' boards, and these new trustees may be affiliated with financial institutions, who tend to seek business from the hospital. It must be made clear that Board membership carries no right to preferential treatment in the placement or handling of the hospital's investments and business accounts. School-Hospital (D) would be well advised to exclude Board members affiliated with financial institutions which have substantial business relationships with School-Hospital (D). Also, we require any trustee newly elected to School-Hospital's (D) Board to read this opinion. Finally, we require School-Hospital (D) to disclose publicly all dealings between School-Hospital (D) and any financial institution of which its own officers/trustees are affiliates, and make summarized records available to patients on request. Judgement for plaintiffs.

Analysis:

Stern illustrates that, just as for-profit corporations' managers may act against the interest of the corporation and its shareholders, so too may non-profit charitable hospitals' trustees subvert the hospital's charitable purpose for personal gain. Here, the allegation was that some of the Trustees (D), who were also directors at affiliated Banks (D), had School-Hospital (D) park its endowment in no-interest or low-interest bank accounts, thus giving their affiliated Banks (D) the ability to re-lend the money at a profit without paying School-Hospital (D) a fair rate of interest. While the court found insufficient evidence of a conspiracy, it conceded the obvious fact that the Trustees (D) were negligent in permitting self-interested Trustees Orem (D) and Ernst (D) to control the Board's entire finance function. Notably, *Stern* explores the doctrinal dichotomy that charitable corporate hospitals may be viewed as either corporations or as charitable trusts, and notes that most courts now view them as more akin to (for-profit) corporations because of their corporate management structure.

■ CASE VOCABULARY

CONSTRUCTIVE NOTICE: Doctrine that, when an employer ignores its agents' obvious wrongdoing, it becomes liable as if it ratified the act. Here, the court notes that a trustee's breach of fiduciary duty creates liability *for the trustee,* separate from constructive notice or respondeat superior (creating liability for the hospital).

INTERLOCKING DIRECTORSHIPS: Arrangement where the same people sit on the Boards of Directors/Trustees of separate entity, often creating risks of conflicted interests and self-dealing.

TRUSTEE: Generally, a person having fiduciary duties to act for the benefit of another. Here, "Trustee" was the title of School-Hospital's (D) directors, since School-Hospital (D) was a charitable "trust" rather than a for-profit corporation.

In re Caremark International Inc. Derivative Litigation

(*Shareholders, for Corporation*) v. (*Directors*)

698 A.2d 959 (Del. Ch. 1996)

CORPORATE DIRECTORS MUST IMPLEMENT CORPORATE MONITORING SYSTEM IN GOOD FAITH

■ **INSTANT FACTS** When a corporation charged with health care bribery is forced to pay $250 million and promise better management in a settlement with government agencies, angry shareholders request the court reject the settlement and permit them to sue the directors for negligently permitting the bribery.

■ **BLACK LETTER RULE** Corporate directors have a duty to make good faith efforts to institute a corporate monitoring system they believe will alert them of material events, but are not liable if the system fails to detect wrongdoing.

■ **PROCEDURAL BASIS**

Motion to approve settlement of derivative action.

■ **FACTS**

Caremark Corporation (P) operated health care centers and prescription drug programs. Caremark (P) and its predecessor often awarded contracts and grants to physicians who prescribed Caremark's (P) services to patients, which may have violated the federal Anti-Referral Payments Law ("ARPL") prohibiting "kickbacks." Eventually, Caremark was investigated by federal and state agencies. Caremark's Directors (D) and managers attempted to curb these payments and improve supervision, though many Directors (D) remained unsure whether the payments were illegal. The Directors (D) (I) revised Caremark's (P) employee guides to be ARPL-compliant, (ii) required payments to be approved by managers, (iii) disclosed the investigations in financial statements, (iv) hired auditors to assess its control structure, (v) reviewed compliance policies, and (vi) trained employees in compliance. Nevertheless, after 4 years of investigations, it was discovered that at least some of the payments were outright bribes, and Caremark (P) was ordered to adopt further safeguards and fined $250 million for criminal and civil violations, most of which began in the predecessor corporation but continued throughout the Directors' cleanup attempt. Shareholders (P) filed several derivative suits, consolidated here, alleging that the Directors (D) breached their duty of care by (*un*intentionally) failing to supervise employees or institute effective controls, causing the fines. Caremark proposed in a settlement with state and federal agencies, which would bar Shareholders' (P) suits, that, in the future, Caremark would (I) have employees stop paying referral fees, (ii) discuss compliance regularly with physicians, (iii) disclose to patients any financial incentives paid to their doctors, (iv) establish a compliance committee with outside directors, and (v) review its contracts—existing and future—to ensure compliance. This settlement was submitted for court approval, as required.

■ **ISSUE**

Should the court allow a settlement which dismisses charges against directors for negligently failing to institute corporate controls which could have prevented fines?

■ DECISION AND RATIONALE

(Allen, J.) Yes. Corporate directors have a duty to make good faith efforts to institute a corporate monitoring system they believe will alert them of material events, but are not liable if the system fails to detect wrongdoing. Courts deciding whether to approve derivative litigation settlements must decide whether the settlement offered is fair compensation for the corporation and its absent shareholders. In doing so, courts should not determine contested facts, but should evaluate the parties' relative claims and defenses, to substitute for an adversarial process. The parties proposing the settlement bear the burden of persuading the court it is fair and reasonable. Directors may be liable in negligence for either (I) making ill advised decisions not protected by the business judgement rule, or (ii) failure to monitor reasonably, if monitoring would have prevented losses. In suits for failure to monitor, directors may be held liable for negligently but unintentionally failing to monitor other employees' actions/decisions. Despite older cases suggesting otherwise, we now hold directors have a duty to make good faith efforts to institute an effective corporate monitoring system (which would alert them to material events and noncompliance), even if they have no reason to suspect wrongdoing. The level of detail necessary for this informational system is a question of business judgement, and directors are obviously not liable every time a reasonable system fails to detect wrongdoing. [Here, we find the settlement fair and reasonable. While the changes demanded by the settlement are small, since they were largely adopted in Caremark's ongoing cleanup effort, they are fully adequate consideration for dismissing the claims against the directors, since the evidence suggest the directors will have the claims against them dismissed. Here, Shareholders (P) would have to prove the Directors (D) (I) knew/should have known about the violations, (ii) took no good faith steps to prevent them, and (iii) proximately caused the losses. Claims of directorial liability for negligent failure to monitor must allege sustained or systematic failures to exercise oversight or create an information system, which would suggest bad faith. Here, the evidence suggests the Directors (D) made good faith efforts to inform themselves. Approving this settlement would dismiss an "extremely weak" claim in return for modest assurances of better management in the future.] Settlement approved.

Analysis:

This case sets a sort of "business judgment rule" for corporate monitoring; directors have a duty to institute a reasonable corporate monitoring system, but are not liable if a reasonable system nevertheless fails to detect wrongdoing. Here, the decision to foreclose shareholder suits seems fair in light of evidence the directors made honest and reasonable efforts to avoid liability. It would have been especially unfair to impose liability in this case because there was apparently real legal uncertainty— among Caremark Directors (D), employees, and even their lawyers—as to whether some types of payments, such as research grants, were actually prohibited as "kickbacks" (though it is admitted that at least some of the payments were intentional bribes).

■ CASE VOCABULARY

DERIVATIVE LITIGATION: Lawsuit filed by corporate shareholders suing on behalf of the corporation for damages done to the corporation. Here, the shareholders are claiming the Directors' (D) crimes harmed the corporation by imposing $250 million in fines.

Manhattan Eye, Ear and Throat Hospital v. Spitzer

(Hospital) v. (Attorney General)

186 Misc.2d 126, 715 N.Y.S.2d 575 (Sup. Ct. 1999)

TRANSACTIONS WITH CHARITABLE CORPORATIONS MUST BE FAIR AND PROMOTE THE PURPOSE OF THE CORPORATION

Gentlemen, we stand to make a killing on this real estate deal. Quick, gimme a "yes" vote.

Maybe we should do some investigation first...

stus.com

■ **INSTANT FACTS** Manhattan Eye, Ear and Throat Hospital (MEETH) (P) brought a petition for approval of a sale of its assets.

■ **BLACK LETTER RULE** In order to obtain judicial approval of a sale of all or substantially all of a non-profit corporation's assets, the board must show that the consideration and terms of the transaction are fair and that the purposes of the corporation will be promoted.

■ **PROCEDURAL BASIS**

Decision on a petition to approve a sale of assets.

■ **FACTS**

MEETH (P) operated a specialty hospital and two outpatient clinics. It also provided advanced training for physicians. In 1999, in order to cope with the changed state of the health care industry, MEETH's (P) board voted to close the hospital and sell the main building, to convert the outpatient clinics to diagnostic and treatment centers, and to add additional diagnostic and treatment centers. MEETH (P) entered into an agreement with New York Presbyterian Hospital (NYPH) that provided that NYPH would become the sole corporate member of MEETH (P).

In mid-January 1999, MEETH (P) received an offer to buy its real estate from Memorial Sloan Kettering Cancer Center (MSKCC). MEETH (P) retained Shattuck Hammond, an investment banking firm, to advise it regarding the transaction. Shattuck Hammond's fee would be a percentage of the sale price MEETH (P) received. Shattuck Hammond concluded that MEETH (P) had no value as an ongoing business. The board of MEETH (P) received an appraisal of the property that put its value between $46 and 55 million, but the board voted in late February 1999 to sell for a price as near as possible to $45 million. On March 11, 1999, Mt. Sinai Hospital offered to purchase the property for $46 million, but the agreement was allowed to lapse. The board of MEETH (P) was told that both MSKCC and Mt. Sinai had backed away from their initial proposals and were interested in purchasing the property only at a price substantially less than $46 million. The board then voted to sell the hospital for a price in excess of $40 million. The board also proposed an amendment to MEETH's (P) certificate of incorporation, which would allow it to close the hospital and operate freestanding diagnostic and treatment centers, but the proposed amendment was never submitted.

The board of MEETH (P) made a decision, according to the minutes of its meeting, to return to the "original mission" of MEETH (P) and to redirect its charitable assets to accomplish this goal. There was no written record of this decision and no studies or plans were provided to the board. By the May 5, 1999 board meeting, MEETH (P) received four separate proposals. One involved sale of the MEETH (P) property to MSKCC and another. MSKCC would use one building for a breast cancer facility, and the remainder of the property would be used to build an apartment building. Mt. Sinai submitted two alternate proposals, one to purchase the real estate with the hospital closed, and another to acquire the hospital and its operations for a "very substantially reduced price." Two alternative purchasers would have continued MEETH (P) as a hospital, by combining it with other facilities. One proposal was rejected because the board had already decided to sell the real estate. The other offeror, Lenox Hill Hospital, was asked to provide more information, but nothing further was done regarding that offer. The board took no further steps to find a bidder. The board voted to accept the offer from MSKCC. After the decision to sell was approved, the board discussed closing the hospital. Without further discussion, the board submitted a closure plan to the Department of Health. There were no studies undertaken regarding the planned use of the sale proceeds to establish diagnostic and treatment centers.

After the board voted to close the hospital, MEETH (P) took steps to effectuate and receive regulatory approval for the closure. In essence, MEETH (P) would ask for approval to close an already closed hospital.

■ ISSUE

Should the sale of MEETH's (P) property be approved?

■ DECISION AND RATIONALE

(Fried, J.) No. In order to obtain judicial approval of a sale of all or substantially all of a non-profit corporation's assets, the board must show that the consideration and terms of the transaction are fair and that the purposes of the corporation will be promoted. MEETH (P) has not satisfied either test. The issue is not the buyer's planned use of the property, which, in this case, is undeniably worthwhile, but whether the seller's use of the sale proceeds will promote its own corporate purposes. In evaluating a proposed sale of all the assets of a non-profit, the court should consider whether due diligence was exercised in deciding to sell, selecting the purchaser, and negotiating the sale; whether the procedures used in making the decision were fair; whether conflicts of interest were disclosed; and whether the seller will receive fair market value for the assets.

The duty of the board of directors of a charitable corporation is to ensure that the mission of the corporation is carried out. The directors must be faithful to the purposes and goals of the organization, since non-profits are defined by their specific objectives. If any fundamental changes in the life of a charitable corporation are undertaken, the Attorney General (D) is involved to ensure that the ultimate beneficiaries of the corporation are represented and protected from improvident transactions.

When considering whether the consideration and terms of the transaction are fair and reasonable to the corporation, the transaction as a whole must be considered, not just the fair market value of the assets sold. In this case, although the real estate may have been fairly valued, that is not enough. Contrary to the conclusion of Shattuck Hammond, the business of MEETH (P) had substantial value, and the transaction did not take that value into account. The proposed transaction does not contemplate preserving the business of MEETH (P), and therefore does not contemplate preserving the total assets of MEETH (P), including the name of MEETH (P) itself. This flaw in the agreement does not prove that the terms are fair and reasonable.

Similarly, there has been no showing that the second test has been met; that is, that the purposes of the corporation will be promoted. When the board proposed an amendment to MEETH's (P) certificate of incorporation, that was behavioral evidence that it knew it was changing the mission of MEETH (P). Although a diagnostic and treatment center is included within the definition of "hospital," it is sophistry to conclude that MEETH (P) is not seeking a new and fundamentally different purpose.

It may be appropriate, in some instances, to sell all the assets of an organization and then undertake a new mission. The board's first duty, however, is to seek to preserve the organization's original mission. In this case, the board did not make a reasoned and studied determination that there was no longer a need for MEETH (P) to function as a hospital, or that financial difficulties made it impossible to continue. Instead, the evidence is that the decision to sell was prompted by the offer of MSKCC to purchase the property. The realization that the real estate could be "monetized" drove subsequent events. The offer from MSKCC drove the decision to retain an advisor that had a direct interest in a sale of the real estate, namely, in the transaction fee. This arrangement may have been customary in the investment banking industry, and may not have actually compromised the result. But the arrangement still gives the appearance that the integrity of the process was flawed and that the board was not receiving the services of a truly independent expert. Moreover, this interest was not disclosed to all members of the board and was not discussed by the board.

The decision to "monetize" the real estate drove the need to change the corporate purpose. This was backwards: an evaluation of whether there was a need to change the purpose of the corporation should have determined the need to sell. The only study of the new plan was made to support an application for regulatory approval, not to evaluate the feasibility of the plan. In addition, the record does not show that the board considered the various alternatives that would have preserved MEETH's (P) mission. The board summarily rejected the alternatives, apparently confusing preservation of the hospital with preservation of the board. Sales transaction disapproved.

Analysis:

The court does not disagree with the decision made, but says that the process by which it was made, or the record of that process, was flawed. Some minor changes may have led to a different decision. For example, suppose the board had voted to sell before retaining Shattuck Hammond, and suppose Shattuck Hammond's fee arrangement had been approved by all the members of the board. These steps would seem to eliminate one of the court's major objections to the transaction. As of this writing, MEETH (P) is still in existence at the East 64th Street location, but it is now affiliated with Lenox Hill Hospital.

Berlin v. Sarah Bush Lincoln Health Center

(Employee) v. *(Corporate Hospital)*

179 Ill.2d 1, 227 Ill.Dec. 769, 688 N.E.2d 106 (1997)

"CORPORATE PRACTICE OF MEDICINE" DOCTRINE EXEMPTS LICENSED CORPORATE HOSPITALS

■ **INSTANT FACTS** A corporate hospital's employee doctor, wishing to escape his non-competition covenant, claims the hospital's hiring of doctors constitutes unauthorized medical practice by the hospital.

■ **BLACK LETTER RULE** While the "corporate practice of medicine" doctrine prevents corporations from providing medical services, it exempts licensed corporate hospitals.

■ **PROCEDURAL BASIS**

In contract action seeking injunction, appeal from appellate affirmation of summary judgement for defendant.

■ **FACTS**

Sarah Bush Lincoln Health Center ("Health Center") (P) is a nonprofit corporation licensed to operate a hospital. Health Center (P) employed Dr. Berlin (D) under an employment agreement containing a restrictive covenant, which prohibited him from working within 50 miles for 2 years after leaving. Later, Berlin (D) quit and immediately went to work for a competing hospital 1 mile away, violating the covenant. Health Center (P) sued to enjoin Berlin (D) from practicing medicine there. Berlin (D) defended, contending the employment contract and restrictive covenant were void, since under it Health Center (D), a corporation, was practicing medicine without a (personal) medical degree. At trial, the county "circuit" court granted summary judgement for Berlin (D), finding the entire employment contract unenforceable. On appeal, the appellate court affirmed. Health Center (P) appeals, contending the "corporate practice of medicine" doctrine should not apply to corporations duly licenced to operate hospitals.

■ **ISSUE**

Does the "corporate practice of medicine" doctrine prevent licensed corporate hospitals from employing doctors?

■ **DECISION AND RATIONALE**

(Nickels, J.) No. While the "corporate practice of medicine" doctrine prevents corporations from providing medical services, it exempts licensed corporate hospitals. Generally, the "corporate practice of medicine" doctrine prohibits corporations from providing professional medical services. Typically, it is inferred from state medical licensure acts, under the rationale that corporations cannot sustain the education, medical training, and character-screening to obtain a medical licence, and thus cannot legally practice medicine. This doctrine means the corporation cannot employ physicians to practice medicine, because their acts would be attributable to the corporate employer, and would thus amount to the (unlicenced) corporation "practicing" medicine. Policy justifications include the danger of lay control over medical judgements, physicians' divided loyalty between their patients and their profit-seeking employers, and the commercialization of medicine. Illinois adopted the corporate practice of medicine doctrine in previous cases *People ex rel. Kerner v. United Medical Service, Inc.* [corporations cannot employ physicians] and *Dr. Allison, Dentist, Inc. v. Allison* [corporations, which cannot be character-screened, may not hire physicians to do their medical work], but our courts never decided whether to exempt licensed corporate hospitals. Therefore, we look to other jurisdictions' guidance. While the "corporate practice" doctrine is recognized widely, many states now allow corporate hospitals to employ physicians, by either (i) deeming that hospitals employing doctors are not themselves "practicing" medicine, or (ii) holding the doctrine inapplicable to nonprofit health care providers, for public policy reasons, or (iii) exempting corporations which are otherwise licensed to provide medical treatment. We find rationales (ii) and (iii) persuasive. Thus, we decline to apply the "corporate practice of medicine" doctrine to licensed hospitals. We find our prior cases are distinguishable, and note Illinois' Hospital Licensing Act specifically authorizes licensed hospital corporations to provide medical services. Further, public policy requires this result. First, the concern over lay control over medical judgement is alleviated in licensed hospitals, where a medical staff of doctors maintains quality control. Second, health care has already become commercialized, without ill effect. Third, quality is assured by independent doctrines setting hospitals' duties. Fourth, we realize that requiring hospitals to provide medical care without employing physicians is illogical. Consequently, the employment agreement between Health Center (D) and Berlin (P) is not unenforceable merely because Health Center (D) is a corporation. Reversed.

■ **DISSENT**

(Harrison) Illinois' "corporate practice of medicine" doctrine was established 60 years ago by *Kerner*, and the state legislature never amended the law. Thus, we assume the doctrine enjoys the legislature's support. This doctrine allows no exception for hospitals.

Analysis:

Berlin introduces the traditional "corporate practice of medicine" doctrine, and the many state law doctrines that chip away at it today. Apparently, the exceptions subsume the rule, and *licensed* corporate hospitals today are allowed to hire doctors to practice medicine. The doctrine's given justifications are inconsistent. First, it is said the corporation itself cannot be character screened and thus should not be allowed to treat patients, but it is not the corporation itself that does so; it is a screened and licensed doctor. A stronger argument is that a corporate hospital runs the risk of having non-doctor administrators dictate the level of care given to patients. While this is potentially problematic, in reality it is tempered by the fact that most hospital administrators are physicians, and that the hospital faces liability for not assigning sufficient or correct treatments.

■ **CASE VOCABULARY**

"CORPORATE PRACTICE OF MEDICINE" DOCTRINE: Generally, common law doctrine whereby corporations cannot provide medical care through agent physicians, because the corporation *itself* has no medical license.

RESTRICTIVE COVENANT: (a.k.a. "covenant not to compete") Employment agreement's provision stating that an employee, on leaving the employer, cannot compete with the employer within a specified time and geographic area. Such covenants are enforceable if reasonable.

Utah County v. Intermountain Health Care, Inc.

(State Taxing Authority) v. *(Nonprofit Hospital)*

709 P.2d 265 (Utah 1985)

NONPROFIT HOSPITALS MAY NOT BE "CHARITIES" FOR TAX PURPOSES

■ **INSTANT FACTS** A wealthy nonprofit hospital applies for property tax exemption as a "charity."

■ **BLACK LETTER RULE** Hospitals seeking "charitable" tax treatment must provide services below cost or reduce government burdens.

■ PROCEDURAL BASIS

In tax assessment, appeal from appellate judgement for government.

■ FACTS

Intermountain Health Care, Inc. ("IHC") (P) is a nonprofit corporation owning 21 hospitals, including Utah Valley Hospital and American Fork Hospital. IHC (P) applied for tax exemption from ad valorem property taxes, as a "charity." The Utah County Board of Equalization (D) ruled against IHC (P). IHC (P) appealed. On appeal, the Utah State Tax Commission reversed. Utah County (D) appeals, contending Utah's constitution allows exemption only of property used "exclusively for . . . . charitable purposes."

■ ISSUE

Is a nonprofit hospital automatically exempt from taxes as a "charity"?

■ DECISION AND RATIONALE

(Durham, J.) No. Hospitals seeking "charitable" tax treatment must provide services below cost or reduce government burdens. Under the Utah Constitution, entities may be granted charitable tax exemptions for their property only if (i) they meet the definition of "charity," or (ii) their property is used for "charitable" purposes exclusively. These standards are strict because they confer indirect subsidies, and are justified by the rationale that charities perform functions which otherwise the state would have to perform, and enhance community values enough to offset the revenue lost. Both standards—"charity" and "charitable purpose" require the element of a gift to the community, which is either substantially-below-cost exchange with a beneficiary, or a lessening of the government's burden. The Utah Constitutional test of whether property is used "exclusively for . . . charitable purposes" includes (i) whether the entity's stated aim is providing significant services to others without immediate expectation of material reward, (ii) how much of the entity's funds come from donations/gifts, (iii) whether charity recipients are expected to pay, partly or fully, (iv) whether the entity actually earns a "surplus" (profit), (v) whether the entity restricts beneficiaries, and if any restrictions are reasonably related to the entity's charitable objectives, (vi) whether the entity provides financial benefits to private interests, and whether such benefits are incidental to its charitable activities. Traditionally, hospitals' "care of the sick" was deemed charitable, but this is no longer true. 19th Century hospitals were true charities, providing custodial care for the poor sick, and funded largely/entirely by voluntary charitable donations. Modern hospitals are professional businesses which demand payments. This is true of both for-profit and nonprofit hospitals alike. Here, we find IHC's (P) articles of incorporation include, among its "corporate purposes," "treatment of the sick ... within and ... outside Utah." IHC's (P) earnings cannot inure to any private benefit, and upon dissolution its assets cannot be distributed to private interests. IHC's (P) revenues come almost entirely from patient charges, not contributions, and its rates are not lower than market. Significantly, IHC's (P) patients are required to pay their full bill, and IHC (P) tries collecting delinquent accounts. IHC (P) has given away less than 1% of gross revenues as free medical care, and avoids advertising free services. IHC's (P) services are not provided substantially below market value, since patient discounts are granted only when the remainder is paid by government or insurers. Finally, IHC's (P) revenues exceed its costs, allowing it to accumulate capital, just like for-profit hospitals. Much of that money has gone to improving salaries among employees and managers. IHC (P) has not proven that its operations do not inure to the (private) benefit of its for-profit and non-profit subsidiaries, e.g., pharmacies, laboratories, etc. Nor has IHC (P) reduced the Utah government's burden, since IHC (P) will turn away patients whose state insurance coverage is inadequate. Reversed.

■ **DISSENT**

(Stewart, J.) Hospitals, to be charitable, need not incur deficits. While IHC (P) received substantial revenues, there is no evidence it was used for any purpose other than providing hospital services to the sick. IHC (D) has a policy against turning away indigents, and ends up providing some free care. Finally, IHC's (D) Utah Valley Hospital was built as a gift by the [Mormon] Church. Under time-honored legal principles, such hospitals qualify as charitable institutions, and should be tax-exempt. Further, evidence shows IHC (D) makes less profit than other hospitals, and charges fees lower than most hospitals. Further, IHC's (D) hospitals relieve a government burden by allowing accessible medical facilities in remote areas.

Analysis:

Whether a hospital qualifies for tax exemption as a "charity" is a difficult legal question. Traditionally, states exempted most nonprofit hospitals with a minimal showing of "charitable" purposes. Recently, some states aggressively challenged even nonprofits' status (e.g., demanding they prove the benefits they purportedly provide to the community), on the more modern understanding that even nonprofit hospitals often charge hefty fees and earn substantial revenue, making them no more beneficial to indigents or communities than their private counterparts. *Intermountain* represents the new trend, though it does not define the law fully. *Intermountain* was not the last word on Utah's taxation of hospitals, while a proposed state constitutional amendment to exempt hospitals automatically failed, Utah's Tax Commission later issued detailed guidelines.

■ **CASE VOCABULARY**

AD VALOREM PROPERTY TAX: Tax "according to the value" of the property.

IHC Health Plans, Inc. v. Commissioner of Internal Revenue

(HMO Operator) v. *(Tax Collector)*

325 F.3d 1188 (10th Cir. 2003)

TAX EXEMPT CORPORATIONS MUST BE FORMED PRIMARILY FOR CHARITABLE PURPOSES

■ **INSTANT FACTS** The Tax Court denied IHC's (P) request for tax-exempt status.

■ **BLACK LETTER RULE** An organization will not be considered charitable unless it is operated primarily to serve a public rather than a private interest.

■ **PROCEDURAL BASIS**

Appeal from an order of the Tax Court denying tax-exempt status.

■ **FACTS**

IHC (P) formed Health Services, a non-profit corporation that provided free hospital and health-care services. The IRS (D) recognized Health Services as a tax-exempt organization.

In order to integrate its provision of health-care services, IHC (P) formed three corporations to operate as HMOs. The three did not provide health-care services directly, but furnished group insurance. All enrollees had to pay a premium to obtain coverage, and dues were not subsidized for those who could not afford to pay. The sole activity of the plans was providing health-care services in exchange for a fee. Although the potential membership in each plan was broad, the services were provided only to members who paid the appropriate fee. The board membership originally was skewed toward members, but the bylaws were later amended to require that a majority of the board be disinterested community members.

The Tax Court held that the HMOs were not entitled to tax-exempt charitable status.

■ **ISSUE**

Do the IHC (P) HMOs qualify for tax-exempt status as a charitable organization?

■ **DECISION AND RATIONALE**

(Tacha, C.J.) No. An organization will not be considered charitable unless it is operated primarily to serve a public rather than a private interest.

The focus of determining if activities are charitable is whether the activities confer a public benefit. In the context of health-care providers, the court must determine whether the provider operates for the benefit of the community. Merely engaging in an activity that promotes health does not, by itself, support tax-exempt status. Providing health-care services to all community members for a fee is not enough; some additional "plus" is required. The "plus" is best described as "a benefit which the society or the community may not itself choose or be able to provide, or which supplements and advances the work of public institutions already supported by tax revenues." Examples provided by IRS (D) rulings include providing free or low cost services, maintaining an emergency room open to all, regardless of ability to pay, and devoting surplus revenues to research or education.

In addition, the primary purpose of the organization must be charitable. Some incidental community benefit is not enough. The inquiry turns on the purpose accomplished by the activity, not on the nature of the activity. In order to be tax-exempt, a health-care provider must make its services available to the entire community, and it must provide additional community or public benefits.

IHC (P) does not operate primarily for the benefit of the community. It is difficult to distinguish IHC's (P) HMOs from traditional insurance companies. IHC (P) provides virtually no free or below-cost services. Members must pay a premium to participate. Although this premium may be relatively low and allow members to obtain services at a lower cost, the discount does not say much about the purpose of IHC (P). Many profit-making businesses sell at a discount. In addition, IHC (P) provided services only to members. Although the class of potential members was large, offering services to a broad segment of the population is as consistent with profit maximization as it is with any charitable purpose. The composition of the board makes little difference, in that there is a dearth of actual community benefit. Affirmed.

Analysis:

Virtually any business can talk itself into believing it provides a benefit to the community at large, and that argument probably is an easier sell for a health-care corporation. The court here is looking not so much at the good works done by IHC (P) as at how IHC (P) generally runs its business. Note that the court does not, in this excerpt, consider state corporate laws when making its decision. Query whether the organization and operation of a corporation under a state's not-for-profit corporation laws would be a factor in the court's analysis.

IHC Health Plans, Inc. v. Commissioner of Internal Revenue

(HMO Operator) v. *(Tax Collector)*

325 F.3d 1188 (10th Cir. 2003)

ORGANIZATIONS THAT EXIST SOLELY TO PROVIDE ESSENTIAL SERVICES TO EXEMPT ENTITIES ARE TAX–EXEMPT

■ **INSTANT FACTS** The Tax Court denied IHC's (P) request for tax-exempt status.

■ **BLACK LETTER RULE** An organization that is not itself tax-exempt may become tax-exempt if it operates solely to provide goods or services to an exempt organization that are essential to the operation of that exempt organization.

■ **PROCEDURAL BASIS**

Appeal from an order of the Tax Court denying tax-exempt status.

■ **FACTS**

IHC (P) formed Health Services, a non-profit corporation that provided free hospital and health-care services. The IRS (D) recognized Health Services as a tax-exempt organization.

In order to integrate its provision of health-care services, IHC (P) formed three corporations to operate as HMOs. The three did not provide health-care services directly, but furnished group insurance. All enrollees had to pay a premium to obtain coverage, and dues were not subsidized for those who could not afford to pay. The sole activity of the plans was providing health-care services in exchange for a fee. Although the potential membership in each plan was broad, the services were provided only to members who paid the appropriate fee. The board membership originally was skewed toward members, but the bylaws were later amended to require that a majority of the board be disinterested community members.

The Tax Court held that the HMOs were not entitled to tax-exempt charitable status. IHC (P) claimed that the HMOs qualified for tax-exempt status as an integral part of Health Services.

■ **ISSUE**

Were the HMOs an integral part of Health Services?

■ **DECISION AND RATIONALE**

(Tacha, C.J.) No. An organization that is not itself tax-exempt may become tax-exempt if its operations are solely used to provide goods or services to an exempt organization that are essential to the operation of the exempt organization. Such an organization would be considered an "integral part" of the tax-exempt organization, but that is not the case here.

The "integral part" doctrine runs counter to two basic tenets of tax law: a corporation is a distinct corporate entity, and exemptions from taxation are to be construed strictly. The doctrine recognizes that the totality of the circumstances should be considered in determining an organization's purpose. An important factor is whether there is an essential nexus between a tax-exempt organization and its affiliate.

In this case, there is no nexus. The enrollees in the HMO received only twenty percent of their physician services from Health Services physicians. Independent physicians provided the remaining eighty percent. Thus, the IHC (P) HMOs do not exist solely to further the functions of Health Services. Affirmed.

Analysis:

Logically, there would seem to be little reason to deny tax-exempt status to an entity that is a true "integral part" of an exempt entity. In this case, however, there was only an incidental connection between the HMOs and Health Services. They were operated by the same entity, but that does not show that there was enough of a connection between them.

Redlands Surgical Services v. Commissioner of Internal Revenue

(Charitable Hospital and Joint Venture Partner) v. *(Federal Taxation Authority)*

113 T.C. 47 (U.S. Tax Ct. 1999)

TAX-EXEMPT HOSPITALS JOINT VENTURING WITH "FOR-PROFIT" ENTITIES MAY LOSE EXEMPTION

■ **INSTANT FACTS** When a tax-exempt nonprofit hospital entered a joint venture with a for-profit hospital, the IRS denied the joint venture tax exemption.

■ **BLACK LETTER RULE** Tax-exempt nonprofit hospitals may jointly venture with for-profit entities, but the joint venture is not tax exempt unless the joint venture is controlled by the nonprofit and is obligated to pursue charitable objectives exclusively.

■ **PROCEDURAL BASIS**

In tax case, appeal from denied application for tax exemption, seeking declaration.

■ **FACTS**

Redlands Surgical Services ("Petitioner") was essentially a nonprofit public-benefit corporation which operated tax-exempt charitable Redlands Hospital. It began a joint venture with for-profit public corporation Surgical Care Affiliates ("SGA"), which owns for-profit subsidiary Redlands-Centers. The joint venture had 2 aspects. First, Petitioner entered a General Partnership with copartner Redlands-Centers. Also, the Petitioner (P) entered an Operating [Limited] Partnership to run nearby Inland Surgery Center ("Surgery Center"), whose general partner was General Partnership and whose limited partners included Petitioner (P) and doctors from [Petitioner (P)-affiliated] Redlands Hospital. Petitioner (P) filed an Application for Recognition of Exemption [on behalf of Surgery Center]. The IRS (D) denied, stating "Basically all you have done is invest in a for-profit entity, Inland, and transfer the profits from this investment to your parent," and contending the joint ventures were controlled by the for-profit organization without guarantees of further charitable purpose. Petitioner (P) sued in Tax Court for recognition of exemption, contending that potential control was irrelevant, since it continued to provide charitable care.

■ **ISSUE**

Is a joint venture between a tax-exempt nonprofit hospital and a for-profit organization tax exempt?

■ **DECISION AND RATIONALE**

(Thornton, J.) No. Tax-exempt nonprofit hospitals may jointly venture with for-profit entities, but the joint venture is not tax exempt unless the joint venture is controlled by the nonprofit and is obligated to pursue charitable objectives exclusively. *IRC § 501(c)(3)* specifies various tax exemptions, including "charitable" purposes. "Charitable" is not defined statutorily, so is interpreted by general principles, including the law of charitable trusts. One purpose deemed "charitable" is promoting health for community benefit. As health care facilities evolved, charitable hospitalization no longer requires caring for indigents, rather than for solvent patients. Rather, the standard for "charitable" care is "insuring . . . adequate . . . care services are actually delivered to those in the community who need them." This standard requires health care providers meet several indicia, which *may* include free care for indigents. Charities purporting to benefit the community must serve a class which is sufficiently large and indefinite, without benefitting private interests substantially. First, we consider whether Petitioner (P) was denied exemption improperly. We hold entities seeking exemption must be operated "in an exclusively charitable manner," not just produce charitable benefits incidentally or occasionally. This requires such entities include structural safeguards prohibiting any revenues from going to for-profit entities. Here, we hold Petitioner (P) was not operated exclusively for charitable purpose, since it had no binding obligation to put charitable purposes ahead of profits. The totality of circumstances shows Petitioner (P) ceded control to (the for-profit) SGA: the General Partnership's charter documents do not require charitable activities, the Operating Partnership's organizational documents retain their for-profit language, Petitioner (P) lacks majority control over Surgery Center to demand charitable priorities, the arbitration clause does not require rulings in favor of charitable aims, manager SCA retains broad management powers under a long-term contract, the nominal medical advisory and quality assurance teams are inactive, and Petitioner (P) lacks informal control sufficient to persuade SGA to pursue charity. Further, evidence shows Surgery Center (D) provides no free care to indigents, and negligible coverage for Medi-Cal [state low-income insurance] patients. Essentially, this joint venture was entered to produce mutual economic benefits for (nonprofit) Petitioner (P) and (for-profit) SGA, by raising capital, utilizing relationships between Redlands Hospital and local physicians, and reducing possible competition. There is no per se proscription against a nonprofit entering contracts with private parties to further its charitable purposes on mutually beneficial terms, so long as the nonprofit organization does not thereby serve private interests impermissibly. Here, however, the joint venture allowed for-profit SCA and affiliates to gain footholds in the area's surgical market, on terms which profited them. Then, SCA is able to operate Surgery Center as a for-profit business, unfettered by charitable objectives which might conflict with commercial ones. Alternately, Petitioner (P) argues it qualifies for exemption under the "integral part" doctrine. In all precedents recognizing this doctrine, the total organization was under the supervision or control of the exempt affiliate, or otherwise expressly limited to advancing the exempt affiliate's interests, and to serving no private interests. Here, we find the (exempt) Petitioner (P)'s activities are controlled by the (private for-profit) SGA. Judgement for IRS (D).

Analysis:

On appeal, the Ninth Circuit denied review of Redlands. Its holding relies heavily on the notion that a joint venture is to be deemed for-profit unless its foundation documents officially cede control to the nonprofit partner and restrict it to running the venture for charitable purposes only. Here, Petitioner (P) argues that, in fact, the joint venture (Inland Surgery Center) was actually run as a nonprofit in practice, but the court disregards this argument as a matter of law (as well as disbelieving it in fact). This led commentators to note that "control is king" under Redlands and Revenue Ruling 98–15, which provides that exempt nonprofit hospitals may merge with for-profit companies, but only if the resulting entity continues to be operated exclusively for exempt purposes, which requires the corporate documents to allow the resulting entity's assets to be used "exclusively" for exempt purposes, except for uses deemed "incidental" to exempt purposes.

CHAPTER FOURTEEN

Fraud and Abuse

United States v. Krizek

Instant Facts: The government filed a civil suit against a psychiatrist, alleging false billing for Medicare and Medicaid patients.

Black Letter Rule: Acting with reckless disregard as to the truth or falsity of Medicare and Medicaid submissions will constitute a violation of the False Claims Act.

United States v. Krizek

Instant Facts: The defendants cross-appealed the District Court's judgment which treated each improperly submitted CPT Code as a separate "claim" for purposes of computing civil penalties.

Black Letter Rule: Reckless disregard lies on a continuum between gross negligence and intentional harm, and in some cases, recklessness serves as a proxy for forbidden intent.

United States ex rel. Mikes v. Straus

Instant Facts: Mikes (P) claimed Straus (D) submitted false claims for reimbursement for tests performed with an inaccurate instrument.

Black Letter Rule: A claim is legally false for purposes of the False Claims Act only when a party certifies compliance with a statute or regulation as a condition to governmental payment.

United States v. Greber

Instant Facts: A physician, the president of a company which produces heart monitors, was convicted of fraud for having tendered remuneration or kickbacks to referring physicians to his monitoring service, in violation of the Medicare statute.

Black Letter Rule: If one purpose of a payment made to a physician for professional services was to induce future referrals, the Medicare statute has been violated.

United States v. Starks

Instant Facts: On appeal from their convictions, the defendants claim that the district court committed reversible error in its jury instructions regarding the Anti–Kickback statute's mens rea requirement, and that the statute is unconstitutionally vague.

Black Letter Rule: The Anti–Kickback statute gives fair warning of conduct which is illegal and, as such, is not unconstitutionally vague.

United States v. Krizek

(Government) v. *(Psychiatrist)*

859 F.Supp. 5 (D.D.C. 1994)

DOCTORS MUST BE HELD STRICTLY ACCOUNTABLE FOR REQUESTS FILED FOR INSURANCE REIMBURSEMENT

■ **INSTANT FACTS** The government filed a civil suit against a psychiatrist, alleging false billing for Medicare and Medicaid patients.

■ **BLACK LETTER RULE** Acting with reckless disregard as to the truth or falsity of Medicare and Medicaid submissions will constitute a violation of the False Claims Act.

■ **PROCEDURAL BASIS**

Original action brought by the government against a psychiatrist, alleging false billing for Medicare and Medicaid patients.

■ **FACTS**

The government (P) brought this civil action against Dr. Krizek (D), a psychiatrist, and his wife, who was responsible for overseeing Krizek's (D) billing operations. The government (P) alleges false billing for Medicare and Medicaid patients, claiming that Dr. Krizek (D) submitted bills coded for services with a higher level of reimbursement than that which Dr. Krizek (D) actually provided, and that he performed services which were not medically necessary. The government (P) has cited 8,002 reimbursement claims in its complaint. It was decided that because of the large number of claims, this case should initially be tried on the basis of seven patients and two hundred claims that the government (P) believed to be representative of Dr. Krizek's (D) improper coding and treatment practices. It was agreed by the parties that a determination of liability on Dr. Krizek's (D) coding practices would be equally applicable to all 8,002 claims in the complaint. A three week bench trial ensued.

■ **ISSUE**

Did the defendant violate the False Claims Act by improperly billing for services and in providing medically unnecessary services?

■ **DECISION AND RATIONALE**

(Sporkin, D.J.) Yes and no. Dr. Krizek (D) testified credibly and persuasively as to the basis for the course of treatment for each of the representative patients. The medical necessity of treating Dr. Krizek's (D) patients through psychotherapy and hospitalization was confirmed via the testimony of other defense witnesses. The Court credits Dr. Krizek's (D) testimony on this question as well as his interpretation of his own notes regarding the seriousness of each patients' condition and the medical necessity for the procedures and length of hospital stay required. The Court finds that the government was unable to prove that Dr. Krizek (D) rendered services that were medically unnecessary. On the question of improper billing, the government (P) contends that for approximately 24% of the bills submitted, Dr. Krizek (D) used the CPT Code for a 45–50 minute psychotherapy session (CPT Code 90844) when he should have billed for a 20–30 minute session (CPT Code 90843). The government (P) also contends that for at least 33% of his patients, Dr. Krizek (D) billed for a full 45–50 minute psychotherapy session, again by using CPT Code 90844, when he should have billed for a "minimal psychotherapy" session (CPT 90862). These two latter procedures are reimbursed at a lower level than 90844, which the government (P) has referred to as the "Cadillac" of psychiatric reimbursement codes. In sum, the government (P) claims that whenever Dr. Krizek (D) would see a patient, regardless of whether he simply checked a chart, spoke with a nurse, or merely prescribed additional medication, his wife or his employee, a Mrs. Anderson, would, on the vast majority of occasions, submit a bill for CPT Code 90844–45–50 minutes of individual psychotherapy. Dr. and Mrs. Krizek (D) freely admit that when a 90844 code bill was submitted on the doctor's behalf, it did not always reflect 45–50 minutes of face-to-face psychotherapy with the patient. Instead, the 45–50 minutes billed captured generally the total amount of time spent on the patient's case, including the "face-to-face" psychotherapy session, discussions with medical staff about the patient's treatment/progress, medication management, and other related services. Dr. Krizek (D) referred to this as "bundling" of services, all of which they reasonably believed were reimbursable under the 90844 Code. The defense witnesses testified that it was a common and proper practice among psychiatrists nationally to bundle a variety of services, whether or not these services took place literally in view of the patient. Thus testimony was credible and persuasive. Therefore, the Court finds that the government's (P) position on this issue is not rational and has been applied in an unfair manner to the medical community, which for the most part is made up of honorable and dedicated professionals. The Court finds that Dr. Krizek (D) did not submit false claims when he submitted a bill under CPT Code 90844 after spending 45–50 minutes working on a patient's case, even though not all of that time was spent in direct face-to-face contact with the patient. The Court finds that Dr. Krizek's (D) "bundled" services interpretation of the CPT Code 90844 is not inconsistent with the plain, common-sense reading of the "description of services" listed by Pennsylvania Blue Shield in its published Procedure Terminology Manual. As for Dr. Krizek's (D) billing system, the same cannot be said. The basic method of billing by Mrs. Krizek (D) and Mrs. Anderson was to determine which patients Dr. Krizek (D) had seen, and then to assume what had taken place was a 50-minute psychotherapy session, unless told specifically by Dr. Krizek (D) that the visit was for a shorter duration. Mrs. Krizek (D) frequently made this assumption without any input from her husband. Mrs. Krizek (D) acknowledged at trial that she never made any specific effort to determine exactly how much time was spent with each patient. Mrs. Krizek (D) felt it was fair and appropriate to use the 90844 Code as a rough approximation of the time spent, because on some days, an examination would last up to two hours and she would still bill 90844. Mrs. Anderson also would prepare and submit claims to Medicare/Medicaid with no input from Dr. Krizek. Routinely, Mrs. Anderson would simply contact the hospital to determine what patients were admitted to various psychiatrists' services, and would then prepare and submit claims to Medicare/Medicaid without communicating with Dr. or Mrs. Krizek (D) about the claims she was submitting and certifying on Dr. Krizek's (D) behalf. While the Court does not find that Dr. Krizek (D) submitted bills for patients he did not see, the Court does find that because of Mrs. Krizek's (D) and Mrs. Anderson's presumption that whenever Dr. Krizek (D) saw a patient he worked at least 45 minutes on the matter, bills were improperly submitted for time that was not spent providing patient services. At the conclusion of trial, both parties agreed that an appropriate bench-mark for excessive billing would be the equivalent of twelve 90844 submissions (or nine patient-service hours) in a single day. Considering the difficulty of reviewing all Dr. Krizek's (D) patient records over a seven-year period, and giving full credence to unrefuted testimony that Dr. Krizek (D) worked very long hours, the Court believes this to be a fair and reasonably accurate assessment of the time Dr. Krizek (D) actually spent providing patient services. Dr. and Mrs. Krizek (D) will therefore be presumed liable for bills submitted in excess of the equivalent of twelve 90844 submissions in a single day. These were not "mistakes" nor merely negligent conduct, as Dr. Krizek (D) contends. Under the statutory definition of "knowing" conduct, the Court is compelled to conclude that Dr. and Mrs. Krizek (D) acted with reckless disregard as to the truth or falsity of the submissions. As such, they will be deemed to have violated the False Claims Act. The Court believes that the Krizeks' (D) billing practices must be corrected before they are permitted to further participate in the Medicare or Medicaid programs. Therefore an injunction will issue, enjoining them from participating in these systems until such time as they can show the Court that they can abide by the relevant rules. The Court also will hold the Krizeks (D) liable under the False Claims Act on those days where claims were submitted in excess of the equivalent of twelve 90844 claims in a single day and where they cannot establish that Dr. Krizek (D) legitimately devoted the claimed amount of time to patient care on the day in question. The government (P) will also be entitled to introduce proof that the Krizeks (D) submitted incorrect bills on days where less than nine hours in a single day were claimed. The assessment of the amount of overpayment and penalty will await these future proceedings.

Analysis:

While Dr. Krizek (D) was a dedicated and competent doctor and was not faulted for his interpretation of the 90844 Code, his billing practices, or at a minimum his oversight of his wife's and Mrs. Anderson's billing system, was seriously deficient. The net result of this system, or more accurately "nonsystem" of billing, was unsubstantiated and inaccurate billings. As a result, Dr. Krizek (D) received reimbursement for services that he did not provide. Dr. Krizek (D) must be held accountable for his billing system, along with those who carried it out. Dr. Krizek (D) was not justified in seeing patients and later not verifying the claims submitted for the services provided to these patients. Doctors must be held strictly accountable for requests filed for insurance reimbursement.

■ CASE VOCABULARY

ENJOIN: To require a person to perform, or to abstain or desist from, some act.

ET SEQ.: "And the following."

INJUNCTION: A court order prohibiting someone from doing some specified act or commanding someone to undo some wrong or injury.

INTER ALIA: Among other things.

UNJUST ENRICHMENT: Occurs when a person has and retains benefits or money which in justice and equity belong to another.

United States v. Krizek

(Government) v. *(Psychiatrist)*

111 F.3d 934 (D.C. Cir. 1997)

RECKLESS DISREGARD CAN BE READ AS AN EXTENSION OF GROSS NEGLIGENCE

■ **INSTANT FACTS** The defendants cross-appealed the District Court's judgment which treated each improperly submitted CPT Code as a separate "claim" for purposes of computing civil penalties.

■ **BLACK LETTER RULE** Reckless disregard lies on a continuum between gross negligence and intentional harm, and in some cases, recklessness serves as a proxy for forbidden intent.

■ **PROCEDURAL BASIS**

Prosecution appeals and defendant cross-appeals from the District Court's judgment against the defendants.

■ **FACTS**

The District Court found the Krizeks (D) liable for knowingly submitting false medical claims for payment and entered judgment against them for $168,105.39. The District Court changed its benchmark for a presumptively false claim, which lowered the damages award substantially. The government (P) appealed (it was seeking $81 million in damages), and the Krizeks (D) cross-appealed on the grounds that the District Court erroneously treated each CPT Code as a separate "claim" for purposes of computing civil penalties. The Krizeks (D) assert that the claim, in this context, is the form submitted (HCFA 1500), even if the form contains a number of CPT Codes.

■ **ISSUE**

Did the District Court err in treating each improper coding as a separate claim for purposes of computing civil penalties, and did the District Court apply the appropriate level of scienter?

■ **DECISION AND RATIONALE**

(Sentelle, C.J.) Yes. Whether a defendant has made one false claim or many is a fact-bound inquiry that focuses on the specific conduct of the defendant. The gravamen of these cases is that the focus is on the conduct of the defendant. The Court asks, "With what act did the defendant submit his demand or request and how many such acts were there?" In this case, the Special Master adopted a position that is inconsistent with this approach. The government (P) contends that fairness or uniformity concerns support treating each CPT Code as a separate claim, arguing that "to count woodenly the number of forms submitted by the Krizeks would cede to medical practitioners full authority to control exposure to the Federal Claims Act simply by structuring their billings in a particular manner." Precisely so. It is conduct of the medical practitioner, not the disposition of the claims by the government, that creates FCA liability. Moreover, even if we considered fairness to be a relevant consideration in statutory construction, we would note that the government's (P) definition of claim permitted it to seek an astronomical $81 million worth of damages for alleged actual damages of $245,392. We therefore remand for recalculation of the civil penalty. We turn now to the question whether, in considering the sample, the District Court applied the appropriate level of scienter. The

FCA imposes liability on an individual who "knowingly presents" a "false or fraudulent claim." A person acts "knowingly" if he (1) has actual knowledge of the information; (2) acts in deliberate ignorance of the truth or falsity of the information; or (3) acts in reckless disregard of the truth or falsity of the information, and no proof of specific intent to defraud is required. 31 U.S.C. Sec. 3729(b). The Krizeks (D) assert that the District Court impermissibly applied the FCA by permitting an aggravated form of gross negligence, "gross-negligence-plus," to satisfy the Act's scienter requirement. We have previously held, as we do now, that reckless disregard lies on a continuum between gross negligence and intentional harm. In some cases, recklessness serves as a proxy for forbidden intent. Such cases require a showing that the defendant engaged in an act known to cause or likely to cause the injury. The question, therefore, is whether "reckless disregard" in this context is properly equated with willful misconduct or with aggravated gross negligence. In determining that gross negligence-plus was sufficient, the District Court cited legislative history equating reckless disregard with gross negligence. While we are not inclined to view isolated statements in the legislative history as dispositive, we agree with the thrust of this statement that the best reading of the Act defines reckless disregard as an extension of gross negligence. Section 3729(b)(2) of the Act provides liability for false statements made with deliberate ignorance. Moreover, as the statute explicitly states that specific intent is not required, it is logical to conclude that reckless disregard in this context is not a "lesser form of intent," but an extreme version of ordinary negligence. We are also unpersuaded by the Krizeks' (D) argument that their conduct did not rise to the level of reckless disregard. The District Court cited a number of factors supporting its conclusion: Mrs. Krizek (D) completed the submissions with little or no factual basis; she made no effort to establish how much time Dr. Krizek (D) spent with any particular patent; and Dr. Krizek (D) "failed utterly" to review bills submitted on his behalf. Most tellingly, there were a number of days within the seven-patient sample when even the shoddiest record keeping would have revealed that false submissions were being made—those days on which the Krizeks' (D) billing approached twenty-four hours in a single day [hard workers!]. In fact, outside the sample, the Krizeks (D) billed for more than twenty-four hours in a single day on three separate occasions. These factors amply support the District Court's determination that the Krizeks (D) acted with reckless disregard. Finally, we note that Dr. Krizek (D) is no less liable than his wife for these false submissions. As noted, an FCA violation may be established without reference to the subjective intent of the defendant. Dr. Krizek (D) delegated to his wife authority to submit claims on his behalf. In failing utterly to review the false submissions, he acted with reckless disregard.

Analysis:

The Special Master concluded in this case that because the government used the CPT Code in processing the claims, the CPT Code, and not the form in its entirety, must be the claim. This conclusion, which was later adopted by the District Court, misses the point. The question turns, not on how the government chooses to process the claim, but on how many times the defendants made a request or demand. The circuit court's conclusion that the claim in this context is the HCFA 1500 form is supported by the structure of the form itself. The CPT codes are listed on the form, and then the charges are totaled to produce one request or demand. The CPT codes function in this context as a type of invoice used to explain how the Krizeks (D) computed their request or demand. The alleged actual damages in this case amounted to $245,392, yet the government, in treating the CPT codes as separate "claims," rather than the whole form itself, sought civil penalties of $81 million!

■ CASE VOCABULARY

RULE OF LENITY: A rule invoked only when the statutory language is ambiguous, whereby the ambiguity should be resolved in favor of lenity in sentencing.

SCIENTER: A mental state; the defendant's guilty knowledge.

SPECIAL MASTER: A person of authority appointed to represent the court in some particular act or transaction.

United States ex rel. Mikes v. Straus

(Terminated Physician) v. *(Physician)*

274 F.3d 687 (2d Cir. 2001)

CLAIMS NOT NECESSARY FOR GOVERNMENTAL PAYMENT ARE NOT "FALSE"

Liar!

Not as defined by the False Claims Act!

stus.com

■ **INSTANT FACTS** Mikes (P) claimed Straus (D) submitted false claims for reimbursement for tests performed with an inaccurate instrument.

■ **BLACK LETTER RULE** A claim is legally false for purposes of the False Claims Act only when a party certifies compliance with a statute or regulation as a condition to governmental payment.

■ **PROCEDURAL BASIS**

Appeal from an order granting summary judgment.

■ **FACTS**

Mikes (P), a pulmonologist, was hired by Straus (D) and his partners to provide pulmonology and critical care services as a part of their medical practice. Shortly after she was hired, Mikes (P) expressed her concerns regarding spirometry tests. Mikes (P) was fired three months later.

Mikes (P) claimed that the spirometry tests were inaccurate because they were performed on improperly calibrated instruments. She claimed that the instruments were so inaccurate as to render the results of the tests "false" under the False Claims Act. Mikes (P) claimed that Straus (D) and his partners (D) submitted Medicare claims for spirometry tests.

At trial, Mikes (P) introduced evidence that showed that spirometers are subject to inaccuracy through time and usage and will provide false readings. Mikes (P) claimed that professional guidelines recommend daily calibration of spirometers. Mikes (P) also claimed that Straus (D) and his partners (D) engaged in a performance of spirometry that yielded inherently unreliable data. Straus (D) testified that Mikes (P) was told to review test results for inaccuracy and train medical assistants in the proper administration of spirometry tests. Mikes (P) never reported any inaccuracies and she did not train the medical assistants.

■ **ISSUE**

Did Straus (D) and his partners submit false claims?

■ **DECISION AND RATIONALE**

(Cardamone, J.) No. A claim is legally false for purposes of the False Claims Act only when a party certifies compliance with a statute or regulation as a condition to governmental payment. The issue of whether the false statement or claim must also be material is not addressed.

Mikes (P) makes the argument that the Medicare claims contain an expressly false certification. The form on which the claim was submitted contained a certification that the claim was "medically necessary for the health of the patient." Certification was a precondition to Medicare reimbursement. But Mikes's (P) objections to the spirometry tests do not implicate the medical necessity of the test. "Medical necessity" does not mandate a particular standard of medical care. The Medicare statute has separate provisions that relate to medical necessity of a procedure and the quality of that procedure.

Mikes (P) also argues that the claims were impliedly false certifications. Implied false certification claims are based on the theory that the act of submitting a claim for reimbursement implies compliance with the governing rules that are a precondition to payment. The implied certification theory does not work well in the medical care context, because the False Claims Act was not meant to enforce compliance with all medical regulations, only those that are a precondition to payment. A limited application of the implied certification theory reconciles the need to enforce the Medicare statute with the role non-federal actors play in assuring that the appropriate standards of medical care are met. Allowing plaintiffs in qui tam actions to assert the failure to meet medical standards would promote the federalization of medical practice. Accordingly, liability under the False Claims Act may be found when a claimant submits a claim knowing that payment expressly is precluded because of some noncompliance by the claimant.

Mikes (P) asserts that compliance with 42 U.S.C. §§ 1395y(a)(1)(A) and 1320c–5a is a precondition to receiving payment, and submission of a claim attests by implication to compliance with both provisions. Section 1395y(a)(1)(A) merely relates to the requirement that the service be reasonable and necessary. Section 1320c–5a relates to the quality of the services rendered, but payment of a Medicare claim is not explicitly conditioned upon compliance with § 1320c–5a. Section 1320c–5a establishes conditions for participation in the Medicare program. Sanctions are authorized for failure to maintain an appropriate standard of care only for serious or continued dereliction. Since the statute does not condition payment on compliance with its terms, Straus's (D) certifications are not legally false.

The United States (P), as *amicus,* argues that the district court erred by not considering whether the submission of claims for substandard spirometry services constituted a claim for worthless services. A worthless services claim is the equivalent of saying that the performance of the service was so deficient as to be the equivalent of no service at all. In this case, however, there can be no liability under this theory, because there is no evidence that Straus (D) and his partners (D) knowingly—as that term is defined in the False Claims Act—submitted a claim for reimbursement for worthless services. The standard of the Ninth Circuit, that the requisite intent is the knowing presentation of what is known to be false, is adopted. Mikes (P) has not substantiated her claim that Straus (D) and his partners (D) knew that the claims they submitted were false. On the other hand, there is ample evidence that they held a good faith belief that the services they rendered had medical value. Affirmed.

Analysis:

The court makes multiple references to the term "knowing" as that term is defined in the False Claims Act. Under the Act, a person acts "knowingly" when he or she has actual knowledge of the information, acts in deliberate ignorance of the truth or falsity of the information, or acts in reckless disregard of the truth or falsity of the information. No specific intent to defraud is required. *See* 31 U.S.C.A. § 3729.

■ CASE VOCABULARY

EX REL.: [Latin, "by or on the relation of."] On the relation or information of. A suit *ex rel.* is typically brought by the government upon the application of a private party (called a *relator*) who is interested in the matter.

FALSE CLAIMS ACT: A federal statute establishing civil and criminal penalties against persons who bill the government falsely, deliver less to the government than represented, or use a fake record to decrease an obligation to the government. 18 U.S.C.A. §§ 286–287; 31 U.S.C.A. §§ 3729–3733. The Act may be enforced either by the attorney general or by a private person in a qui tam action.

QUI TAM ACTION: [Latin, *qui tam pro domino rege quam pro se ipso in hac parte sequitur,* "who as well for the king as for himself sues in this matter."] An action brought under a statute that allows a private person to sue for a penalty, part of which the government or some specified institution will receive. Often shortened to *qui tam* (Q.T.).

United States v. Greber

(Government) v. *(Heart Doctor)*

760 F.2d 68 (3d Cir.), cert. denied, 474 U.S. 988, 106 S.Ct. 396, 88 L.Ed.2d 348 (1985)

PAYMENTS TO A PHYSICIAN INTENDED TO INDUCE FUTURE REFERRALS ARE VIOLATIONS OF THE MEDICARE STATUTE

■ **INSTANT FACTS** A physician, the president of a company which produces heart monitors, was convicted of fraud for having tendered remuneration or kickbacks to referring physicians to his monitoring service, in violation of the Medicare statute.

■ **BLACK LETTER RULE** If one purpose of a payment made to a physician for professional services was to induce future referrals, the Medicare statute has been violated.

■ **PROCEDURAL BASIS**

Appeal from the jury's verdict convicting the defendant on 20 of 23 counts in the indictment.

■ **FACTS**

Greber (D) is an osteopathic physician who is board certified in cardiology. He was also the president of Cardio-Med, Inc., an organization which he formed to provide physicians with diagnostic services. Cardio-Med bills Medicare for its monitor service and when payment is received, forwards a portion to the referring physician. Based on these billing practices, the indictment charged Greber (D) with having tendered remuneration or kickbacks to the referring physicians in violation of the Medicare statute. Dr. Greber (D) had paid referring physicians "interpretation feed" for their initial consultation services, even though there was evidence that Greber (D) had actually evaluated the monitoring data. Moreover, the fixed percentage paid to the referring physician was more than Medicare allowed for such services. The government (P) also introduced testimony that Greber had stated that "if the doctor didn't get his consulting fee, he wouldn't be using our service. So the doctor got a consulting fee." The evidence as to mail fraud was the Greber (D) repeatedly ordered monitors for his own patients even though use of the device was not medically indicated. Additionally, the monitors are required to be in operation for eight hours or more in order for Medicare to pay for the monitoring. Greber (D) routinely certified that the condition had been met, although in fact it had not. After a jury trial, Greber (D) was convicted on 20 of 23 counts in an indictment charging violations of the mail fraud, Medicare fraud, and false statement statutes. Post-trial motions were denied, and Greber (D) has appealed.

■ **ISSUE**

Can payments made to a physician for professional services in connection with tests performed by a laboratory be the basis of Medicare fraud?

■ **DECISION AND RATIONALE**

(Weis, C.J.) Yes. The district judge instructed the jury that the government (P) was required to prove that Cardio-Med paid the referring physicians some part of the amount received from Medicare, that Dr. Greber (D) caused Cardio-Med to make the payment, and did so knowingly and willfully as well as with the intent to induce the referring physicians to use Cardio-Med's services for patients covered by Medicare. The judge further charged that even if the physician interpreting the test did so as a

---

consultant to Cardio-Med, that fact was immaterial if a purpose of the fee was to induce the offering of services from Cardio-Med. Greber (D) contends that the charge was erroneous. He insists that absent a showing that the only purpose behind the fee was to improperly induce future services, compensating a physician for services actually rendered could not be a violation of the statute. The government (P) argues that Congress intended to combat financial incentives to physicians for ordering particular services patients did not require. The language and purpose of the statute support the government's (P) view. Even if the physician performs some service for the money received, the potential for unnecessary drain on the Medicare system remains. The statute is aimed at the inducement factor. The potential for increased costs to the Medicare-Medicaid system and misapplication of federal funds is plain, where payments for the exercise of such judgments are added to the legitimate cost of the transaction. These are among the evils Congress sought to prevent by enacting the kickback statutes. We therefore hold that the district court correctly instructed the jury. If the payments were intended to induce the physicians to use Cardio-Med's services, the statute was violated, even is the payments were also intended to compensate for professional services. A review of the record also convinces us that there was sufficient evidence to sustain the jury's verdict. Having carefully reviewed all of Greber's (D) allegations, we find no reversible error. Accordingly, the judgment of the district court will be affirmed.

Analysis:

Kickbacks are payments back by a seller of a portion of the purchase price to the buyer or a public official, in order to induce the purchase or to improperly influence future purchases or leases. The amended text of the Medicare statute refers to "any remuneration." Remuneration refers to a payment in return for services rendered, which includes not only sums for which no actual service was performed, but also those amounts for which some professional time was expended. By including such items as kickbacks and bribes, the statute expands "remuneration" to cover such situations where no service is performed. That a particular payment was a remuneration (which implies that a service was rendered) rather than a kickback does not foreclose the possibility that a violation nevertheless could exist. Thus, in this case, although Dr. Greber (D) claims his intent was not to improperly induce future services, he could nevertheless properly be convicted under the Medicare fraud statute. Most courts have followed the lead in this case, and also hold that the purpose to induce referrals need not be the dominant or sole purpose of the scheme in order to fall within the antikickback law's prohibition.

■ CASE VOCABULARY

BRIBE: Any money, property, thing of value, or any preferment, advantage, or privilege, or any promise or undertaking asked, given or accepted, with a corrupt intent to induce or influence the action, vote or opinion of a person in any public or official capacity.

KICKBACK: Payment back by a seller of a portion of the purchase price to the buyer or a public official to induce the purchase or to improperly influence future purchases or leases.

REMUNERATION: Payment in return for services rendered.

United States v. Starks

(Government) v. (Drug Treatment Counselors)

157 F.3d 833 (11th Cir. 1998)

IGNORANCE OF THE LAW IS NO EXCUSE; KNOWLEDGE THAT CONDUCT IS UNLAWFUL IS ALL THAT IS REQUIRED

■ **INSTANT FACTS** On appeal from their convictions, the defendants claim that the district court committed reversible error in its jury instructions regarding the Anti-Kickback statute's mens rea requirement, and that the statute is unconstitutionally vague.

■ **BLACK LETTER RULE** The Anti-Kickback statute gives fair warning of conduct which is illegal and, as such, is not unconstitutionally vague.

■ **PROCEDURAL BASIS**

Appeal from the district court's judgment against the defendant.

■ **FACTS**

Siegel (D) was the president and sole shareholder of Future Steps, Inc., a corporation that developed and operated treatment programs for drug addiction. Future Steps contracted with Florida CHS to run a drug program for pregnant women at CHS's Hospital. In return, CHS promised to pay Future Steps a share of the Hospital's profits from the program. Before executing the contract, Siegel (D) initialed each page of the agreement, which included a provision explicitly prohibiting Future Steps from making any payment for patient referrals in violation of the Anti-Kickback statute. Starks (D) and Henry, employees of the Department of Health and Rehabilitative Services (HRS), worked in a federally-funded research project called "Project Support." As part of their duties, they advised pregnant women about possible treatment for drug abuse. Upon beginning their work at HRS, Starks (D) and Henry were advised that they could not accept any outside employment that might pose a conflict of interest with their work at HRS, and that they were obligated to report any outside employment to HRS. Future Steps was having difficulty attracting patients. One of its salaried "liaison workers," Doud-Lacher, identified Project Support as a potential source of referrals. When Doud-Lacher's initial efforts to establish a referral relationship between Future Steps and Project Support failed, Siegel (D) suggested to Doud-Lacher that she spend more time at Project Support, give diapers to them, take the workers lunch, and otherwise build a relationship with Project Support's employees. During one of her visits, Doud-Lacher learned from Starks and Henry that cuts in federal spending threatened to reduce their work hours. She promised them she would inquire about opportunities at Future Steps. Doud-Lacher spoke to Siegel (D) about hiring the two women. Despite the women's extant employment with HRS, Siegel agreed to pay them for patients they referred. After accepting Siegel's (D) terms, Starks (D) and Henry did not report their referral arrangement to anyone at Project Support or HRS. At the outset of their work for Future Steps, Starks (D) and Henry received checks written on Future Step's account and signed by Siegel. They were only paid for their referrals; at no time did Siegel (D) pay them for their time or expenses. After some time, Future Steps began paying the women in cash. The women didn't want to be seen accepting payments from Future Steps, so they would meet covertly to exchange the reimbursement. Beyond the impropriety of Starks' (D) and Henry's acceptance of referral payments from Siegel (D), the referral arrangement directly affected Starks (D) and Henry's counseling of the pregnant women who relied on them and Project Support for help. At trial, several women testified that

Starks and Henry threatened that HRS would take away their babies if they didn't go to Future Steps specifically for treatment. In total, Starks (D) and Henry referred eighteen women from Project Support to Future Steps. From these referrals, the Hospital received $323,023.04. A federal grand jury indicted Siegel, Starks, Henry, and Doud-Lacher on five counts related to the referrals. On appeal from their convictions, Starks and Siegel renew two contentions from their trial. First, they claim that the district court committed reversible error when it refused to instruct the jury that, because of the Anti-Kickback statute's mens rea requirement, Starks and Siegel had to have known that their referral arrangement violated the Anti-Kickback statute in order to be convicted. Second, Starks and Siegel argue that the Social Security Act's prohibition on paid referrals, when considered together with the Act's safe harbor provision, is unconstitutionally vague.

■ ISSUE

Did the district court err in its instruction to the jury, and is the Anti-Kickback statute unconstitutionally vague?

■ DECISION AND RATIONALE

(Birch, C.J.) No. Starks (D) and Siegel (D) argue that the district court erred in its instruction concerning the mens rea required under the Anti-Kickback statute. Since we heard oral argument on this case, however, the Supreme Court has issued an opinion in *Bryan v. United States* that clearly refutes their position. According to the *Bryan* Court, a jury may find a defendant guilty of violating a statute employing the word "willfully" if it believes that the defendant acted with an evil-meaning mind, that is to say, that he acted with knowledge that his conduct was unlawful. Because the jury finds that the defendant knew that his conduct was unlawful, the danger of convicting individuals engaged in apparently innocent activity is not present. Thus, the willfulness requirement does not carve out an exception to the traditional rule that ignorance of the law is no excuse; knowledge that conduct is unlawful is all that is required. Analogously, the Anti-Kickback statute does not constitute a special exception. It is not a highly technical regulation that poses a danger of ensnaring persons engaged in apparently innocent conduct. Thus, we see no error in the district court's refusal to give Starks' (D) and Siegel's (D) requested instruction. Starks (D) and Siegel (D) also argue that the Anti-Kickback statute is unconstitutionally vague because people of ordinary intelligence in either of their positions could not have ascertained from a reading of its Safe Harbor provision that their conduct was illegal. Under the Safe Harbor provision, the Anti-Kickback statute's prohibition on referral payments shall not apply to any amount paid by an employer to an employee (who has a bona fide employment relationship with such employer) for employment in the provision of covered items and services. Starks (D) and Siegel (D) are correct that a criminal statute must define an offense with sufficient clarity to enable ordinary people to understand what conduct is prohibited. Both the particular facts of this case and the nature of the Anti-Kickback statute, however, undercut Starks' (D) and Siegel's (D) vagueness argument. Persons in either Siegel's (D) or Starks' (D) position could hardly have thought that either Starks (D) or Henry was a bona fide employee. Unlike all of Future Steps' other workers, Starks (D) and Henry did not receive regular salary checks at the Hospital. Instead, they clandestinely received their checks (often bearing false category codes) or cash in parking lots and other places outside the Project Support clinic so as to avoid detection by other Project Support workers. Moreover, the statute requires "knowing and willful" conduct, a mens rea standard that mitigates any otherwise inherent vagueness in the Anti-Kickback statute's provisions. In sum, we agree with the district court that the Anti-Kickback statute gave Starks (D) and Siegel (D) fair warning that their conduct was illegal and that the statute therefore is not unconstitutionally vague. Thus, with regard to Starks' (D) and Siegel's (D) appeal, we affirm the district court's judgment on these two issues.

Analysis:

A person acts willfully if he acts intentionally and purposely and with the intent to do something the law forbids, that is, with the bad purpose to disobey or to disregard the law. A person need not be aware of the specific law or rule that his conduct may be violating, but he must act with the intent to do something that the law forbids. The government produced ample evidence here from which the jury could reasonably have inferred that Starks (D) and Siegel (D) knew that they were breaking the law—

even if they may not have known that they were specifically violating the Anti-Kickback statute. Indeed, the giving or taking of kickbacks for medical referrals is hardly the sort of activity a person might expect to be legal. According to Starks (D) and Siegel (D), this provision is vague because ordinary people in their position might reasonably have thought that they were "bona fide employees" who were exempt from the Anti-Kickback statute's prohibition on remuneration for referrals. However, even if Starks (D) and Siegel (D) believed that they were bona fide employees, they were not providing "covered items or services" as required by the statute. As the government (P) has shown, Starks (D) received payment from Siegel (D) and Future Steps only for referrals and not for any legitimate service for which the Hospital received any Medicare reimbursement.

CASE VOCABULARY

BONA FIDE: In or with good faith.

MALUM IN SE: An act wrong in itself, without regard to the laws of the state.

MALUM PROHIBITUM: An act which is wrong because it is prohibited by law.

MENS REA: A guilty or wrongful purpose; a criminal intent.

SAFE HARBOR PROVISION: A provision in a law which gives a person protection as long as efforts were made to comply with the law.

VAGUENESS DOCTRINE: Under this principle, a law which does not fairly inform a person of what is commanded or prohibited is unconstitutionally as violative of due process.

CHAPTER FIFTEEN

Antitrust

In Re Michigan State Medical Society

Instant Facts: The defendant was found to have violated the Sherman Antitrust Act by unlawfully conspiring with its members to influence third-party reimbursement policies.

Black Letter Rule: The success or failure of a group boycott or price-fixing agreement is irrelevant to the question of either its existence or its legality.

California Dental Association v. Federal Trade Commission

Instant Facts: The defendant appeals the FTC's decision holding that its advertising restrictions relating to discounted fees and the quality of dental services violated the FTC Act under an abbreviated rule-of-reason analysis.

Black Letter Rule: The Commission's jurisdiction under the FTC Act extends to an association that provides substantial economic benefit to its for-profit members, but where any anticompetitive effects of given restraints are far from intuitively obvious, the rule of reason demands a thorough inquiry into the consequences of those restraints.

Wilk v. American Medical Association

Instant Facts: The AMA (D) is appealing a judgment of the district court which held that it had conducted an illegal boycott in restraint of trade directed at chiropractors, and which ordered injunctive relief.

Black Letter Rule: Since the purpose of the inquiries into market definition and market power is to determine whether an arrangement has the potential for genuine adverse effects on competition, proof of actual detrimental effects, such as reduction of output, can obviate the need for an inquiry into market power, which is only a surrogate for detrimental effects.

Arizona v. Maricopa County Medical Society

Instant Facts: The State has claimed that a group of competing physicians have violated the Sherman Act by agreements which set the maximum fees that they may claim in full payment for health services provided to policyholders of specified insurance plans.

Black Letter Rule: Section one of the Sherman Act is violated by a price restraint that tends to provide the same economic rewards to all practitioners regardless of their skill, their experience, their training, or their willingness to employ innovative and difficult procedures in individual cases.

Kartell v. Blue Shield of Massachusetts, INC.

Instant Facts: Blue Shield (D) is alleged to have violated the Sherman Act in its policy which pays doctors for treating patients who are Blue Shield health insurance subscribers, but only if each doctor promises not to make any additional charge to the subscriber.

Black Letter Rule: A "ban on balance billing" practice does not violate either section 1 of the Sherman Act, which forbids agreements in "restraint of trade," or section 2 of the Sherman Act, which forbids "monopolization" and "attempts to monopolize."

In the Matter of Hospital Corporation of America

Instant Facts: A hospital chain was found to have violated the Clayton Act and the FTC Act and was ordered to divest its acquisitions of hospitals in Tennessee.

Black Letter Rule: An acquisition violates Section 7 of the Clayton Act and Section 5 of the Federal Trade Commission Act where in any line of commerce in any section of the country, the effect of such acquisition may be substantially to lessen competition, or tend to create a monopoly.

Federal Trade Commission v. Tenet Healthcare Corp.

Instant Facts: When two area hospitals agreed to merge to improve medical services, the Federal Trade Commission (FTC) claimed a violation of federal antitrust law.

Black Letter Rule: Prospective mergers do not violate federal antitrust law so long as consumers in the relevant geographic market have practicable alternatives to the merged entity.

In the Matter of Evanston Northwestern Healthcare Corp.

Instant Facts: Evanston Northwestern Healthcare Corp. (D) substantially raised its prices shortly after merging with a competitor, prompting charges from the Federal Trade Commission of antitrust violations.

Black Letter Rule: A merger that creates such market leverage so as to enable a business to substantially inflate its prices violates federal antitrust law.

In re Michigan State Medical Society

(Professional Association of Doctors)

101 F.T.C. 191 (1983)

CONCERTED ACTIVITY FOR A COMMON PURPOSE CONSTITUTES A SHERMAN ACT VIOLATION, WHETHER OR NOT AN ACTION SUCCEEDS

WE'VE GOT TO BAND TOGETHER SO WE CAN GET WHAT WE WANT!

■ **INSTANT FACTS** The defendant was found to have violated the Sherman Antitrust Act by unlawfully conspiring with its members to influence third-party reimbursement policies.

■ **BLACK LETTER RULE** The success or failure of a group boycott or price-fixing agreement is irrelevant to the question of either its existence or its legality.

■ **PROCEDURAL BASIS**

Appeal from the administrative law judge's judgment against the defendants.

■ **FACTS**

The Michigan State Medical Society (MSMS) (D), a group of doctors, unsuccessfully attempted to negotiate with Blue Cross and Blue Shield of Michigan (BCBSM) on issues regarding reimbursement for services to patients. As a result, MSMS's Negotiating Committee recommended that MSMS members (the individual doctors) be urged to write letters to BCBSM withdrawing from participation (refusing to provide services to BCBSM insureds), but mail them to the Negotiating Committee to be held as "proxies." The House of Delegates authorized the committee to collect the proxies, but to use them only at the discretion of the Council, with prior notice to the members who submitted them, if a negotiating impasse develops with BCBSM [ooh, *leverage!*]. The letters contained two blank revocable powers of attorney, one for BCBSM and one for Medicaid, empowering the Negotiating Committee to cancel the signer's participation in either program if such action was deemed warranted by the Council. As a result of this response, a dispute over reimbursement was resolved in MSMS's (D) favor with the status quo being preserved and BCBSM withdrawing its proposal for a new reimbursement program. These proxies also played a role in MSMS's (D) dealings with Medicaid. BCBSM filed a complaint regarding MSMS's (D) actions. The administrative law judge found that MSMS (D) unlawfully conspired with its members to influence third-party reimbursement policies by seeking to negotiate collective agreements with insurers, by agreeing to use coercive measures like proxy solicitation and group boycotts, and by actually making coercive threats to third party payers.

■ **ISSUE**

Did the defendants, acting through a professional association, conspire to restrain trade by organizing boycotts and tampering with the fees from third party insurers of their services?

■ **DECISION AND RATIONALE**

(Clanton, C.) Yes. The MSMS (D) members, acting through their House of Delegates, established a Division of Negotiations for the purpose of working out differences with third party payers. Thus, at the outset we find that the very creation of the Division of Negotiations reveals a collective purpose on the part of MSMS (D) and its members to go beyond the point of giving advice to third party payers. In fact, it reveals a purpose to organize and empower a full-fledged representative to negotiate and resolve controversies surrounding physician profiles, screens and other similar matters. Turning to the boycott issue, the law is clear that the definition of that term is not limited to situations where the target of the concerted refusal to deal is another competitor or potential competitor. And although BCBSM and Medicaid—the targets of the boycott—are not in competitive relationships with MSMS (D), that fact alone does not preclude a finding of a boycott. MSMS (D) argues that the proxies were not exercised and, in the case of the departiciation letter campaign, that there was no adverse effect on BCBSM. However, the success or failure of a group boycott or price-fixing agreement is irrelevant to the question of either its existence or its legality. Whether or not the action succeeds, it is the concerted activity for a common purpose that constitutes the violation of the Sherman Antitrust Act. Furthermore, an agreement among competitors affecting price does not have to be successful in order to be condemned. It would appear that MSMS's (D) conduct approaches the kind of behavior that previously had been classified as per se illegal. Nevertheless, since this conduct does not involve direct fee setting, we are not prepared to declare it per se illegal at this juncture and close the door on all asserted pro-competitive justifications. Where horizontal arrangements so closely relate to prices or fees as they do here, a less elaborate analysis of competitive effects is required. The collective actions under scrutiny clearly interfere with the rights of physicians to compete independently on the terms of insurance coverage offered by BCBSM and Medicaid. Moreover, the joint arrangements directly hamper the ability of third party payers to compete freely for the patronage of individual physicians and other physician business entities. While we understand MSMS's (D) concerns about the effects of physician withdrawal from Medicaid, we observe that MSMS (D) clearly had public forums available to it to correct perceived mistakes made by the state legislature or administrators of Medicaid. It could have expressed its views in ways that fell well short of organized boycott threats. In fact, there are many less anti-competitive ways of providing information to insurers. Thus, the order that we impose on MSMS (D) allows it to provide information and views to insurers on behalf of its members, so long as the Society does not attempt to extract agreements, through coercion or otherwise, from third party payers on reimbursement issues. In allowing MSMS (D) to engage in non-binding, non-coercive discussions with health insurers, we have attempted to strike a proper balance between the need for insurers to have efficient access to the views of large groups of providers and the need to prevent competitors from banding together in ways that involve the unreasonable exercise of collective market power.

Analysis:

It is the contract, combination, or conspiracy in restraint of trade or commerce that the Sherman Act strikes down, whether the concerted activity be ineffectual or successful. Moreover, even if less than all members of an organization or association agree to participate, that fact does not negate the presence of a conspiracy or combination as to those who do participate. As for the collection of proxies that were never exercised, the law does not require that a competitor actually refuse to deal before a boycott can be found or liability established. Rather, the threat to refuse to deal may suffice to constitute the offense. The threat implicit in the collection of departiciation proxies and the attendant publicity can be as effective as the actual execution of the threatened action. Indeed, it may be assumed that parties to a concerted refusal to deal hope that the announcement of the intended action will be sufficient to produce the desired response. That is precisely what happened in this case, and the court correctly rejected this strategy as improper and illegal.

■ **CASE VOCABULARY**

ANTITRUST LAW: Federal and state statutes to protect trade and commerce from unlawful restraints, price discriminations, price fixing, and monopolies.

BOYCOTT: Concerted refusal to do business with a particular person or business in order to obtain concessions or to express displeasure with certain acts or practices of a person or business.

INTER ALIA: Among other things.

POWER OF ATTORNEY: An instrument in writing whereby one person, as principal, appoints another as his agent and confers authority to perform certain specified acts or kinds of acts on behalf of the principal.

STATUS QUO: The existing state of things at a given time.

California Dental Association v. Federal Trade Commission

(Nonprofit Professional Association) v. *(Government)*

526 U.S. 756, 119 S.Ct. 1604, 143 L.Ed.2d 935 (1999)

QUICK-LOOK ANALYSIS IS ONLY APPROPRIATE IN SITUATIONS WHERE THE LIKELIHOOD OF ANTICOMPETITIVE EFFECTS CAN BE EASILY ASCERTAINED

■ **INSTANT FACTS** The defendant appeals the FTC's decision holding that its advertising restrictions relating to discounted fees and the quality of dental services violated the FTC Act under an abbreviated rule-of-reason analysis.

■ **BLACK LETTER RULE** The Commission's jurisdiction under the FTC Act extends to an association that provides substantial economic benefit to its for-profit members, but where any anticompetitive effects of given restraints are far from intuitively obvious, the rule of reason demands a thorough inquiry into the consequences of those restraints.

■ **PROCEDURAL BASIS**

Appeal from the Court of Appeals' affirmance of the Commission's (P) decision against the defendant.

■ **FACTS**

California Dental Association (D) is a nonprofit association of local dental societies, to which about 75% of the State's dentists belong. CDA (D) provides desirable insurance and preferential financing arrangements for its members, and engages in lobbying, litigation, marketing, and public relations for members' benefit. Members agree to abide by CDA's (D) Code of Ethics which, inter alia, prohibits false or misleading advertising. The FTC (P) claimed that in applying its guidelines relating to advertising so as to restrict two types of truthful, nondeceptive advertising (price advertising, particularly discounted fees, and advertising relating to the quality of dental servies), the CDA (D) violated the FTC Act. In its administrative proceedings, the Commission (P) held that the advertising restrictions violated the Act under an abbreviated rule-of-reason analysis. The Court of Appeals affirmed, and this appeal followed.

■ **ISSUE**

Does the jurisdiction of the Federal Trade Commission extend to the California Dental Association, a nonprofit professional association, and does a "quick look" suffice to justify finding that certain advertising restrictions adopted by the CDA violated the antitrust laws?

■ **DECISION AND RATIONALE**

(Souter, J.) Yes and No. The dentists who belong to the CDA (D) agreed to abide by a Code of Ethics. Responsibility for enforcing the Code rests in the first instance with the local dental societies, to which applicants for CDA membership must submit copies of their own advertisements and those of their employers or referral services to assure compliance with the Code. The local societies also actively seek information about potential Code violations by applicants or CDA members. Applicants who refuse to withdraw or revise objectionable advertisements may be denied membership, and members who, after a hearing, remain similarly resistant are subject to censure, suspension, or expulsion from the CDA (D). There are two issues in this case: whether the jurisdiction of the FTC extends to the CDA (D), and whether a "quick look" sufficed to justify finding that certain advertising restrictions adopted by the CDA (D) violated antitrust laws. We first hold that the Commission's (P) jurisdiction extends to associations that, like the CDA (D), provide substantial economic benefit to their for-profit members. The FTC Act, which gives the Commission (P) authority over a corporation that is organized to carry on business for its own profit or that of its members, confers jurisdiction over nonprofit associations whose activities provide substantial economic benefits to their for-profit members. The abbreviated or "quick-look" analysis under the rule of reason is appropriate when an observer with even a rudimentary understanding of economics could conclude that the arrangements in question would have an anticompetitive effect on customers and markets. And in such cases, quick-look analysis carries the day when the great likelihood of anticompetitive effects can easily be ascertained. The case before us, however, fails to present a situation in which the likelihood of anticompetitive effects is comparably obvious. Whereas the Ninth Circuit seems to accept that the restrictions here were like restrictions on advertisement of price and quality generally, it seems to us that the CDA's (D) advertising restrictions might plausibly be thought to have a net procompetitive effect, or possibly no effect at all on competition. The restrictions on both discount and nondiscount advertising are, at least on their face, designed to avoid false or deceptive advertising in a market characterized by striking disparities between the information available to the professional and the patient. The existence of such significant challenges to informed decisionmaking by the customer for professional services immediately suggests that advertising restrictions arguably protecting patients from misleading or irrelevant advertising call for more than cursory treatment as obviously comparable to classic horizontal agreements to limit output or price competition. In this case, the CDA's (D) rule appears to reflect the prediction that any costs to competition associated with the elimination of across-the-board advertising will be outweighed by gains to consumer information (and hence competition) created by discount advertising that is exact, accurate, and more easily verifiable (at least by regulators). As a matter of economics this view may or may not be correct, but it is not implausible, and neither a court nor the Commission (P) may initially dismiss it as presumptively wrong. Although the Court of Appeals acknowledged the CDA's (D) view that claims about quality are inherently unverifiable and therefore misleading, it responded that this concern does not justify banning all quality claims without regard to whether they are, in fact, false or misleading. As a result, the court said the restriction justified quick look analysis. The court assumed, in these words, that some dental quality claims may escape justifiable censure, because they are both verifiable and true. But its implicit assumption fails to explain why it gave no weight to the countervailing, and at least equally plausible suggestion that restricting difficult-to-verify claims about quality or patient comfort would have a procompetitive effect by preventing misleading or false claims that distort the market. It is, indeed, entirely possible to understand the CDA's (D) restrictions on unverifiable quality and comfort advertising as nothing more than a procompetitive ban on puffery. Saying here that the Court of Appeals' conclusion at least required a more extended examination of the possible factual underpinnings than it received is not, of course, necessarily to call for the fullest market analysis. As the circumstances here demonstrate, there is generally no categorical line to be drawn between restraints that give rise to an intuitively obvious inference of anticompetitive effect and those that call for more detailed treatment. The object is to see whether the experience of the market has been so clear, or necessarily will be, that a confident conclusion about the principal tendency of a restriction will follow from a quick (or at least quicker) look, in place of a more diligent one. And of course what we see may vary over time, if rule-of-reason analyses in case after case reach identical conclusions. For now, at least, a less quick look was required for the initial assessment of the tendency of these professional advertising restrictions. Because the Court of Appeals did not scrutinize the assumption of relative anticompetitive tendencies, we vacate the judgment and remand the case for a fuller consideration of the issue.

■ CONCURRENCE AND DISSENT

(Breyer, J.) I agree with the Court that the FTC has jurisdiction over CDA (D), and I join Parts I and II of its opinion. I also agree that in a "rule of reason" antitrust case, the quality of proof required should vary with the circumstances, and that the object is a "confident conclusion about the principal tendency of a restriction." But I do not agree that the Court has properly applied those principles here. In my view, a traditional application of the rule of reason to the facts as found by the Commission (P) requires affirming the Commission—just as the Court of Appeals did below. In the Court's view, the legal analysis conducted by the Court of Appeals was insufficient, and the Court remands the case for a more thorough application of the rule of reason. But in what way did the Court of Appeals fail? I find the Court's answers to this question unsatisfactory when one divides the overall Sherman Act question into its traditional component parts and adheres to traditional judicial practice for allocating the burdens of persuasion in an antitrust case. The upshot, in my view, is that the Court of Appeals, applying ordinary antitrust principles, reached an unexceptional conclusion. Thus, I respectfully dissent from Part III of the Court's opinion.

Analysis:

That false or misleading advertising has an anticompetitive effect, as that term is customarily used, has been long established. The fact that a restraint operates upon a profession as distinguished from a business is, of course, relevant in determining whether that particular restraint violates the Sherman Act. It would be unrealistic to view the practice of professions as interchangeable with other business activities, and automatically to apply to the professions antitrust concepts that originated in other areas. The public service aspect, and other features of the professions, may require that a particular practice, which could properly be viewed as a violation of the Sherman Act in another context, be treated differently. In a market for professional services, in which advertising is relatively rare and the comparability of service packages not easily established, the difficulty for customers or potential competitors to get and verify information about the price and availability of services magnifies the dangers to competition associated with misleading advertising.

■ CASE VOCABULARY

A PRIORI: From the cause to the effect which necessarily must follow.

CENSURE: An official reprimand or condemnation.

DE NOVO: Hearing a matter anew, the same as if it had not been heard before and as if no decision had been previously made.

IBID: In the same place; in the same book; on the same page, etc.

PRIMA FACIE: A fact presumed to be true on its face unless it is disproved by some evidence to the contrary.

PUFFERY: Exaggeration concerning the quality of goods or services, which usually concerns opinions rather than facts.

"QUICK LOOK" ANALYSIS: An abbreviated rule-of-reason analysis.

Wilk v. American Medical Association

(Chiropractors) v. *(Medical Society)*

895 F.2d 352 (7th Cir.), cert. denied, 498 U.S. 982, 111 S.Ct. 513, 112 L.Ed.2d 524 (1990)

THE THRESHOLD ISSUE IN ANY RULE OF REASON CASE IS MARKET POWER

■ **INSTANT FACTS** The AMA (D) is appealing a judgment of the district court which held that it had conducted an illegal boycott in restraint of trade directed at chiropractors, and which ordered injunctive relief.

■ **BLACK LETTER RULE** Since the purpose of the inquiries into market definition and market power is to determine whether an arrangement has the potential for genuine adverse effects on competition, proof of actual detrimental effects, such as reduction of output, can obviate the need for an inquiry into market power, which is only a surrogate for detrimental effects.

■ PROCEDURAL BASIS

Appeal from the Court of Appeals' reversal of the jury's verdict for the defendants.

■ FACTS

Pedigo, Arthur, Bryden, and Wilk (P) are licensed chiropractors. Their complaint charged the American Medical Association (AMA) (D) with violating the Sherman Act by conducting an illegal boycott in restraint of trade directed at chiropractors generally, and the four plaintiffs in particular. It sought both damages and an injunction, claiming that the AMA engaged in a conspiracy to eliminate the chiropractic profession by refusing to deal with chiropractors. A jury returned a verdict for the AMA (D), and an earlier panel of this Court reversed that judgment. In reversing and ordering a new trial, the Court held that, in applying the rule of reason, the jury had been allowed to consider factors beyond the effect of the AMA's (D) conduct on competition. The district court had improperly failed to confine the jury's consideration to the patient care motive as contrasted with the generalized public interest motive. The AMA's (D) present position regarding chiropractic is that it is ethical for a medical physician to professionally associate with chiropractors if the physician believes that the association is in his patient's best interests. The district court found that the AMA (D) had not previously communicated this position to its membership. Based on these findings, the court held that the AMA and its members violated the Sherman Act by unlawfully conspiring to restrain trade. Despite the fact that the district court found that the conspiracy had ended, it concluded that the illegal boycott's "lingering effects" still threatened the chiropractors (P) with current injury and ordered injunctive relief.

■ ISSUE

Does a boycott by the American Medical Association (D) of chiropractors (P) constitute an unreasonable restraint of trade in violation of the Sherman Act?

■ DECISION AND RATIONALE

(Manion, C.J.) Yes. The threshold issue in any rule of reason case is market power. Whether market power exists in an appropriately defined market is a fact-bound question, and appellate courts normally defer to district court findings on that issue. Thus, we find that the district court properly relied on the AMA membership's substantial market share in finding market power. While we cautioned against relying solely on market share as a basis for inferring market power, we did not rule out that approach. This is especially so where there are barriers to entry and no substitutes from the consumer's perspective. The district court also found there was substantial evidence that the boycott adversely affected competition, and that a showing of such adverse effects negated the need to prove in any elaborate fashion market definition and market power. Since the purpose of the inquiries into market definition and market power is to determine whether an arrangement has the potential for genuine adverse effects on competition, proof of actual detrimental effects, such as reduction of output, can obviate the need for an inquiry into market power, which is only a surrogate for detrimental effects. Moving on, the AMA (D) argues that even if market power existed, it escapes liability under the rule of reason because the AMA (D) rule against associating with chiropractors had overriding pro-competitive effects. The AMA's (D) conduct, the theory goes, ensured that physicians acquired reputations for quality, and thus allowed consumers to be assured that physicians would use only scientifically valid treatments. This in effect simultaneously provided consumers with essential information and protected competition. Getting needed information to the market is a fine goal, however it cannot be said that the AMA (D) was motivated solely by such altruistic concerns. Indeed, the district court found, and we agree, that the AMA (D) intended to destroy a competitor, namely, chiropractors. It is not enough to carry the day to argue that competition should be eliminated in the name of public safety. In the AMA's (D) first appeal, we modified the rule of reason to allow the AMA (D) to justify its boycott of chiropractors if it could show that it was motivated by a concern for "patient care." Although doubting the AMA's (D) genuineness regarding its concern for scientific method in patient care, the district court concluded that the AMA (D) established that element. The court, however, found that the AMA (D) failed to carry its burden of persuasion as to whether its concern for scientific method in patient care was objectively reasonable. Moreover, the AMA's (D) own evidence suggested that at some point during its lengthy boycott, there was no longer an objectively reasonable concern that would support a boycott of the entire chiropractic profession. In sum, we agree with the district court that the AMA's (D) boycott constituted an unreasonable restraint of trade under the Sherman Act and the rule of reason. Therefore, the district court's findings that the AMA's (D) boycott was anti-competitive, and was not counter-balanced by any pro-competitive effects were not erroneous.

Analysis:

The district court relied on substantial evidence of adverse effects on competition caused by the boycott to establish the AMA's (D) market power. It is anti-competitive and it raises costs to interfere with the consumer's free choice to take the product of his liking. Additionally it is anti-competitive to prevent physicians from referring patients to a chiropractor. The AMA's (D) plan is anti-competitive in imposing higher costs on chiropractors by forcing them to pay for their own x-ray equipment rather than obtaining x-rays from hospital radiology departments or radiologists in private practice. Finally, it is anti-competitive to prevent chiropractors from improving their education in a professional setting by preventing physicians from teaching or lecturing to chiropractors. The Court was correct in affirming the district court's decision that the AMA's (D) boycott was anti-competitive and was thus a violation of the Sherman Act.

■ CASE VOCABULARY

BURDEN OF PERSUASION: The obligation of a party to establish by evidence a requisite degree of belief concerning a fact in the mind of the trier of fact or the court.

MARKET POWER: The ability to raise prices above the competitive level by restricting output.

Arizona v. Maricopa County Medical Society

(Government) v. *(Medical Foundations)*

457 U.S. 332, 102 S.Ct. 2466, 73 L.Ed.2d 48 (1982)

A PRICE-FIXING AGREEMENT IS UNLAWFUL ON ITS FACE

■ **INSTANT FACTS** The State has claimed that a group of competing physicians have violated the Sherman Act by agreements which set the maximum fees that they may claim in full payment for health services provided to policyholders of specified insurance plans.

■ **BLACK LETTER RULE** Section one of the Sherman Act is violated by a price restraint that tends to provide the same economic rewards to all practitioners regardless of their skill, their experience, their training, or their willingness to employ innovative and difficult procedures in individual cases.

■ PROCEDURAL BASIS

Certiorari granted to review the Court of Appeals' decision that the issue must go to trial to be decided.

■ FACTS

The Maricopa Foundation (D) is a nonprofit corporation composed of licensed physicians, organized for the purpose of promoting fee-for-service medicine and to provide the community with a competitive alternative to existing health insurance plans. The Foundation (D) establishes the schedule of maximum fees that participating doctors agree to accept as payment in full for services performed for patients insured under plans approved by the Foundation (D). It reviews the medical necessity and appropriateness of treatment provided by its members to such insured persons. It is authorized to draw checks on insurance company accounts to pay doctors for services performed for covered patients. In performing these functions, the Foundation (D) is considered an "insurance administrator." The Foundation (D) uses "relative values" and "conversion factors" in compiling its fee schedule. The fee schedules limit the amount that the member doctors may recover for services performed for patients insured under plans approved by the Foundation (D). The doctors are free to charge higher fees to uninsured patients, and they also may charge any patient less than the scheduled maximum. A patient who is insured by a Foundation-endorsed plan is guaranteed complete coverage for the full amount of his medical bills only if he is treated by a foundation member. The impact of the Foundation (D) fee schedules on medical fees and on insurance premiums is a matter of dispute. The State (P) contends that the periodic upward revisions of the maximum-fee schedules have the effect of stabilizing and enhancing the level of actual charges by physicians, and that the increasing level of their fees in turn increases insurance premiums. The Foundation (D), on the other hand, argue that the schedules impose a meaningful limit on physicians' charges, and that the advance agreement by the doctors to accept the maximum enables the insurance carriers to limit and to calculate more efficiently the risks they underwrite and therefore serves as an effective cost-containment mechanism that has saved patients and insurers millions of dollars.

■ ISSUE

Is section one of the Sherman Act violated by agreements among competing physicians setting, by majority vote, the maximum fees that they may claim in full payment for health services provided to policyholders of specified insurance plans?

■ DECISION AND RATIONALE

(Stevens, J.) Yes. The Foundation (D) recognizes that our decisions establish that price-fixing agreements are unlawful on their face. But they argue that the per se rule does not govern this case because the agreements at issue are horizontal and fix maximum prices, are among members of a profession, are in an industry with which the judiciary has little antitrust experience, and are alleged to have pro-competitive justifications. However, we believe that the cases place horizontal agreements to fix maximum prices on the same legal—even if not economic—footing as agreements to fix minimum or uniform prices. The per se rule is grounded on faith in price competition as a market force and not on a policy of low selling prices at the price of eliminating competition. In this case, the rule is violated by a price restraint that tends to provide the same economic rewards to all practitioners regardless of their skill, their experience, their training, or their willingness to employ innovative and difficult procedures in individual cases. Such a restraint also may discourage entry into the market and may deter experimentation and new developments by individual entrepreneurs. We are equally unpersuaded by the argument that we should not apply the per se rule in this case because the judiciary has little antitrust experience in the health care industry. The argument that the per se rule must be rejustified for every industry that has not been subject to significant antitrust litigation ignores the rationale for per se rules, which in part is to avoid the necessity for an incredibly complicated and prolonged economic investigation into the entire history of the industry involved, as well as related industries, in an effort to determine at large whether a particular restraint has been unreasonable—an inquiry so often wholly fruitless when undertaken. The Foundation's (D) argument is that the per se rule is inapplicable because their agreements are alleged to have pro-competitive justifications. The argument indicates a misunderstanding of the per se concept. The anti-competitive potential inherent in all price-fixing agreements justifies their facial invalidation even if pro-competitive justifications are offered for some. Those claims of enhanced competition are so unlikely to prove significant in any particular case that we adhere to the rule of law that is justified in its general application. Even when the Foundation (D) is given every benefit of the doubt, the limited record in this case is not inconsistent with the presumption that the Foundation's (D) agreements will not significantly enhance competition. Having declined the Foundation's (D) invitation to cut back on the per se rule against price fixing, we are left with their argument that their fee schedules involve price fixing in only a literal sense. If a clinic offered complete medical care for a flat fee, the cooperating doctors would have the type of partnership arrangement in which a price-fixing agreement among the doctors would be perfectly proper. But the fee arrangements disclosed by the record in this case are among independent competing entrepreneurs. They fit squarely into the horizontal price-fixing mold. The judgment of the Court of Appeals is reversed.

■ DISSENT

(Powell, J.) The medical care plan condemned by the Court today is a comparatively new method of providing insured medical services at predetermined maximum costs. It involves no coercion. Medical insurance companies, physicians, and patients alike are free to participate or not as they choose. On its face, the plan seems to be in the public interest. I do not think today's decision on an incomplete record is consistent with proper judicial resolution of an issue of this complexity, novelty, and importance to the public. I therefore dissent.

Analysis:

Litigation of the effect or purpose of a business practice is often extensive and complex. Judges often lack the expert understanding of industrial market structures and behavior to determine with any confidence a practice's effect on competition. And the result of the process in any given case may provide little certainty or guidance about the legality of the same business practice in another context. However, to make it a bit easier for the judges, it is settled law that once an arrangement has been labeled as "price fixing," it is to be condemned per se. The most that can be said for having doctors fix the maximum prices is that doctors may be able to do it more efficiently than insurers, but there is no reason to believe that any savings that might accrue from this arrangement would be sufficiently great to affect the competitiveness of these kinds of insurance plans. It is entirely possible that the power of the Foundation (D) to dictate the terms of such insurance plans may more than offset the theoretical efficiencies upon which its defense ultimately rests. Therefore, the Foundation's (D) business practice at issue in this case must be struck down as unreasonable.

■ CASE VOCABULARY

CERTIORARI: A writ issued in order that a superior court may inspect the proceedings in the lower court to determine whether there have been any irregularities.

DISCOVERY: The pre-trial devices that can be used by one party to obtain facts and information about the case from the other party in order to assist the party's preparation for trial.

PRICE-FIXING: A violation of the Sherman Act which involves the cooperative setting of price levels or range by competing firms, which would otherwise be set by natural market forces.

Kartell v. Blue Shield of Massachusetts, Inc.

(Doctors) v. (Health Insurer)

749 F.2d 922 (1st Cir. 1984), cert. denied, 471 U.S. 1029, 105 S.Ct. 2040, 85 L.Ed.2d 322 (1985)

ANTITRUST LAW RARELY STOPS THE BUYER OF A SERVICE FROM TRYING TO DETERMINE THE PRICE OR CHARACTERISTICS OF THE PRODUCT THAT WILL BE SOLD

■ **INSTANT FACTS** Blue Shield (D) is alleged to have violated the Sherman Act in its policy which pays doctors for treating patients who are Blue Shield health insurance subscribers, but only if each doctor promises not to make any additional charge to the subscriber.

■ **BLACK LETTER RULE** A "ban on balance billing" practice does not violate either section 1 of the Sherman Act, which forbids agreements in "restraint of trade," or section 2 of the Sherman Act, which forbids "monopolization" and "attempts to monopolize."

■ PROCEDURAL BASIS

Appeal from the district court's judgment in favor of the plaintiff, and a cross-appeal from other rulings of the district court in favor of the defendant.

■ FACTS

The consumers of Blue Shield insurance can see any "participating doctor," i.e. a doctor who has entered into a standard agreement with Blue Shield (D). Under the standard agreement, a participating doctor promises to accept as payment in full an amount determined by Blue Shield's (D) "usual and customary charge" method of compensation. Blue Shield (D) pays this amount directly to the doctor; the patient pays nothing out of his own pocket and therefore receives no reimbursement. Virtually all practicing doctors agree to take Blue Shield (D) subscribers as patients and to participate in its fee plan. This practice is known as a "ban on balance billing," and the issue in this case is whether this is a violation of the Sherman Act. The district court held that the practice constituted an unreasonable restraint of trade in violation of section 1. The district court found that, the effect of this payment system, when combined with Blue Shield's (D) size and buying power, was to produce an unreasonably rigid and unjustifiably low set of prices. In the court's view, the fact that doctors cannot charge Blue Shield (D) subscribers more than the Blue Shield payment-schedule amounts interferes with the doctors' freedom to set higher prices for more expensive services and discourages them from developing and offering patients more expensive (and perhaps qualitatively better) services.

■ ISSUE

Does a "ban on balance billing" practice violate the Sherman Act?

■ DECISION AND RATIONALE

(Breyer, C.J.) No. We disagree with the district court because we do not believe that the facts that it found show an unreasonable restraint of trade. To find an unlawful restraint, one would have to look at Blue Shield (D) as if it were a "third force," intervening in the marketplace in a manner that prevents willing buyers and sellers from independently coming together to strike price/quality bargains. Antitrust law typically frowns upon behavior that impedes the striking of such independent bargains. The persuasive power of the district court's analysis disappears, however, once one looks at Blue Shield (D) not as an inhibitory "third force," but as itself the purchaser of the doctors' services. Antitrust law rarely stops the buyer of a service from trying to determine the price or characteristics of the product that will be sold. Thus, the more closely Blue Shield's (D) activities resemble, in essence, those of a purchaser, the less likely that they are unlawful. The district court here found that Blue Shield (D) is a buyer with significant "market power"—i.e. the power to force prices below the level that a freely competitive market would otherwise set. They argue that Blue Shield's (D) "market power" makes a significant difference. We do not agree. To resolve this argument about the existence of market power—an issue hotly debated by the expert economists who testified at trial—would force us to evaluate a record that the district court described as "two competing mountains of mostly meaningless papers." Rather than do so, we shall assume that Blue Shield (D) possesses significant market power. We shall also assume, but purely for the sake of argument, that Blue Shield (D) uses that power to obtain "lower than competitive" prices. We next ask whether Blue Shield's (D) assumed market power makes a significant legal difference. In essence, the lawfulness of the term in question stems from the fact that it is an essential part of the price bargain between buyer and seller. Whether or not that price bargain is, in fact, reasonable is, legally speaking, beside the point, even in the case of a monopolist. As Blue Shield (D) stresses in its brief, HMOs, independent practice associations, and preferred provider organizations all routinely agree with doctors that the doctors will accept payment from the plan as payment in full for services rendered to subscribers. We can find no relevant analytical distinction between this type of purchasing decision and the practice before us—even on the assumption that Blue Shield possesses market power. A legitimate buyer is entitled to use its market power to keep prices down. The claim that Blue Shield's (D) price scheme is "too rigid" because it ignores qualitative differences among physicians is properly addressed to Blue Shield (D) or to a regulator, not to a court. There is no suggestion that Blue Shield's (D) fee schedule reflects, for example, an effort by, say, one group of doctors to stop other doctors from competing with them. Here, Blue Shield (D) and the doctors sit on opposite sides of the bargaining table. And Blue Shield (D) seems simply to be acting as every rational enterprise does, i.e. to get the best deal possible. Three additional circumstances militate strongly here against any effort by an antitrust court to supervise the Blue Shield/physician price bargain. First, the prices at issue here are low prices, not high prices. Of course, a buyer, as well as a seller, can possess significant market power; and courts have held that *agreements* to fix prices—whether maximum or minimum—are unlawful. Nonetheless, the Congress that enacted the Sherman Act saw it as a way of protecting consumers against prices that were too *high*, not too low. Second, the subject matter of the present agreement—medical costs—is an area of great complexity where more than solely economic values are at stake. This fact too warrants judicial hesitancy to interfere. Third, the price system her at issue is one supervised by state regulators. While that fact alone does not automatically carry with it antitrust immunity, it suggests that strict antitrust scrutiny is less likely to be necessary to prevent the unwarranted exercise of monopoly power. These general considerations do not dictate our result in this case. They do, however, counsel us against departing from present law or extending it to authorize increased judicial supervision of the buyer/seller price bargain.

Analysis:

It is not surprising the courts have unanimously upheld contracts analogous in various degrees to the one at issue here—contracts in which those who directly provide goods or services to insureds have agreed to cap or forego completely additional charges to these insureds in return for direct payment by the insurer. The district court rested its decision in large part upon the decision in *Arizona v. Maricopa County Medical Society*. That case, however, involved a *horizontal* agreement among competing doctors about what to charge. A horizontal agreement among competitors is typically unlawful because the competitors prevent themselves from making *independent* decisions about the terms as to which they will bargain. The antitrust problems at issue when a single firm sets a price—whether, when, and how courts can identify and control an individual exercise of alleged market power—are very different from those associated with agreements by competitors to limit independent decision-making. A decision about the latter is not strong precedent for a case involving only the former. *Maricopa* is simply not on point, and the Court correctly rejected the district court's reliance upon it.

In the Matter of Hospital Corporation of America

(Proprietary Hospital Chain)

106 F.T.C. 361 (1985)

AN ACQUISITION WHICH MAY SUBSTANTIALLY LESSEN COMPETITION VIOLATES SECTION 7 OF THE CLAYTON ACT AND SECTION 5 OF THE FEDERAL TRADE COMMISSION ACT

■ **INSTANT FACTS** A hospital chain was found to have violated the Clayton Act and the FTC Act and was ordered to divest its acquisitions of hospitals in Tennessee.

■ **BLACK LETTER RULE** An acquisition violates Section 7 of the Clayton Act and Section 5 of the Federal Trade Commission Act where in any line of commerce in any section of the country, the effect of such acquisition may be substantially to lessen competition, or tend to create a monopoly.

■ **FACTS**

Hospital Corporation of America (HCA) (D) acquired Hospital Affiliates International (HAI) in a stock transaction valued at approximately $650 million. At the time of the acquisition, HAI owned or leased 57 hospitals and managed 78 hospitals nationwide. Four months later, HCA (D) acquired another hospital corporation, Health Care Corporation (HCC) in a stock transaction valued at approximately $30 million. As a result of these acquisitions, HCA (D) increased its hospital operations from one acute care hospital to ownership or management of five of the Chattanooga, Tennessee area's eleven acute care hospitals. Additionally, within the metropolitan area, HCA (D) changed its position from owner of one hospital to owner or manager of seven of the fourteen acute care hospitals. The Administrative Law Judge found that the acquisitions violated Section 7 of the Clayton Act and Section 5 of the Federal Trade Commission Act, and ordered HCA (D) to divest two of the hospitals of which it had acquired ownership. The Judge also ordered that HCA (D) provide prior notification to the Commission of certain of its future hospital acquisitions. HCA (D) appeals this decision.

■ **ISSUE**

Did the defendant's acquisition of several area hospitals violate Section 7 of the Clayton Act and Section 5 of the Federal Trade Commission Act?

■ **DECISION AND RATIONALE**

(Calvani, C.) Yes. The Administrative Law Judge (ALJ) determined that the market should include outpatient services provided by hospitals but excluded outpatient services provided by non-hospital providers, holding that only hospitals can provide the "unique combination" of services which the acute care patient needs. He defined the relevant product market to be the cluster of services offered by acute care hospitals, including outpatient as well as inpatient care, "since acute care hospitals compete with each other in offering both kinds of care and since acute care outpatient facilities feed patients to the inpatient facilities." Neither HCA (D) nor Complaint Counsel appeal the ALJ's product market definition. Accordingly, for purposes of this proceeding only we accept the finding on this issue. However, we do note that the ALJ's definition does not necessarily provide a very happy medium between the two competing positions. The evidence in this case tended to show *both* that free-

---

standing outpatient facilities compete with hospitals for many outpatients and that hospitals offer and inpatients consume a cluster of services that bears little relation to outpatient care. If so, it may be that defining the cluster of hospital inpatient services as a separate market better reflects competitive reality in this case. Certainly, it is clear that anti-competitive behavior by hospital firms could significantly lessen competition for hospital inpatients that could not be defeated by competition from non-hospital outpatient providers. Our analysis will hence proceed with primary reference to the cluster of services provided to inpatients. Because we are concerned only with an area in which competition could be harmed, the relevant geographic market must be broad enough that buyers would be unable to switch to alternative sellers in sufficient numbers to defeat an exercise of market power by firms in the area. Sellers may exercise market power by raising prices, reducing output or reducing quality. With few exceptions, every physician who admitted to Chattanooga urban area hospitals admitted exclusively to other hospitals in the Chattanooga urban area. Conversely, physicians admitting and treating patients at hospitals outside the Chattanooga urban area rarely admitted and treated patients at hospitals in the Chattanooga urban area. One of the major dimensions of HCA's (D) purchase of HAI was the acquisition of some 75 to 80 hospital management contracts. HCA (D) argues, and the ALJ agreed, that two of the contracts in the Chattanooga urban area should be treated as entities completely separate from HCA (D), incapable of being significantly influenced by HCA (D) in its role as administrator. We conclude that treating the two managed hospitals as entities completely independent of HCA (D) is contrary to the overwhelming weight of the evidence in this case. As manager, HCA (D) controls the competitive variables needed for successful coordination with the activities of HCA-owned hospitals in Chattanooga. Moreover, as manager, it knows the competitive posture of managed hospitals so well that the likelihood of any anti-competitive behavior HCA (D) wished to engage in is greatly increased. The evidence compels us to consider the market shares of the two hospitals as part of HCA's market share in considering the effect on competition in this case. Even were the evidence not as compelling, we would consider HCA's (D) management of the two hospitals to greatly enhance the likelihood of collusion in this market. Traditionally, hospitals have competed for patients in three ways: first, by competing for physicians to admit their patients; second, by competing directly for patients on the basis of amenities and comfort of surroundings; and third, by competing to a limited degree on the basis of price. The first two constitute "non-price" or "quality" competition, and by far have been in the past the most important of the three. The increasing concern of employers and employees with the costs of insurance means that differences in prices between hospitals matter to them and their third-party payors, since insurance will cost less when hospital care costs less. The result is that hospitals are now far more likely to present themselves to insurers, employers and employee groups as less costly than their competitors as one method of attracting more business. Price competition, fostered by these new insurance mechanisms, is therefore growing in the hospital industry. Thus, it is obvious that price has been a competitively sensitive matter among Chattanooga hospitals. We do not here conclude that price has been the prime arena in which hospitals in Chattanooga compete. However, we do think it clear that even though rates are not constantly adjusted due to a changing price structure, they have been periodically set with some reference to what the market will bear in face of the prices of other hospitals. It is clear that section 7 protects whatever price competition exists in a market, however limited. In sum, evidence of the increased concentration caused by these acquisitions points toward a finding of likely harm to competition, all other things being equal. HCA's (D) acquisitions have made an already highly concentrated market more conducive to collusion by eliminating two of the healthiest sources of competition in the market and increasing concentration substantially. But all other things are not equal in this market, and statistical evidence is not the end of our inquiry. In the absence of barriers to entry, an exercise of market power can be defeated or deterred by the entry or potential entry of new firms regardless of the structure of the existing market. We now turn to the issue of entry barriers and conclude that they confirm and even magnify the inference to be drawn from the concentration evidence in this case. There is hardly free entry into the acute care hospital industry in either Tennessee or Georgia. Indeed, the CON (certificate of need) laws at issue here create a classic "barrier to entry" under every definition of that term. The evidence is clear that the costs are significant in this market. We agree with the ALJ that because incumbent hospitals can oppose new entry, even an unsuccessful opposition to a CON application may delay its disposition by several years. In sum, it is not merely the costs of obtaining a CON that a potential entrant faces, but the significant risk of being denied entry once those costs have been incurred. This risk, which incumbents did not have to face when building their hospitals, in effect raises the costs of entry a significantly greater amount. As a result, many potential entrants may decide not to even attempt entry. Indeed, the evidence shows that CON regulation has had a deterrent effect in the Chattanooga market. Hospitals compete in a myriad of ways that could be restricted anti-competitively through a collision. Thus, it appears that a merger analysis in this case need be no different than in any other case; market share and concentration figures, evidence of entry barriers and other market evidence taken together appear to yield as accurate a picture of competitive conditions as they do in other settings. Nevertheless, although HCA (D) concedes that many of the above described forms of collusion *could* occur, the heart of HCA's (D) case is that collusion in this market is inherently unlikely, and to that contention we now turn. Section 7 of the Clayton Act prohibits acquisitions that may have the effect of substantially lessening competition or tending to create a monopoly. Because Section 7 applies to "incipient" violations, actual anti-competitive effects need not be shown; an acquisition is unlawful if such an effect is reasonably probable. The small absolute number of competitors in this market, the high concentration and the extremely high entry barriers indicate a market in which anti-competitive behavior is reasonably probable after the acquisitions. The fact that industry members recognize the enormity of entry barriers makes collusion even more probable. In addition, hospital markets have certain features that evidence a likelihood of collusion or other anti-competitive behavior when they become highly concentrated. In addition, administrators of non-profit hospitals may seek to maximize their personal benefits and comfort through what would otherwise be known as profit-seeking activity. HCA's (D) analysis of the likelihood of collusion distorts competitive reality. HCA (D) would have us believe that the world of possible collusion is limited to complicated formulae concerning every aspect of hospital competition - that market power can only be exercised with respect to the entire cluster of services that constitutes the acute care hospital market through a conspiracy fixing the overall quantity or quality of treatment running to each patient in the market. Rather than focus on the likely avenues of collusion among hospitals, HCA (D) assumes into existence a world in which collusion is infeasible. We hold that HCA's (D) acquisitions of HAI and HCC may substantially lessen competition in the Chattanooga urban area acute care hospital market in violation of Section 7 of the Clayton Act and Section 5 of the Federal Trade Commission Act.

Analysis:

Over the last decade, two major trends increasing competition among hospitals beyond its traditional limits have developed. First, both non-price and price competition are now being directed much more toward patients themselves than in the past. Second, beginning in the late 1970s, the hospital industry has seen the clear emergence of direct price competition. At the same time, traditional non-price competition for patients on the basis of amenities has intensified somewhat, through the provision of such amenities as private rooms. Non-price competition for physicians remains pervasive, since physicians still largely determine the disposition and treatment of their patients. It is true that the undisputed evidence shows that more vigorous competition, including more direct price competition, is emerging in the health care industry, but it is a fallacy to conclude that growing competition in health care markets means that these acquisitions pose no threat to that competition. In fact, it is just that emerging competition that must be protected from mergers that facilitate the suppression of such competition.

■ CASE VOCABULARY

CLAYTON ACT: A Federal law enacted as an amendment to the Sherman Act dealing with antitrust regulations and unfair trade practices.

COLLUSION: An agreement between two or more persons to defraud a person of his rights by the forms of law, or to obtain an object forbidden by law.

DIVEST: In anti-trust law, the order of a court to a defendant corporation to dispose of or sell off property, securities or other assets.

Federal Trade Commission v. Tenet Healthcare Corp.

(*Government Agency*) v. (*Hospital*)

186 F.3d 1045 (8th Cir. 1999)

A HOSPITAL MERGER DID NOT DEPRIVE PATIENTS OF PRACTICABLE HEALTHCARE ALTERNATIVES

Quick! Rush him to the cheapest hospital!

AMBULANCE

stus.com

■ **INSTANT FACTS** When two area hospitals agreed to merge to improve medical services, the Federal Trade Commission (FTC) claimed a violation of federal antitrust law.

■ **BLACK LETTER RULE** Prospective mergers do not violate federal antitrust law so long as consumers in the relevant geographic market have practicable alternatives to the merged entity.

■ **PROCEDURAL BASIS**

On appeal to review a preliminary injunction.

■ **FACTS**

Tenet Healthcare Corp. (D) owned and operated Lucy Lee Hospital in Poplar Bluff, Missouri and another ten outpatient clinics in the area. The 210–bed hospital provided general in-patient primary and secondary care. Doctors' Regional Medical Center also provided general in-patient care in the area. Because both facilities were underutilized and therefore found it difficult to attract specialists to the area, Tenet Healthcare Corp. (D) entered into an agreement to purchase Doctors' Regional Medical Center, use it as a long-term care facility, and move all in-patient care to Lucy Lee Hospital, where more specialists could be employed. The FTC (P) challenged the proposed merger in federal district court, claiming that the merger would substantially lessen competition between hospitals in the geographic market in violation of the Clayton Act. At the hearing, the evidence showed that Lucy Lee and Doctors' Regional were the only two general care hospitals in Poplar Bluff and covered an eight-county area, with a fifty-mile radius service area. Employers, health plan administrators, and network providers testified that they often negotiated discounted rates by playing the two hospitals against one another. Managed care organization representatives further testified that because of physician loyalty, perceptions of quality, and other considerations, it was unlikely that it could steer patients to facilities outside of Poplar Bluff to nearby hospitals in Cape Girardeau, because they were too expensive. However, the evidence indicated that significant numbers of Poplar Bluff residents did travel out of town for primary and secondary treatment that was also available in Poplar Bluff. After considering the evidence, the district court ordered a preliminary injunction against the merger. Tenet Healthcare Corp. (D) appealed.

■ **ISSUE**

Did the FTC (P) provide sufficient evidence that the proposed merger would result in a merged entity possessing excessive market power within the relevant geographic market?

■ **DECISION AND RATIONALE**

(Beam, J.) No. Prospective mergers do not violate federal antitrust law so long as consumers in the relevant geographic market have practicable alternatives to the merged entity. The FTC (P) has the burden of proving the relevant geographic market by presenting evidence on where consumers of hospital services could reasonably turn for alternative services should the merger be consummated and prices increase. This critical question requires a showing of where consumers could practically go, not where they actually go. The FTC (P) proposes that this geographic market constitutes the fifty-mile radius from Poplar Bluff, in which the two hospitals derive ninety percent of their patients. This service area, however, is not necessarily the relevant geographic market for antitrust purposes. Despite finding that no statistical evidence supported the fifty-mile radius service area as the relevant geographic market, the district court nonetheless determined that the merger was anticompetitive.

However, the evidence shows that there are numerous practical alternatives in neighboring towns in the area. Over twenty-two percent of the population in the primary zip codes within the area already use hospitals outside the service area. Others in the service area actually work or live closer to hospitals outside the service area, serving as a check on the anticompetitive price increases feared by the FTC (P). Moreover, the geographic market proposed by the FTC (P) conveniently stops short of a large regional hospital, which, for many residing within the service area, is actually closer to their home than is Poplar Bluff. These considerations demonstrate that the market established by the FTC (P) is too narrow.

Additionally, the managed care payers' testimony that it would accept a price increase rather than steer patients to more economical healthcare is suspect, in that it is contrary to these payers' economic interests as for-profit businesses. The evidence shows that, as in the past, these large organizations likely will bargain for the best healthcare rates possible, especially given the cost savings realized by Tenet (D) as a result of the merger. Consumer habit and sentiment do nothing to eliminate other inpatient service providers as a practicable alternative. Moreover, the trial court discounted the non-price-competitive factors, such as the quality of care, involved with hospitals in nearby communities such as Cape Girardeau. Healthcare decisions are more often driven by quality considerations than price factors, and the fact that Cape Girardeau hospitals are more expensive than Poplar Bluff hospitals does not make them anticompetitive. In fact, the Tenet (D) merger and resulting cost efficiencies will likely lead to more competition by attracting more qualified physicians to Poplar Bluff and raising the level of care available there. Finally, the days of physician loyalty have been replaced by large-scale healthcare management. Patients rarely have the luxury of choosing the physician they desire, for they are more often compelled to select among those covered by their insurance plans.

Poplar Bluff cannot economically support two thriving hospitals, and third-party payers have reaped the benefits through negotiated discounts for years. While prices will increase by eliminating Tenet's (D) biggest competitors, other practicable alternatives will not be eliminated through the merger. The FTC (P) has not shown a likelihood of success on the merits of its claim, and the court erred in issuing an injunction.

Analysis:

From a pure economic perspective, a merger of two competing businesses into one appears to necessarily impact the competitive balance in the industry. However, in healthcare, not all competitors are equal because, as the court points out, financial considerations are rarely the first priority when making a choice among competing healthcare providers. Issues like access to medical facilities and the quality of care are often more important considerations for patients than are healthcare costs, especially for those covered under health insurance plans.

■ CASE VOCABULARY

ANTITRUST LAW: The body of law designed to protect trade and commerce from restraints, monopolies, price-fixing, and price discrimination.

CLAYTON ACT: A federal statute—enacted in 1914 to amend the Sherman Act—that prohibits price discrimination, tying arrangements, and exclusive-dealing contracts, as well as mergers and interlocking directorates, if their effect might substantially lessen competition or create a monopoly in any line of commerce.

INJUNCTION: A court order commanding or preventing an action. To get an injunction, the complainant must show that there is no plain, adequate, and complete remedy at law and that an irreparable injury will result unless the relief is granted.

In the Matter of Evanston Northwestern Healthcare Corp.

(Federal Trade Commission) v. *(Hospital)*
Federal Trade Commission, Aug. 6, 2007

A HOSPITAL FAILED TO ESTABLISH NON–MERGER JUSTIFICATIONS FOR PRICE HIKES

Give me one good reason we shouldn't promote teamwork.

The government calls it "antitrust".

stus.com

■ **INSTANT FACTS** Evanston Northwestern Healthcare Corp. (D) substantially raised its prices shortly after merging with a competitor, prompting charges from the Federal Trade Commission of antitrust violations.

■ **BLACK LETTER RULE** A merger that creates such market leverage so as to enable a business to substantially inflate its prices violates federal antitrust law.

■ **PROCEDURAL BASIS**

Federal Trade Commission consideration of an initial administrative decision.

■ **FACTS**

In 2000, Evanston Northwestern Healthcare Corp. (D), which owned Evanston Hospital and Glenbrook Hospital, merged with Highland Park Hospital. After doing so, Evanston (D) substantially raised its prices. Four years later, the FTC issued an administrative complaint challenging Evanston's (D) acquisition of Highland Park under the Clayton Act. The Commission argued that by acquiring Highland Park, Evanston (D) reduced competition so that it had greater market power to increase its prices. Evanston (D) claimed that it had been previously charging prices well below market rates, and that only during the merger discussions did it learn the true market value of its services. An administrative law judge determined that the merger violated the Clayton Act and ordered Evanston (D) to divest Highland Park.

■ **ISSUE**

Did the evidence surrounding Evanston's (D) merger establish an antitrust violation?

■ **DECISION AND RATIONALE**

(Judge Undisclosed.) Yes. A merger that creates such market leverage so as to enable a business to substantially inflate its prices violates federal antitrust law. The evidence here shows that senior officials at Evanston (D) and Highland Park contemplated a price increase as a result of greater market leverage during their merger discussions. Additionally, economists for both parties concluded that the price increases coincided with the merger and ruled out Evanston's (D) explanation for substantial portions of its price increases. There is no support for Evanston's position that it had been charging substantially less than market prices in the years preceding the merger. However, given the merged entity's operation for seven years, the cost of divestiture is too substantial and is an inappropriate remedy. Any lost competition caused by the merger should instead be restored through injunctive relief. Affirmed in part.

Analysis:

In its decision, the Commission does not focus on what alternatives may be available for area residents to obtain healthcare, nor whether Evanston (D) received increased market power to raise its prices

---

compared to surrounding healthcare facilities. Rather, the opinion illustrates that, even absent these considerations, a merger designed to enable the merged entity to raise its prices is anticompetitive in violation of federal antitrust law. However, in urban areas such as Chicago, where more healthcare options exist, the anticompetitive effect of even a merger designed for the purpose of a price increase will be limited by prevailing market rates.

■ CASE VOCABULARY

ANTITRUST LAW: The body of law designed to protect trade and commerce from restraints, monopolies, price-fixing, and price discrimination.

CLAYTON ACT: A federal statute—enacted in 1914 to amend the Sherman Act—that prohibits price discrimination, tying arrangements, and exclusive-dealing contracts, as well as mergers and interlocking directorates, if their effect might substantially lessen competition or create a monopoly in any line of commerce.

DIVESTITURE: A court order to a defendant to rid itself of property, securities, or other assets to prevent a monopoly or restraint of trade.

INJUNCTION: A court order commanding or preventing an action. To get an injunction, the complainant must show that there is no plain, adequate, and complete remedy at law and that an irreparable injury will result unless the relief is granted.

CHAPTER SIXTEEN

Human Reproduction and Birth

Roe v. Wade

Instant Facts: Roe (P) argues that Texas (D) abortion statutes improperly invade what she contends is her constitutional right to decide to have an abortion.

Black Letter Rule: The Constitution protects a right of privacy which includes a pregnant woman's right to decide to have an abortion.

Planned Parenthood of Southeastern Pennsylvania v. Casey

Instant Facts: Abortion clinics (P) challenged several provisions of a Pennsylvania (D) statute regulating abortions.

Black Letter Rule: An abortion regulation constitutes an undue burden and is unconstitutional if it has the purpose or effect of placing a substantial obstacle in the path of a woman seeking an abortion of a nonviable fetus.

Gonzales v. Carhart

Instant Facts: An abortion doctor challenged the federal Partial–Birth Abortion Act as void for vagueness, overbroad, and placing an undue burden on a woman's right to obtain an abortion.

Black Letter Rule: A law limiting abortions is valid so long as it promotes the government's legitimate interest in protecting the health of the woman and the life of the fetus without placing an undue burden on the woman's right to terminate her pregnancy.

Smith v. Cote

Instant Facts: Smith (P), who gave birth to Heather (P), born with birth defects, claims she would have had an abortion if Cote (D) had timely diagnosed her exposure to rubella and advised her of the risks to Heather (P).

Black Letter Rule: (1) New Hampshire recognizes a cause of action for wrongful birth by the mother of a child born with birth defects. (2) New Hampshire does not recognize a cause of action for wrongful life by a child born with birth defects.

In the Interest of K.M.H.

Instant Facts: D.H. (D) provided sperm to S.H. (P) for artificial insemination, and then brought an action to determine his paternity of the children born as a result of that insemination.

Black Letter Rule: The gender classification in the sperm donor statute substantially furthers, and is thus substantially related to, legitimate legislative purposes and important government objectives, and the requirement that a sperm donor agreement be in writing does not deprive donors of rights that have already arisen and attached.

Davis v. Davis

Instant Facts: A husband and wife stored frozen embryos they had created through in vitro fertilization (IVF), then, when they divorced, could not agree about what to do with them.

Black Letter Rule: Courts should resolve disputes over the disposition of preembryos produced by IVF by looking first to the preferences of the gamete-providers, then to a prior agreement, and if no agreement exists, then to weighing each gamete-provider's interests in gestating or discarding the preembryos and the burdens different resolutions would impose upon them.

In the Matter of Baby M

Instant Facts: The Sterns (P) entered into a surrogacy contract with Whitehead (D), but after giving birth Whitehead changed her mind and wanted to keep her baby.

Black Letter Rule: Surrogacy contracts violate state law and policy and are invalid and unenforceable unless the surrogate acts voluntarily and without payment and retains the right to change her mind and assert her parental rights.

Johnson v. Calvert

Instant Facts: The Calverts (D) entered into a gestational surrogacy contract with Johnson (P), but during the pregnancy they sought a judicial declaration of their parental rights because Johnson (P) threatened to keep the child.

Black Letter Rule: If genetic parenthood and gestational parenthood do not coincide in one woman, then in California the natural mother of the child is she who intended to bring about the birth of the child to raise as her own.

Prato-Morrison v. Doe

Instant Facts: The Morrisons (P) believed that their genetic material was given to the Does (D), and the Morrisons (P) claimed they were the parents of the Does' (D) children.

Black Letter Rule: A person may not bring an action to establish parentage unless that person can produce evidence that he or she is the genetic parent of the child.

In re A.C.

Instant Facts: Finding a dying pregnant woman incompetent and her fetus in danger, a trial court ordered the hospital to perform a caesarean to attempt to save the fetus.

Black Letter Rule: A court must make a substituted judgment to decide the course of medical treatment for an incompetent pregnant patient even when her interests may conflict with those of her fetus.

State v. Wade

Instant Facts: One day after giving birth, Wade (D) was charged with child endangerment when both she and her son tested positive for marijuana and methamphetamine.

Black Letter Rule: In the absence of specific legislative direction, illegal drug use by a pregnant mother does not constitute child endangerment.

In re J.D.S.

Instant Facts: J.D.S., an incapacitated woman, was pregnant, and a petition was filed to name a guardian of her fetus.

Black Letter Rule: An unborn child is not a "person" within the meaning of the statutes authorizing the appointment of a guardian over a person.

Roe v. Wade

(Pregnant Woman) v. *(District Attorney)*

410 U.S. 113, 93 S.Ct. 705, 35 L.Ed.2d 147 (1973)

STATING THAT IT "NEED NOT RESOLVE THE DIFFICULT QUESTION OF WHEN LIFE BEGINS," THE SUPREME COURT DECLARES A CONSTITUTIONAL RIGHT TO HAVE AN ABORTION

■ **INSTANT FACTS** Roe (P) argues that Texas (D) abortion statutes improperly invade what she contends is her constitutional right to decide to have an abortion.

■ **BLACK LETTER RULE** The Constitution protects a right of privacy which includes a pregnant woman's right to decide to have an abortion.

■ **PROCEDURAL BASIS**

Appeal and cross-appeal from District Court's denial of injunctive relief and grant of declaratory relief, respectively, in facial constitutional challenge of state abortion statutes.

■ **FACTS**

Roe (P), a pregnant woman, argues that Texas (D) statutes improperly invade her right to decide to have an abortion. Roe (P) argues that this right is either part of the concept of personal "liberty" embodied in the Fourteenth Amendment's Due Process Clause; or is one of the privacy rights protected by the Bill of Rights or its penumbras; or is one of the rights reserved to the people by the Ninth Amendment.

■ **ISSUE**

Does the Constitution protect a right of a pregnant woman to decide to have an abortion?

■ **DECISION AND RATIONALE**

(Blackmun, J.) Yes. The restrictive criminal abortion laws in effect in most states today were generally enacted in the latter half of the 19th century. One possible reason for their enactment was the danger of the abortion procedures of the time to the pregnant woman. Modern medical techniques have altered this situation. In the first trimester abortion is now relatively safe [for the woman, he means]. Mortality rates for women who undergo legal early abortions are at least as low as the rates for women who give birth. Thus, any State interest in protecting the woman from a procedure that is inherently dangerous has largely disappeared. Another reason for the enactment of these criminal abortion statutes is the State's interest—some phrase it in terms of duty—in protecting prenatal life. This case is concerned with balancing these interests. Although it does not explicitly mention it, this Court has recognized that the Constitution includes a right of personal privacy. In various contexts, the Court has found at least the roots of this right in the First, Fourth and Fifth, or Ninth Amendments; in the penumbras of the Bill of Rights; or in the liberty guaranteed by the first section of the Fourteenth Amendment. This guarantee of personal privacy includes only "fundamental" personal rights which are "implicit in the concept of ordered liberty." It extends to activities relating to marriage, family relationships, and child rearing. Whether this privacy right is founded in the Fourteenth Amendment, as we feel it is, or the Ninth Amendment's reservation of rights to the people, we find it broad enough to include a woman's decision whether or not to have an abortion. The detriment that the State would impose upon a pregnant woman by denying her this choice is apparent. A woman may suffer medical or psychological harm. Maternity or additional offspring, or having a child she does not want, may cause her a distressful life. Child care may tax her mental and physical health. Some women may also have to face the difficulties and stigma of unwed motherhood. Based on factors such as these, Roe (P) argues that she has an absolute right to abort her child no matter when, how, or why she chooses to do so. We disagree. A State has important interests in safeguarding health, maintaining medical standards, and in protecting potential life. At some point in pregnancy these interests become sufficiently compelling to sustain State regulation of abortion. In light of present medical knowledge, the compelling point as to the woman's health is at approximately the end of the first trimester because until then mortality in abortion may be less than mortality in childbirth. After this point a State may regulate abortion in a way that reasonably relates to the preservation and protection of maternal health. Before this point, however, a physician, after consulting with a woman, may make a medical judgment that the woman should have an abortion and may carry out that abortion free from State regulation or interference. As to the State's important and legitimate interest in potential life, the compelling point is at viability, because at this point the fetus can live outside the mother's womb. Because State regulation protective of fetal life after viability has both logical and biological justifications, after this point a State may go so far as to proscribe abortion, except when it is necessary to preserve the life or health of the mother. Thus, the Texas (D) statute, which provides an exception only for procedures to save the life of the mother and which does not distinguish between different stages of pregnancy, violates the Due Process Clause of the Fourteenth Amendment. Before the end of a woman's first trimester, the State must leave the abortion decision to her physician's medical judgment. After the first trimester, a State may regulate the abortion procedure in ways that are reasonably related to maternal health. After viability, a State may regulate and even proscribe abortion, except where it is medically necessary to preserve the life or health of the mother. Affirmed.

Analysis:

In *Roe* the Court held that the Fourteenth Amendment Due Process Clause protects a fundamental right to privacy, which includes the right to have an abortion. States can limit a fundamental right only when necessary to serve a compelling state interest. The Court found two interests that might be sufficiently compelling to justify regulation of abortion. The first is the state's interest in protecting the life and health of the pregnant woman, which the Court held becomes compelling at the point abortion becomes more dangerous than childbirth. The Court found that this point was at the end of the first trimester. The second is the state's interest in protecting potential human life, which the Court held becomes compelling at viability. Thus, under this framework, the state could regulate abortion to promote the health of the mother only after the first trimester, and could regulate or proscribe abortion to protect fetal life only after viability. Texas (D) argued that life begins at conception and is present throughout pregnancy, and that Texas (D) therefore had a compelling interest in protecting that life from and after conception. The Court responded that it "need not resolve the difficult question of when life begins," and that when those trained in medicine, philosophy, and theology cannot arrive at a consensus on this question, the judiciary cannot speculate as to the answer. One of the legal arguments against *Roe* was that it amounted to a return to the days of substantive due process, when the Court acted as if it could make social policy decisions notwithstanding any legal or constitutional restrictions. Indeed, courts have found it difficult to support the creation and application of the "right to privacy" that *Roe* found in the Fourteenth Amendment, and have applied this right in only a few cases, primarily in other abortion cases. The Supreme Court has refused to extend this right to other areas, including areas involving health care. Legally, *Roe* is a misfit, and the number of justices on the Court that support it has declined. In 1973 the Court decided *Roe* by a 7-2 margin, but in 1986 it reaffirmed it by only 5-4, and in 1989 it appeared to be evenly divided between retaining *Roe's* analysis and overruling it. In 1992, in the next case, *Planned Parenthood of Southeastern Pennsylvania v. Casey*, *Roe* survived, but in a substantially revised form and only by the narrowest of majorities.

■ CASE VOCABULARY

VIABILITY: The point at which a fetus is reasonably likely to be able to survive outside the womb, with or without artificial support.

Planned Parenthood of Southeastern Pennsylvania v. Casey

(Abortion Providers) v. *(Pennsylvania Governor)*

505 U.S. 833, 112 S.Ct. 2791, 120 L.Ed.2d 674 (1992)

THE SUPREME COURT LETS ROE SURVIVE, BUT REWRITES THE RULES

■ **INSTANT FACTS** Abortion clinics (P) challenged several provisions of a Pennsylvania (D) statute regulating abortions.

■ **BLACK LETTER RULE** An abortion regulation constitutes an undue burden and is unconstitutional if it has the purpose or effect of placing a substantial obstacle in the path of a woman seeking an abortion of a nonviable fetus.

■ PROCEDURAL BASIS

Certiorari granted in facial constitutional challenge of state abortion statute after the Court of Appeals reversed the trial court's grant of declaratory and injunctive relief as to all but one statutory provision, which it affirmed.

■ FACTS

The Pennsylvania Abortion Control Act of 1982 (the Act) [statute regulating abortions] requires that a woman give her informed consent before having an abortion, and requires that a physician provide her certain information at least 24 hours before the abortion. Before a minor may obtain an abortion, the Act requires the informed consent of one of her parents, but it also provides a judicial bypass option if the minor does not obtain parental consent. With certain exceptions, the Act also requires a married woman to notify her husband before obtaining an abortion. The Act exempts compliance with these provisions in a medical emergency. Finally, the Act imposes reporting requirements on facilities that provide abortions.

■ ISSUE

Are state abortion regulations still limited by *Roe v. Wade's* [declared constitutional right to abortion] holding that the Constitution protects the right to have an abortion?

■ DECISION AND RATIONALE

(O'Connor, J.) Yes. Liberty finds no refuge in a jurisprudence of doubt. Yet 19 years after *Roe,* there is still doubt about whether it rightly defined liberty to include the right to have an abortion. After taking the constitution, institutional integrity, and stare decisis into consideration [not necessarily in that order], we reaffirm *Roe. Roe's* essential holding includes three parts. First it recognizes a woman's right to have an abortion before viability without undue interference from the State. Before viability, a State may not prohibit abortion or impose a substantial obstacle to obtaining an abortion. Second, *Roe* confirms the State's power to restrict abortions after viability as long as the law contains exceptions for pregnancies which endanger a woman's life or health. Third, *Roe* recognizes the State's legitimate interests in protecting the health of the woman and the life of the fetus from the outset of pregnancy. We adhere to each of these principles. People can disagree about the profound moral and spiritual implications involved in abortion, even in the earliest stages of pregnancy. Some of us find abortion offensive to our most basic principles of morality, but that cannot control our decision. We must define liberty for all. Abortion is a unique act fraught with consequences for others: for the woman who must live with her decision; for the abortionists and their assistants; for the spouse, family and society, which must confront the existence of abortion, which some consider an act of violence against innocent human life; and finally, for the unborn life that is aborted. However, carrying a child to term also has consequences for the mother, including anxieties, physical constraints and pain. This suffering is too intimate for the State to insist that she make these sacrifices only because women have made them with pride from the dawn of the human race. The woman must shape her own destiny. While we appreciate the weight of the State's arguments for overruling *Roe*, individual liberty and stare decisis outweigh them. *Roe* has not been unworkable and is not a doctrinal anachronism discounted by society. An entire generation has grown up relying upon *Roe's* definition of women's capacity to make reproductive decisions. No changes of fact have rendered viability more or less appropriate as the point at which the balance of interests tips. Under our stare decisis analysis, then, the stronger argument is for reaffirming *Roe's* central holding, despite whatever personal reluctance any of us have in doing so. *Roe* is distinguishable from *Lochner* [condemned substantive due process case protecting "liberty of contract"] and the "separate but equal" cases, where we did overrule well-settled precedents. Further, we should not risk public respect for the Court by reversing *Roe*. However, while a woman does have some freedom to have an abortion, this liberty is not unlimited. From the outset a State can show its concern for the life of the unborn. At a later point in fetal development, the State's interest in life is sufficient to restrict the woman's right to have an abortion. This point is at viability. We adhere to this principle for two reasons: first, stare decisis, and second, viability is the point at which there is a realistic possibility of maintaining life outside the womb. At this point the independent existence of the second life can in all fairness be the object of State protection which can override the rights of the woman. As *Roe* holds, the woman has the right to have an abortion before viability. However, *Roe* not only establishes this right, but also speaks of the State's "important and legitimate interest" in protecting fetal life. This Court has failed to sufficiently acknowledge and implement this portion of *Roe*. We decided in subsequent cases that any abortion regulation must survive strict scrutiny, but this does not follow *Roe's* holding that the State has legitimate interests in protecting both the health of the woman and the life within her. We now follow *Roe* over the later cases. We thus reject the trimester framework, not an essential holding of *Roe* [surprise!], because it is a rigid prohibition on all previability regulation aimed at protecting the life of the unborn. Measures aimed at ensuring that a woman's decision about abortion contemplates the consequences for the fetus do not necessarily interfere with her right to make that decision, although courts have found such measures inconsistent with *Roe's* trimester framework. A law which has a valid purpose which does not strike at the right to procure an abortion is not invalid simply because it has the incidental effect of making the exercise of that right more difficult or expensive. Such a law is invalid only if it imposes an undue burden on a woman's ability to decide whether to have an abortion. The trimester framework contradicts *Roe's* own holding that the State has a substantial interest in protecting the life of the unborn throughout pregnancy in that it forbids any regulation designed to advance that interest before viability. We find it incompatible with recognition of this State interest to treat all governmental attempts to influence a woman's decision on behalf of the unborn life within her as unwarranted. Not all burdens on the woman's right are undue. We find that the undue burden standard appropriately reconciles the State's interest with the woman's right. A regulation is an undue burden if it has the purpose or effect of placing a substantial obstacle in the path of a woman seeking an abortion of a nonviable fetus. The means the State chooses to further its interest in fetal life must be calculated to inform the woman in making her decision, not to hinder her. Even if its purpose is valid, an abortion regulation would be invalid if it has the effect of placing a substantial obstacle in the woman's path because it would not be a permissible means of serving its legitimate ends. We must clarify that what is at stake is the woman's right to make the ultimate decision, not the right to be insulated from others in doing so. Regulations which merely create a means by which the State, or a parent or guardian, may express respect for the life of the unborn are permissible if they are not a substantial obstacle to the woman's exercise of her right. To promote its profound interest in the life of the unborn, the State may, throughout pregnancy, take measures to persuade a woman to choose childbirth over abortion, as long as these measures do not place an undue burden on her right to make the ultimate decision. The State may also enact regulations to further the health or safety of a woman seeking an abortion, as long as they do not have the purpose or effect of placing a substantial obstacle in her path. We reaffirm *Roe's* central holding that a State may not prohibit a woman from making the ultimate decision to have an abortion before viability. We also reaffirm *Roe's* holding that after viability, the State may regulate, and even proscribe, abortion except where it is necessary in appropriate medical judgment to preserve the life or health of the mother. The statute at issue in this case defines a medical emergency as a condition which necessitates an immediate abortion to avert the death of the pregnant woman or for which a delay would create a serious risk of substantial and irreversible impairment of a major bodily function. We agree with the Court of Appeals that such a definition does not impose an undue burden on a woman's right to have an abortion. The statute's informed consent requirement is also valid. Except in a medical emergency, the statute requires that at least 24 hours before an abortion the physician must inform the woman of the nature of the procedure, the health risks of abortion and childbirth, and the probable gestational age of the unborn child. The physician or other qualified person must also inform the woman of the availability of printed State materials providing information about the fetus; medical assistance for childbirth; child support; and agencies which provide adoption and other services as alternatives to abortion. The government does not violate the constitution when it requires the giving of truthful, nonmisleading information. We overrule prior cases which find such requirements invalid because these cases are inconsistent with *Roe's* acknowledgment of an important interest in the life of the unborn child. A State may also require doctors to inform a woman seeking an abortion of the availability of materials about the consequences of an abortion to the fetus, even when those consequences have no direct relation to the woman's health.

The State may further its legitimate goal of protecting the life of the unborn through legislation aimed at ensuring that the woman's decision is mature and informed, even if the State expresses a preference for childbirth over abortion. Requiring the giving of information about fetal development and the assistance available if the woman chooses childbirth is a reasonable way to ensure an informed decision. Such a requirement is not a substantial obstacle to obtaining an abortion, and therefore there is no undue burden. Planned Parenthood (P) argues that a physician has a First Amendment right not to provide information about the risks of abortion and childbirth in the manner mandated by the State. The physician's First Amendment right not to speak arises only as part of the practice of medicine, subject to reasonable State regulation. The requirement that the physician provide the information mandated here does not violate the Constitution. We also uphold the Act's requirement that a physician, rather than an assistant, provide the information relevant to a woman's informed consent. This requirement is not an undue burden, and the Constitution gives States broad latitude to decide that particular functions be performed only by licensed professionals. Again, we uphold this provision as a reasonable means to ensure that the woman's consent is informed. We must also apply the undue burden standard to the Act's 24-hour waiting period between the provision of the information necessary for informed consent and the abortion. In *Akron I* [invalidated a 24-hour waiting period], we stated that we were not convinced that a 24-hour waiting period reasonably served the State's legitimate concern that a woman's consent be informed. We now consider this conclusion wrong. The idea that important decisions will be more informed after some period for reflection is not unreasonable, especially where the statute requires the giving of important information beforehand. Whether a 24-hour waiting period places a substantial obstacle in a woman's path is a closer question. Due to the distance many women must travel to reach an abortion provider, the practical effect of this waiting period will often be a delay of more than a day because the woman must make at least two visits to the doctor. While troubling in some respects, the increased cost and delay the waiting period may cause do not constitute an undue burden. Planned Parenthood (P) argues that these aspects of the Act's informed consent requirement are unconstitutional because they place barriers to abortion on demand. However, *Roe* does not suggest a constitutional right to abortion on demand, but only a right to decide to have an abortion free of undue interference by the State. Rather than interfere with this right, the Act's informed consent requirement facilitates the wise exercise of it, and therefore does not unduly burden it. The Act also prohibits physicians from giving a married woman an abortion unless she provides a signed statement that she has notified her spouse of her intent to obtain one, except in cases of a medical emergency. However, because many men are physically or psychologically abusive to their wives or children, many women may reasonably fear that notifying their husbands of their intent to have an abortion may provoke further abuse. Because the spousal notification requirement does not provide an adequate exemption for these women, it is likely to prevent a significant number of women from obtaining an abortion. This requirement does not merely make abortions a little more difficult or expensive for such women. For them, it imposes a substantial obstacle which is as likely to deter them from having an abortion as surely as if the State had outlawed all abortions. Pennsylvania (D) argues that the spousal notification requirement imposes almost no burden for the vast majority of women seeking abortions. Because only 20% of women who seek abortions are married, and some of them will be able to notify their husbands without adverse consequences or will qualify for an exception, this provision affects less than 1% of women seeking abortions. For this reason, Pennsylvania (D) argues that this provision cannot be invalid on its face. We disagree. We must measure the constitutionality of legislation by its impact on those whose conduct it affects. The Act's target is those women seeking abortions who are married, do not qualify for an exception, and do not wish to notify their husbands of their intent. In a large fraction of those cases, the Act will operate as a substantial obstacle to a woman's decision to have an abortion, and is therefore an undue burden and invalid. On the other hand, we reaffirm that a State may require a minor seeking an abortion to obtain the consent of a parent or guardian, provided there is an adequate judicial bypass procedure. The Act's one-parent consent requirement and judicial bypass procedure are constitutional. We reject Planned Parenthood's (P) argument that this requirement is invalid because it requires informed parental consent for the same reasons we upheld the general informed consent requirement. Indeed, the requirement's waiting period may have particular force in this context because it would provide a parent the opportunity to consult with their daughter in private and discuss the consequences of her decision in the context of the family's moral principles. Except for those relating to spousal notification, we uphold the Act's record keeping requirements as well. Affirmed in part and reversed in part.

■ CONCURRENCE AND DISSENT

(Rehnquist) The joint opinion uses a new variation on stare decisis to retain the outer shell of *Roe* while retreating from its substance. *Roe* was wrongly decided, and we can and should overrule it under traditional stare decisis analysis. *Roe* adopted a "fundamental right" standard which permitted only State regulations which could survive strict scrutiny. After all its praise for stare decisis and the legitimacy of the Court, the joint opinion has created out of whole cloth a new standard for evaluating a woman's right to have an abortion which the majority of this Court does not support: the "undue burden" standard. To apply this standard, judges must decide whether a regulation places a "substantial obstacle" in the path of a woman seeking an abortion. Because this standard relies on a judge's subjective determinations, it permits judges to decide constitutional matters guided only by their personal views. The joint opinion leaves *Roe* as a judicial Potemkin Village, a monument to the importance of adhering to precedent. Behind the facade, however, is an entirely new method of analysis with no roots in constitutional law. This serves neither stare decisis nor "legitimacy."

■ CONCURRENCE AND DISSENT

(Scalia) It should be citizens, through debate and voting, that decide the permissibility of abortion and its limitations. As the Court acknowledges, where reasonable people disagree, the State may adopt either position, as long as its choice does not intrude upon a protected liberty. The State's choice may intrude upon a "liberty" in the absolute sense. For example, entire societies of reasonable people disagree about bigamy, but because bigamy is not a liberty specially protected by the Constitution, States may enact laws against it. The issue here is not whether the power of a woman to abort her unborn child is a "liberty" in the absolute sense, or even whether it is a liberty that is important to many women. It is both. The issue is whether this liberty is protected by the Constitution. It is not. As with bigamy, this conclusion rests on the fact that the Constitution says absolutely nothing about it, and on the fact that the longstanding traditions of American society have permitted States to prohibit it. Whether the Court has saved the "central holding" of *Roe* is not clear because it is not clear what the "undue burden" test means. However, there are portions of *Roe* which the joint opinion did not save. The joint opinion applies its undue burden test to uphold: (1) a requirement that a woman receive truthful information designed to influence her decision before she may give informed written consent; (2) a requirement that a physician, rather than a nonphysician counselor, provide this information; (3) a requirement of a 24-hour waiting period; and (4) a requirement of detailed reports of demographic data about each woman seeking abortion and about each abortion. All of these requirements were unconstitutional under *Roe*.

Analysis:

In this case the Court reaffirmed what the joint opinion called the "central" or "essential" holding of *Roe*, which it identified as the holding "that viability marks the earliest point at which the State's interest in fetal life is constitutionally adequate to justify a legislative ban on nontherapeutic abortions." However, the Court also rejected some of *Roe's* other significant holdings. In *Roe* the Court held that a woman had a fundamental right to an abortion, but the joint opinion rejects that view. Likewise, the *Roe* Court held that abortion regulations were subject to "strict scrutiny," which requires them to be narrowly tailored to serve a compelling state interest. The joint opinion rejects that holding. *Roe* also used a rigid trimester framework to analyze abortion regulations, which the Court continued to use for nineteen years. The joint opinion rejects that framework as well. While purporting to adhere to precedent, the joint opinion instead revises it and overrules decisions that followed it. As Justice Scalia stated, "[i]t seems to me that stare decisis ought to be applied even to the doctrine of stare decisis, and I confess never to have heard of this new, keep-what-you-want-and-throw-away-the-rest version." The decision in *Casey*, like many of the abortion cases before it, failed to command a majority of the Court. As Justice Scalia points out, *Roe* did not resolve the abortion controversy, but inflamed it. The undue burden standard itself, for which this case is known, commanded the support of only four justices, with one applying it differently than the other three. This standard reigns as the new standard for abortion cases under the rule that when no rationale for a decision commands a majority of the Court, the narrowest standard or rationale in support of the judgment may stand as the holding of the Court. One of the key changes in abortion law after *Casey* is that the Court no longer treats abortion as a fundamental right. Justice Rehnquist, representing the reasoning of four justices, explained that the Court has considered a right to be fundamental if it is "implicit in the concept of ordered liberty," or where it is part of a "principle of justice so rooted in the traditions and conscience of our people as to be ranked as fundamental." He argued that the historical traditions of the American people do not support the view that the right to have an abortion is fundamental. The joint opinion also abandoned *Roe's* trimester framework, which it found overly rigid and inconsistent with *Roe's* holding that the state has an interest in protecting unborn life from conception throughout pregnancy. Further, the joint opinion found that in practice the trimester framework undervalued the state's interest in the life of the unborn and misconceived the nature of the pregnant woman's interest. The joint opinion replaced the trimester framework with a two-part framework that centers on viability. After viability a state may freely regulate abortions and even prohibit them, except when they are necessary to preserve the life or health of the mother. Another clarification that the Court made in *Casey* was that the specific right the Constitution protects is the woman's right to make the ultimate decision about whether to have an abortion, not the right to make this decision without input from others, or from the state in particular. The Court explained that despite *Roe's* statement that this right was not absolute, subsequent cases have invalidated regulations that did not deprive women of the ultimate decision, and those decisions went too far. The Court also overruled its previous determination that a 24-hour waiting period was invalid. Although the waiting period could increase the cost and delay of abortions, the Court upheld it as a justifiable way to encourage reflection and as a reasonable way for the state to protect the life of the unborn. Waiting periods between the time a woman receives required information and the time she has the abortion, such as the 24-hour waiting period in *Casey*, usually have the effect of requiring the woman to make two trips to the doctor. Although the Court found that such a requirement was not an undue burden, it is not clear whether it would uphold a longer waiting period or a "three-trip" requirement. The Court also permitted Pennsylvania to require this two-visit informed consent process of parents as part of its parental consent requirement.

■ CASE VOCABULARY

PAEANS: Ancient Greek hymns of praise.

POTEMKIN VILLAGE: Something that looks impressive, but is actually only a facade intended to divert attention from something void of real substance.

UNDUE BURDEN STANDARD: A standard under which an abortion regulation is unconstitutional if its purpose or effect is to place a substantial obstacle in the path of a woman seeking an abortion before viability.

Gonzales v. Carhart

(Attorney General) v. *(Abortion Doctor)*

550 U.S. 124, 127 S. Ct. 1610, 167 L. Ed. 2d 480 (2007)

A FEDERAL PARTIAL–BIRTH ABORTION BAN IS CONSTITUTIONAL

Stu, we need an abortion cartoon that's both funny and memorable, but doesn't offend anyone.

No problem. I'll do it right after I create peace in the Middle East.

stus.com

■ **INSTANT FACTS** An abortion doctor challenged the federal Partial–Birth Abortion Act as void for vagueness, overbroad, and placing an undue burden on a woman's right to obtain an abortion.

■ **BLACK LETTER RULE** A law limiting abortions is valid so long as it promotes the government's legitimate interest in protecting the health of the woman and the life of the fetus without placing an undue burden on the woman's right to terminate her pregnancy.

■ **PROCEDURAL BASIS**

Supreme Court review of an undisclosed lower court opinion.

■ **FACTS**

Between eighty-five and ninety percent of the 1.3 million abortions performed in the U.S. each year take place in the first trimester (three months) of pregnancy. Most of the remainder take place in the second trimester, usually by "dilation and evacuation" (D & E). A doctor may have to make ten to fifteen passes with a forceps to complete the "evacuation" part of this process, and the fetus is usually ripped apart as it is removed. The procedure that was the impetus for various bans on "partial-birth" abortions is a variation of the D & E.

In 2003, following the Supreme Court's decision in the *Stenberg* case (striking down a Nebraska abortion statute), Congress passed a new late-term abortion law that is the subject of this lawsuit. The Act makes it a crime to perform certain partial-birth abortions known as "intact" D & Es. The law provides an exception when the woman's life, but not her health, is in danger. An abortion doctor challenged the Act as being facially invalid.

■ **ISSUE**

Is the 2003 federal law banning certain partial-birth abortions, with no exception for when a woman's health is at risk, facially unconstitutional?

■ **DECISION AND RATIONALE**

(Kennedy, J.) No. A law limiting abortions is valid so long as it promotes the government's legitimate interest in protecting the health of the woman and the life of the fetus without placing an undue burden on the woman's right to terminate her pregnancy. An undue burden exists if the law places substantial obstacles in the woman's path to obtaining an abortion before the fetus attains viability. Moreover, if the language of the Act is vague or its reach overbroad, it must be invalidated. Here, the Act in question is not void for vagueness because it uses explicit terms and departs in material ways from the one struck down in *Stenberg*. The Act specifically requires that a person "vaginally deliver a living fetus," clearly excluding delivery of an expired fetus or delivery via non-vaginal means. Likewise, the Act specifically

---

provides easily definable points at which a permissible abortive procedure becomes a partial-birth abortion prohibited by the Act. Finally, the Act requires an "overt act" done "deliberately and intentionally" to kill the fetus. The Act similarly does not present an undue burden because its restrictions are overbroad. Unlike the language at issue in *Stenberg*, the Act adopts the phrase "delivers a living fetus" instead of "delivering ... a living unborn child, or a substantial portion thereof." Partial-birth abortion, as defined in the Act, differs from a standard D & E. The Act is not void for vagueness or overbreadth.

We reject the contention that the purpose of the Act was to place a substantial obstacle in the path of a woman seeking an abortion. The prohibition on partial-birth abortions in the Act would be unconstitutional if it subjected women to significant health risks. The Act, both by its terms and the Court's abortion jurisprudence, establishes its purpose as serving the government's legitimate interests in regulating the integrity of the medical profession, protecting the life of the unborn fetus, and safeguarding the health of the mother. In enacting the legislation, it was reasonable for Congress to think that partial-birth abortions, more so than standard D & E's, "undermine[] the public's perception of the appropriate role of a physician during the delivery process, and pervert[] the process during which life is brought into the world." The Act's purpose was not to place a substantial obstacle in a woman's path to terminating her pregnancy.

Despite no such purpose, the Act may nonetheless create such an obstacle if it does not further its interest in protecting the woman's health. The Act considerably limits the practice of partial-birth abortions even for the preservation of the health of the mother. These limitations would be unconstitutional if they were certain to present significant health risks to the mother. However, whether the Act creates such risks is a factual question equally supported by diverging medical views. When such uncertainty exists, legislatures have wide discretion. The Act is not invalid on its face where there is uncertainty over whether the procedure is ever necessary to preserve a woman's health, given the availability of other abortion procedures that are considered safe alternatives.

■ CONCURRENCE

(Thomas, J.) I agree with the Court's conclusion here, but write separately to reiterate that the Court's abortion jurisprudence, including *Casey* and *Roe*, has no basis in the Constitution.

■ DISSENT

(Ginsburg, J.) The Court refuses to take *Casey* and *Stenberg* seriously. It applauds federal intervention to ban a procedure found to be necessary under certain circumstances by the American College of Obstetricians and Gynecologists. It blurs the line between post-and pre-viability abortions. Moreover, the Act does not further the asserted governmental interest of protecting the life of the fetus, for the Act attacks merely the method of abortion, not the right of abortion. No fetus is saved by operation of this Act. The Court admits that "moral concerns" are at work, but still finds the ban constitutional because the respondents failed to show it would be unconstitutional in a large fraction of relevant cases. But the very purpose of the health exception is to protect women in those exceptional cases. The absence of a health exception burdens all women for whom it is relevant: women who, in their doctors' opinions, require an intact D & E because other procedures would put their health at risk. The Court continues to chip away at a right declared again and again to be central to women's lives.

Analysis:

The Court found that, under the most reasonable interpretation, the Act in question applies only to intact D & Es and not to the more common D & E procedure. The Act's application was also limited to cases in which the doctor *intends* to perform an intact D & E, and delivers the living fetus past certain "anatomical landmarks." Because the Act applies only to this specific method of abortion, the ban was not unconstitutionally vague, overbroad, or an undue burden on the decision to obtain an abortion. The Court also held that Congress, after finding intact D & E never to be medically necessary, could validly omit a health exception, even if some part of the medical community considered the procedure to be necessary. To require a health exception whenever such medical uncertainty exists would be too exacting a standard to impose on the legislative power to regulate the medical profession, the Court opined. The Court did leave open the possibility that an "as-applied" challenge could be raised if the Act were ever applied in a situation in which an intact D & E was in fact necessary to protect the woman's health.

■ CASE VOCABULARY

ABORTION: An artificially induced termination of a pregnancy for the purpose of destroying an embryo or fetus. In *Roe v. Wade*, the Supreme Court first recognized a woman's right to choose to end her pregnancy as a privacy right stemming from the Due Process Clause of the 14th Amendment. Sixteen years later, in *Webster v. Reproductive Health Services*, the Court permitted states to limit this right by allowing them to enact legislation that (1) prohibits public facilities or employees from performing abortions, (2) prohibits the use of public funds for family planning that includes information on abortion, or (3) severely limits the right to an abortion after a fetus becomes viable—that is, could live independently of its mother. In 1992, the Court held that (1) before viability, a woman has a fundamental right to choose to terminate her pregnancy, (2) a law that imposes an undue burden on the woman's right to choose before viability is unconstitutional, and (3) after viability, the state, in promoting its interest in potential human life, may regulate or prohibit abortion unless it is necessary to preserve the life or health of the mother. *Planned Parenthood of Southeastern Pa. v. Casey*, 505 U.S. 833, 112 S. Ct. 2791 (1992). In 2000, the Court again considered abortion rights and reaffirmed *Casey* in holding the Nebraska law at issue unconstitutional because (1) it failed to provide an exception to preserve the health of the mother, and (2) it unduly burdened a woman's right to choose a late-term abortion, thereby unduly burdening her right to choose abortion itself. *Stenberg v. Carhart*, 530 U.S. 914, 120 S. Ct. 2597 (2000).

FACIAL CHALLENGE: A claim that a statute is unconstitutional on its face—that is, that it always operates unconstitutionally.

LATE–TERM ABORTION: An abortion performed during the latter stages of pregnancy, usually after the middle of the second trimester.

OVERBREADTH DOCTRINE: The doctrine holding that if a statute is so broadly written that it deters free expression, then it can be struck down on its face because of its chilling effect—even if it also prohibits acts that may legitimately be forbidden. The Supreme Court has used this doctrine to invalidate a number of laws, including those that would disallow peaceful picketing or require loyalty oaths.

PARTIAL–BIRTH ABORTION: An abortion in which a viable fetus is partially delivered before being destroyed.

VOID FOR VAGUENESS: Establishing a requirement or punishment without specifying what is required or what conduct is punishable, and therefore void because violative of due process.

Smith v. Cote

(*Pregnant Woman*) v. (*Obstetrician/Gynecologist*)

128 N.H. 231, 513 A.2d 341 (1986)

WRONGFUL BIRTH ACTIONS GAIN ACCEPTANCE AFTER *ROE*, BUT NOT WRONGFUL LIFE

■ **INSTANT FACTS** Smith (P), who gave birth to Heather (P), born with birth defects, claims she would have had an abortion if Cote (D) had timely diagnosed her exposure to rubella and advised her of the risks to Heather (P).

■ **BLACK LETTER RULE** (1) New Hampshire recognizes a cause of action for wrongful birth by the mother of a child born with birth defects. (2) New Hampshire does not recognize a cause of action for wrongful life by a child born with birth defects.

■ **PROCEDURAL BASIS**

Questions of law transferred from Superior Court in wrongful birth and wrongful life actions for damages.

■ **FACTS**

Linda Smith (Smith) (P) became pregnant in early 1979, and Cote (D), an obstetrician/gynecologist, cared for her. Smith (P) consulted Cote (D) about her nausea, abdominal pain and a late menstrual period in April 1979. In August 1979, while in her second trimester, Cote (D) directed her to undergo a rubella titre test, which indicated that she had been exposed to rubella. Smith (P) gave birth to her daughter Heather (P) in January 1980, who was born with congenital rubella syndrome. At age six, Heather (P) has multiple congenital heart defects, motor retardation, significant hearing impairment, and is legally blind. Smith (P) alleges that she contracted rubella early in her pregnancy and that Cote (D) negligently failed to test for and discover the disease in a timely manner. Smith (P) further alleges that Cote (D) negligently failed to advise her of the potential birth defects of a fetus exposed to rubella, thus depriving her of knowledge necessary to make an informed decision about whether to give birth to a potentially impaired child. Smith (P) claims that if she had known of the risks, she would have had an abortion. Smith (P) argues that her wrongful birth claim fits within the framework of a wrongful conception claim and is consistent with established tort principles. Cote (D) argues that tort principles cannot accommodate wrongful birth, he did not cause Smith's (P) injury, and damages cannot be fairly and accurately ascertained. In addition, Heather (P) argues that she has a wrongful life action based on Cote's (D) duty to both Smith (P) and Heather (P) during Smith's (P) pregnancy. Heather (P) argues that Cote (D) breached this duty when he failed to discover Smith's (P) exposure to rubella and to inform Smith (P) of the possible effects of that exposure on Heather (P). Because Smith (P) would have had an abortion had she been so informed, Heather (P) argues that Cote's (D) breach caused her to bear the burden of her defects for the rest of her life.

■ **ISSUE**

(1) Will New Hampshire recognize a cause of action for wrongful birth by the mother of a child born with birth defects? (2) Will New Hampshire recognize a cause of action for wrongful life by a child born with birth defects?

■ DECISION AND RATIONALE

(Batchelder, J.) (1) Yes. The surrounding controversy notwithstanding, the Supreme Court has held in *Roe v. Wade* [declares a right to have an abortion] that a woman has a constitutional right to have an abortion. Given the existence of a woman's right to decide to have an abortion, we must decide whether our common law should recognize a duty to exercise care in providing information that bears on that decision. A wrongful birth claim is one brought by the parents of a child born with severe defects against a physician who negligently fails to timely inform them of an increased possibility that the child would be born with such defects, precluding their informed decision about whether to give birth to the child. A wrongful life claim is a corresponding claim brought by the child born with defects. The child claims that the physician negligently failed to inform her parents of the risk of bearing a child with defects, thus preventing the parents from deciding to abort the child. Although we have never expressly considered a cause of action for wrongful birth, we have considered a similar claim for wrongful conception. In *Kingsbury v. Smith* [recognizes a claim for wrongful conception], Mrs. Kingsbury had a tubal ligation because she and her husband wanted no more children. The operation failed and she gave birth to another child, and sued the doctors for the injury their negligence caused. We allowed a claim for wrongful conception, a claim which arises when a negligently performed sterilization or a negligently filled birth control prescription contributes to the birth of a child. We reasoned that recognizing this claim was necessary to avoid a void in the area of medical malpractice that would dilute the standard of professional conduct in family planning. In general, one who suffers an injury to his person or property because of another's negligence has a tort claim. An action for negligence requires a person to show the existence of a duty the breach of which proximately caused his injury. If Smith (P) establishes a physician-patient relationship with Cote (D) with respect to her pregnancy, it follows that Cote (D) owed her a duty of reasonable care in treating her. Given *Roe*, this "due care" standard may have required Cote (D) to ensure that Smith (P) had an opportunity to make an informed decision about her procreative options. Whether this required Cote (D) to test for, diagnose and disclose her exposure to rubella at a particular stage of her pregnancy is a question of fact. The standard depends on circumstances including the recommended practices of the medical profession and the training and skill of an average medical practitioner. This standard does not require a physician to identify and disclose every chance of every possible birth defect. Cote (D) only breached his duty of due care if (1) the applicable standard of care required him to test for and diagnose Smith's (P) rubella infection in a timely manner and to inform her of the possible effects of the virus on her child, and (2) he failed to do so. The element of causation in this case depends on a finding that Smith (P) would have chosen to have an abortion if she had known of the risks of birth defects. Cote (D) argues that this hypothetical chain of events is too remote to prove causation. We disagree. Smith (P) can prove causation if she can show that but for Cote's (D) negligent failure to inform her of the risks of bearing a child with birth defects, she would have had an abortion. On the final element of injury, Smith (P) argues that in bearing a child with birth defects after being deprived of an opportunity to make an informed procreative decision, she sustained injury. Cote (D) argues that because both benefits (the joys of parenthood) and harms (alleged emotional and pecuniary damages) have resulted from Heather's (P) birth, Smith (P) cannot prove injury. In effect, Cote (D) argues that the birth of a child can never constitute an injury to its parents, and therefore a physician can never be liable for negligently causing a child to be born. We disagree. Under *Roe*, parents may have constitutionally cognizable reasons for avoiding the emotional and pecuniary burdens that may attend having a child with birth defects. Advances in prenatal health care provide the basis upon which parents may make informed decisions about whether to have an abortion. We cannot hold that as a matter of law those who act negligently in providing this care cannot cause harm. The difficulty of measuring damages is also insufficient reason to deny recovery to an injured party. We hold that New Hampshire recognizes a cause of action for wrongful birth. Notwithstanding the controversy surrounding abortion, we are bound by the law that protects a woman's right to have one. We do not encourage or discourage abortion, and we do not conclude that Heather (P) should never have been born. We must, however, deter negligent conduct and compensate the victims of those who act unreasonably. The wrongful birth cause of action is unique in medical malpractice because it does not involve physical injury, but the invasion of a parental right to decide whether to abort a child with congenital birth defects. The denial of the opportunity to make this decision may impair interests in avoiding the expenses attending a child born with defects, in preventing the anguish the parents may feel, and in preserving personal autonomy. Quantifying the impairment of these interests is challenging. Smith (P) seeks compensation for the extraordinary medical and educational costs she will sustain in raising Heather (P), for the maternal care that she must provide, and for the emotional distress which she claims is a foreseeable consequence of her injury. The usual rule for compensatory damages is that the wronged person should receive a sum which would restore him to the position he would have been in but for the wrong. Here, this would include all the costs of raising Heather (P), ordinary and extraordinary. On the other hand, the rule requiring the mitigation of tort damages and the "avoidable consequences" rule, rigidly applied, would require parents claiming wrongful birth to place their child for adoption. Because of our profound respect for the sanctity of the family, we are loathe to apply this rule in these circumstances, but if we do not, parents claiming wrongful birth may receive windfalls. Hence, a special rule limiting recovery to extraordinary costs is warranted in these cases, and this is the course most jurisdictions have chosen. This extraordinary costs rule coincides with contract law's expectancy rule of damages, which would put the parents in the position they expected to be in at the outset, since parents claiming wrongful birth usually start out intending to give birth to and support a child. In addition to extraordinary educational and medical costs, recovery should include compensation for the extraordinary maternal care that Smith (P) must provide as a result of Heather's (P) condition. Avoiding the extra burdens of caring for a child with birth defects is often one of the primary motivations of parents who decide to abort such children. To the extent that a parent's emotional distress results in tangible pecuniary losses, such as medical expenses or counseling fees, these losses are recoverable as well. Intangible damages for emotional distress are not recoverable, however, just as they are not recoverable by a parent for distress that results from a child's injury or death. (2) No. With respect to Heather's (P) wrongful life action, the crucial problem is the question of injury. To recognize her wrongful life action, we must assume that Heather (P), as a fetus, had an interest in avoiding her own birth. We must assume that it would have been best *for Heather (P)* if she had not been born. The law can assert no competence to resolve this issue, particularly in view of the very nearly uniform high value which the law has placed on human life. Policy reasons also weigh against wrongful life claims. One is that courts should not become involved in deciding whether a particular person's life is or is not worthwhile. Another is that to characterize a disabled life as an injury would be damaging both to the disabled and to the growing public awareness that the disabled can be valuable and productive members of society. Finally, because in wrongful life cases the finding of injury hinges on intensely personal notions about the intangible value of life, there is a danger of disparate and unpredictable outcomes. We recognize that our rejection of the wrongful life action may cause the recovery of some impaired children's medical expenses to depend on whether their parents are available to claim wrongful birth. However, our paramount regard for the value of human life and our adherence to fundamental principles of justice outweigh this cost. We will not recognize a right not to be born, and we will not permit a person to recover damages from one who has done him no harm.

Analysis:

This case is a wrongful birth action, a special type of medical malpractice action that gained general acceptance after *Roe v. Wade* and illustrates the difference between actions for wrongful birth, wrongful life, and wrongful conception. Before *Roe*, courts usually denied recovery for wrongful birth and wrongful life. The gravamen of these actions is the claim that but for the doctor's negligence, the mother would have had an abortion, and she and the child, respectively, would never have had to experience the pain and expense that come with the physical problems that the doctor could have foreseen. Absent a right to decide whether to give birth to a child, the elements of these claims would not exist. After *Roe*, most states accepted wrongful birth actions. Their number is declining, however. Courts have always been less willing to accept wrongful life actions. One argument for this is that a physician cannot have a duty to a person who did not exist when the tortious action took place. However, the law has recognized such a duty under some circumstances, such as when a doctor negligently transfused a woman and thereby caused injury to a child she bore several years later. There is also a presumption that being born is always better than not being born. In *Smith* the court distinguished wrongful life cases from "right to die" cases, reasoning that while the judiciary has a role to play in protecting the right of the dying, it has no business declaring that there are those among the living that never should have been born. Finally, some argue that acceptance of wrongful life actions would constitute a social judgment that disabled lives are worth less than other lives. This argument also has begun to affect wrongful birth actions and is a factor in their waning acceptance. One state that banned wrongful birth actions in 2001 cited the inherent discrimination against disabled persons that these suits promote.

■ CASE VOCABULARY

AVOIDABLE CONSEQUENCES RULE: A person seeking damages for a tort has a duty to minimize damages and may not recover for any harm that he could have avoided by reasonable effort after the tort occurred.

EXPECTANCY RULE: A rule from contract law that damages should put a person in the position he expected to be in absent a breach.

WRONGFUL BIRTH: A malpractice claim by parents of a child born with birth defects against a person whose negligent treatment or advice precluded their informed decision about whether to give birth to the child.

WRONGFUL CONCEPTION: Also called "wrongful pregnancy," a malpractice claim by parents of a healthy child against a person whose negligently performed sterilization or negligently filled birth control prescription contributed to the conception of the child.

WRONGFUL LIFE: A malpractice claim by a child born with birth defects against a person whose negligent advice to the child's parents precluded them from aborting the child.

In the Interest of K.M.H.

(Children Conceived Through Artificial Insemination)

285 Kan. 53, 169 P.3d 1025 (2007)

REQUIRING WRITTEN AGREEMENTS TO ESTABLISH SPERM DONOR PATERNITY DOES NOT VIOLATE EQUAL PROTECTION OR DUE PROCESS

No, the way it actually works is that your right to your soul is automatically terminated unless you specifically contracted otherwise.

stus.com

■ **INSTANT FACTS** D.H. (D) provided sperm to S.H. (P) for artificial insemination, and then brought an action to determine his paternity of the children born as a result of that insemination.

■ **BLACK LETTER RULE** The gender classification in the sperm donor statute substantially furthers, and is thus substantially related to, legitimate legislative purposes and important government objectives, and the requirement that a sperm donor agreement be in writing does not deprive donors of rights that have already arisen and attached.

■ PROCEDURAL BASIS

Appeal from an order granting a motion to dismiss an action to determine paternity.

■ FACTS

D.H. (D), an unmarried man, agreed to provide sperm to S.H. (P), an unmarried woman, for artificial insemination. D.H. (D) and S.H. (P) were both residents of Kansas and made their oral agreement for donation in Kansas. The insemination took place in Missouri. There was no formal written agreement between D.H. (D) and S.H. (P) regarding the donation, the insemination, or any expectations of the parties regarding what, if any, parental rights D.H. (D) would have.

S.H. (P) gave birth to twins—K.M.H. and K.C.H.—as a result of the insemination. The children were born in Kansas. S.H. (P) brought an action to establish that D.H. (D) had no parental rights. D.H. (D) brought an action to determine his paternity.

Kansas Statute § 38–114(f) (based in part on section 5 of the Uniform Parentage Act) provided that the donor of semen who provides semen to a licensed physician for use in artificial insemination of a woman other than the donor's wife is regarded as not being the birth father of the child thereby conceived "unless agreed to in writing by the donor and the woman." D.H. (D) alleged that the Kansas statute was unconstitutional. The trial court held that the statute was constitutional, and that D.H. (D) had no parental rights regarding K.M.H. and K.C.H. The court dismissed D.H.'s (D) petition to determine paternity. On appeal, D.H. (D) argued that the trial court erred in upholding the constitutionality of the Kansas statute, and that the statute was unconstitutional as applied to him, a known sperm donor who alleges he had an oral agreement that granted him parental rights. He also argued that the court misinterpreted the "licensed physician" requirement of the statute, and that the pleadings in S.H.'s (P) action satisfied the "written agreement" requirement. D.H. (D), a non-lawyer, also argued that S.H. (P) had unclean hands, because S.H. (P), a lawyer, failed to advise him of the statute or that he should have independent legal advice. D.H. (D) also argued that S.H. (P) told him that a written agreement was not necessary. The court found in S.H.'s (P) favor and D.H. (D) appealed.

■ ISSUE

Is the Kansas artificial insemination statute constitutional?

■ DECISION AND RATIONALE

(Beier, J.) Yes. The gender classification in the sperm donor statute substantially furthers, and is thus substantially related to, legitimate legislative purposes and important government objectives, and the requirement that a sperm donor agreement be in writing does not deprive donors of rights that have already arisen and attached. Equal protection principles require that similarly situated individuals be treated alike. In order to pass muster under the Equal Protection Clause, a classification of individuals based solely on gender must substantially further a legitimate legislative purpose. The government's objective in enacting the law with the classification must be important, and the classification must be substantially related to the achievement of that purpose.

The evolution of the law regarding artificial insemination in other states provides context for the analysis of the Kansas statute. The statutes in most states that have laws on this subject provide that the husband of a married woman bears all parental rights and obligations as to a child conceived by artificial insemination, regardless of who the donor was. The original version of the Uniform Parentage Act did not address the issue of an unmarried woman. The earliest case to deal with the issue, a case from New Jersey, relied on common law principles regarding the "natural fathers" of "illegitimate children" to award visitation rights to an unmarried sperm donor. The court held that, if the parties had been married, the donor would have been considered the child's father, and the court applied the same principle, even though the parties were not married, given the evidence that the parties intended to raise the children together.

A subsequent case, from Colorado, explicitly rejected the idea that an unmarried sperm donor lost the protection of the parentage Act merely because the donee knew the donor. On the other hand, an Oregon case held that the Parentage Act made an acceptable classification between males and females, because only females can conceive and bear children, and only males can donate sperm. The classification was also rationally related to the purposes of the statute, which were to allow married couples to have children even if the husband was infertile, to allow unmarried women to bear children without engaging in sexual intercourse, to resolve potential disputes regarding parentage, to encourage men to be sperm donors, and to legitimize children. The court also held that the statute would violate the Due Process Clause as applied to donors who could prove an agreement to share the rights and responsibilities of parenthood. A similar result was reached in an Ohio case.

The Parentage Act was amended in 2000 to provide that a sperm donor "is not a parent of a child conceived by means of assisted reproduction." In a California case, the trial court found that the new statute was constitutional, but upheld a claim of paternity on equitable grounds: the donor and donee had tried artificial insemination, but when that resulted in a miscarriage, tried to conceive through sexual intercourse. When that did not work, the couple successfully tried artificial insemination. The donor was involved in the pregnancy and birth of the child. The appellate court, however, reversed, holding that the words of the statute were clear and operated as an absolute bar to a claim of paternity in that case.

The Kansas statute differs from the Uniform Act, in that it applies to married and unmarried women, and it allows for an agreement to opt out of the paternity bar. The statute draws a gender-based line between sperm recipients, who are necessarily female, and sperm donors, who are necessarily male. Under the statute, the female is always the parent or potential parent; the male is never a parent or potential parent unless there is a written agreement with the female. The right of the male to be a parent disappears when he donates sperm. Up until that time, he may refuse to participate unless there is a written agreement about the terms. The female can unilaterally decide whether to use the donation for insemination, or she can deny the male parental rights by refusing to enter into a written agreement.

It is doubtful whether females and males are similarly situated with respect to conceiving and bearing a child. Assuming that they are, there are several legitimate legislative purposes behind the statute. The statute envisions that both married and unmarried women may become pregnant through artificial means, wither by choice, or because their partners are infertile, impotent, or ill. The statute also encourages men to be donors by protecting them from unwanted claims for support. Women are also protected from unwanted paternity claims. The requirement that agreements be in writing enhances predictability and clarity, and encourages early resolution of the elemental question of paternal rights. The statute's gender classification substantially furthers and is thus substantially related to those legitimate legislative purposes. A clear default pattern is established, and the parties are free to modify that pattern, provided they do so in writing.

D.H.'s (D) substantive due process claim must also fail. The statute does not eliminate any existing rights. Instead, it ensures that no rights attach without a written agreement. The fact that a woman may be the sole arbiter of whether a sperm donor is to have parental rights does not make the statute unconstitutional. It is consistent with precedent that makes a woman the sole arbiter of whether to carry a child to term.

Kansas law applies to this case, because such agreement as existed between the parties was made in Kansas between two residents of Kansas, D.H. (D) performed his obligations in Kansas, and the twins were born and reside in Kansas. The only connection this case has with Missouri is that the medical procedure was performed there. Significant contacts and a significant aggregation of contacts with Kansas make the application of Kansas law appropriate and constitutional.

D.H.'s (D) lack of knowledge of the statute, and S.H.'s (P) failure to explain the effect of a lack of a written agreement, is not grounds for reversal. Ignorance of the law is no excuse for failure to abide by it. While there may be a future case in which a donor could prove that the existence of the statute was concealed, or that a donor was fraudulently induced not to obtain independent legal advice or seek a written agreement, this is not such a case. Nor did the trial court misinterpret the requirement that sperm be provided to a licensed physician. The sperm was provided to S.H. (P), who in turn provided it to the medical personnel who performed the insemination. In addition, the pleadings in the case are insufficient to establish a "written" agreement. Affirmed

■ DISSENT

(Caplinger, J.) The majority states that it was D.H.'s (D) "inaction" that made him unable to meet the requirements of the statute, and that is the constitutional problem with the statute .. Fundamental rights must be actively waived, not lost through passivity. The expression "opt out" used by the majority is a misnomer, in that donors must choose, or "opt in," to parenthood if their rights are not to be lost forever. D.H.'s (D) rights to parenthood are fundamental, and he is entitled to the full protection of the Due Process Clause. Giving up a fundamental right should involve an intentional, free, and meaningful choice. In the instant case, D.H. (D) was not aware of the Kansas statute or of the writing requirement.

In addition, the court should be able to consider S.H.'s (P) pleadings, in which she referred to D.H. (D) as the "father" of K.M.H. and K.C.H. at least fifty-six times, as evidence of an agreement between S.H. (P) and D.H. (D) regarding the role he was to play in the children's lives.

Analysis:

In its opinion, the court discusses some of the policy issues raised by the statute. The court notes that some European countries have banned anonymous sperm donations, the "near-perfect analogs to donations from known donors who will have no role beyond facilitating artificial insemination." Banning anonymous donations recognizes the desire of some children conceived through artificial insemination to know "the males from whom they have received half of their genes." The Kansas statute, like most American statutes on this subject, does not take this desire or interest into account.

Davis v. Davis

(*Husband*) v. (*Wife*)

842 S.W.2d 588 (Tenn. 1992)

COURT DETERMINES THE FATE OF FROZEN EMBRYOS BY BALANCING THE GAMETE-PROVIDERS' INTERESTS BUT NOT STATE INTERESTS

■ **INSTANT FACTS** A husband and wife stored frozen embryos they had created through *in vitro* fertilization (IVF), then, when they divorced, could not agree about what to do with them.

■ **BLACK LETTER RULE** Courts should resolve disputes over the disposition of preembryos produced by IVF by looking first to the preferences of the gamete-providers, then to a prior agreement, and if no agreement exists, then to weighing each gamete-provider's interests in gestating or discarding the preembryos and the burdens different resolutions would impose upon them.

■ **PROCEDURAL BASIS**

Review granted of Court of Appeals decision reversing trial court regarding control of frozen embryos.

■ **FACTS**

Junior Davis (Junior) (P) and Mary Davis (Mary) (D) were once a happily married couple attempting to achieve a pregnancy through in vitro fertilization (IVF). When Junior (P) later sued Mary (D) for divorce, they could not agree on who would have custody of the seven frozen embryos they had stored at a fertility clinic. Mary (D) first asked for the embryos with the intent to have them implanted into her own uterus after the divorce. Junior (P) objected, preferring to leave them frozen. The trial court determined that the frozen embryos were human beings from the moment of fertilization, awarded custody to Mary (D), and directed that she be permitted the opportunity to bring the children to term through implantation. The Court of Appeals reversed, holding that Junior (P) had a constitutional right not to beget a child where no pregnancy has taken place, and that there was no compelling state interest to justify ordering implantation against the will of either Junior (P) or Mary (D) [the sorry-my-hands-are-tied rationale]. The court held that Junior (P) and Mary (D) shared an interest in the embryos and remanded the case to the trial court to vest them with joint control and an equal voice over their disposition. Mary (D) appealed to this Court, contesting the constitutional basis of the appellate court's decision. Mary (D) has remarried and now wishes to donate the embryos to a childless couple. Junior (P) wants to discard them.

■ **ISSUE**

May a court balance the interests of gamete-providers to resolve disputes over the disposition of their frozen embryos?

■ **DECISION AND RATIONALE**

(Daughtrey, J.) Yes. There is no statutory or common law precedent on this issue, but much comment in the legal journals. Scholars have proposed various models for disposing of frozen embryos when certain contingencies arise, ranging from requiring the gamete-providers to either use the embryos or donate them to requiring that all unused embryos be automatically discarded. Some models give the female gamete-provider control over the embryos because of her greater physical and emotional contribution to the IVF process. There are also two "implied contract" models. One infers from a couple's enrollment in an IVF program that the clinic has authority to resolve impasses by deciding whether to donate or discard the embryos or use them for research. The other infers an irrevocable commitment to reproduction from the couple's participation in the creation of the embryos, and therefore requires implantation into either the female provider or a donee. One of the "equity models" would divide the embryos equally between the parties. The other would give veto power to whichever party wishes to avoid parenthood. While any of these models would provide a bright line rule that would be easy to apply, constitutional law principles, Tennessee policy regarding unborn life, emerging reproductive technologies and ethical considerations leave us no easy answers. We must weigh the interests of each party to resolve this type of dispute in a fair and responsible manner. One fundamental issue here is whether frozen embryos, or preembryos, are "persons" or "property" under the law. Neither Tennessee law nor federal law protects preembryos as "persons." The trial court's ruling would have given the preembryos the legal status of "persons" and vested them with their own legal interests. Such a decision would have effectively outlawed IVF programs in Tennessee. The American Fertility Society discusses three major ethical positions on the status of preembryos. One views the preembryo as a human subject after fertilization which necessarily has the rights of a person. This position therefore requires an opportunity for implantation and bans any action before then that might harm the preembryo or that is not therapeutic. The opposite view is that the preembryo is no different from any other human tissue. This position would place no limits on actions taken with preembryos with the consent of those who have decision-making authority over them. The middle and most widely held view is that the preembryo deserves more respect than human tissue, but does not consider it a person. The Ethics Committee thus urges IVF programs to establish policies which give "special respect" to preembryos and suggests that decision-making authority regarding preembryos belongs to the gamete-providers. We conclude that preembryos are not strictly either "persons" or "property," but something in between, and that they deserve special respect. While Mary (D) and Junior (P) cannot have a true property interest in the preembryos, they do have an interest similar to ownership to the extent they have decision-making authority over their disposition. Any agreement regarding the disposition of preembryos in the event of contingencies such as death, divorce, financial reversals, or abandonment of the program is presumptively valid and enforceable. Here, Mary (D) and Junior (P) made no such agreement. Asking whether a preembryo is "property" is not altogether helpful because the value of preembryos is their potential to develop into children. The essential dispute here is not where or how or how long to store the preembryos, but whether the parties will become parents. The right to individual privacy encompasses the right of procreational autonomy, which in turn is composed to two equally significant rights: the right to procreate and the right to avoid procreation. The equivalence of and tension between these rights are most evident in the IVF context. The concerns about a woman's bodily integrity that have precluded men from controlling abortion decisions are not present here. We recognize that women undergo more emotional stress and physical discomfort in the IVF process than men. However, with respect to the joys of parenthood versus a lifetime of unwanted parenthood, we must consider Mary (D) and Junior (P) equivalent gamete-providers. Further, no one other than the gamete-providers has any decision-making authority to interfere with their decision. At least with respect to Tennessee's policy and right to privacy, the state's interest in the life of the preembryos is insufficient to justify infringement on the gamete-providers' procreational autonomy. If the state's interest is not sufficiently compelling to justify regulating abortion until the end of the first trimester, then it cannot overcome the interests of the gamete-providers in this context. Under the Tennessee abortion statute, the state's interest increases with each developmental stage, supporting the conclusion that the state's interest at the preembryo stage is slight and that the interests of the gamete-providers outweigh it. Prior cases have dealt with the childbearing and child-rearing aspects of parenthood, and abortion cases have dealt with gestational parenthood. This case deals with genetic parenthood. We conclude that an interest in avoiding genetic parenthood can be significant enough to trigger the protections of all other aspects of parenthood. Even if someone else gestated these preembryos, Mary (D) and Junior (P) would become parents at least genetically, and the profound impact this would have on them supports their right to sole decisional authority over whether to attempt to gestate them. When, as here, the gamete-providers disagree about whether to continue the IVF process, to resolve the dispute a court may consider the positions of the parties, the significance of their interests, and the relative burdens that different resolutions would impose upon them. We start by considering the burdens imposed on Mary (D) and Junior (P) by solutions that would prevent them from exercising their procreative autonomy. For Junior (P), the gestation of the preembryos would impose unwanted parenthood on him, with all of its possible financial and psychological consequences. To understand the impact this would have on him, we must consider his circumstances. He is one of six children of parents who divorced when he was five years old. His mother had a nervous breakdown and he and three of his brothers went to live at a Lutheran home for boys. Another brother lived with an aunt, and his sister stayed with their mother. He visited his mother monthly, and saw his father three times before he died. Junior (P) feels that he suffered because of his lack of a relationship with his parents and especially because of the absence of his father. Because of these experiences, Junior (P) is vehemently opposed to fathering a child that would not live with both parents because the child's bond with the non-custodial parent would not be satisfactory. He also opposes donation because the recipient couple might divorce and leave the child, which he would consider his child, in a single-parent setting. For Mary (D), refusal to permit donation of the preembryos would impose on her the burden of knowing that the IVF procedures she underwent were futile and that the preembryos would never become children. While this emotional burden is not insubstantial, we must conclude that her interest in donation is not as significant as Junior's (P) interest in avoiding parenthood. Junior (P) testified that if the preembryos were brought to term he would fight for custody of the children. Donation would rob him twice, of his procreational autonomy and of a relationship with his children. The case would be closer if Mary (D) wanted to gestate the preembryos herself, but only if she could not achieve parenthood by any other reasonable means. Since IVF and adoption are both available to her, she would have other means. We hold that courts should resolve disputes over the disposition of preembryos produced by IVF by first looking to the preferences of the progenitors, then to a prior agreement, and if no agreement exists, then to weighing the relative interests of each progenitor in gestating or discarding the preembryos and the burdens different resolutions would impose upon them. Ordinarily the party wishing to avoid procreation should prevail, assuming the other party has a reasonable possibility of achieving parenthood by other means. If no other reasonable alternatives exist, then the court should consider the argument in favor of gestating the preembryos. However, if the party seeking to gestate the preembryos intends to donate them to another couple for gestation, the objecting party has a greater interest and should prevail. This rule does not create an automatic veto. Affirmed.

Analysis:

This is the first case to address the issue of how to resolve a dispute between a man and woman who use the IVF process and then disagree about whether to implant the remaining frozen embryos. The trial court here found, after weighing expert testimony, that "human life begins at the moment of conception." From this it concluded that the eight-cell entities at issue were "children in vitro" and held, under the doctrine of parens patriae, that it was "in the best interest of the children" to be born rather than destroyed. Because Mary (D) was willing to give them this opportunity and Junior (P) was not, the trial court awarded Mary (D) "custody." The Court of Appeals rejected this and, treating the preembryos as "property" rather than "persons," held that Mary (D) and Junior (P) each had an equal share in them and gave them joint control over their disposition. This court, like the Court in *Roe*, presumes, consciously or unconsciously, that life does not begin at conception (fertilization) by presuming that parenthood, even genetic parenthood, does not begin until some time after that point. Today states vary in the rules they use to resolve disputes over preembryos. Virginia, for example, treats preembryos as property subject to ordinary bailment laws. Louisiana, on the other hand, forbids the destruction of preembryos, requires that the couple who created them either implant them or donate them to another couple for implantation, and applies a "best interest of the preembryo" standard to resolve disputes. In *Davis* the court held that no one other than the gamete-providers has any decision-making authority over the disposition of frozen embryos because the state's interest in the life of the preembryos is insufficient to justify infringement on the gamete-providers' procreational autonomy.

■ CASE VOCABULARY

CRYOGENICALLY-PRESERVED: Frozen in nitrogen and stored at sub-zero temperatures.

GAMETE: A mature sperm or egg cell.

IN VITRO FERTILIZATION: An assisted reproduction technique by which sperm fertilize egg cells, usually several, outside the body [the romantic Petri dish], with the intent to implant the resulting embryo later in the uterus to complete the pregnancy.

PROGENITOR: A direct biological ancestor.

In the Matter of Baby M

(Child of Surrogacy Arrangement)

109 N.J. 396, 537 A.2d 1227 (1988)

HOLDING SURROGACY CONTRACTS VOID, ILLEGAL, AND AGAINST PUBLIC POLICY; COURT REINSTATES "SURROGATE" MOTHER'S PARENTAL RIGHTS

■ **INSTANT FACTS** The Stems (P) entered into a surrogacy contract with Whitehead (D), but after giving birth Whitehead changed her mind and wanted to keep her baby.

■ **BLACK LETTER RULE** Surrogacy contracts violate state law and policy and are invalid and unenforceable unless the surrogate acts voluntarily and without payment and retains the right to change her mind and assert her parental rights.

■ **PROCEDURAL BASIS**

Direct certification granted of appeal of trial court's order awarding custody, terminating parental rights and granting adoption in action for specific performance of a surrogacy contract.

■ **FACTS**

Under a "surrogacy contract," for a fee of $10,000 a woman agrees to be artificially inseminated with semen from another woman's husband, to conceive and carry a child to term, and to surrender it after its birth to the natural father and his wife. The intent of the contract is for the wife to adopt the child and to forever separate the child from its natural mother, inappropriately called the "surrogate mother." William Stem (P) and Mary Beth Whitehead (D) entered into such a surrogacy contract. The contract stated that Stern's (P) wife was infertile, that they wanted a child, and that Whitehead (D) was willing to provide that child as the mother with Stern (P) as the father. Whitehead (D) did bear a child. The Sterns (P) call the baby Melissa and Whitehead (D) calls her Sara. [After giving birth, Whitehead (D) changed her mind and wanted to keep her child. The Sterns (P) sued to enforce the contract.]

■ **ISSUE**

Is a "surrogacy contract" valid and enforceable?

■ **DECISION AND RATIONALE**

(Wilentz, J.) No. We invalidate this surrogacy contract because it conflicts with the law and public policy of this State. We find the payment of money to a "surrogate" mother illegal, perhaps criminal, and potentially degrading to women. We grant custody to the natural father here because this is in the child's best interests. However, we void the termination of the surrogate mother's parental rights and the adoption of the child by the father's wife, and thus restore the "surrogate" as the mother of the child. Our present law permits a woman to act as a surrogate mother, voluntarily and without payment, as long as she is not subject to a binding agreement to surrender her child. Private adoptions are disfavored in New Jersey, but they are legal. However, a surrogacy contract's use of money for a private adoption is illegal and perhaps criminal. We have no doubt that the money exchanged under this contract is for the adoption and not for Whitehead's (D) personal services. Further, the natural mother's irrevocable agreement, prior to birth and even prior to conception, to surrender her child is coercion of contract and is totally unenforceable in private placement adoption. Even when an adoption occurs through an approved agency, the agreement to surrender the child occurs only after birth and after the mother has been offered counseling. Also invalid are the natural mother's agreement to cooperate with proceedings to terminate her parental rights, and her contractual concession that giving custody of the child to the natural father and his wife would be in the child's best interests. In a surrogacy contract the natural mother agrees to all of this even before she conceives the child, and before she has any idea what the natural father and adoptive mother are like. These critical provisions directly conflict with New Jersey statutes and offend long-established state policies, and are therefore invalid and unenforceable. The statutes with which a surrogacy contract conflicts include laws prohibiting the use of money in connection with adoptions; laws requiring proof of parental unfitness or abandonment before the termination of parental rights; and laws making the surrender of custody and the consent to adoption revocable in private placement adoptions. The goals and means of a surrogacy contract also conflict with New Jersey public policy. The contract's basic premise, that the natural parents can decide before birth who will have custody of the child, conflicts with the settled law that the child's best interests shall determine custody. This is the sale of a child, or at least the sale of a mother's right to her child. The only mitigating factor is that one of the purchasers is the child's father. In this surrogacy contract scheme, a middleman, propelled by profit, promotes the sale, and this profit motive predominates and ultimately governs the transaction. The demand for children is great and the supply small. The availability of contraception and abortion and the greater willingness of single mothers to keep their children has led to a shortage of babies offered for adoption. Middlemen enter the market to increase the supply by using money. One argument against surrogacy contracts is that surrogacy will benefit the rich at the expense of the poor. While the Sterns (P) are not rich and the Whiteheads (D) are not poor, we doubt that low-income infertile couples will find rich surrogates. While it is true that Whitehead (D) agreed to this arrangement fully understanding the consequences, her consent is irrelevant. In civilized society, there are some things that money cannot buy. Possible, though unknown, long-term effects of surrogacy contracts might include the impact on the child who learns that her mother gave birth to her only for money; the impact on the natural mother as she feels the full weight of the sale of her body and her child; and the impact on the natural father and the adoptive mother once they realize the consequences of their conduct. In New Jersey the surrogate mother's agreement to sell her child is void. Further, under New Jersey law the termination of parental rights cannot rest upon contract, but only on proof of the statutory requirements. Because there is no statutory basis for termination of Whitehead's (D) parental rights, she may retain her rights as a mother. Both parties also raise constitutional arguments based on the right of privacy, the right to procreate, and the right to the companionship of one's child, fundamental rights which both the federal and state constitutions protect. The Sterns (P) assert the right of procreation and Whitehead (D) asserts the right to the companionship of her child. The right to procreate is simply the right to have natural children, and is no more than that. Stern (P) has not been deprived of this right; Baby M is his child. The custody, care, companionship, and nurturing of the child are not parts of the right to procreation. We have already restored Whitehead's (D) (D) right to the companionship of her child, limited by the child's best interests, by restoring her as the child's mother. It is in the child's best interests here for Stern (P) to have custody and for Whitehead (D) to have visitation. It is desirable for the child to have contact with both parents, and the parents' interests must be considered, but the child's best interests are paramount in determining what visitation would be appropriate. Surrogacy has apparently provided positive results for some infertile couples. This case illustrates that unregulated surrogacy contracts can also bring suffering to the surrogate mother and her family, the natural father and his wife, and most important, the child. Affirmed in part, reversed in part.

Analysis:

In this world-famous early surrogacy case the court discussed many of the perils of surrogacy. One argument against surrogacy arrangements is that they exploit women who are willing to rent their bodies to carry other people's children. The fact that many women may see surrogacy as an opportunity does not diminish its potentially devastating consequences for other women. The court explains that under a surrogacy contract, "the natural mother is irrevocably committed before she knows the strength of her bond with her child. She never makes a totally voluntary, informed decision, for quite clearly any decision prior to the baby's birth is, in the most important sense, uninformed, and any decision after that, compelled by a pre-existing contractual commitment, the threat of a lawsuit, and the inducement of a $10,000 payment, is less than totally voluntary." In adoptions the mother's consent to surrender her child is revocable, even after surrender, unless it is to an approved agency, and then regulations protect against an ill-advised surrender. For example, adoption statutes require that the birth mother be offered counseling before surrendering her child. Here, Mrs. Whitehead (D) did undergo a psychological evaluation, but not for her benefit. The psychologist warned the infertility center that facilitated the surrogacy arrangement that Mrs. Whitehead (D) demonstrated certain traits that might make surrender of the child difficult, and that there should therefore be further inquiry into this issue. However, to inquire further might have jeopardized the center's fee, so it did not inform Mrs. Whitehead (D) or the Stems (P) of the results of the evaluation. Another argument against surrogacy contracts is that they advance the interests of the parties, but totally disregard the best interests of the child. Some believe that learning about the surrogacy arrangement later will harm the child, as will the use of the child by the surrogate mother as an instrument for profit. In *Baby M* the court explained that there was never any inquiry into the effect on the child of not living with her natural mother, or into the fitness of the Sterns (P) as custodial parents or of Mrs. Stern (P) as an adoptive parent. Courts usually look to the child's best interests to resolve custody disputes between parents. Surrogacy contracts ignore this principle, and lead the mother to the highest paying adoptive parents rather than the ones best-suited for parenthood. Both of these arguments lead many to condemn surrogacy arrangements as baby selling, but given rising infertility rates and improvements in the legal process, the arrangement's popularity has increased nonetheless.

■ CASE VOCABULARY

SURROGATE MOTHER: A woman who is artificially inseminated with sperm from another woman's husband under a prior agreement to relinquish her parental rights and to surrender the child to the couple after she gives birth.

Johnson v. Calvert

(Gestational Surrogate) v. *(Genetic Parents)*

5 Cal.4th 84, 19 Cal.Rptr.2d 494, 851 P.2d 776 (1993)

COURT DECIDES GESTATIONAL SURROGACY DISPUTE BASED ON THE INTENT OF THE PARTIES

■ **INSTANT FACTS** The Calverts (D) entered into a gestational surrogacy contract with Johnson (P), but during the pregnancy they sought a judicial declaration of their parental rights because Johnson (P) threatened to keep the child.

■ **BLACK LETTER RULE** If genetic parenthood and gestational parenthood do not coincide in one woman, then in California the natural mother of the child is she who intended to bring about the birth of the child to raise as her own.

■ **PROCEDURAL BASIS**

Review granted after court of appeal affirmed trial court judgment granting declaratory relief and enforcing surrogacy contract.

■ **FACTS**

Mark and Crispina Calvert (D) are a married couple who wanted to have a child. Because Crispina (D) had a hysterectomy, but could still produce eggs, they considered surrogacy. Anna Johnson (P) offered to serve as a surrogate for the Calverts (D). Johnson (P) and the Calverts (D) signed a contract providing that an embryo created with the sperm and egg of the Calverts (D) would be implanted in Johnson (P), that the Calverts (D) would take the child into their home "as their child" after the birth, and that Johnson (P) would relinquish "all parental rights" to the child in favor of the Calverts (D). In return, the Calverts (D) would pay Johnson (P) $10,000 in installments and would pay for a life insurance policy on Johnson's (P) life. After Johnson (P) became pregnant, the Calverts (D) learned that Johnson (P) had previously suffered several stillbirths and miscarriages. Johnson (P) felt the Calverts (D) did not do enough to obtain the life insurance policy for her, and she felt abandoned during an onset of premature labor. When she was seven months pregnant, Johnson (P) demanded the balance of the payments due or she would refuse to give up the child. The Calverts (D) sued Johnson (P) seeking a declaration that they were the legal parents of the unborn child, and Johnson (P) responded with an action to declare her the mother of the child. After the child was born, blood samples excluded Johnson (P) as the genetic mother. The court ordered that the child would remain with the Calverts (D) temporarily, with visits by Johnson (P).

■ **ISSUE**

When genetic parenthood and gestational parenthood do not coincide in one woman, is the natural mother of the child she who intended to bring about the birth of the child to raise as her own?

■ **DECISION AND RATIONALE**

(Panelli) Yes. It is clear that Johnson (P) gave birth to the child in this case, but that Crispina (D), not Johnson (P), is genetically related to him. Both women, therefore, have evidence of motherhood under the Uniform Parentage Act of 1973 (the Act) [defines methods for determining parentage in connection with replacing the concept of illegitimacy with the concept of parentage]. However, California law recognizes only one natural mother per child, despite the reproductive technology that made this situation possible. We decline to find that the child has two mothers. The Calverts (D) are the genetic and intended parents of their son and have provided him [with the assistance of a court order] with a stable, nurturing home. To recognize parental rights in Johnson (P) would diminish Crispina's (D) role as mother. With respect to proving parenthood, we see no clear legislative preference between genetic evidence and proof of having given birth. Because both women have given acceptable proof of maternity under the Act, we must look to the intentions of the parties as manifested in the surrogacy agreement. The Calverts (D) wanted a child of their own genes, but needed the help of reproductive technology. They intended the birth of the child and underwent *in vitro* fertilization for that purpose. But for their intentions and actions, this child would not exist. Johnson (P) agreed to aid the procreation of the Calverts' (D) child. Johnson's (P) purpose was to give birth to the Calverts' (D) child, not for the Calverts (D) to donate a zygote to her. The Calverts (D) would not have given Johnson (P) the opportunity to gestate the child if she manifested an intent to become the child's mother. Johnson's (P) later change of heart should not detract from the determination that Crispina (D) is the child's natural mother. Thus, although the Act recognizes both genetic consanguinity and giving birth as means of establishing maternity of a child, if these do not coincide in one woman, then in California the natural mother of the child is she who intended to bring about the birth of the child to raise as her own. Relying on her claim that she is the child's natural mother, Johnson (P) argues that surrogacy contracts violate the adoption policies against the prebirth waiver of parental rights and the Penal Code's prohibition of payment for consent to adoption. However, gestational surrogacy differs from adoption and is not governed by adoption statutes. When Johnson (P) entered into this surrogacy contract, she was not subject to financial inducements to part with her own offspring because she was not the genetic mother of the child. The payments due to Johnson (P) under the contract were compensation for gestating the fetus and undergoing labor, not for giving up "parental" rights to the child. Johnson (P) also argues that surrogacy contracts exploit or dehumanize women, especially poor women, and that giving up a child after giving birth to him may cause a woman psychological harm. Others argue that surrogacy may encourage society to view children as commodities. We are not sufficiently persuaded that gestational surrogacy arrangements are likely to cause these results to invalidate them on public policy grounds. We reject the argument that a woman cannot knowingly and intelligently agree to gestate and deliver a baby for intended parents. We will not foreclose this personal and economic choice of surrogate mothers, and will not deny intended parents what may be their only means of procreating a child of their own genes. Johnson (P) also argues that she has a constitutional right to the continued companionship of the child, relying mainly on theories of substantive due process, privacy, procreative freedom, and the fundamental liberty interest of natural parents in the custody and care of their children. However, these theories all depend upon a prior determination that she is the child's natural mother. Here Crispina (D) is the natural mother because she provided the ovum for *in vitro* fertilization intending to raise the child as her own. Whatever constitutional interests Johnson (P) has in this situation are less that those of a mother. Affirmed.

■ CONCURRENCE

(Arabian, J.) I agree with the majority's application of the Uniform Parentage Act in this case, but I would leave it to the legislature to decide whether surrogacy contracts are consistent with public policy.

■ DISSENT

(Kennard, J.) In my view, both the woman who provides the fertilized ovum and the woman who gives birth to a child have a substantial claim to legal motherhood. I do not agree that intent to have a child should be determinative. Pregnancy and the contribution of an ovum are each unique and substantial commitments to an unborn child. When two woman share the reproductive development of one child, California law requires courts to decide which one is the natural mother, but provides no standards for making that decision. The majority's resort to "intent" is unsupported by statute, and, absent legal protections against the abuse of surrogacy arrangements, is also ill-advised. To resolve this dispute, I would apply the standard most protective of the child, the best interests of the child standard. Proponents of surrogacy argue that gestational surrogacy enhances individual freedom by enabling people to procreate who could not otherwise do so. They would allow women to freely agree to serve as gestational surrogates for payment. As long as the surrogate's decision is voluntary, proponents argue, we should hold her responsible for it to fulfill the expectations of the other parties. Critics of surrogacy argue that payment for the gestation and relinquishment of a child threatens the exploitation of poor women, who might engage in commercial surrogacy out of financial need, and the development of a "breeder" class. Some suggest that the surrogate may underestimate the psychological impact of relinquishing the child. Critics also argue that gestational surrogacy dehumanizes and commodifies women and children by treating reproduction capacity and children as products for trade, and that this commodification reinforces oppressive gender stereotypes and threatens the well-being of children. To resolve disputes such as the one in this case, surrogacy proponents propose pre-conception contracts in which the surrogate agrees to relinquish parental rights, and would make the bargained-for intentions of the parties determinative of legal parenthood. The intent of the parties would override legal presumptions of paternity and maternity. Critics consider the unique female role in reproduction as determinative, reasoning that although both men and women contribute genetic material to a child, only women can gestate the fetus. They would consider the woman who gives birth to a child to be its mother regardless of whether she is also genetically related to the child, and would apply adoption laws to determine her parental rights. Critics would therefore allow a gestational mother to wait until the birth of the child to decide whether to relinquish her parental rights. The majority offers four arguments to support its decision to rely upon the intent of the genetic mother as determinative, but none of them mandates its conclusion. First the majority relies upon "but-for" causation: the child would not have been born but for the efforts of the intended parents. However, application of the [tort law] "but-for" test is unprecedented and unjustified in this [family law] situation, [and in any case it can support either "mother"]. A second argument, taken from intellectual property, is that a mental concept of the child is a controlling factor in its creation, and therefore those who originate that concept merit full credit as conceivers. This argument fails here because children are not property. Rights in children cannot be sold or made freely available to the public. Third, the majority reasons that bargained-for expectations of the parties support its conclusion. Courts will not compel performance of all contractual obligations, however, and particularly not where specific performance would determine the course of a child's life. Children are not personal [commercial] property any more than they are intellectual property. Courts cannot order their delivery as a contract remedy. Finally, the majority reasons that preferring the intended mother serves the child's interests, which are unlikely to run contrary to the people who chose to bring the child into being. The problem here is that this inflexible rule will not serve the child's best interests in every case. Absent legislation addressing the problems of gestational surrogacy, courts should look to family law to resolve this type of dispute. In issues of child welfare, the standard courts use is the best interests of the child. I would use this standard to determine who can best assume the responsibilities of motherhood for a child born of a gestational surrogate. Relevant factors include the ability to nurture the child physically, psychologically, ethically and intellectually, as well as stability and continuity. The intent of the genetic mother to procreate is also relevant, but not dispositive.

Analysis:

This case further examines the legal and policy issues present in surrogacy arrangements, but this time in the context of gestational surrogacy. Unlike in the Matter of Baby M, where the court gave great weight to the fact that the surrogate was the biological mother of the child, here the surrogate was not the biological mother and the court denied her petition for parental rights. The court here distinguishes this case from Baby M by noting that the case of a gestational surrogate does not involve a woman parting with her own biological offspring. While significant, that is not the only difference between this case and Baby M. The New Jersey court found surrogacy contracts against public policy, but this California court found the opposite. While there was some indication of legislative acceptance of surrogacy contracts in California in a bill the legislature passed to regulate it, the governor, expressing reservations about surrogacy, vetoed the bill. The court therefore made its own policy choice, although not unanimously as the New Jersey court did in Baby M.

■ CASE VOCABULARY

CONSANGUINITY: Related by blood or common ancestry.

GESTATIONAL SURROGATE: A woman who carries and bears a child to whom she is not genetically related pursuant to a prior agreement to surrender the child to another couple, usually the genetic parents, to raise as their own.

Prato-Morrison v. Doe

(Claimed Parentage) v. *(Parents of Twins)*
103 Cal.App.4th 222, 126 Cal.Rptr.2d 509 (2002)

STANDING TO CLAIM PARENTAGE REQURIES A GENETIC LINK

How do I know that you're my wife's egg?

Keep asking questions. I'm sure one of the seventy million guys right behind you won't be so picky.

stus.com

■ **INSTANT FACTS** The Morrisons (P) believed that their genetic material was given to the Does (D), and the Morrisons (P) claimed they were the parents of the Does' (D) children.

■ **BLACK LETTER RULE** A person may not bring an action to establish parentage unless that person can produce evidence that he or she is the genetic parent of the child.

■ **PROCEDURAL BASIS**

Appeal from an order of the family law court dismissing the action.

■ **FACTS**

In 1988, Prato–Morrison (P) and her husband, Morrison (P) were patients at a fertility clinic. They provided their eggs and sperm to the clinic to be used to produce a child through *in vitro* fertilization. The attempts were unsuccessful, and the Morrisons (P) abandoned their efforts. They assumed that any remaining eggs or sperm would be destroyed.

Several years later, the fertility clinic learned that stealing had occurred. Eggs were taken from one patient and implanted in another patient, without the consent of the woman who produced the eggs. The Morrisons (P) and others sued the clinic, the University with which it was affiliated, and the doctors involved. The Morrisons (P) settled their case, after learning through discovery that their genetic material may not have been destroyed. The Morrisons (P) learned that Prato–Morrison's (P) eggs may have been implanted in Judith Doe (D). Doe (D) gave birth to twin daughters in December 1988, and the Morrisons (P) claimed that they were the genetic parents of the twins. The Morrisons (P) brought a suit for custody of the children, but then amended their complaint. The amended complaint did not ask for custody, but asked for blood tests to establish parentage and for visitation. The Morrisons (P) also requested the appointment of a mental health professional to help determine the degree of contact the Morrisons (D) should have with the twins.

The Does (D) alleged that Judith Doe (D) became pregnant by her husband, that they have two older children, and that Jacob Doe (D) was neither impotent nor sterile at the time the twins were conceived. The Does (D) further alleged that they received the twins into their home when they were born, that the twins were raised in their culture and religion, and that the Does (D) were the only parents the twins had ever known. The Does (D) claimed that the Morrisons' (P) suit caused great emotional stress in their family life. The Does (D) asked the court to seal the records of the case, issue protective orders to prevent disclosure of the litigation to the children, and issue an order quashing the petition on the grounds that the Does (D) were the presumed natural parents of the twins and the Morrisons (P) lacked standing to pursue the petition.

The family court sustained the Does' (D) objections and found that the Morrisons (P) lacked standing to pursue their claim. The court continued the matter to allow the Morrisons (P) to present additional evidence. The Morrisons (P) submitted a copy of a handwritten list and a declaration from Ord, a former employee of the fertility clinic. The declaration stated that Ord participated in the transfer of genetic materials from patients, and that both Prato–Morrison (P) and Doe (D) were patients at the clinic. Ord's declaration stated that she prepared the handwritten list to show that Doe (D) received eggs from Prato–Morrison (P). The Morrisons (P) also submitted evidence that the original patient and laboratory records were unavailable, since the FBI confiscated them in 1995. The court sustained the Does' (D) objections to this evidence on the grounds that it was hearsay and that it violated the physician-patient privilege and the Does' (D) right to reproductive privacy. The trial court dismissed the Morrisons' (P) action.

■ ISSUE

Did the Morrisons (P) have standing to claim they were the parents of the Doe twins after they learned of the thefts and mix-ups at the fertility clinic?

■ DECISION AND RATIONALE

(Vogel, J.) No. A person may not bring an action to establish parentage unless that person can produce evidence that he or she is the genetic parent of the child. The question for the court is whether the declaration of the former employee and the handwritten list were properly excluded. If the exclusion was proper, there is no evidence to suggest that either of the Morrisons (P) is related to the twins.

The handwritten list was compiled from other records that are not identified. Ord did not attempt to establish her personal knowledge of the information on the list. The list was not made at or near the time of the events, but was made almost eight years later. There is no reason given as to why the list was made. The preparation of the list shows a lack of trustworthiness, so the list cannot come within the business record exception to the hearsay rule.

The Morrisons (P) claim that the unavailability of the original records is sufficient to make Ord's evidence admissible. Evidence offered to show the contents of a missing document must be "otherwise admissible," and the list and Ord's statements are inadmissible hearsay.

The Morrisons (P) claim they should be allowed to "discover" whether the twins were born as a result of the theft of their genetic material, and that their rights as alleged genetic parents should trump the right of the Does (P) as the presumed parents. The Morrisons' (P) rights were vindicated when they settled their claim for theft of their genetic materials. The rights at issue are the rights of the Does (D) and the twins to be free of the claims of the Morrisons (P). The trial court found that dismissal of the action is in the best interests of the children. Even if the Morrisons (P) had presented evidence to establish a genetic link, it would not be in the best interests of the twins to have the Morrisons (P) intrude into their lives and disrupt their family relationship. The social relationship established by the Does (D) and the twins is more important than a genetic relationship with a stranger. Affirmed.

Analysis:

The court's decision technically just affirms a decision that the Morrisons (P) did not have standing to pursue their action. Ordinarily, a court will not make a detailed factual analysis to determine if a party has standing, but will focus on the claims of the party whose standing is challenged. Here, the Morrisons (P) are asked to introduce evidence to bolster their allegations in order to establish their standing. The court strongly implies that there is no way for the Morrisons (P) to establish parentage now, and so it is doubtful whether any evidence would suffice.

■ CASE VOCABULARY

BUSINESS–RECORDS EXCEPTION: A hearsay exception allowing business records (such as reports or memoranda) to be admitted into evidence if they were prepared in the ordinary course of business. Fed R. Evid. 803(6).

In re A.C.

(Dying Pregnant Woman)

573 A.2d 1235 (D.C. Ct. App. 1990)

COURT FINDS THAT BALANCING FETAL AND MATERNAL INTERESTS ALMOST NEVER JUSTIFIES COERCIVE MEDICAL TREATMENT ON A PREGNANT WOMAN

■ **INSTANT FACTS** Finding a dying pregnant woman incompetent and her fetus in danger, a trial court ordered the hospital to perform a caesarean to attempt to save the fetus.

■ **BLACK LETTER RULE** A court must make a substituted judgment to decide the course of medical treatment for an incompetent pregnant patient even when her interests may conflict with those of her fetus.

■ **PROCEDURAL BASIS**

Appeal of trial court order declaring a pregnant patient incompetent and ordering medical treatment on behalf of her fetus.

■ **FACTS**

A.C. was diagnosed with cancer at age thirteen. She underwent several surgeries, radiation treatments and chemotherapy. When she was twenty-seven, during a period of remission, A.C. married and soon became pregnant. A.C. very much wanted her child. Because of her medical history, in her fifteenth week she began to attend a high risk pregnancy clinic at George Washington University Hospital (Hospital). At twenty-five weeks A.C. went to the Hospital for a checkup and learned that she had an inoperable tumor which nearly filled her right lung. The Hospital admitted A.C. as a patient. Her condition improved temporarily, but then worsened considerably. The doctors informed A.C. that her illness was terminal, and she agreed to palliative treatment that would extend her life until her twenty-eighth week, when the potential outcome for her fetus would be better if it became necessary to "intervene." A.C. knew the treatment she chose presented some risk to the fetus, but she opted for this course to prolong her life and to maintain her comfort. When asked if she still wanted the baby, A.C. was equivocal, saying she didn't know, but she thought so. The Hospital petitioned the emergency judge for declaratory relief as to how it should treat A.C., then in her twenty-sixth week, and the court held a three-hour hearing at the Hospital. The court appointed counsel for A.C. and the fetus, and the District of Columbia intervened for the fetus as *parens patriae.* There was no evidence that A.C. consented to or even contemplated having a caesarean before her twenty-eighth week, and there was considerable dispute as to whether she would have consented to a caesarean at the time of the hearing. A.C.'s mother opposed surgery, testifying that A.C. wanted to and expected to live long enough to hold the baby. Her physician testified that given her medical problems, he did not think she would have chosen to deliver a substantially impaired child. The court found that A.C. would probably die within the next twenty-four to forty-eight hours, and that she was pregnant with a twenty-six and a half week viable fetus. The court further found that there was some testimony that a caesarean might hasten A.C.'s death, but that the fetus had a fifty to sixty percent chance of survival if a caesarean were performed immediately, and delay would greatly increase the risk to the fetus. The court found that because it was viable, the state had an important and legitimate interest in protecting the life of the fetus. Finally, the court found that it did not clearly know what A.C.'s views were with respect to whether the child should live or die, and that she was presently unconscious. A few days earlier she wanted the baby to live, but the day before she wasn't sure. After making these findings, the court ordered a caesarean section to deliver A.C.'s fetus. A.C. then regained consciousness, learned of the court's decision, and consented to the caesarean. The court reconvened and suggested moving the hearing to A.C.'s bedside. The doctors discouraged this, but went to A.C., with her mother and husband, to confirm her consent. When they returned, they told the court that A.C. asked whether she would survive the operation and whether her doctor would perform it. He told her he would not perform it unless she consented, but that it would be done in any case. She understood that, and then, after a pause, mouthed several times, "I don't want it done. I don't want it done." A.C. was under considerable stress and in intensive care, but the doctors thought she was understanding and capable of making decisions, and that she did not consent. The court found that it was still not clear what her intent was, and again ordered the caesarean. Physicians performed the caesarean and delivered a baby girl. The baby died within two and one-half hours. A.C. died two days later.

■ ISSUE

Must a court make a substituted judgment to decide the course of medical treatment for an incompetent patient when the patient is pregnant and her interests may conflict with those of her fetus?

■ DECISION AND RATIONALE

(Terry, J.) Yes. Any person has the right to make an informed choice, if competent to do so, to accept or forgo medical treatment. A court will not compel a person to permit a significant intrusion upon his or her bodily integrity for the benefit of another. The common law has consistently held that one human being is under no legal compulsion to aid or take action to save another human being. Further, rather than protecting the health of women and children, court-ordered caesareans erode the trust that permits a pregnant woman to communicate to her physician all information relevant to her proper diagnosis and treatment. Even more serious, court-ordered intervention drives women with high-risk pregnancies out of the health care system to avoid coerced treatment. Judicial proceedings in cases such as this ordinarily take place under pressing time constraints that make it difficult or impossible for the mother to communicate adequately with counsel, or for counsel to organize an effective defense of the mother's liberty, privacy, and bodily integrity. However, sometimes a once competent patient will be unable to render an informed decision. In such cases, we hold that courts must make substituted judgments on behalf of the patient based on all the evidence. The duty of the court, as surrogate for the incompetent, is to determine what that individual, if competent, would choose with respect to medical procedures. Despite the lack of precedent involving an incompetent pregnant patient whose life may be shortened by a caesarean but whose unborn child's survival may depend on one, we conclude that substituted judgment is the best procedure to follow here because it most clearly respects the right of the patient to bodily integrity. The court should give the greatest weight to the patient's previously expressed wishes. It is also important to probe the patient's value system to help the court discern what the patient would choose. The trial court here did not make a finding as to what A.C. would have chosen if she were competent. Instead, the court balanced the state's and the fetus's interests in having the caesarean with A.C.'s interest in not having it. In cases such as this the court must determine whether the patient is capable of making an informed decision about her medical treatment. If she is, her wishes control in virtually all cases. If she is not, then the court must make a substituted judgment. We need not decide whether the state's interests can ever prevail over the interests of a pregnant patient. Vacated.

■ CONCURRENCE AND DISSENT

(Belson, J.) The state's interest in preserving human life and the viable unborn child's interest in survival are entitled to more weight than the majority assigns them when it states that in virtually all cases the patient's decision will control. I would hold that in cases in which a viable unborn child's interest in living and the state's interest in protecting human life conflict with a mother's decision to forgo a procedure such as a caesarean, the court should balance the interests and should give the unborn child's and the state's interest substantial weight. This balancing test should apply when a woman's unborn child reaches viability. Such a woman's circumstances differ fundamentally from other potential patients who might undergo procedures to aid another person. The woman has undertaken to bear another human being, and the unborn child is singularly dependent upon the mother. Unlike a person called upon to donate an organ for transplant, an expectant mother has placed herself in a special class of persons who are bringing another person into existence, upon whom that other person's life is totally dependent, and within whose body the other person is literally captive. No other potential beneficiary of a surgical procedure on another is in that position. When exercising substituted judgment, in the rare case in which the court concludes that the patient would probably opt not to have the caesarean section, the court should assign a weight to this factor in proportion to the confidence it has in the accuracy of its conclusion. When the indicia of an incompetent patient's judgment are equivocal, the court should assign this factor less weight. Other considerations may also merit special attention, such as a danger to the mother's life or health and the mother's religious beliefs with respect to the operation. It is also appropriate to consider the likelihood of the unborn child's survival and the child's interest in being born with as little impairment as possible. The most important factor on this side, however, is life itself, because the viable unborn child that dies because its mother refuses a caesarean loses, entirely and irrevocably, the life on which it was about to embark.

Analysis:

This case, involving a woman named Angela Carder, focused national attention on the question of whether courts should determine medical treatment for pregnant patients. When her parents pursued this case after her death, the American Medical Association (AMA), the American College of Obstetricians and Gynecologists (ACOG), and more than 120 other medical groups, women's groups, religious and civil rights groups, and bioethicists joined their condemnation of coercive medical treatment by filing amicus briefs supporting her case. Because of this participation and the extensive legal briefing that resulted, this case is a leading opinion on compelled medical treatment during pregnancy that has influenced courts nationwide. At the hearing at the hospital, the court focused on the balance of Angela's interests against those of her fetus, but gave very little attention to what was clinically best for Angela or what she would want. Her family opposed the caesarean because her doctors did not expect her to be able to survive it, and they all agreed Angela would oppose it. Her treating physicians also opposed it based on their understanding of Angela's wishes and on the clinical status of both Angela and her fetus. A neonatologist with little familiarity with Angela's medical case testified that the fetus had only a slightly lower than normal chance of survival for a fetus at that age. However, both Angela and her fetus had already suffered from oxygen deprivation, and other medical experts later concluded that there was virtually no chance of survival because the fetus was already brain dead. Carder's attorney tried to get the Court of Appeals to block the order even as she was on her way into surgery. A three-judge panel of the court refused to do so and later upheld the trial court's order. When Angela died shortly after the surgery, her death certificate listed the caesarean as a contributing cause of death. Later, in *In re A.C.*, the entire D.C. Court of Appeals vacated the order. The Supreme Court has long held that an individual has a constitutionally protected liberty interest in refusing unwanted medical treatment. In this case the court found that only in a truly exceptional case, if any, could a state interest be so compelling as to justify overriding the pregnant woman's interests, and that this was not such a case even though it involved a dying woman and a viable fetus.

■ CASE VOCABULARY

IN EXTREMIS: Near death.

PALLIATIVE TREATMENT: Treatment to alleviate the effects of a disease, though without curing it.

PARENS PATRIAE: Literally "father of his country," the doctrine by which the state acts as the protector of all citizens unable to protect themselves.

SUBSTITUTED JUDGMENT: A decision about medical treatment that one person makes on behalf of, and in accordance with the wishes of, another who is incompetent to decide for herself.

State v. Wade

(Government) v. *(Mother)*

232 S.W.3d 663 (Mo. Ct. App. 2007)

MISSOURI'S CHILD ENDANGERMENT STATUTE DOES NOT PROTECT UNBORN CHILDREN

Child endangerment for drug use while pregnant? But, your honor, my reproductive strategy is quantity, not quality.

stus.com

■ **INSTANT FACTS** One day after giving birth, Wade (D) was charged with child endangerment when both she and her son tested positive for marijuana and methamphetamine.

■ **BLACK LETTER RULE** In the absence of specific legislative direction, illegal drug use by a pregnant mother does not constitute child endangerment.

■ **PROCEDURAL BASIS**

On appeal to review a trial court order dismissing criminal charges against the defendant.

■ **FACTS**

One day after giving birth, Wade (D) and her newborn son tested positive for marijuana and methamphetamine. Wade (D) was charged with first-degree child endangerment for causing a substantial risk to her child's health by using illegal drugs during her pregnancy. The circuit court dismissed the charge after determining that the state's child endangerment statute could not be applied to conduct directed toward an unborn child.

■ **ISSUE**

Does the state's child endangerment statute protect unborn children from otherwise criminal conduct?

■ **DECISION AND RATIONALE**

(Hardwick, J.) No. The Missouri child endangerment statute provides that a person commits a felony by "knowingly act[ing] in a manner that creates a substantial risk to the life, body, or health of a child less than seventeen years old." The State (P) contends that this language necessarily protects Wade's (D) unborn child since he is less than seventeen years old. While the statute does not define the term "child," the term is defined in the state criminal nonsupport statute as "any biological or adoptive child, or any child whose relationship to the defendant has been determined, by a court of law in a proceeding for dissolution or legal separation, to be that of child to parent." This definition appears to exclude unborn children and the plain language of the endangerment statute suggests a similar construction.

It is true that Missouri law generally supports protection of the rights of unborn children, but these protections have principally been from harm caused by third parties, such as in murder convictions and wrongful death actions. The law does not protect against any harm caused by a mother to her unborn child. It would be difficult to determine what types of prenatal conduct would give rise to criminal charges. For instance, a mother could be criminally charged for smoking, failing to wear a seatbelt, imbibing alcohol, or any other conduct that may harm her unborn child. Here, Wade (D) properly faces criminal charges for illegal drug use. But the legislature has enacted a series of statutes that call for prenatal education and treatment for mothers suffering from addiction, not criminal responsibility. Any criminal charges for endangerment would serve only to protect the unborn child and deviate from legislative intent. Whether illegal drug use by a pregnant mother is to constitute child endangerment must be established by the legislature.

Analysis:

It is difficult to see how criminal charges for child endangerment to a mother's own unborn child could pass constitutional muster. As the court suggests, if actions such as smoking, drinking, and failing to wear a seat belt could lead to criminal charges, abortion would certainly fall within the category of conduct constituting child endangerment. Under the current state of the law, a legislature's ability to protect a fetus from child endangerment appears limited.

■ CASE VOCABULARY

ENDANGERMENT: The act or an instance of putting someone or something in danger; exposure to peril or harm.

Wixtrom v. Dept. of Children and Family Services (In re J.D.S.)

(Incapacitated Woman)
864 So.2d 534 (Fla. Dist. Ct. App. 2004)

AN UNBORN CHILD IS NOT A PERSON

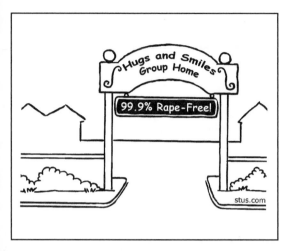

■ INSTANT FACTS J.D.S., an incapacitated woman, was pregnant, and a petition was filed to name a guardian of her fetus.

■ BLACK LETTER RULE An unborn child is not a "person" within the meaning of the statutes authorizing the appointment of a guardian over a person.

■ PROCEDURAL BASIS

Appeal from an order denying a petition to be appointed guardian.

■ FACTS

J.D.S. was a twenty-two year old incapacitated woman who suffered from severe mental retardation, cerebral palsy, autism, and seizure disorder. She was nonverbal, unable to make decisions, and did not understand her own limitations. She could not take care of herself. J.D.S. became pregnant after a sexual battery, and she was taking numerous medications that could have been detrimental to the fetus. The Department of Children and Family Services (P) filed a petition authorizing temporary emergency protective services for J.D.S., and then filed an amended petition, seeking a guardian for J.D.S. and a separate guardian for her fetus. The Department (P) claimed that J.D.S.'s interests and needs were potentially adverse to the interests and needs of the fetus, and that a conflict of interest was likely because J.D.S.'s medications could be harmful to the fetus.

Wixtrom (P) filed a petition to be named the guardian of the fetus. She claimed that the appointment was necessary because J.D.S. could not provide proper prenatal care and make necessary decisions. The trial court denied the petition and held that it was error to appoint a guardian for a fetus.

■ ISSUE

May a guardian be appointed for an unborn child?

■ DECISION AND RATIONALE

(Thompson, J.) No. An unborn child is not a "person" within the meaning of the statutes authorizing the appointment of a guardian over a person. The statutes do not define "fetus," and no section of the law entitles a fetus or unborn child to a guardian. The legislature has, in other contexts, expressly provided for the protection of fetuses. If the legislature had intended that fetuses should receive the protections of the guardianship statutes, it would have done so.

A "guardian" is defined as a person appointed to act on behalf of a ward's person, property, or both. A "ward" is a person for whom a guardian has been appointed. A fetus must be determined to be a "person" before a guardian may be appointed. No statute or case law contains such a definition. In fact, courts have repeatedly declined to include a fetus within the definition of "person."

Wixtrom (P) has alleged that she is concerned that J.D.S.'s guardian could have authorized an abortion. Florida law provides safeguards to insure that a guardian does not act cavalierly or capriciously. Affirmed.

■ CONCURRENCE

(Orfinger, J.) Florida has adhered to the common-law rule that the unborn have no rights unless and until a live birth occurs. The state has an interest in the potentiality of human life, but if the Legislature intends to depart from the traditional meanings of "person" and "human being," it must do so expressly.

The legislature is the proper forum in which to debate the proper balance between the state's interest in protecting the unborn and the mother's constitutional right to privacy.

■ DISSENT

(Pleus, J.) Under the statute, the court has the power to appoint a plenary guardian, as opposed to a guardian *ad litem*, for an unborn child. Appointment of a guardian is not an undue burden and is necessary to ensure that the state's compelling interest in the health, welfare, and life of an unborn child is protected. The U.S. Supreme Court has ruled that a state's legitimate interest in protecting fetal health becomes a compelling interest when the unborn child becomes viable.

The appointment of a guardian for an unborn child in the third trimester is consistent with both *Roe v. Wade,* 410 U.S. 113 (1973) and *Planned Parenthood of Southeastern Pennsylvania v. Casey,* 505 U.S. 833 (1992). The appointment of a guardian advances the state's interest in the life of the unborn child by insuring compliance with all statutory requirements and by appointing an advocate for the state's interest in preserving the life of the unborn child. In this case, the only interests at stake are the state's interest in preserving the life of the unborn child and the guardian's interest in determining whether preserving the life or health of the mother requires terminating the pregnancy. Absent clear and convincing evidence that the mother's health is at risk, the balance tips in favor of preserving the life of the unborn child.

The legislature should overturn the majority's decision. Terms such as "embryo" and "fetus" are meaningless in this context and only serve to cloud the issue. The better view would be for the legislature to adopt a bright-line rule that life begins at conception.

Analysis:

At the oral argument on this case, Judge Orfinger is reported to have asked why the concern for the life of the fetus did not extend to cases in which the mother is healthy. The attorney who argued the case for the state supporting appointment of a guardian acknowledged that it would be difficult to find a "narrow, yet encompassing solution." Note that the alleged father of J.D.S.'s child was the seventy-five year old husband of the owner of the group home in which J.D.S. lived. He was arrested, but charges were dropped when he was found incompetent to stand trial.

■ CASE VOCABULARY

GUARDIAN AD LITEM: A guardian, usually a lawyer, appointed by the court to appear in a lawsuit in behalf of an incompetent or minor party.

PLENARY: Full; complete; entire, as in "plenary authority"; (of an assembly) intended to have the attendance of all members or participants, as in "plenary session."

VIABLE: Capable of living, especially outside the womb, as in "a viable fetus."

CHAPTER SEVENTEEN

Legal, Social and Ethical Issues in Human Genetics

Safer v. Pack

Instant Facts: A physician is sued for failing to warn the family members of a patient who were known to be at risk of a genetic disease, after the daughter of the patient developed the same condition, which may have been prevented upon early diagnosis and treatment.

Black Letter Rule: Physicians have a duty to warn those known to be at risk of avoidable harm from a genetically transmissible condition.

Greenberg v. Miami Children's Hospital Research Institute

Instant Facts: Greenberg (P) donated genetic material for research done by Matalon (D) and claimed unjust enrichment when Matalon (D) obtained a patent on the results of his research.

Black Letter Rule: A donor has no property rights in body tissue and genetic matter donated for purposes of research.

Safer v. Pack

(Patient's Daughter) v. *(Doctor)*

291 N.J.Super. 619, 677 A.2d 1188 (App. Div. 1996)

PHYSICIANS MUST TAKE REASONABLE STEPS TO WARN THOSE LIKELY TO BE AFFECTED BY A HEREDITARY CONDITION

■ **INSTANT FACTS** A physician is sued for failing to warn the family members of a patient who were known to be at risk of a genetic disease, after the daughter of the patient developed the same condition, which may have been prevented upon early diagnosis and treatment.

■ **BLACK LETTER RULE** Physicians have a duty to warn those known to be at risk of avoidable harm from a genetically transmissible condition.

■ **PROCEDURAL BASIS**

Appeal to the Superior Court of New Jersey, Appellate Division, of the trial court's dismissal of the complaint.

■ **FACTS**

In November 1956, Robert Batkin (Batkin), father of Donna Safer (Safer) (P), was admitted to the hospital with a preoperative diagnosis of retroperitoneal cancer, Dr. George T. Pack (Dr. Pack) (D) performed a total colectomy and an ileosigmoidectomy for multiple polyposis of the colon with malignant degeneration in one area. The discharge summary noted the finding in a pathology report of the existence of adenocarcinoma developing in an intestinal polyp, and diffuse intestinal polyposis from one end of the colon to the other. Dr. Pack (D) continued to treat Batkin postoperatively. In October 1961, Batkin was again hospitalized and Dr. Pack (D) performed an ileoabdominal perineal resection with an ileostomy. The discharge summary reported pathology findings of ulcerative adenocarcinoma of colon and adenomatous polyps. In December 1963, Batkin was once again hospitalized, and it was found that the carcinoma of the colon had metastasized to the liver with secondary jaundice and probable retroperitoneal disease causing pressure on the sciatic nerve plexus. After some treatment, Batkin died on January 3, 1964, when Safer (P) was ten years old. In February 1990, Safer (P), then thirty-six, began to experience lower abdominal pain, and was diagnosed with a cancerous blockage of the colon and multiple polyposis. In March, Safer (P) underwent a total abdominal colectomy with ileorectal anastomosis. A primary carcinoma in the sigmoid colon was found to extend through the serosa of the bowel and multiple polyps were seen throughout the entire bowel. As a result of the detection of additional metastatic adenocarcinoma and carcinoma, Safer's (P) left ovary was also removed, and Safer (P) underwent chemotherapy treatment. In September 1991, Safer (P) obtained Batkin's medical records and discovered that he had suffered from polyposis. In March 1992, Safer (P) filed a complaint alleging a violation of duty on the part of Dr. Pack (D) in his failure to warn Safer (P) of the risk to her health, and asrguing that multiple polyposis is a hereditary condition that, if undiscovered and untreated, invariably leads to metastatic colorectal cancer. Safer (P) further contended that the hereditary nature of the disease was known at the time Dr. Pack (D) was treating Batkin and that the physician was required, by medical standards then prevailing, to warn those at risk so that they might have the benefits of early examination, monitoring, detection and treatment. In a deposition, Ida Batkin (Ida), Safer's (P) mother, testified that neither Batkin nor Dr. Pack (D) had ever told her that Batkin suffered from cancer, and that when Ida had inquired of Dr.Pack (D) as to whether the infection would affect her children, she was told not to worry. The trial court dismissed the claim holding that a physician had no legal duty to warn a child of a patient of a genetic risk. In the absence of any evidence whether Dr. Pack (D) had warned Batkin to provide information concerning his disease for the benefit of his children, the motion judge assumed that Dr. Pack (D) did not tell Batkin of the genetic disease. Safer (P) appeals.

■ ISSUE

Does a physician have the duty to warn those known to be at risk of a hereditary condition?

■ DECISION AND RATIONALE

(Kestin, J.A.D.) Yes. Physicians have a duty to warn those known to be at risk of avoidable harm from a genetically transmissible condition. The motion judge assumed that in order for a doctor to have a duty to warn, there must be a patient/physician relationship or circumstances requiring the protection of the public health or the community at large. Finding that there was no physician-patient relationship between Safer (P) and Dr. Pack (D), the court held genetically transmissible diseases to differ from contagious or infectious diseases, or threats of harm in respect of the duty to warn, since the harm is already present within the non-patient child, rather than being introduced by a patient who was not warned to stay away. In *Pate v. Threlkel*, The Florida Supreme Court, while hearing a case that had initially been decided on a motion to dismiss the complaint for failure to state a claim, accepted as true that pursuant to the prevailing standard of care, the health care providers were under a duty to warn the patient of the importance of testing her children for the genetically transmissible carcinoma. The court then held that because in most instances the physician is prohibited from disclosing the patient's medical condition to others without consent, that the patient ordinarily can be expected to pass on the warning, and because to require the physician to seek out and warn various members of the patient's family would be often difficult and overly burdensome, the physicians duty to warn of genetically transferable diseases will be satisfied by warning the patient. Since the issue before us arose on a motion for summary judgment, we too must accept Safer's (P) proffer through their medical expert, that the prevailing standard of care at the time Dr. Pack (D) treated Batkin, required the physician to warn of the known genetic threat. Whether Dr. Pack's (D) conduct comported with the prevailing standards of care, is a question for the finder of fact and not amenable to resolution on summary judgment. Whether a legal duty exists, however, is a matter of law. We see no impediment to recognizing a physician's duty to warn those known to be at risk of avoidable harm from a genetically transmissible condition. As in cases where there exist the menace of infection or a threat of physical harm, the individuals at risk are easily identifiable, and substantial future harm may be averted or minimized by a timely and effective warning. The trial court gave too little significance to the proffered expert view that early monitoring of those at risk can effectively avert some of the more serious consequences a person with multiple polyposis might otherwise experience. We cannot conclude that Dr. Pack (D) breached no duty because avoidable harm to Donna was foreseeable, since such a determination would ignore the presumed state of medical knowledge at the time. While an overly broad and general application of the physician's duty to warn might lead to confusion, conflict or unfairness in many types of circumstances, we are confident that the duty to warn of avertible risk from genetic causes, by definition a matter of familial concern, is sufficiently narrow to serve the interest of justice. We need not presently decide how that duty is to be discharged, especially with respect to young children who may be at risk, except to require reasonable steps be taken to assure that the information reaches those likely to be affected or is made available for their benefit. Although we are aware of no direct evidence that has been developed concerning the nature of the communications between physician and patient regarding Batkin's disease, there may be enough from Mrs. Batkin's testimony and other evidence for inferences to be drawn. It may be necessary, at some stage, to resolve a conflict between the physician's broader duty to warn and his fidelity to an expressed preference of the patient that nothing be said to family members about the details of the disease. Although we cannot know presently whether there is any likelihood that such a conflict may be shown to have existed in this matter, it is possible that such conflict will be shown to have existed and that the only evidence on the issue will be Mrs. Batkin's testimony. We note, in addition, the possible existence of some offsetting evidence that Donna was rectally examined as a young child, suggesting that the risk to her had been disclosed. This case implicates serious and conflicting medical, social, and legal policies, and leaves issues of fact to be resolved. While we are led to understand from the experts' reports that the risk of multiple polyposis was significant, and that upon detection, an early full colectomy may well have been the treatment of choice to avoid resultant cancer, full factual development may cast a different light on these issues of fact and others. Because of the necessarily limited scope of our consideration, we have highlighted only a few of the potentially troublesome issues presented by this case. Such questions are best conceived and considered in the light of a fully developed record rather than in the abstract. Reversed.

Analysis:

This case serves as an introduction to the legal, social, and ethical issues surrounding the area of human genetics. An individual's genetic information is the unique property of that individual, and may not be disclosed to unauthorized third parties without express, willing, and written consent. The instant case leaves open the possibility that a doctor may be found liable when he or she fails to warn those in danger of a hereditary or genetic condition. On the one hand, genetic information may not always be a "unique" concern of the patient, especially when hereditary conditions threaten the well being of others in a patient's family. Here, it may seem just to require a doctor to warn more than just the patient, especially when it would not prove too burdensome. On the other hand, there are many reasons why a doctor's duty should not extend beyond warning his or her patient, and why a patient may also have valid reasons for not disclosing genetic information to outside parties, one of the most important being possible discrimination based on genetic conditions.

■ CASE VOCABULARY

ADENOCARCINOMA: Malignant tumor cells occurring in glandular tissue.

COLECTOMY: Excision of part of the large intestine or colon.

ILEOABDOMINAL PERINEAL: Pertaining to the area between the scrotum and anus in a male.

ILEOSIGMOIDECTOMY: The removal of all or part of the small intestine and colon.

POLYPOSIS: Formation of multiple polyps.

RETROPERITONEAL CANCER: Cancer located behind the membrane which lines the entire internal surface of the abdominal cavity and envelops the viscera [interior organs—especially the abdomen and throat].

Greenberg v. Miami Children's Hospital Research Institute

(Genetic Information Donor) v. *(Patent Holder)*

264 F.Supp.2d 1064 (S.D. Fla. 2003)

DONORS HAVE NO PROPERTY RIGHTS IN DONATED GENETIC MATERIAL

I've isolated the Canavan gene from tissue donated by afflicted people.

Great! I'll file the patent application and put together a business plan to screw the terminally ill.

stus.com

■ **INSTANT FACTS** Greenberg (P) donated genetic material for research done by Matalon (D) and claimed unjust enrichment when Matalon (D) obtained a patent on the results of his research.

■ **BLACK LETTER RULE** A donor has no property rights in body tissue and genetic matter donated for purposes of research.

■ **PROCEDURAL BASIS**

Decision on a motion to dismiss for failure to state a claim.

■ **FACTS**

Greenberg (P) asked Matalon (D), a research physician, for assistance in discovering the genes responsible for Canavan disease, a fatal, inherited brain disease. Greenberg (P) and the local chapter of the National Tay–Sachs and Allied Disease Association, Inc. located Canavan families and convinced them to provide tissue samples, financial support, and help finding other Canavan families internationally. Greenberg (P) and the Tay–Sachs Association also created a database with medical and other information about the Canavan families. Greenberg (P) and the other plaintiffs alleged that they provided Matalon (D) with the samples and confidential information with the understanding and expectation that it would be used for research that could lead to detection of Canavan carriers. Greenberg (P) and the other plaintiffs also alleged that it was their understanding that any testing developed would be made available on an affordable basis, and that Matalon's (D) research would remain in the public domain. This understanding stemmed from their experience in community testing for Tay–Sachs disease.

Matalon (D) became associated with Miami Children's Hospital (D) in 1990. Matalon (D) continued to accept tissue donations, as well as financial support. In 1993, Matalon (D), using the samples and information provided by Greenberg (P) and the other plaintiffs, was able to isolate the gene responsible for Canavan disease. In 1997, Matalon (D) and Miami Children's Hospital (D) received a patent on the genetic sequence that was identified. Miami Children's (D) announced that it would limit Canavan disease testing through restrictive licensing of the patent. Miami Children's (D) also restricted public accessibility through exclusive licensing agreements and royalty fees.

Greenberg (P) and the other plaintiffs alleged that they did not know that Matalon (D) or Miami Children's (D) intended to seek a patent or to commercialize the research.

■ **ISSUE**

Did Matalon (D) and Miami Children's (D) unlawfully convert the samples and information from Greenberg (P) and the other plaintiffs?

■ **DECISION AND RATIONALE**

(Moreno, J.) No. A donor has no property rights in body tissue and genetic matter donated for purposes of research. The use of the results of medical research inconsistent with the wishes of the donor of bodily material is not conversion, because the donor has no property interest at stake after the donation. The patented result of research is factually and legally distinct from the material used in the research. Cases cited by Greenberg (P) and the other plaintiffs do not involve voluntary donations to medical research.

The Florida statute on genetic testing, Fla. Stat. § 760.40, does not apply to the question of conversion. That statute provides for penalties for disclosure or lack of informed consent if a person is subject to genetic testing. The statute does not create a property right in genetic material donated for medical research. Even assuming that it did, it is not clear whether that right would confer a property right for a common-law conversion action.

Greenberg (P) and the other plaintiffs do not claim that the donated material was used for any purpose other than research. The claim is that the fruits of the research were commercialized. This is a distinction and a step in the chain of attenuation that renders conversion liability inapplicable. The theory used by Greenberg (P) would cripple medical research, as donors would have a right to possess the results of any research.

Greenberg (P) and the other plaintiffs have, however, alleged sufficient facts for a claim of unjust enrichment. The complaint alleges a picture of a continuing research collaboration that goes beyond a donor-donee relationship. Miami Children's (D) acknowledges that Greenberg (P) and the other plaintiffs have conferred a benefit by supplying samples and providing financial support. The detriment is the use of the benefit for unauthorized purposes. Greenberg (P) and the other plaintiffs would not have provided the benefits under the same terms if they had known that Miami Children's (D) intended to commercialize their genetic material. Miami Children's (D) claims that it invested substantial sums in the research with no guarantee of success, but the same may be said of the plaintiffs. The patent on the gene sequence does not defeat an unjust enrichment claim. Complaint dismissed, except for the unjust enrichment claim.

Analysis:

The unjust enrichment claim is based on an allegation that, if Greenberg (P) or the other plaintiffs had known the truth about the plans to commercialize the research, they would not have given the genetic material. The court does not say that Miami Children's (D) or Matalon (D) misled anyone about their intentions. It was just assumed, based on earlier experiences researching another disease, that the results of the research would not be commercialized. Note that claims for breach of fiduciary duty and fraudulent concealment were alleged in the complaint, too, but were dismissed by the court for failure to state a claim.

■ CASE VOCABULARY

UNJUST ENRICHMENT: The retention of a benefit conferred by another, without offering compensation, in circumstances where compensation is reasonably expected; a benefit obtained from another, not intended as a gift and not legally justifiable, for which the beneficiary must make restitution or recompense; the area of the law dealing with unjustifiable benefits of this kind.

CHAPTER EIGHTEEN

Defining Death

In Re T.A.C.P.

Instant Facts: The parents of T.A.C.P. (P), an anencephalic baby with a functioning brain stem, wished to have T.A.C.P. (P) declared dead in order to donate her organs for transplant, but her health care providers refused.

Black Letter Rule: Anencephaly does not equate with death for organ donation purposes.

In the Matter of Baby "K"

Instant Facts: When the mother of an anencephalic baby insisted that the Hospital (P) give the baby respiratory support when needed, the Hospital (P) sought judicial permission to refuse to provide this treatment.

Black Letter Rule: The Emergency Medical Treatment and Active Labor Act (EMTALA) prohibits physicians from "allowing" anencephalic babies to die by refusing to provide them requested stabilizing treatment for an emergency condition.

In re T.A.C.P.

(Anencephalic Baby)

609 So.2d 588 (Fla. 1992)

COURT REFUSES TO CREATE A NEW DEFINITION OF DEATH FOR ANENCEPHALIC BABIES

■ **INSTANT FACTS** The parents of T.A.C.P. (P), an anencephalic baby with a functioning brain stem, wished to have T.A.C.P. (P) declared dead in order to donate her organs for transplant, but her health care providers refused.

■ **BLACK LETTER RULE** Anencephaly does not equate with death for organ donation purposes.

■ **PROCEDURAL BASIS**

Review granted after certification by appellate court of order denying parents' petition for declaration of their daughter's death and permission to donate her organs.

■ **FACTS**

T.A.C.P. (P) was born with anencephaly and survived only a few days. Anencephaly is a severe birth defect which involves the absence of major portions of the brain, skull and scalp. It is always lethal. T.A.C.P. (P) was incapable of developing any cognitive process and needed a respirator to assist her breathing part of the time. All anencephalic babies are permanently unconscious because they lack a cerebral cortex, but if they have a functioning brain stem, as T.A.C.P. (P) did, they may have spontaneous breathing, heartbeat, reflexes, and even some facial expressions. Anencephalic babies have been used as organ donors. However, by the time their whole brain stem ceases to function and they meet the criteria for "whole brain death," they are usually no longer suitable as organ donors. T.A.C.P.'s (P) parents agreed to undergo a caesarean with the hope of donating her organs for transplant in other children. However, when T.A.C.P.'s (P) parents requested a declaration of death for this purpose, T.A.C.P.'s (P) health care providers refused for fear of civil or criminal liability.

■ **ISSUE**

Does an anencephalic baby's deformity render it "dead" for organ donation purposes?

■ **DECISION AND RATIONALE**

(Kogan, J.) No. Florida common law applies the cardiopulmonary definition of death. Florida has not adopted a comprehensive statutory definition of death, but does permit the use of the "irreversible cessation of the functioning of the entire brain" as the standard for determining death when mechanical devices maintain the functioning of the heart and lungs. Under this Florida definition, an anencephalic baby is alive until the entire brain stem ceases to function. The question is whether public policy reasons justify our creating an additional common law definition of death for only anencephalics. After reviewing medical, ethical, and legal literature, we find no consensus that doing so would better serve public necessity or fundamental rights. There is no medical consensus as to the utility of anencephalic organs for transplant. Further, there is no consensus as to the ethical issues and constitutional problems involved in this type of case. Thus, we find no basis for creating a common law standard that equates anencephaly with death. Because the Florida statute does not apply in this case, the cardiopulmonary standard applies to the determination of death. Since T.A.C.P.'s (P) heart and lungs were functioning at the times in question, she was alive, and no donation of her organs would have been legal.

Analysis:

The "dead donor rule" requires that a person be dead before their life-necessary nonrenewable organs may be taken. In this case the parents of T.A.C.P. (P), or "Baby Theresa" Pearson, sought a court order declaring Baby Theresa dead so that they could donate her organs for transplant. Baby Theresa was born with anencephaly, which involves the absence of part of the brain, skull, and scalp. Part of the incomplete brain is exposed to the air and thus susceptible to infection. Anencephalic babies are permanently unconscious because they have no cerebral cortex, and thus are similar to those in a persistent vegetative state. Anencephaly is always fatal, usually, as with T.A.C.P. (P), within a few days. The rarity of longer survival may be due to the scarcity of effort to help anencephalic babies survive. When their caregivers make every medical effort to help them survive, they may live much longer. While anencephalic babies have no "higher brain" functions, they may have a functioning brain stem which supports the functioning of their heart, lungs, and other organs. Under current law, anencephalic babies are alive until their brain stem activity ceases. Although the organs of an anencephalic baby may be suitable for transplant shortly after birth, they are usually not suitable by the time whole brain death occurs because they usually deteriorate during the dying process. Because at the time anencephalic babies' organs are suitable for transplant some affirmative act would be necessary to end their lives, anencephalics usually will not be eligible to donate organs under current law. To make these organs available for transplant earlier, some, like the parents in this case, have proposed changing the law defining death to permit physicians to declare the death of anencephalic babies earlier in the dying process. In this case, the Pearsons wished to donate Baby Theresa's organs, but Baby Theresa's health care providers refused because her heart could beat on its own and they feared legal liability. The Pearsons then sought a judicial determination that Baby Theresa was dead, notwithstanding her heartbeat, and that her organs could be donated. Both the trial court and the appellate court refused their petition. However, the appellate court certified the case to the Florida Supreme Court as a question of great public importance requiring immediate resolution. A few hours later, Baby Theresa died. Nevertheless, because the case did present an issue of great public importance that was "capable of repetition yet evading review," the Florida Supreme Court chose to review the case. In this unanimous opinion, the court refused to expand the common law definition of death to include anencephaly. In addition to the lack of consensus on this matter and the uncertainty about the utility of anencephalic organs for transplant, the court recognized the concern that defining anencephalic babies as dead in order to harvest their organs could lead down a slippery slope toward defining other groups of human beings as dead to meet other societal needs. Three years after *T.A.C.P.*, In 1995, the AMA reversed its 1988 position applying the dead donor rule to anencephalic babies. The AMA announced that it found it ethically acceptable to harvest organs from anencephalic babies even before they die, as long as certain procedural "safeguards" are met. Because many physicians objected to this opinion, the AMA withdrew it almost immediately, but never reinstated its 1988 opinion prohibiting the harvesting of anencephalics' organs before death. The harvesting of organs from anencephalic newborns involves the fundamental question of whether it is ethical to destroy one human life in an attempt to save or improve another. Under the dead donor rule, the answer to this question is clearly no.

■ CASE VOCABULARY

ANENCEPHALY: The congenital absence of major portions of the brain, skull and scalp, including the cerebral cortex and cerebral hemispheres.

In the Matter of Baby "K"

(Anencephalic Baby)

16 F.3d 590 (4th Cir. 1994)

COURT FINDS ANENCEPHALIC BABIES ENTITLED TO THE SAME EMERGENCY MEDICAL TREATMENT AS OTHER INDIVIDUALS

■ **INSTANT FACTS** When the mother of an anencephalic baby insisted that the Hospital (P) give the baby respiratory support when needed, the Hospital (P) sought judicial permission to refuse to provide this treatment.

■ **BLACK LETTER RULE** The Emergency Medical Treatment and Active Labor Act (EMTALA) [requires hospitals to provide stabilizing treatment for emergency medical conditions] prohibits physicians from "allowing" anencephalic babies to die by refusing to provide them requested stabilizing treatment for an emergency condition.

■ **PROCEDURAL BASIS**

Appeal of denial of petition for declaratory judgment interpreting EMTALA regarding treatment for anencephalic babies.

■ **FACTS**

Baby K was born at the Hospital (P) with anencephaly. When Baby K had difficulty breathing on her own, Hospital physicians (P) placed her on a ventilator. The physicians (P) explained to Ms. H, Baby K's mother, that most anencephalic babies die within a few days of birth from breathing difficulties and other complications. The physicians (P) told Ms. H that aggressive treatment would serve no therapeutic purpose and recommended that Baby K receive only nutrition, hydration, and warmth. The physicians also suggested a "Do Not Resuscitate Order" under which they would withhold lifesaving measures. Ms. H rejected the physicians' (P) recommendations and insisted that they provide Baby K respiratory support whenever necessary. The Hospital (P) tried to transfer Baby K to another hospital, but none would accept her. One month later, when Baby K no longer needed the Hospital's (P) services, they transferred her to a nearby nursing home. Baby K returned to the Hospital (P) three times due to breathing difficulties. Each time the Hospital (P) stabilized her and discharged her to the nursing home. The Hospital (P) brought this action seeking a declaratory judgment that the Hospital (P) need not provide Baby K respiratory support or other aggressive treatments which it considers medically and ethically inappropriate. The district court denied this request and found that EMTALA requires the Hospital (P) to provide respiratory support to Baby K when she comes to the Hospital (P) in respiratory distress and treatment is requested for her.

■ **ISSUE**

Does EMTALA permit physicians to "allow" anencephalic babies to die by refusing to provide them stabilizing treatment for an emergency condition?

■ **DECISION AND RATIONALE**

(Wilkins, J.) No. We agree with the district court. The Hospital (P) concedes that its failure to give Baby K "immediate medical attention" when she arrives in respiratory distress would probably cause serious impairment of her bodily functions. Thus, her breathing difficulty qualifies as an emergency medical condition triggering the Hospital's (P) duty to provide stabilizing treatment. The Hospital (P) states that aggressive treatment, including the use of a respirator, is necessary to stabilize Baby K's condition. Straightforward application of EMTALA obligates the Hospital (P) to provide Baby K respiratory support when she comes to the Hospital (P) in respiratory distress and treatment is requested for her. To avoid the plain language of EMTALA, the Hospital (P) argues that it only requires uniform treatment of all patients exhibiting the same condition. However, if only uniform treatment were necessary, the Hospital (P) could provide Baby K with any level of treatment, even a level that would allow her condition to materially deteriorate, as long as it provided the same level of care to other individuals. This directly conflicts with the plain language of EMTALA. The stabilizing treatment EMTALA requires is not simply uniform treatment, but the treatment necessary to prevent material deterioration of each patient's emergency medical condition. When Baby K is in respiratory distress, this treatment includes respiratory support. The Hospital (P) further argues that by prohibiting disparate emergency medical treatment, Congress did not intend to require treatment outside the prevailing standard of medical care. The Hospital (P) contends that the life expectancy of anencephalic babies is extremely limited and that treatment is futile, and that the prevailing standard of medical care for them requires only warmth, nutrition, and hydration. The Hospital (P) maintains that providing respiratory support exceeds this standard of care. However, we cannot ignore the plain language of EMTALA, which requires stabilizing treatment for any individual who comes to the Hospital (P) with an emergency medical condition and who cannot be transferred. The Hospital (P) also argues that interpreting EMTALA to require a physician to provide respiratory support to an anencephalic baby fails to recognize a physician's legal right under Virginia law to refuse to provide medical treatment that he considers medically or ethically inappropriate. However, EMTALA is federal legislation which preempts any state or local law that directly conflicts with its requirements. It is not our function to address the moral or ethical propriety of providing emergency stabilizing treatment to anencephalic babies. We must only interpret federal statutes in accordance with their plain language and Congressional intent. EMTALA does not provide an exception for anencephalic babies in respiratory distress any more than for patients who are comatose or who have lung cancer or other conditions which require repeated emergency treatment for respiratory distress and which ultimately result in death. Affirmed.

■ DISSENT

(Sprouse, J.) I do not believe that Congress intended EMTALA to control cases such as this, which involve sensitive, private, end-of-life issues. Further, I agree with the Hospital (P) that it is anencephaly that is the condition which the court should review under EMTALA, and that respiratory failure is only a subsidiary condition found in anencephalics. EMTALA was not designed for conditions such as anencephaly. [No, it was designed for subsidiary emergency conditions like respiratory failure.] This case demonstrates the need to take a case-by-case approach to determine whether EMTALA applies to a particular emergency. We should consider the treatment for anencephaly as a continuum, not a series of isolated medical emergencies.

Analysis:

The previous case, *In re T.A.C.P.*, involved a situation in which the parents of an anencephalic baby wanted to have their baby declared dead before her cardiopulmonary functions ceased. There the court refused to equate anencephaly with death. This case deals with the opposite end of the spectrum of treatment possibilities for anencephalic babies. Baby K's mother wanted the Hospital (P) to treat Baby K as fully alive and to give her whatever care she needed to stay alive, while the Hospital (P) wanted to "allow" her to die by not giving her this stabilizing treatment. Baby K, or Stephanie, was born with anencephaly in October 1992 at Fairfax Hospital (P) in Virginia. Stephanie lacked a cerebrum and was therefore permanently unconscious. However, she had a functioning brain stem that supported her independent heartbeat, breathing, and reflex actions. These reflexes included feeding reflexes such as sucking, swallowing, and rooting, and reflexive responses to noxious stimuli, such as avoidance and crying. Stephanie's heart rate, blood pressure, digestion, and liver, kidney and bladder functions were all normal. When she was one month old the Hospital (P) discharged Stephanie to a nursing home. Stephanie sometimes suffered from respiratory distress and returned to the Hospital (P) for emergency treatment six times before she died. She died of cardiac arrest in April 1995, when she was two and a half years old. As illustrated in *T.A.C.P.*, anencephalic babies who have a functioning brain stem do not meet the legal definition of either cardiopulmonary death or brain death. However, standard treatment for anencephalic babies is to keep them warm and offer them fluids and nutrition, but to allow their organs to fail. Thus, most anencephalic babies die within hours or days from respiratory failure because the brain stem usually cannot sustain adequate breathing. As Stephanie proved, anencephalic babies can live much longer if they receive the same care any other individual would receive for the same emergency conditions. The question facing the caregivers of anencephalic babies, therefore, is whether to seek stabilizing treatment to save a life of permanent unconsciousness. This question requires a value-based decision. Many medical professionals consider preserving such a life to be medically "futile." Families that believe strongly in the sanctity of life, as Stephanie's mother did in *Baby K*, disagree. In *Baby K*, the court supported the mother's right to make this life-and-death decision for her child.

CHAPTER NINETEEN

Life and Death Decisions

Cruzan v. Director, Missouri Department of Health

Instant Facts: The parents of a woman reduced to a persistent vegetative state after a car accident seek a court order allowing them to terminate the delivery of life-sustaining hydration and nutrition to their daughter and thereby end their daughter's life.

Black Letter Rule: Because the State has an unqualified interest in preserving human life without regard to the quality of life, the Due Process clause of the United States Constitution does not prohibit a state from allowing a surrogate decisionmaker to decide whether to terminate the delivery of life-sustaining medical treatment to an incompetent patient or from imposing procedures designed to limit the surrogate's decisionmaking power.

Bouvia v. Superior Court

Instant Facts: A woman hospitalized in a California public facility and rendered quadriplegic and bedridden, but not incompetent, by cerebral palsy petitions for court authorization to remove a nasogastric tube that delivers her life-sustaining hydration and nutrition.

Black Letter Rule: Under California law, a competent patient has the right to refuse medical treatment, even when that treatment is life-sustaining and even when the patient is not terminally ill.

Public Health Trust of Dade County v. Wons

Instant Facts: A Florida public hospital seeks court authorization to give a competent patient a life-sustaining blood transfusion despite the fact that the patient, a Jehovah's Witness, refused to receive the transfusion on religious grounds.

Black Letter Rule: Under Florida law, a competent adult patient may refuse life-sustaining medical treatment on religious grounds.

In re Eichner

Instant Facts: When a member of a Catholic religious order is reduced to a persistent vegetative state during a heart operation, his surrogate decision maker petitions for court authorization to terminate his life support.

Black Letter Rule: Under New York law, a surrogate decision maker may direct the termination of a life support system only when he can provide clear and convincing evidence that the incompetent patient would have desired the termination of life support.

In re Conroy

Instant Facts: In a case involving an incompetent patient that had never clearly expressed her desires about life support systems, the Supreme Court of New Jersey formulates two "best interests" tests to determine whether it will authorize the removal or withholding of life support.

Black Letter Rule: Under New Jersey law, life-sustaining medical treatment may be withheld or withdrawn from an incompetent patient when that patient had clearly expressed his desire that treatment be withheld or withdrawn while competent, or when the patient's surrogate decision maker can present some trustworthy evidence that the patient would have wanted the termination of treatment or can show that the net burdens of the patient's life with the life-sustaining treatment should clearly and markedly outweigh the benefits.

Conservatorship of Wendland

Instant Facts: Wendland was incapacitated after a truck accident and two years later, his conservator/wife (P) requested permission to remove his feeding and hydration tubes.

Black Letter Rule: The decision to withdraw life-sustaining treatment must be supported by clear and convincing evidence that the patient either wished to refuse the treatment or that the withdrawal would be in the best interest of the patient.

Guardianship of Schiavo

Instant Facts: Theresa Schiavo's husband Michael (P) sought to have her life support terminated, and her parents (D) objected.

Black Letter Rule: In the absence of instructions, the court may make a decision on whether life support should be withdrawn, based on clear and convincing evidence of what the patient would want.

Superintendent of Belchertown State School v. Saikewicz

Instant Facts: In a case involving a severely retarded and uncommunicative man that had never been competent to make his own medical decisions, the court is asked to determine whether to authorize the termination of life-sustaining chemotherapy.

Black Letter Rule: Under Massachusetts law, in cases involving a patient that has never been competent, a surrogate decision maker should make the decision that the patient would have made if he were competent and should take into account the patient's present and future incompetence as one factor in the decision-making process.

In re Storar

Instant Facts: After a severely retarded man is diagnosed with terminal cancer and demonstrates a reluctance to undergo life-sustaining blood transfusions, his mother seeks court authorization to terminate the transfusions.

Black Letter Rule: Under New York law, adults that have never been competent are treated as children and although a surrogate decision maker may provide consent to treatment, he may not direct the termination of life-sustaining medical treatment.

Newmark v. Williams

Instant Facts: The parents of a terminally ill child, both practicing Christian Scientists, seek court authorization to refuse an aggressive course of chemotherapy treatment for their son that would only stand a 40% chance of success but would stand a greater chance of causing emotional trauma and severe physical side effects.

Black Letter Rule: A parent does not neglect his child when he chooses to forego life-sustaining medical treatment for that child in favor of spiritual treatment and prayer by an accredited religious practitioner and in accordance with the tenets and practices of a recognized religious faith.

Miller v. HCA

Instant Facts: The Millers' (P) baby was born in distress after only twenty-three weeks' gestation and she was provided with resuscitative care without the Millers' (P) consent.

Black Letter Rule: A physician does not commit a legal wrong when he or she provides treatment to a minor without parental consent under emergent circumstances, that is, if death is likely to result immediately upon the failure to perform the treatment.

Washington v. Glucksberg

Instant Facts: Physicians and terminally ill patients bring a constitutional due process challenge to Washington's statutory prohibition of assisted suicide.

Black Letter Rule: Assisted suicide is not a fundamental right protected by the Due Process Clause of the Fourteenth Amendment to the United States Constitution.

Vacco v. Quill

Instant Facts: A group of physicians and terminally ill patients bring an Equal Protection challenge to New York's statutory prohibition of assisted suicide.

Black Letter Rule: A state statutory ban on assisted suicide does not violate the Equal Protection Clause of the Fourteenth Amendment to the United States Constitution.

Cruzan v. Director, Missouri Department of Health

(*Comatose Patient*) v. (*State of Missouri*)

497 U.S. 261, 110 S.Ct. 2841, 111 L.Ed.2d 224 (1990)

SUPREME COURT LEAVES TO THE STATES THE DEFINITION OF PROCEDURAL RIGHTS SURROUNDING THE REFUSAL OF MEDICAL TREATMENT

■ **INSTANT FACTS** The parents of a woman reduced to a persistent vegetative state after a car accident seek a court order allowing them to terminate the delivery of life-sustaining hydration and nutrition to their daughter and thereby end their daughter's life.

■ **BLACK LETTER RULE** Because the State has an unqualified interest in preserving human life without regard to the quality of life, the Due Process clause of the United States Constitution does not prohibit a state from allowing a surrogate decisionmaker to decide whether to terminate the delivery of life-sustaining medical treatment to an incompetent patient or from imposing procedures designed to limit the surrogate's decisionmaking power.

■ **PROCEDURAL BASIS**

Certiorari to the Supreme Court of Missouri in a declaratory judgment action seeking a court order to terminate life-sustaining hydration and nutrition delivered to an incompetent patient.

■ **FACTS**

In January 1983, Nancy Beth Cruzan (P) got into a car accident in Jasper County Missouri. Her car overturned and when she was found, Nancy Beth Cruzan (P) was lying facedown in a ditch. She was not breathing and her heart had stopped. Paramedics restored her breathing and heartbeat and transported her to a hospital. At the hospital, a neurosurgeon determined that Nancy (P) had sustained probable cerebral contusions compounded by lack of oxygen. At trial, the Missouri court found that permanent brain damage usually results after six minutes of oxygen-deprivation and that Nancy (P) had been deprived of oxygen for 12 to 14 minutes. Nancy (P) was in a coma for three weeks, but then progressed to a state where she was still unconscious but could ingest food. With the permission of her then husband, surgeons implanted a gastrostomy in Nancy (P) in order to ease her feeding and hydration. Since then, Nancy (P) has been living in a state hospital in a persistent vegetative state, which means that she exhibits some motor reflexes but otherwise shows no indication of any cognitive function. The state is paying for her care. Nancy's parents (P2) asked hospital employees to terminate the artificial hydration and feeding procedures, which were keeping Nancy (P) alive. When the employees refused to honor this request without a court order, Mr. and Mrs. Cruzan (P2) sought and received such an order. The trial court found that an individual in Nancy's (P) condition has a fundamental right under both the Missouri and the United States Constitutions to refuse or ask for the withdrawal of "death prolonging procedures." The trial court also found that when Nancy (P) was 25, she had told her roommate that she would not want to continue life in a vegetative state. The Supreme Court of Missouri reversed the trial court, and the United States Supreme Court granted certiorari.

■ **ISSUE**

Does the United States Constitution permit a state to establish a procedural requirement that has the effect of restricting a surrogate decisionmaker's ability to terminate the delivery of life-sustaining medical treatment to an incompetent patient?

■ DECISION AND RATIONALE

(Rehnquist, C.J.) Yes. Under the Fourteenth Amendment to the United States Constitution, a state may not deprive an individual of life, liberty, or property without due process of law. The fact that an individual has a liberty interest in refusing unwanted medical treatment can be inferred from prior Supreme Court decisions. After determining that an individual has a liberty interest, a court must then balance that interest against the relevant state interests in order to determine whether the individual's constitutional rights have been violated. For the purposes of this case, the Court will assume that a competent person has a constitutional right to refuse hydration and nutrition that would prolong life. Mr. and Mrs. Cruzan (P2) argue that an incompetent person should have the same right. However, an incompetent person is incapable of making an informed or voluntary choice to exercise a constitutional right to refuse medical treatment, therefore the constitutional right must be exercised by someone else on the incompetent person's behalf. Missouri allows a surrogate to act for the patient in choosing to withdraw hydration and nutrition but has established a procedural safeguard to assure that the surrogate's decision conforms as much as possible to the patient's wishes. Under Missouri law, a surrogate must provide clear and convincing evidence that the incompetent's wishes are to discontinue treatment. The United States Constitution does not prohibit a state from imposing such a procedural requirement. Missouri's (D) interest in this case is in the preservation of human life. Missouri (D) also has an interest in protecting the personal nature of a choice between life and death. Because not all incompetent patients will have loved ones to act as surrogates, a state has an interest preventing abuses. A judicial proceeding to determine an incompetent patient's wishes may not always be adversarial, and the state has an interest in ensuring that even if the proceeding is not adversarial the court will have to engage in accurate fact-finding. A state may also choose to refrain from making judgments about the "quality of life" an individual may enjoy. Missouri (D) has chosen to advance all of these interests by imposing a clear and convincing evidence standard. The standard of proof applied in a civil action reflects not only the importance of that action, but also society's determination of how the risk of error should be distributed among the parties. Missouri law has placed an increased risk of an erroneous decision on persons that seek to terminate an incompetent patient's treatment, so that an erroneous decision would lead to the maintenance of the status quo. This means that an erroneous decision may be corrected in the event that new medical technology becomes available, or new evidence about the patient's wishes comes to light. A state may apply a clear and convincing evidence standard in a proceeding in which a guardian seeks to discontinue the nutrition and hydration of a patient diagnosed to be in a persistent vegetative state.

■ CONCURRENCE

(O'Connor, J.) A protected liberty interest in refusing medical treatment may be inferred from prior Supreme Court decisions and that liberty interest includes the refusal of life-prolonging nutrition and hydration. The liberty interest in refusing medical treatment is inferred from decisions involving the State's invasions of the body. Because our notions of liberty are entwined with our notions of physical freedom the Supreme Court has often found that State invasions of the body are prevented by the Due Process clause. A state's decision to impose medical treatment on a competent adult always involves some type of restraint or intrusion. The Due Process Clause protects an individual's personal decision to reject medical treatment, including the artificial delivery of water and nutrition. The court's decision that a state may require clear and convincing evidence of an incompetent patient's wishes to have treatment withdrawn does not prevent the Court from determining in the future that a state is required to implement a decision made by a patient's appointed surrogate.

■ CONCURRENCE

(Scalia, J.) The Court should have taken the opportunity to announce that the federal courts have no role in this type of determination. The states have always had the power to prevent suicide and the point at which a life becomes worthless and the point at which the means to save life becomes inappropriate are not set forth in the Constitution or known to any of the Supreme Court justices. If it is determined by clear and convincing evidence that an individual wishes to refuse medical treatment, it is up to the state legislature to determine whether that wish will be honored. The Due Process clause protects individuals from deprivations of liberty without due process of law. In order to maintain a substantive due process claim, a claimant must demonstrate that the State has deprived him of a right that is traditionally and historically protected from State interference. There is no indication that the right to suicide is rooted in American tradition to the point that it is a fundamental right implicit in the concept of ordered liberty.

■ DISSENT

(Brennan, J.) Nancy Beth Cruzan (P) has a fundamental right to be free of unwanted medical attention and this right is not outweighed by any interest of the state of Missouri (D). The right to refuse medical treatment is the right to make a personal decision according to one's values and after the evaluation of the benefits and detriments of treatment. The only benefit to Nancy (P) from continued medical treatment will be to remain metabolically alive. The only state interest asserted in this case is the general interest in preserving human life. The State has no legitimate interest in an individual's life that could outweigh that individual's choice to refuse medical treatment. The State's general interest cannot outweigh the personal interest in self-determination. Missouri (D) could assert that it has a paternalistic interest in making as accurate as possible a determination of an incompetent patient's true wishes. Missouri (D) may impose a procedural requirement that would lead to the accurate determination of Nancy's (P) wishes, but the clear and convincing evidence standard it currently applies is not designed to achieve an accurate determination of her wishes. It imposes an asymmetrical evidentiary burden by not requiring proof to support a finding that the incompetent patient would wish to continue medical treatment and by allowing only clear and convincing evidence of specific statements about choice of medical treatment made by the patient while competent to show that the patient would wish to avoid medical treatment while in a vegetative state. The Missouri Supreme Court did not describe what types of evidence would meet its high standard of proof, but its discussion suggests that only a living will or other formal document would do. The majority opinion here suggests that when it is impossible to tell what decision an incompetent person would make, the State may make the decision itself. The State should not be allowed to protect an individual's right to make a choice simply by appropriating that choice for itself.

■ DISSENT

(Stevens, J.) Missouri's (D) treatment of Nancy Beth Cruzan (P) is both unconstitutional and unjust. Nancy's (P) interest in her own life includes an interest in how she will be remembered after her death. The trial court order allows Nancy's parents (P2) to achieve closure by terminating their daughter's treatment. Missouri's (D) objection to the order subordinates Nancy's (P) family, her body, and her life to the interest of the State. To be considered constitutional, Missouri's (D) action must bear a rational relationship to some legitimate state end. Missouri (D) argues that it has an interest in the protection of human life, but the state's policy has more to do with defining life than protecting it. In defining "life," Missouri (D) has abstracted the concept of "life" from the human body, treating it as a physiological condition rather than as an activity constituting the integration of a person's interests or as the manifestation of a person's spirit. Because Missouri (D) has decided to give itself the power to define life, and because the Court is willing to allow Missouri (D) this power, Nancy's (P) constitutionally protected interest in life is put in conflict with her constitutionally protected liberty interest in choosing whether she will continue to receive medical treatment. If we define Nancy's (P) life with reference to her own interests, in such a way that her life could be considered to have ended at the moment her existence stopped serving any of her interests, then her constitutional interests in life and in liberty will not be in conflict.

Analysis:

Cruzan is the first case in which the United States Supreme Court directly addressed the issue of the right to refuse life-sustaining medical treatment. The holding in *Cruzan* is that Missouri's (D) requirement that a surrogate decisionmaker provide clear and convincing evidence of an incompetent patient's wish to terminate life-sustaining hydration and nutrition does not violate the Due Process clause. But Justice Rehnquist's majority is weakened by concurrences from Justices O'Connor and Scalia, and the effect of the case has been to force those seeking an interpretation of the right to refuse life-sustaining medical treatment to do so at the state level. One thing that emerges clearly from *Cruzan* is that the Constitution allows states a great deal of freedom to develop their own procedures to govern surrogate decisionmaking. *Cruzan* leaves other important issues unresolved. The decision does not address the issue of whether a competent person has the constitutional right to terminate medical treatment or whether a competent person has the constitutional right to die. The Court does not address the issues of whether the cost of medical care and who bears that cost are relevant considerations in the determination of the state's interests and the patient's interests. The Supreme Court in *Cruzan* has abandoned the field in favor of the states, and this has allowed states to develop wildly different procedures governing the termination of life-sustaining medical treatment.

■ CASE VOCABULARY

PARENS PATRIAE: Literally, "the parent of his country." The term "parens patriae" is used to describe the state when it is acting in its capacity to protect the interests of, or to represent, citizens that are unable to protect or represent their own interests.

SIMPLICITER: Simply.

Bouvia v. Superior Court

(*Paralyzed Patient*) v. (*State of California*)

179 Cal.App.3d 1127, 225 Cal.Rptr. 297 (1986)

COMPETENT CALIFORNIA PATIENTS MAY REFUSE LIFE-SUSTAINING MEDICAL TREATMENT

■ **INSTANT FACTS** A woman hospitalized in a California public facility and rendered quadriplegic and bedridden, but not incompetent, by cerebral palsy petitions for court authorization to remove a nasogastric tube that delivers her life-sustaining hydration and nutrition.

■ **BLACK LETTER RULE** Under California law, a competent patient has the right to refuse medical treatment, even when that treatment is life-sustaining and even when the patient is not terminally ill.

■ **PROCEDURAL BASIS**

Appeal to the California Court of Appeal of a trial court's denial of a petition to remove the feeding tube of a mentally competent quadriplegic patient in a public hospital.

■ **FACTS**

Elizabeth Bouvia (P) was a 28-year-old patient in a California hospital that was maintained by the County of Los Angeles (D). She suffered from severe cerebral palsy, which had rendered her quadriplegic and completely bedridden. Though she could move a few fingers on one hand and had the ability to make slight head and facial movements, Bouvia (P) was otherwise immobile. She also suffered from severe arthritis and was in constant pain. Although almost completely immobile, Bouvia (P) was intelligent and mentally competent. When her husband left her, she went to live with her parents. When her parents could no longer care for her, she stayed with friends and in public hospitals. Because she lacks the financial means to support herself, searches for a permanent place to live where she might have received constant care were unsuccessful. Bouvia (P) expressed the desire to die several times. In 1983 a court in Riverside County denied her the right to be cared for in a public hospital while she starved herself to death. After that, her friends moved her from hospital to hospital until she finally arrived at the present one (D). Bouvia (P) had to be spoon-fed soft foods as she could not retain solids. The medical staff at her current hospital (D) were concerned about her weight, which hovered around 70 pounds, and given her previously expressed desire to starve herself, the medical staff decided to insert and maintain a nasogastric feeding tube against Bouvia's (P) wishes. Bouvia (P) seeks a court order to remove the feeding tube.

■ **ISSUE**

Under California law, does a mentally competent patient have the right to refuse any medical treatment or attention, even when the treatment is the delivery of nutrition and hydration and the withdrawal of that treatment would create a life-threatening condition?

■ **DECISION AND RATIONALE**

(Beach, Associate Justice) Yes. An adult of sound mind has the right to determine whether or not he will submit to medical treatment. A patient has the right to refuse any medical treatment, even if that treatment would save or prolong his life. The Presidential Commission for the Study of Ethical Problems in Medicine and Biomedical and Behavioral Research has concluded that it is the voluntary choice of the competent and informed patient that should determine whether or not he should receive life-sustaining medical treatment. The American Hospital Policy and Statement of Patient's Choices of Treatment Options, which was approved by the American Hospital Association in 1985 states that the authority to choose the course of treatment and the right to refuse a specific treatment or all treatment rests with the patient. In 1986 the Council on Ethical and Judicial Affairs of the American Medical Association stated that although the physician has the social commitment to sustain life and relieve suffering, when those commitments come into conflict, the choice of the patient or the patient's family, if he is incompetent, should prevail. The county hospital (D) argues that the state's interests should prevail over Bouvia's (P) right to refuse treatment. The state's interests include the interest in preserving life and preventing suicide, the interest in protecting innocent third parties, and the interest in maintaining the ethical standards of the medical profession. The county hospital (D) also argues that because Bouvia (P) is a patient at a public hospital, the state will be a party to the result of her actions; that Bouvia (P) is not comatose, terminally ill, or in a vegetative state; that Bouvia (P) has asked for other medical treatment and cannot accept it while cutting off the treatment that would make it effective; and that she is trying to starve herself and the state will not be a party to suicide. The trial court held that with the feeding tube, Bouvia (P) could prolong her life by 15 to 20 years and that the state's interest in preserving her life for that amount of time outweighed her right to refuse treatment. The trial court erred in attaching so much importance to the amount of time left to Bouvia (P) while not granting equal weight and consideration to the quality of her life. Courts that have allowed the cessation of medical treatment have all done so in part because the quality of life in the time remaining for the patient had deteriorated. Bouvia's (P) quality of life has diminished to the point where she is bedridden, immobile, helpless, and in constant pain. If her right to choose to refuse treatment cannot be exercised because she could live an arbitrary number of years, her right will have lost all meaning. The right to refuse treatment belongs to Bouvia (P). It is not a medical decision for doctors to make. It is not a legal issue for judges to resolve. It is a personal, philosophical, and moral decision that belongs to Bouvia (P) alone. Medical practitioners cannot assert their right to preserve a life, or painful existence, that someone else must live for 15 to 20 years. It is not the state's policy to force an ordeal like Bouvia's (P) on anyone. Because she is a competent adult, Bouvia (P) has the right to live her life in dignity and peace. Personal dignity is part of an individual's right to privacy. The trial court also erred in basing part of its decision on Bouvia's (P) "motives" in exercising her right. If an individual has a right, it does not matter what motivates its exercise. Bouvia (P) is entitled to the immediate removal of her feeding tube.

Analysis:

Bouvia rests in part on the doctrine of informed consent. If a patient has the right to consent to medical treatment after receiving adequate information from his doctor, then that patient necessarily has the right to refuse consent when informed of the possible consequences of treatment. The doctrine of informed consent grants a competent, informed patient the right to refuse life-sustaining medical treatment. This means that although there may not be a constitutional right to die, in California there is a common-law right. The court also attaches great weight to the quality of Bouvia's (P) life. In his concurrence in the *Cruzan* case, justice Scalia makes the point that pain and physical incapacity have never been considered defenses to a charge of suicide. In *Bouvia* the California Court of Appeal makes the opposite point, implying that because Bouvia (P) is incapacitated and in pain, her quality of life has diminished to the point where her right to refuse the medical treatment that would prolong her life outweighs the state interest in preserving life and preventing suicide. The *Bouvia* court makes a point that the United States Supreme Court expressly avoided making in *Cruzan* by declaring that the right to personal dignity, and by implication the right to choose to die with dignity, is part of an individual's "right to privacy."

■ CASE VOCABULARY

REAL PARTY IN INTEREST: The person that will be benefitted by the suit, in other words, the person that will discharge the claim upon which suit is brought and control the action brought to enforce the claim.

Public Health Trust of Dade County v. Wons

(Jehovah's Witness) v. (Florida Public Hospital)

541 So.2d 96 (Fla. 1989)

IN FLORIDA A COMPETENT ADULT MAY REFUSE LIFE-SUSTAINING MEDICAL TREATMENT ON RELIGIOUS GROUNDS

■ **INSTANT FACTS** A Florida public hospital seeks court authorization to give a competent patient a life-sustaining blood transfusion despite the fact that the patient, a Jehovah's Witness, refused to receive the transfusion on religious grounds.

■ **BLACK LETTER RULE** Under Florida law, a competent adult patient may refuse life-sustaining medical treatment on religious grounds.

■ **PROCEDURAL BASIS**

Appeal to the Supreme Court of Florida of the Third District Court of Appeals' reversal of a circuit court order authorizing a hospital to give a blood transfusion over the patient's objection.

■ **FACTS**

Norma Wons (D) entered a hospital run by the Public Health Trust of Dade County (Health Trust) (P) with a medical condition called dysfunctional uterine bleeding. Mrs. Wons (P) required a blood transfusion in order to save her life. However, as a practicing Jehovah's Witness, Mrs. Wons (D) refused the transfusion on the grounds that to receive a blood transfusion would violate the prohibition her sect places on receiving blood from outside her own body. When she refused consent, Mrs. Wons (D) was conscious and competent to reach an informed decision regarding her medical care. The Health Trust (P) petitioned the circuit court to order a blood transfusion. The court granted the petition, reasoning that Mrs. Wons' (D) two minor children had a right to be raised by two parents, a right that overrides a mother's right to freely exercise her religion. The Health Trust medical staff (P) performed the transfusion while Mrs. Wons (D) was unconscious. When she regained consciousness, she appealed to the Third District Court of Appeals, which reversed the circuit court's order, holding that an individual's rights to free exercise of religion and to privacy could not be overridden by the state's interest in protecting a child's right to a two-parent home.

■ **ISSUE**

Does a competent adult have the right to refuse life-sustaining medical treatment on religious grounds?

■ **DECISION AND RATIONALE**

Yes. The Health Trust (P) argues that the state has a compelling interest in the protection of innocent third parties, in this case, Mrs. Wons' (D) two minor children. Although the environment created by a two-parent home is important to a child's development, the state's interest here is not sufficient to override Mrs. Wons' (D) fundamental constitutional rights to free exercise and to privacy. An individual's religion, or philosophical and moral outlook on life is sacred and the courts have traditionally given great deference to an individual's right to make decisions that vitally affect his private life. This right is "the very bedrock on which this country was founded" and cannot be overstated. The Court of Appeals is affirmed.

Analysis:

No court wants to make a mistake that a higher court cannot rectify because one of the parties has died as a result of the mistake However, the trial court's decision here may represent an unacceptable level of paternalism. In the *Georgetown College* case, Judge Wright did not seem to take Mrs. Jones's religious beliefs very seriously when he determined first that she was incompetent and second that her religion did not prohibit the transfusion itself, but only the patient's verbal acceptance. Where Judge Wright seemed to say that he knew more about what was in Mrs. Jones's best interests as a person and as a practicing Jehovah's Witness, the Florida Supreme Court in *Wons* determined that only Mrs. Wons (D) could decide how to exercise her own religious beliefs and how much weight to give her beliefs in balancing them against the interests of her children.

■ CASE VOCABULARY

FUNDAMENTAL RIGHTS: The idea of "fundamental rights" is primarily an Anglo-American concept meant to encompass those rights that are deemed common to all citizens except where those rights that are declared to be forfeited by the law of the land.

In re Eichner

(Surrogate Decision Maker for Comatose Patient) v. *(State of New York)*

52 N.Y.2d 363, 438 N.Y.S.2d 266, 420 N.E.2d 64 (Ct. App. 1981)

IN NEW YORK, SUBSTITUTED JUDGMENT IS ALLOWED ONLY WHEN THERE IS CLEAR AND CONVINCING EVIDENCE OF THE PATIENT'S WISHES

■ **INSTANT FACTS** When a member of a Catholic religious order is reduced to a persistent vegetative state during a heart operation, his surrogate decision maker petitions for court authorization to terminate his life support.

■ **BLACK LETTER RULE** Under New York law, a surrogate decision maker may direct the termination of a life support system only when he can provide clear and convincing evidence that the incompetent patient would have desired the termination of life support.

■ **PROCEDURAL BASIS**

Appeal to the New York Court of Appeals of a surrogate decision maker's petition for court authorization of the termination of a life support system.

■ **FACTS**

Brother Joseph Fox was a member of a Catholic religious order known as the Society of Mary for over 66 years. The religious order operated Chaminade High School in Mineola. While Fox was undergoing an operation he had a heart attack, which resulted in loss of oxygen to the brain and substantial brain damage. Fox was reduced to a persistent vegetative state. Because he had lost the ability to breathe on his own, Fox was placed on a respirator. Fox's doctors informed Father Philip Eichner (P), the president of Chaminade and the director of the society at the school, that Fox had no reasonable chance of recovery. Father Eichner (P) obtained confirmation of the diagnosis and then asked the hospital to remove Fox's respirator. The hospital refused to remove the respirator without a court order, so Father Eichner (P) applied to the court to be appointed committee of the person and property of Brother Fox with the authority to remove his respirator. Fox's surviving relatives supported Father Eichner's (P) petition. The court appointed a guardian ad litem and held a hearing at which the District Attorney opposed Father Eichner's (P) petition. At the hearing, all the expert witnesses agreed that there was no reasonable likelihood that Brother Fox would recover from his coma. There was also evidence that Fox had, before he was rendered incompetent, expressed the view that in those circumstances he would want his respirator removed. Fox had expressed this view in 1976 when the Chaminade community held formal discussions of the moral implications of the *Karen Ann Quinlan* case, in which the parents of a New Jersey woman in a coma requested the hospital to remove the respirator that was keeping her alive. At that time, the Pope had stated that Catholic religious principles allowed the termination of extraordinary life-sustaining treatment when the patient had no reasonable chance of recovery. Catholic church officials in New Jersey had determined that the use of the respirator in *Quinlan* amounted to an "extraordinary measure" and Fox expressed his agreement with this view at the Chaminade discussions. He also expressed his desire that none of this "extraordinary business" be done for him under those circumstances. A couple of months before his final hospitalization, Fox reiterated this desire.

■ ISSUE

Can a surrogate decision maker be appointed to direct the removal of a life-support system where the patient is currently incompetent, but in the past has clearly expressed his desire to have life support systems removed if he were ever in a vegetative state with no hope of recovery?

■ DECISION AND RATIONALE

(Wachtler, J.) Yes. In this case, there was compelling proof of the patient's wishes. He had carefully reflected on the subject, concluded that he would not wish his life to be prolonged artificially if there were no chance of recovery, and expressed this view. The fact that Fox reiterated this view a couple of months before entering the hospital for the last time shows his commitment to this view. In this case, there is clear and convincing evidence that Fox did not want his life to be prolonged by use of a respirator if he were in a vegetative coma and had no reasonable hope of recovery.

Analysis:

New York, like Missouri, does not allow substituted judgment in cases involving incompetent patients unless that judgment is based on the formally articulated desires of the patient. In *Cruzan*, the court could not find clear and convincing evidence of the patient's desires. In this case, Father Eichner (P) was able to show that Brother Fox would not have wanted a hospital to take extraordinary measures to prolong his life if he had no chance of recovery and that in Fox's opinion, a respirator constituted such an "extraordinary measure." In New York, Missouri, and also Michigan, a court may only look to the patient's expressed preferences in deciding whether to permit a surrogate decision-maker to direct the removal of life-support. In other states, courts may look to a variety of additional factors, including the surrogate's knowledge of the patient's religious beliefs and personal value system and the patient's quality of life.

■ CASE VOCABULARY

GUARDIAN AD LITEM: An individual appointed by a court during the course of litigation to represent and protect the interests of an incompetent person who is a party to the action.

In re Conroy

(Comatose Patient) v. *(State of New Jersey)*

98 N.J. 321, 486 A.2d 1209 (1985)

NEW JERSEY APPLIES "BEST INTERESTS" ANALYSIS TO DETERMINE WHETHER TO TERMINATE INCOMPETENT PATIENT'S LIFE SUPPORT

■ **INSTANT FACTS** In a case involving an incompetent patient that had never clearly expressed her desires about life support systems, the Supreme Court of New Jersey formulates two "best interests" tests to determine whether it will authorize the removal or withholding of life support.

■ **BLACK LETTER RULE** Under New Jersey law, life-sustaining medical treatment may be withheld or withdrawn from an incompetent patient when that patient had clearly expressed his desire that treatment be withheld or withdrawn while competent, or when the patient's surrogate decision maker can present some trustworthy evidence that the patient would have wanted the termination of treatment or can show that the net burdens of the patient's life with the life-sustaining treatment should clearly and markedly outweigh the benefits.

■ **PROCEDURAL BASIS**

Appeal to the Supreme Court of New Jersey.

■ **FACTS**

Claire Conroy was a patient that had been reduced to a state where she was incompetent to make an informed decision on whether or not to receive life-sustaining medical treatment. She had never clearly expressed her wishes regarding her placement on a life support system.

■ **ISSUE**

Can a life support system be removed from an incompetent patient that has never clearly expressed her desires in regards to such treatment?

■ **DECISION AND RATIONALE**

(Schreiber, J.) Yes. Life-sustaining medical treatment may be withheld or withdrawn from an incompetent patient when that patient has clearly expressed his desire that treatment be withheld or withdrawn under the circumstances involved. Life-sustaining medical treatment may also be withheld or withdrawn from an incompetent patient if one of two best interests tests are met. Under the first test, the limited-objective test, treatment may be withdrawn when there is trustworthy evidence that the patient would have refused the treatment if he were competent and when the decision maker is satisfied that the burdens of the patient's prolonged life would outweigh the benefits of continued medical treatment. The limited-objective test allows the termination of life-sustaining medical treatment when a patient has not expressed a clear desire in regards to treatment before becoming incompetent. The limited-objective test does require some trustworthy evidence that the patient would have wanted the termination of treatment, but this evidence could take other forms besides the patient's formal articulations on the subject. If there is no trustworthy evidence or any evidence at all of the patient's wishes, life-sustaining treatment may still be withdrawn or withheld if the second best interests test is met. Under the pure-objective test the net burdens of the patient's life with the life-sustaining treatment should clearly and markedly outweigh the benefits. The recurring, unavoidable, and severe pain of the patient's life with continued medical treatment should be such that continuing treatment would be inhumane. However, treatment should not be withdrawn where the patient, while competent, had expressed a wish to be kept alive in spite of any pain. The court will not hold that the decision-making process may be based on any assessment of the worth or utility of the patient's life or the value of that life to others. It may sometimes be difficult to determine that the evidence presented would support termination of treatment under either best interests test. In such cases, the termination of life-sustaining treatment cannot be justified and the court must err on the side of preserving life.

Analysis:

In this case, the court recognizes that there are certain circumstances under which a patient's autonomy interest cannot be served. The court creates two "best interests" tests that can be applied when a surrogate decision maker cannot apply the principle of substituted judgment because there is simply no evidence of what the patient's judgment would have been. Under the best interests tests outlined in Conroy, the surrogate makes a choice that he has reason to believe is in the incompetent patient's best interests. Under the pure-objective test the surrogate will not make any inquiry into the patient's wishes unless the patient had expressed a desire to receive treatment regardless of how painful his existence became. Unlike courts in New York and Missouri, the New Jersey Supreme Court will allow the principle of beneficence to prevail in cases where it is impossible to serve the principle of individual autonomy.

■ CASE VOCABULARY

INCOMPETENT PERSON: In general, a person that lacks the mental ability to make a contract or engage in business; the term can include any person that is incapacitated for the purposes of contract formation or business transactions whether that incapacity is due to youth or mental disability.

Conservatorship of Wendland

(Injured in Truck Accident)

26 Cal.4th 519, 110 Cal.Rptr.2d 412, 28 P.3d 151 (2001)

A CONSERVATOR MUST PROVE THE WISH TO DISCONTINUE TREATMENT

When I vowed "in sickness and in health", I really only envisioned a bad cold.

stus.com

■ **INSTANT FACTS** Wendland was incapacitated after a truck accident and two years later, his conservator/wife (P) requested permission to remove his feeding and hydration tubes.

■ **BLACK LETTER RULE** The decision to withdraw life-sustaining treatment must be supported by clear and convincing evidence that the patient either wished to refuse the treatment or that the withdrawal would be in the best interest of the patient.

■ **PROCEDURAL BASIS**

Appeal from an order of the court of appeal reversing a determination of the trial court.

■ **FACTS**

Wendland was seriously hurt when he rolled his truck at a high speed. The accident injured Wendland's brain. He was in a coma for several months after the accident. Although he regained consciousness, he was mentally and physically disabled and dependent on artificial nutrition and hydration. He was able to perform simple tasks and follow two-step instructions, but he was unable to walk, talk, feed himself, eat, drink, and control his bowel and bladder functions. It was very difficult for him to swallow, so he was dependent on the feeding tube. Wendland was able to communicate at times by blinking his eyes, but no consistent communication was achieved.

Wendland's feeding tube was dislodged three times after Wendland regained consciousness, and each time, his wife (P) authorized reinsertion. When it became dislodged a fourth time, she refused to allow it to be reinserted. Wendland's wife (P) discussed her decision with her daughters and Wendland's brother, all of whom believed that Wendland would not have approved of the reinsertion. The decision was also discussed with Wendland's physician, the hospital ombudsman, and other physicians, all of whom supported the decision not to allow reinsertion. The decision not to reinsert was approved by the hospital's ethics committee.

Wendland's mother and sister learned of the decision not to reinsert the tube from an anonymous phone call. They obtained a temporary restraining order against removal of the tube. Wendland's wife (P) petitioned to be named Wendland's conservator and asked that her authority to withdraw or withhold treatment, including nutrition and hydration, be sustained. Wendland's wife (P) was named conservator. After a sixty-day observation period went by with no significant improvement in Wendland's condition, Wendland's wife (P) renewed her request. Pursuant to a mandate from the court of appeal, counsel was appointed for Wendland, and the appointed attorney also supported the conservator's (P) decision.

At trial, the physicians all testified that Wendland was not likely to recover any further. His wife (P), brother, and daughter recounted statements that Wendland had made about life-sustaining health care. Wendland's wife (P) recalled two specific conversations in which Wendland said he would not want to live on life support, but on cross-examination she admitted that he said only that he would not want to live as a "vegetable" or in a comatose state. Wendland's brother said that when they were discussing the possibility of Wendland getting into a serious accident because of his drinking, Wendland said that he would just want to be let alone. His daughter testified that her father said on that occasion that if he could not provide for his family or do what he enjoyed doing, or do the basic things of life, he would not want to live.

The trial court found that Wendland's wife (P) had not met her burden of proving that Wendland, who was not in a persistent vegetative state or suffering from a terminal illness, would want to die. The court denied her request. The court of appeal reversed, holding that the trial court should have limited itself to asking if Wendland's wife (P) had acted in good faith.

■ ISSUE

Did the trial court err in refusing the conservator/wife's request to remove her husband's feeding tube?

■ DECISION AND RATIONALE

(Werdegar, J.) No. The decision to withdraw life-sustaining treatment must be supported by clear and convincing evidence that the patient either wished to refuse the treatment, or that the withdrawal would be in the best interest of the patient. It is certain that a competent adult has the right to refuse any medical treatment, even life-saving treatment. This right has its basis in the common law and in the privacy clause in the California Constitution. Federal law is not to the contrary. Furthermore, the right to decline treatment survives incapacity, if exercised while the patient is competent. The Health Care Decisions Law gives competent adults extremely broad power to direct all aspects of their health care if they should become incompetent. Decisions made by conservators on behalf of an incompetent person, however, have authority derived from the *parens patriae* power of the state to protect incompetent persons.

The purpose of requiring conservators to make decisions in accordance with a conservatee's wishes is to enforce the fundamental principle of personal autonomy. Unlike an agent designated by a competent person to make health care decisions, the conservator is not an agent and cannot be presumed to have special knowledge of the conservatee's wishes. When the decision to be made is the decision to end the conservatee's life, a high standard of proof will help to ensure the reliability of the decision.

The clear and convincing standard of proof has been applied when necessary to protect important rights. In a case involving the decision to end medical treatment, the importance of the ultimate decision and the risk of error are manifest. Likewise, the degree of confidence required in the necessary findings of fact is manifest. The risk is that a conservator will make a decision to end the conservatee's life, contrary to the subjective wishes of the conservatee. This would represent the gravest possible affront to a conservatee's state constitutional right to privacy, in the sense of unwanted bodily intrusions, and to life. The decision to treat is reversible. The decision to withdraw treatment is not. The differences between a choice made by a competent person to refuse treatment and the choice made on behalf of an incompetent person by someone else, to refuse treatment, justify the high degree of proof required.

The clear and convincing standard also applies to determining the best interests of the conservatee in the exceptional case where the conservator proposes to end the life of a conscious but incompetent conservatee. The decision threatens the conservatee's fundamental rights to privacy and life. The extreme factual predicates that might justify such a decision are not defined. In this case, on this record, the conservator did not meet her burden of proof. Reversed.

Analysis:

The court carefully limits its opinion to conscious conservatees who have not left formal instructions regarding their health care, and whose conservators propose withdrawing life-sustaining treatment. Conservatees who are comatose, or whose conservators are making less drastic decisions, are specifically not included under the rule of this case. The California constitutional provision relating to the right to privacy reads, in its entirety, "[a]ll people are by nature free and independent and have inalienable rights. Among these are enjoying and defending life and liberty, acquiring, possessing, and protecting property, and pursuing and obtaining safety, happiness, and privacy." Cal. Const. art. I, § 1.

■ CASE VOCABULARY

CLEAR AND CONVINCING EVIDENCE: Evidence indicating that the thing to be proved is highly probable or reasonably certain. This is a higher burden than preponderance of the evidence, the standard applied in most civil trials, but less than evidence beyond a reasonable doubt, the norm for criminal trials.

PARENS PATRIAE: [Latin, "parent of his or her country."] The state regarded as a sovereign; the state in its capacity as provider of protection to those unable to care for themselves, as in "the attorney general acted as *parens patriae* in the administrative hearing; a doctrine by which a government has standing to prosecute a lawsuit on behalf of a citizen, especially on behalf of someone who is under a legal disability to prosecute the suit, as in '*parens patriae* allowed the state to institute proceedings.'" The state ordinarily has no standing to sue on behalf of its citizens, unless a separate, sovereign interest will be served by the suit.

Guardianship of Schiavo

(Woman in Persistent Vegetative State)

780 So.2d 176 (Fla. Dist. Ct. App. 2001)

COURTS WILL MAKE A DECISION ON END–OF–LIFE CARE, ABSENT DIRECTION

The court said it should have decision-making authority over end-of-life decisions. That's only okay if I get to pick which court.

stus.com

■ **INSTANT FACTS** Theresa Schiavo's husband Michael (P) sought to have her life support terminated, and her parents (D) objected.

■ **BLACK LETTER RULE** In the absence of instructions, the court may make a decision on whether life support should be withdrawn, based on clear and convincing evidence of what the patient would want.

■ **PROCEDURAL BASIS**

Appeal from an order authorizing the discontinuation of life support.

■ **FACTS**

Theresa Schiavo suffered a cardiac arrest in 1990. She never regained consciousness. Since 1990, she has lived in nursing homes and has received constant care. Theresa was fed and hydrated by tubes. Her condition was diagnosed as a permanent or persistent vegetative state. Theresa was not asleep or in a coma. She had periods of wakefulness and apparent sleep, but did not show any signs of cognition or awareness. Due to the lack of oxygen at the time of her cardiac arrest, Theresa's brain had deteriorated. Scans of her brain showed a severely abnormal structure, and her cerebral cortex was gone, replaced by spinal fluid. Medicine could not cure her condition. Unless a miracle happened and her brain was reconstructed, Theresa would always remain in the vegetative state, totally dependent upon others for her care. She could remain in that state for many years.

Theresa's husband Michael (P) had cared for her since her cardiac arrest. He watched over her care and visited her regularly. Theresa's parents (D) also continued to visit her often. After her cardiac arrest, Michael (P) had filed a medical malpractice lawsuit on Theresa's behalf. The suit resulted in an award of a large sum of money, sufficient to provide for Theresa's care for many years.

Michael (P) and Theresa's parents (D) could not agree on whether Theresa's life support should be terminated. Michael (P) wanted to terminate, but her parents (D) disagreed. Each party claimed that the money awarded in the malpractice suit was the other party's motivation. If Theresa died, the laws of intestacy would direct that the money would go to Michael (P). If Michael (P) divorced Theresa, the remainder of the money would go to her parents on her death.

Michael (P) petitioned the court for an order allowing termination of life support. Theresa's parents (D) disagreed with the request, and asked that a guardian *ad litem* be appointed. The court refused to appoint a guardian and granted the petition to allow termination of life support.

■ **ISSUE**

Did the trial court err in allowing termination of life support of a woman when her husband and parents disagreed on whether it should be terminated?

■ **DECISION AND RATIONALE**

(Altenbernd, J.) No. In the absence of instructions, the court may make a decision on whether life support should be withdrawn, based on clear and convincing evidence of what the patient would want.

Either Michael (P) or Theresa's parents (D) would have been a suitable surrogate decision-maker; however, because of their disagreement, and because of an apparent conflict of interest caused by the inheritance issue, the court would serve as the surrogate decision-maker.

Although the evidence on Theresa's wishes was conflicting, it was still sufficient for the court to make a decision. The court's default position is to favor life. Theresa did not have a will or a living will. She was raised Roman Catholic, but did not attend mass regularly or have a spiritual advisor who could advise the court regarding her religious attitudes about life-support methods. She made a few statements to family and friends about the dying process. These statements, along with other evidence, were sufficient to give the court a basis for its decision.

The trial court was within its discretion not to appoint a guardian *ad litem.* The fact that Michael (P) stood to inherit from Theresa did not automatically compel appointment of a guardian. When there is no advance directive or living will, it is natural that the surrogate decision-maker will be someone close to the patient, and thus likely to inherit from him or her. There may be occasions when an inheritance gives a reason to question a surrogate's objectivity. In this case, Michael (P) has not made a decision to disconnect life support; he has invoked the court's jurisdiction to serve as surrogate decision-maker. The trial court essentially serves as guardian and is charged with weighing all the evidence. Appointment of a guardian in this case would have added little of value.

The trial court should not have heard evidence regarding American attitudes and values about the decision to end life support. There is a risk that a judge could rely on this type of evidence to make a "best interests" decision. In this case, it does not appear that the judge gave the evidence undue weight. Affirmed.

Analysis:

"Terri's Law," the legislative effort to overturn the result in this case, was declared unconstitutional by the Florida Supreme Court. *See Bush v. Schiavo,* 885 So.2d 321 (Fla. 2004), *cert. den.,* 543 U.S. 1121 (2005). On March 21, 2005, President Bush signed P.L. 109-3, which granted the U.S. District Court for the Middle District of Florida jurisdiction to decide whether Theresa's rights were violated by the removal of her feeding tube. Theresa's parents' (D) request in federal court to have the feeding tube reinserted was denied, and that denial was affirmed by the Eleventh Circuit Court of Appeals. *See Schiavo ex rel. Schindler v. Schiavo,* 403 F. 3d 1289 (11th Cir. 2005). On March 30, 2005, the U.S. Supreme Court refused to stay the proceedings pending a petition for a writ of certiorari. Theresa Schiavo died on March 31, 2005.

■ CASE VOCABULARY

ADVANCE DIRECTIVE: A durable power of attorney that takes effect upon one's incompetency and designates a surrogate decision-maker for health-care matters; a legal document explaining one's wishes about medical treatment if one becomes incompetent or unable to communicate.

LIVING WILL: An instrument, signed with the formalities statutorily required for a will, by which a person directs that his or her life not be artificially prolonged by extraordinary measures when there is no reasonable expectation of recovery from extreme physical or mental disability. Most states have living-will legislation.

Superintendent of Belchertown State School v. Saikewicz

(Massachusetts Institution for the Mentally Disabled) v. *(Profoundly Retarded Cancer Patient)*

373 Mass. 728, 370 N.E.2d 417 (1977)

MASSACHUSETTS APPLIES OBJECTIVE STANDARD TO DETERMINE OUTCOME IN CASE INVOLVING A PATIENT THAT WAS NEVER COMPETENT

■ **INSTANT FACTS** In a case involving a severely retarded and uncommunicative man that had never been competent to make his own medical decisions, the court is asked to determine whether to authorize the termination of life-sustaining chemotherapy.

■ **BLACK LETTER RULE** Under Massachusetts law, in cases involving a patient that has never been competent, a surrogate decision maker should make the decision that the patient would have made if he were competent and should take into account the patient's present and future incompetence as one factor in the decision-making process.

■ **PROCEDURAL BASIS**

Appeal to the Supreme Judicial Court of Massachusetts of an action for court authorization to withhold life-sustaining treatment from an incompetent patient.

■ **FACTS**

Joseph Saikewicz (D) was a 67-year old profoundly retarded and uncommunicative adult, who had spent most of his life in institutions. He suffered from leukemia and although chemotherapy might be provided to others suffering from this disease, Saikewicz (D) had no family willing to take part in the decision-making regarding his medical care, and the court was called upon to determine whether this treatment should be withheld.

■ **ISSUE**

Under the law of Massachusetts, may a surrogate decision maker direct the withdrawal of life-sustaining medical treatment from an incompetent patient who had never been competent to make his own medical decisions?

■ **DECISION AND RATIONALE**

(Liacos, J.) Yes. The determination of what legal standards govern the decision of whether to withhold or terminate the life-sustaining treatment of an incompetent person involves two important subissues. The first is: Does a choice exist in the case of an incompetent person, or is it always the responsibility of the State to order medical treatment in all circumstances where the patient is incompetent to make his own decisions? The second is: if there is a choice in certain circumstances, what considerations should be taken into account during the decision-making process? Massachusetts recognizes a general right, for all individuals, to refuse medical treatment in appropriate circumstances. The State, however, retains the traditional responsibility, under the doctrine of parens patriae, to protect the best interests of the incompetent patient. The best interests of an incompetent person may not always be served by requiring that these individuals receive treatment that competent individuals might refuse under similar circumstances. The State is obligated to recognize the dignity and worth of each individual and must afford to the incompetent person the same rights and choices it affords to

---

competent people. The issue of whether or not to terminate the life-sustaining treatment of an incompetent patient cannot be resolved merely by examining statistical reports of what the majority of competent patients have chosen in the past. An individual's resolution of the most complex and significant issues in life is based on his unique perspective, not on a majority vote. An inquiry into what the majority of competent people have chosen to do in a given set of circumstances approaches an objective standard or a "reasonable person" inquiry. However, the appropriate legal standard in this area is actually a subjective one. The court's goal is to determine the wishes and needs of the individual patient as accurately as possible. In cases involving the termination of medical treatment from an incompetent patient who has never been competent, the Massachusetts courts will apply the following substituted judgment doctrine: The guardian ad litem and trial court should try to ascertain the patient's actual interests and preferences. The decision maker should make the decision that the patient would have made if he were competent and should take into account the patient's present and future incompetence as one factor in the decision-making process. In this case, the facts on the record support the proposition that Saikewicz (D) would have refused treatment.

Analysis:

The substituted judgment standard seems impossible to apply in cases involving patients that have never been competent. As a result, courts are divided on whether an objective standard should be applied in these cases rather than the subjective standard that governs in cases involving once-competent patients. The *Saikewicz* court decided to forgo an objective standard out of the desire to extend the same level of protection to the dignity and individual worth of an incompetent person as it does to the dignity and worth of a competent person. Although the court expressed a noble intention, the standard it chooses to adopt seems to raise more issues than it resolves. The court requires decision-makers to determine as accurately as possible the desires and needs of the patient in order to make the choice that the patient would have made if competent, while all the time taking into account that patient's present and future incompetence as a factor in the decision-making. The court does not explain how the patient's present and future incompetence should be taken into account. If the patient has been totally uncommunicative throughout his life, how can any accurate determination of his wishes be made? If no subjective determination can be made, it would appear that the State's interest in preserving human life would prevail.

■ CASE VOCABULARY

GUARDIAN AD LITEM: An individual appointed by a court during the course of litigation to represent and protect the interests of an incompetent person who is a party to the action.

PARENS PATRIAE: Literally, "the parent of his country." The term "parens patriae" is used to describe the state when it is acting in its capacity to protect the interests of, or to represent, citizens that are unable to protect or represent their own interests.

In re Storar

(*New York Institution for the Mentally Disabled*) v. (*Mother of Profoundly Retarded Patient*)

52 N.Y.2d 363, 438 N.Y.S.2d 266, 420 N.E.2d 64 (Ct. App. 1981)

IN NEW YORK, PATIENTS THAT HAVE NEVER BEEN COMPETENT ARE TREATED AS CHILDREN FOR THE PURPOSES OF SURROGATE DECISIONMAKING

■ **INSTANT FACTS** After a severely retarded man is diagnosed with terminal cancer and demonstrates a reluctance to undergo life-sustaining blood transfusions, his mother seeks court authorization to terminate the transfusions.

■ **BLACK LETTER RULE** Under New York law, adults that have never been competent are treated as children and although a surrogate decision maker may provide consent to treatment, he may not direct the termination of life-sustaining medical treatment.

■ FACTS

John Storar was a profoundly retarded, 52-year-old man with a mental age of 18 months. Since the age of five he had been living in a state institution, the Newark Development Center (Center) (P). In 1979, after noticing blood in Storar's urine, physicians at the Center (P) requested permission from Storar's mother (D) to conduct diagnostic tests. The physicians discovered that Storar had cancer of the bladder and recommended that he receive radiation therapy. Mrs. Storar (D) applied to the court to be appointed guardian of her son's person and property and gave her consent to the radiation therapy. After six weeks of radiation, Storar's cancer went into remission. In March 1980, physicians at the Center (P) again discovered blood in Storar's urine. The physicians diagnosed the cancer as terminal. In May, the physicians requested Mrs. Storar's (D) permission to administer blood transfusions. Although she refused at first, she later changed her mind and for a few weeks Storar received blood transfusions when necessary. Mrs. Storar (D) asked that the transfusions be discontinued on June 19. The Center (P) then initiated this action under the Mental Hygiene Law seeking court authorization to continue the transfusions because without them Storar would die within weeks. At the hearing all the medical experts testified that John Storar had irreversible terminal cancer, that he had three to six months to live, and that he was continuously losing blood. They also agreed that he had the mental capacity of an infant and was unable to make a reasoned decision regarding his medical treatment. The Center (P) conceded that Storar did not like the transfusions, that he found the blood in his urine distressing, and that he had displayed some resistance to receiving transfusions on one or two occasions in the past. He received sedatives prior to the transfusions and was given narcotics to alleviate the pain caused by his cancer. Mrs. Storar (D) presented evidence that there was some support in the medical community for the idea that transfusions at this stage of the disease only prolong suffering and that medical treatment could be limited to administering painkillers. Mrs. Storar (D) testified that she had directed the termination of the transfusions because she wanted her son to be comfortable and because he obviously disliked the procedures.

■ ISSUE

Under New York law, may a surrogate decision maker direct the termination of life-sustaining medical treatment in a case involving a patient that has never been competent and has the mental capacity of an infant?

■ DECISION AND RATIONALE

(Wachtler, J.) No. Because John Storar has never been competent it is unrealistic to try to determine what his wishes would be if he were competent. Storar has the mental capacity of an infant and the only realistic way to make a determination in this case is to accord to him the rights and protections accorded to infants. Although a parent or guardian may consent to medical treatment on a child's behalf, a parent may not deprive a child of life-sustaining medical treatment, however well intentioned he is. This case is further complicated by the fact that there are two threats to Storar's life. His cancer is terminal, but the related blood loss also poses a threat to his life. Although blood transfusions will not cure Storar's cancer, they will prevent his death from another cause. Although Storar resisted the transfusions, the evidence presented shows that the procedures did not involve excessive pain. Without the transfusions, Storar's mental and physical state would deteriorate, while with the treatment he would remain in the same condition, albeit with a fatal illness. The trial court should have granted the Center (P) permission to continue treatment.

Analysis:

In the *Saikewicz* case, the Massachusetts court based its decision on the principle of individual autonomy and decided to adopt a subjective standard in cases involving patients that had never been competent. The *Storar* court takes a paternalistic approach. The court recognizes the impossibility of determining with any accuracy what the wishes of an incompetent person would be if he had never been competent. Instead of attempting to serve the principle of autonomy it adopts an objective "best interests" standard, declaring that adults that have been incompetent since birth must be treated as children. The *Storar* court first concludes that the blood transfusions were not excessively painful and then analogizes Storar's position to that of a terminally ill child. Because a parent has no right to terminate the life-sustaining medical treatment of his child, the New York approach would prohibit the termination of life-sustaining medical treatment in virtually every case. Although this position is simpler than the subjective standard adopted in Massachusetts, it can be equally problematic.

■ CASE VOCABULARY

PETITION: An application or a pleading in a civil action that sets out the plaintiff's cause of action and invokes the court's jurisdiction to hear the case.

Newmark v. Williams

(*Christian Science Parents of Terminally Ill Child*) v. (*Delaware Department of Child Protective Services*)

588 A.2d 1108 (Del. 1991)

CHRISTIAN SCIENTISTS ALLOWED TO REFUSE MEDICAL TREATMENT ON BEHALF OF THEIR CHILDREN ON RELIGIOUS GROUNDS

■ **INSTANT FACTS** The parents of a terminally ill child, both practicing Christian Scientists, seek court authorization to refuse an aggressive course of chemotherapy treatment for their son that would only stand a 40% chance of success but would stand a greater chance of causing emotional trauma and severe physical side effects.

■ **BLACK LETTER RULE** A parent does not neglect his child when he chooses to forego life-sustaining medical treatment for that child in favor of spiritual treatment and prayer by an accredited religious practitioner and in accordance with the tenets and practices of a recognized religious faith.

■ PROCEDURAL BASIS

Appeal to the Supreme Court of Delaware of the State's petition for temporary custody of the child of Christian Scientist parents in order to obtain medical treatment for the child.

■ FACTS

Colin Newmark, a three-year-old child, suffered from an aggressive and advanced form of Burkitt's Lymphoma, a type of pediatric cancer. Colin's parents (D) were well-educated, prosperous people, who were members of the First Church of Christ, Scientist. As Christian Scientists, they rejected the medical treatment physicians proposed for Colin, proposing to treat their son's illness with spiritual assistance and prayer. Dr. Meek, Colin's physician, had proposed treating Colin with an extremely intensive course of chemotherapy. She testified that chemotherapy had about a 40% chance of curing Colin's disease and that without it, he would certainly die within six to eight months. She had diagnosed Colin's condition and testified that the cancer was an advanced tumor that was disseminated throughout his body and not localized to any one section. The chemotherapy Dr. Meek proposed is the most aggressive type of cancer treatment short of a bone marrow transplant and its side effects include hair loss, reduced immunological function, and neurological problems. Each cycle of chemotherapy would have brought Colin near death. Because of the damage to his immune system, Colin would have needed to be placed in a foster home where he could receive intensive and specialized in-home monitoring. Additionally, Dr. Meek testified that there was a possibility that the chemotherapy itself could cause Colin's death. And if he underwent chemotherapy, there was still a possibility that he could suffer additional tumors. The Newmarks (D) refused to authorize the chemotherapy and placed their son under the care of a Christian Science practitioner. The Delaware Division of Child Protective Services (DCPS) (P) petitioned the Family Court for temporary custody of Colin so that it could authorize the Alfred I. DuPont Institute, a children's hospital, to treat Colin's cancer with chemotherapy. The Newmarks (D) opposed the DCPS' (P) petition.

■ ISSUE

Under Delaware law, may a parent refuse to authorize medical treatment for his child on religious grounds where the child's condition is terminal but the medical treatment offers less than a 50% chance of success?

■ DECISION AND RATIONALE

(Moore, J.) Yes. Parents enjoy a legal right to make important decisions for their children. This right is not absolute, but the State must prove by clear and convincing evidence that it is necessary for the State to intervene in the parent-child relationship in order to ensure the safety of the child or to protect the public at large. DCPS (P) does not meet this burden. Under Delaware statutory law, a neglected child is defined as a child whose physical, mental, or emotional health is threatened or impaired because of inadequate care or protection by the child's custodian, or a child that has been abused or neglected. Abuse and neglect are defined as physical injury by other than accidental means, injury resulting in a mental or emotional condition caused by neglect, negligent treatment, abandonment, exploitation, sexual abuse, maltreatment, mistreatment, or non-treatment. The Delaware Code does contain spiritual treatment exemptions to its child abuse and neglect statutes that directly affect Christian Scientists. Under the exemptions, a child that is under a good-faith course of treatment through solely spiritual means through prayer by a duly accredited practitioner and in accordance with the tenets and practices of a recognized church shall not be considered neglected. Neither party in this case has raised the issue of the constitutionality of this provision of the Delaware Code. To determine whether under the circumstances Colin was a neglected child when the Newmarks (D) refused to consent to Colin's physician's prescribed course of treatment, the court will apply a balancing test. Under this test, the court will balance the interests of Colin's parents against the interests of the State. A parent's right to make important decisions regarding the care of his child is sacred and can only be invaded for the most compelling reasons. This parental right is a recognized common-law principle and courts have recognized that maintaining the autonomy of the parent-child relationship is integral to the preservation of the integrity of the family. Because in many circumstances the State cannot serve as an adequate surrogate for a loving parent, courts give great deference to parental decisions regarding the care of minor children. However, the parental right is not absolute. The State can intervene in the parent-child relationship in order to protect the health and safety of the child and the public. The State has a duty to protect the youngest and most helpless citizens under the doctrine of parens patriae. The parens patriae doctrine traditionally has been used to give the State the right to act on behalf of children in certain marital and property disputes. Courts have begun to use the doctrine to justify State intervention in cases involving a parent's religious objection to the medical treatment of a child's life-threatening illness. The principle that underlies the doctrine's use in this area is the State's interest in the preservation of human life. But the State's interest in preserving life is not unlimited and, under *Cruzan*, must be weighed against the constitutionally protected rights of the individual. In addition to the Newmarks' (D) parental right, the individual interests at stake here include Colin's right to life. Because Colin is three years old and lacks the ability to make informed decisions regarding his medical care, the court must substitute its objective judgment to determine what is in his best interests. There are two elements in the best interests analysis. The first is the consideration of the effectiveness of the proposed treatment and the child's chances of survival with and without the treatment. The second is the consideration of the nature of the treatment and how it might affect the child. Under the best interests analysis adopted here, the DCPS' (P) petition must be denied. The proposed medical treatment was highly invasive, painful, and involved terrible side effects. It also posed an unacceptably low chance of success and a high risk that the treatment itself would cause death. The treatment would have involved placing Colin in foster care, which would have had a severe emotional effect on him. The court can best serve Colin's best interests by allowing his parents (D) to retain custody.

Analysis:

Because a parent's right to make important decisions regarding the care of her child is recognized as a matter of state and federal constitutional law as well as common law, a parent is in a stronger position when it comes to directing the withholding of medical treatment than a surrogate decision-maker of an incompetent adult patient. However, as the *Newmark* court makes clear, the parental right is not absolute. The most important limitation of this right comes from state child abuse and neglect statutes. Under most child abuse and neglect statutes a parent that denies her child adequate medical care is guilty of neglect and the State may exercise its authority under the parens patriae doctrine to take custody of the child to assure that his needs are met. In *Storar* the New York Court of Appeals applied the rule that no parent may deprive a child of life-sustaining treatment, no matter how well intentioned that parent is. However, most states, like Delaware, have enacted safe harbors for Christian Scientists. These safe harbors were created after extensive lobbying by Christian Scientists at both the state and federal level and allow parents such as the Newmarks (D) to terminate painful and traumatic life-sustaining treatment on behalf of their children, while similarly situated parents with no *religious* objection to such medical treatment would not be allowed to order its termination. These safe harbors are arguably unconstitutional violations of the First Amendment Establishment Clause because they provide special status for the Church of Christ, Scientist, perhaps in violation of the constitutional prohibition on governmental actions that advance or inhibit any particular religion.

■ CASE VOCABULARY

EXEMPTION: The freedom or release from a legal obligation or duty that is extended to some individuals or groups but that is not granted indiscriminately to others.

Miller v. HCA

(Parents) v. *(Hospital)*

118 S.W.3d 758 (Tex. 2003)

PARENTAL CONSENT IS NOT REQUIRED TO GIVE LIFE SUSTAINING TREATMENT TO INFANTS

■ **INSTANT FACTS** The Millers' (P) baby was born in distress after only twenty-three weeks' gestation and she was provided with resuscitative care without the Millers' (P) consent.

■ **BLACK LETTER RULE** A physician does not commit a legal wrong when he or she provides treatment to a minor without parental consent under emergent circumstances, that is, if death is likely to result immediately upon the failure to perform the treatment.

■ **PROCEDURAL BASIS**

Appeal from an order of the court of appeals reversing a trial court judgment.

■ **FACTS**

Karla Miller (P) went into premature labor approximately four months before her due date. An ultrasound showed that her fetus weighed about 629 grams. She was given a drug to stop labor, but her physician later found that she had a serious infection that required the inducement of labor. Physicians at the hospital (D) told her that if delivery were induced, there was little chance that the baby would be born alive. If the baby were born alive, it would most likely suffer severe impairments, including cerebral palsy, mental retardation, blindness, and lung disease. Mark Miller (P), the baby's father, also testified that the physicians told him that they had never had such a premature infant survive, and that anything they did to sustain the infant's life would be guesswork. The Millers (P) informed the physicians that they wanted no heroic measures performed on the infant, and that they wanted nature to take its course. Mark (P) testified that he understood heroic measures to mean resuscitation, chest massage, and the use of life support machines. The Millers' (P) request was recorded in the medical records.

One of the physicians informed the staff of the hospital (D) that no neonatologist would be present at the delivery. Meetings were held to discuss the situation, and Mark (P) was informed that the hospital (D) had a policy that required the resuscitation of any baby born weighing more than 500 grams. The physicians and the hospital (D) agreed that a neonatologist would be present at the delivery, and the decision to resuscitate would be made based on the infant's condition at that time. Mark (P) was asked to sign a consent form allowing resuscitation according to the hospital's (D) rules, but he declined. He was told that the only way he could prevent resuscitation would be to remove Karla (P) from the hospital (D), which was not a viable option, given her condition.

The baby was born alive, and the Millers (P) named her Sidney. Initially, Sidney responded well to her treatment, but sometime during the first few days, she suffered a brain hemorrhage. There was conflicting testimony regarding the cause of the hemorrhage. The hemorrhage caused Sidney to suffer severe mental and physical impairment. The evidence indicated that Sidney's circumstances would not change.

The Millers (P) sued the hospital (D), but not the physicians, claiming battery and negligence. Their claims were based on the treatment of Sidney without the Millers' (P) consent and on the use of

---

experimental treatments and drugs. The trial court entered judgment for the Millers (P), but that judgment was reversed on appeal.

■ ISSUE

Was the hospital (D) wrong to treat the premature infant against the wishes of her parents?

■ DECISION AND RATIONALE

(Enoch, J.) No. A physician does not commit a legal wrong when he or she provides treatment to a minor without parental consent under emergent circumstances, that is, if death is likely to result immediately upon the failure to perform the treatment. As a general rule, consent is required before medical treatment may be provided. That rule is based on the patient's right to receive adequate information to make an informed decision about treatment. In addition, in an emergency situation, consent may be implied. The emergent circumstances doctrine does not imply consent. The doctrine acknowledges that the harm from the failure to treat outweighs the harm from the treatment. It is impossible for the courts to calculate the relative value of an impaired life versus no life at all.

The Millers (P) argue that there was no emergent situation that would excuse treatment without their consent or a court order. There were numerous discussions held before Sidney's birth, and the Millers (P) stated that they did not want any heroic measures. The Millers' (P) argument ignores the fact that Sidney could be properly evaluated only after she was born. No pre-birth decision could be made regarding Sidney's best interests.

In addition, when Sidney was born, she was in distress. The physician had to make an immediate decision regarding her treatment. There was no time to obtain the Millers' (P) consent, or to start legal proceedings to challenge the withholding of that consent. Hospitals and physicians should always strive to obtain consent, but if that consent is denied or not forthcoming, physicians will not be held liable for providing life-sustaining treatment to a newborn infant without that consent.

The Millers' (P) negligence claim is based on their lack of consent to treatment, just like their battery claim. It was not negligence or hospital (D) policy that caused the treatment without consent, it was the emergent circumstances.

The hospital (D) raises the issue that the federal "Baby Doe" regulations are a part of Texas law. Those regulations, if they apply here, mean only that the state of Texas must provide a mechanism for notifying child protective services to prevent the withholding of medical treatment. The hospital also argues that parents may withhold medical treatment only if the child is terminally ill. That argument does not relate to this case, in that the claim is that treatment should have been withheld. The emergent circumstances doctrine prevents liability in this situation. Affirmed.

Analysis:

Note that the jury was never instructed regarding the emergent circumstances doctrine, and the hospital (D) never objected to the lack of such an instruction. The court here decided on its own that the evidence showed an emergent circumstance existed; instead of remanding for a jury's determination of the issue, it proceeded to uphold the court of appeals. Query whether the Millers (P) had, under the court's analysis, any real right to consent. They were apprised of the likely condition of Sidney eleven hours before her birth and were asked for their instructions at that time. Those instructions were overruled before her birth, even though the court stressed that there could be no evaluation of Sidney's condition until after her birth.

Washington v. Glucksberg

(State of Washington) v. *(Physicians and Terminally Ill Patients)*

521 U.S. 702, 117 S.Ct. 2258, 138 L.Ed.2d 772 (1997)

SUPREME COURT HOLDS NO DUE PROCESS RIGHT TO ASSISTED SUICIDE

■ **INSTANT FACTS** Physicians and terminally ill patients bring a constitutional due process challenge to Washington's statutory prohibition of assisted suicide.

■ **BLACK LETTER RULE** Assisted suicide is not a fundamental right protected by the Due Process Clause of the Fourteenth Amendment to the United States Consitution.

■ FACTS

A statute enacted in the state of Washington provided that anyone that knowingly aided or caused another person to commit suicide was guilty of a felony. Several plaintiffs, including Harold Glucksberg (P), a physician, brought suit in federal district court to obtain a declaratory judgment that the statute was unconstitutional on its face. The district court recognized a constitutionally protected liberty interest in the right of a terminally ill, mentally competent adult to make a personal choice to commit physician-assisted suicide. The court held that Washington's prohibition of physician-assisted suicide placed an unconstitutional burden on that liberty interest. A panel of the Court of Appeals for the Ninth Circuit reversed the district court on the grounds that no court of final jurisdiction had ever recognized a constitutional right to aid another in killing himself. The Ninth Circuit then reheard the case en banc and reversed the panel's decision.

■ ISSUE

Does a state prohibition against causing or aiding a suicide violate the Due Process Clause of the Fourteenth Amendment to the United States Constitution?

■ DECISION AND RATIONALE

(Rehnquist, C.J.) No. First, as in all due process cases, the Court examines this country's history, tradition, and practices. It is a crime to assist a suicide in almost every state. State prohibitions of assisted suicide are not innovations but are rather the traditional expressions of the State interest in protecting and preserving human life. Although society's attitude toward suicide has changed since the original thirteenth century bans on suicide, the law has consistently condemned assisted suicide. Having examined legal history and tradition, the Court will turn to Glucksberg's (P) constitutional claim. The Due Process Clause of the Fourteenth Amendment protects against government interference with an individual's fundamental rights and liberty interests. Although the Court has held that in addition to the specific liberties protected by the Bill of Rights, protected liberty interests include the rights to abortion, to marital privacy, to use contraception, and to bodily integrity. However, the Court has always tried to exercise the utmost care when called upon to expand the concept of substantive due process so that the freedoms protected by the Due Process Clause do not become transformed into the policy preferences of the members of the Court. The Court's due process analysis is based on two principles. The first is that the Due Process Clause protects fundamental rights and liberties that are, objectively, deeply rooted in the nation's history and traditions and that are implicit in the concept of ordered liberty in such a way that liberty and justice would cease to exist if these rights were sacrificed.

The second is that the Court has required in all substantive due process cases a careful description of the fundamental right being asserted. The Court of Appeals stated the issue in this case was whether there is a liberty interest in an individual's determination of the time and manner of his death. The statute at issue here prohibits aiding another person to commit suicide, so the question before the Court is whether the liberty protected by the Due Process Clause includes the right to commit suicide, which in turn includes the right to assistance in doing so. In *Cruzan*, the Court assumed that the constitution would grant a competent person the right to refuse life-sustaining nutrition and hydration. The right the Court assumed in *Cruzan* was derived from the traditional common law rule that forced medication constitutes a battery and a long legal tradition that protected the right to refuse unwanted medical attention. The Court's assumption was in accordance with the nation's tradition and history. However, although the decision to commit suicide with another person's assistance may be a personal and profound one, it has never had the same kind of legal protection as the decision to refuse unwanted medical treatment. Glucksberg (P) has also relied on *Casey*. In that case, the Court held that a woman has a right to an abortion, before the fetus is viable, without undue State interference, that the State may restrict post-viability abortions, and that the State has a legitimate interests in protecting the health of the unborn child and the life of the mother throughout her pregnancy. The majority opinion in *Casey* discussed the Court's tradition of interpreting the Due Process Clause to protect fundamental rights and liberties that involve the most intimate and personal choices an individual makes in life. But the fact that the Due Process Clause protects some rights and liberties that sound in personal autonomy does not mean that all important personal decisions are protected. This country has rejected nearly all efforts to allow assisted suicide. This is enough to permit the Court to conclude that the right to assisted suicide is not a fundamental liberty interest that is protected by the Due Process Clause. However, the constitution still requires that Washington's prohibition be rationally related to legitimate State interests. This requirement is met as Washington's prohibition of assisted suicide serves a number of state interests. First, the State has an unqualified interest in the preservation of human life. Second, the State has an interest in protecting the integrity and ethics of the medical profession. Third, the State has an interest in protecting vulnerable groups, including the poor and the elderly, from abuse, neglect, and mistakes. Legalizing assisted suicide would pose a risk to individuals whose autonomy is weakened by poverty, old age, lack of access to good medical care, or membership in a stigmatized group. Fourth, the State has an interest in preventing itself from placing itself on the slippery slope toward voluntary, or even involuntary, euthanasia. All of these interests are important and legitimate and Washington's prohibition of assisted suicide is rationally related to their promotion and protection. Washington's prohibition is not unconstitutional on its face or as applied. The Court of Appeals is reversed.

■ CONCURRENCE

(In both *Glucksberg* and *Vacco*) (O'Connor, Justice) The Court is not required to address the issue of whether a suffering patient has a constitutionally cognizable interest in obtaining medical treatment that would relieve his suffering during the last days of his life. A dying patient in Washington can obtain medical treatment to relieve his pain, even if doing so would hasten his death. What justifies the state prohibition that this Court upholds is the difficulty in defining "terminal illness" and the concern that a patient's request for assistance in committing suicide might not be entirely voluntary.

■ CONCURRENCE

(In both *Glucksberg* and *Vacco*): (Stevens, Justice) The Court's holding is consistent with the continuation of society's debate about the limits that the constitution places on the power of a State to punish the practice of physician-assisted suicide. In its capital punishment cases, the Supreme Court has concluded that the State does in fact have the power to determine that some lives have a lesser value than others and that there is no absolute requirement that a State treat all human life as equally deserving of its protection. The Court in *Glucksberg* holds that Washington's prohibition of assisted suicide is not unconstitutional on its face. However, there might be some applications of that statute that could be unconstitutional. There are situations where there exists a legitimate interest in hastening death. The source of the right to refuse medical treatment recognized in *Cruzan* was not just common law. Instead, this right is an aspect of a broader individual interest in dignity and determining the character of the memories that will survive after death. *Cruzan* recognizes an interest in making decisions about how to confront imminent death. An individual that is already on the threshold of death has a constitutional interest that might outweigh the traditional State interest in preserving life at all costs. Although the State has an interest in the contributions an individual might make to society, that interest is weakened in a case where the individual is terminally ill and his choice is not whether to live, but how to die. The State's interest in protecting the integrity of the medical profession is weakened in a case where a patient sees the physician's role as one of easing his suffering and making his death tolerable and dignified. There may be cases where there is only a slight difference between a patient that decides to remove his life-support and a patient that seeks a physician's assistance in ending his life. It is clear that the unqualified State interest in preserving life is not sufficient by itself to outweigh a liberty interest in preserving a dying person's dignity and alleviating his suffering.

■ CONCURRENCE

(Souter, J.) In evaluating and protecting substantive due process rights under the constitution, the Court must assess the relative weights of the asserted interests. This exercise is similar to the sort of balancing of interests performed at common law. However, common law is subject to two important constraints. The first is that a court is bound to confine the liberty interests that it recognizes to those truly deserving constitutional protection. The interests must be expressed in the constitution or else exemplified by the nation's legal traditions or revealed by contrast with the traditions the nation has broken. The second constraint is that the Court's role is judicial review, not lawmaking. The Washington legislature could reasonably have decided that a statute that prohibits physician-assisted suicide protects terminally ill patients. The Court's role is not to intervene in the legislature's decision but to allow reasonable legislative consideration.

■ CONCURRENCE

(In *Glucksberg* and *Vacco*): (Breyer, Justice) The majority formulated the liberty interests asserted in this case as the right to commit suicide with another person's assistance. The interest could have been better expressed as the right to die with dignity. This Court does not need at this point to determine whether such a right is fundamental because the avoidance of severe pain would comprise an essential part of a successful claim and the Washington statute at issue in this case does not force a dying person to undergo that kind of pain. The statute does not prohibit a doctor from providing a patient with sufficient drugs to ease suffering even if those drugs would themselves cause death.

Analysis:

Because the individual interest in committing suicide or in obtaining assistance in committing suicide are not deeply rooted in the nation's history and legal traditions, they cannot be held to be constitutionally protected fundamental rights necessary to the concept of ordered liberty. There is an ongoing debate in the United States about the morality and legality of physician-assisted suicide, and this debate is best resolved through the legislative process. However, Justices O'Connor, Stevens, and Breyer suggest that they would reconsider their position if they were ever presented with a statute or an application of a statute that prohibited a doctor from administering the kind of palliative care that would alleviate suffering but would also hasten death. In that case, the State interest in preserving life would presumably be outweighed by the terminally ill patient's individual interest in avoiding severe pain.

■ CASE VOCABULARY

EN BANC: The court, in this case the appellate court, with all qualified judges sitting on the case.

Vacco v. Quill

(Physicians and Terminally Ill Patients) v. *(New York Attorney General)*

521 U.S. 793, 117 S.Ct. 2293, 138 L.Ed.2d 834 (1997)

SUPREME COURT HOLDS STATE BAN OF ASSISTED SUICIDE DOES NOT VIOLATE EQUAL PROTECTION CLAUSE

■ **INSTANT FACTS** A group of physicians and terminally ill patients bring an Equal Protection challenge to New York's statutory prohibition of assisted suicide.

■ **BLACK LETTER RULE** A state statutory ban on assisted suicide does not violate the Equal Protection Clause of the Fourteenth Amendment to the United States Constitution.

■ **PROCEDURAL BASIS**

Challenge in the United States Supreme Court of a ruling by the United States Court of Appeals for the Second Circuit that New York's prohibition of physician-assisted suicide violated the Equal Protection Clause of the Fourteenth Amendment of the United States Constitution.

■ **FACTS**

Several plaintiffs, including Vacco (P) and three terminally ill patients that had died by the time the case reached the United States Supreme Court, brought suit in federal district court to obtain a declaratory judgment that New York's statutes prohibiting physician-assisted suicide violated the Equal Protection Clause of the Fourteenth Amendment. The district court rejected their claim. The Court of Appeals for the Second Circuit reversed the district court on the grounds that New York law did not treat all terminally ill patients equally. Under New York law, a terminally ill patient was allowed to hasten his death through the removal of a life-support system but a similarly situated patient that was not attached to a life-support machine was not allowed to hasten his death through the self-administering of prescribed drugs. Additionally, according to the Court of Appeals the New York statutes that prohibit physician-assisted suicide were not rationally related to any legitimate State interest.

■ **ISSUE**

Does a state prohibition against causing or aiding a suicide violate the Equal Protection Clause of the Fourteenth Amendment to the United States Constitution?

■ **DECISION AND RATIONALE**

(Rehnquist, C.J.) No. The Equal Protection Clause does not create any substantive rights. Rather, it expresses the general rule that a State must treat all similar cases alike but is not required to treat dissimilar cases alike. Under the Equal Protection Clause, if a State classification or distinction does not burden a fundamental right or target a suspect class the Court will uphold it as long as it bears a rational relationship to some legitimate State purpose. The New York statutes banning assisted suicide do not impinge a fundamental right or target a suspect class and therefore they are entitled to a presumption of validity. New York's prohibition of assisted suicide and its statutes that permit a patient to refuse unwanted medical treatment do not on their faces draw distinctions between persons. Everyone is entitled to refuse medical treatment, and no one is allowed to assist a suicide. The Court of Appeals, however, concluded that New York law treats terminally ill patients on life support differently from those that are not on life support. This conclusion is based on the idea that terminating or refusing life-sustaining medical treatment is the same as assisted suicide. Unlike the Court of Appeals, the Supreme Court believes the distinction between assisting suicide and refusing medical treatment is rational, logical, and important. The distinction is in accordance with the basic legal principles of causation and intent. First, as a matter of causation, when a terminally ill patient refuses medical treatment he dies as a result of the underlying fatal illness but when he ingests lethal prescribed medication he is killed by that medication. Second, as a matter of intent, when a physician withdraws life-sustaining treatment he intends only to respect his patient's wishes and to stop taking futile steps where his patient can no longer benefit from them. When a physician provides aggressive palliative care he intends only to ease pain, even when the drugs used themselves hasten his patient's death. However, when a physician assists a suicide he intends primarily to end his patient's life. The law has traditionally used an actor's intent to distinguish between actions. Given the general principles of causation and intent, it is unsurprising that New York courts, like those of many other states, have distinguished between the action of refusing life-sustaining medical treatment and the action of assisting a suicide. The majority of state legislatures have also drawn this distinction by allowing the refusal of unwanted medical treatment and prohibiting assisted suicide. The United States Supreme Court has also recognized the distinction between letting a person die and causing a person's death. In *Cruzan*, the Court's assumption of the right to refuse treatment was not based on the proposition that a patient has the right to hasten death but on traditional rights to bodily integrity and freedom from unwanted touching. *Cruzan* does not support the idea that refusing medical treatment is nothing more or less than suicide. New York may distinguish between the act of refusing medical treatment and the act of assisting suicide without violating the Equal Protection Clause. As an additional matter, New York's prohibition is rationally related to important legitimate State interests, including those of prohibiting intentional killing, preserving life, preventing suicide, protecting the integrity and ethics of the medical profession, protecting vulnerable people from abuse, and avoiding a slide toward legalized euthanasia. The Court of Appeals is reversed.

■ CONCURRENCE

(Souter, J.) Assisted suicide is not a fundamental right deserving of Court recognition at this time. However, the physicians and patients in this case and in the related case of *Glucksberg*, present highly important claims that require a commensurate justification.

Analysis:

Vacco is the companion case to *Glucksberg*. Under *Vacco* and *Glucksberg* a state's prohibition of physician-assisted suicide does not violate the Fourteenth Amendment to the United States constitution. In *Vacco*, the Court determined that New York's prohibition of assisted suicide does not burden a fundamental right or target a suspect class. It does not accord inappropriately different treatment to two different types of terminally ill patients. All patients may refuse unwanted medical treatment, whether they are on a life support machine or not. No patient may seek another's help in committing suicide, again whether they are on a life-support machine or not. Both *Vacco* and *Glucksberg* may be seen as Supreme Court expressions that the courtroom is not the appropriate forum to resolve American society's ongoing debate about the legalization of physician-assisted suicide. Chief Justice Rehnquist makes it clear in *Glucksberg* that when the Court assumed in *Cruzan* that a competent individual would have a constitutionally protected right to refuse unwanted life-sustaining hydration and nutrition, it was acting in accordance with longstanding legal traditions Legal history and traditions provided the Court with some guidance on how to proceed. In the case of physician-assisted suicide, there was no such tradition to guide the Court in its determination.

■ CASE VOCABULARY

ARBITRARY: Without reason, in accordance with a whim rather than in accordance with the law.

CHAPTER TWENTY

Regulation of Research Involving Human Subjects

Grimes v. Kennedy Krieger Institute, Inc.

Instant Facts: As a part of a research project, Kennedy Krieger (D) encouraged families with young children to move into homes with some lead paint.

Black Letter Rule: The relationship between researchers and human subjects in nontherapeutic research projects may create special duties, the breach of which may be the basis for a negligence action.

Grimes v. Kennedy Krieger Institute, Inc.

(Research Subject) v. (Research Institute)

366 Md. 29, 782 A.2d 807 (Ct. App. 2001)

HUMAN EXPERIMENTATION CREATES DUTIES OF DISCLOSURE BY THE RESEARCHER

"To disclose, or not to disclose?" That is the question.

You experimented on children with lead paint. "What the hell were you thinking?" is the question.

stus.com

■ **INSTANT FACTS** As a part of a research project, Kennedy Krieger (D) encouraged families with young children to move into homes with some lead paint.

■ **BLACK LETTER RULE** The relationship between researchers and human subjects in nontherapeutic research projects may create special duties, the breach of which may be the basis for a negligence action.

■ **PROCEDURAL BASIS**

Appeal from an order granting summary judgment.

■ **FACTS**

Kennedy Krieger Institute (KKI) (D) developed a nontherapeutic research project to study the effectiveness of varying degrees of lead paint abatement procedures. A "nontherapeutic" study is one that is not designed to directly benefit the subjects of the research, but is designed to benefit the public at large. The project involved doing different types of lead abatement on residential property, and then encouraging or requiring landlords to rent the properties to families with young children. The experiment required that the children remain in their homes even after lead was detected in their system, so that the continuing accumulation could be measured.

The consent form signed by the parents of the children (P) involved in the study did not state clearly that the success of the abatement methods would be measured by the accumulation of lead in the systems of the children (P). The form was developed in conjunction with an institutional review board. The board suggested changes to the form to make it more acceptable to federal regulators, but did not suggest changes in the experiment or the testing protocol. The consent form signed by Grimes's (P) parent stated only that Grimes (P) would be tested periodically for lead, as would their home. Testing was to be done without charge, and KKI (D) made small payments for answering questions and completing questionnaires. During Grimes's (P) participation in the experiment, she was given periodic blood tests, and their home was tested for lead. Grimes's (P) mother was notified of the results of the blood tests soon after they were taken. After several months, Grimes (P) was found to have a highly elevated level of lead in her blood. The home testing revealed high levels of lead, but the results of these tests were not revealed until after Grimes (P) showed elevated lead levels in her system.

Grimes (P) and other children (P) in the experiment brought suit against KKI (D), claiming that KKI (D) had a duty to warn them about the presence of lead in their homes. In addition, it was alleged that KKI (D) did not adequately inform them of the risks of the research. The trial court granted KKI's (D) motion for summary judgment, holding that KKI (D) had no duty to warn of the presence of lead.

■ **ISSUE**

Did the trial court err in holding that KKI (D) did not have a duty to warn of the presence of lead?

■ DECISION AND RATIONALE

(Cathell, J.) Yes. The relationship between researchers and human subjects in nontherapeutic research projects may create special duties, the breach of which may be the basis for a negligence action. The basis may be created by the informed consent, which would create a contract, or it may be based on governmental regulation of human experimentation.

The researcher and subject relationship is not one that has been recognized by case law or by statute as one that creates a duty of care. The record indicates, however, that the relationship involves a duty or duties that would ordinarily exist, based on the facts of the individual cases.

The consent form signed by Grimes's (P) mother and KKI (D) created a bilateral contract between the parties. At the very least, the forms show that Grimes's (P) mother expected to be to be compensated and to be informed of anything that might affect their willingness to continue in the study. KKI (D), in return, got access to the houses and to the children. A reasonable parent in these circumstances would expect to be clearly informed that it was contemplated that his or her child would ingest lead particles, and that the extent of the lead contamination of the child's system would be one of the ways in which the success of the experiment would be measured. The human subject is entitled to all material information, and the informed consent form used did not supply that information.

Regulations or statutes may also create a duty of care. Federal regulations that govern federally funded research projects create a duty to warn of all risks that are reasonably foreseeable. In this case, the risks of lead exposure were not only foreseeable, but were well known to KKI (D). The consent forms did not directly inform that it was not only possible, but contemplated, that some level of lead might contaminate the blood of the children (P).

Consent or compliance with internal regulations will not suffice to immunize researchers from liability, especially when the information furnished to the subject of the experiment is incomplete. The duty to a vulnerable research subject is independent of consent, particularly when children are the subject of the research. Such legal duties and protections may be warranted because of the conflict of interest between the goal of the researcher and the health of the human subject. The knowledge gap between the researchers and the subjects creates an additional reason why full disclosure is necessary. Participants in an experiment should not be solely responsible for their own protection.

Parents or other surrogates have no right to consent to the participation of children in nontherapeutic research or studies in which there is any risk of injury or damage to the health of the subject. The "best interests of the child" has long been the overriding concern of the courts in matters that relate to children. To think otherwise, to turn over human and legal ethical concerns solely to the scientific community, is to risk embarking on a slippery slope that has all too often in the past resulted in practices that no community should ever be willing to accept. Reversed.

■ CONCURRENCE

(Raker, J.) The majority makes findings of fact that are more appropriate for the jury. The factual record before the court is sparse, so remand is appropriate. The conduct of KKI (D) was not *per se* illegal, and the majority goes too far in holding that a parent or guardian may never consent to the participation of a child in a nontherapeutic research study in which there is any risk of injury. The majority comes close to adopting the Nuremberg Code into Maryland tort law.

Analysis:

Experimentation on human beings is an area that generates strong reactions, most of them negative. At the same time, it can yield important scientific information that is unavailable by any other means. The scientific community has often been criticized for overlooking the ethical aspects of some unlawful and unquestionably unethical experiments because of the useful data obtained. This may be one reason why, rightly or wrongly, the majority is so pointedly opposed to leaving the ethical questions of human experimentation entirely to the scientists.
